The
HARPER HANDBOOK
of College Composition

The
HARPER HANDBOOK
of College Composition

By **GEORGE S. WYKOFF,** Professor of English, Purdue
University, and **HARRY SHAW,** Humanities Editor, Harper
& Brothers, Formerly Director, Workshops in Composition,
New York University

New York

HARPER & BROTHERS, PUBLISHERS

THE HARPER HANDBOOK OF COLLEGE COMPOSITION

Portions of this book are adapted from *Writing and Rewriting*, by Harry Shaw. Copyright, 1937, 1945, 1949, 1951, by Harper & Brothers.

Library of Congress catalog number: 51-11967

Contents

Contents

Contents

Contents

Foreword

A course in freshman English means many things to many people. For some teachers its important aim is training students to read carefully and critically. For others the course provides opportunity to teach literature, a sort of survey leading to advanced or specialized literary work. With still others first-year English constitutes an approach to aesthetics, a method of fostering "good taste." Still other instructors use the discipline of the course to emphasize speaking or listening or principles of clear thinking.

We have no particular quarrel with any of these approaches. Each is important, legitimate, and defensible. But many years of classroom experience have convinced us that no course can be a successful coverall, that primary emphasis must be placed somewhere, that one unassailable charge against the efficacy of the first-year English course is that in attempting much it sometimes accomplishes too little.

We believe that the needs of most beginning college students—perhaps all—are best served by genuinely solid work, under supervision, in thinking, writing, and rewriting. *The Harper Handbook* has only this major aim: *to help students to think and write correctly, clearly, and effectively and to assist teachers in achieving this aim for their students.* Such a purpose, we hold, is both significant and far from pedestrian. Learning to think logically and learning to write effectively are worth-while intellectual processes valuable not only in composition classes but in all other outreachings of the mind.

Throughout, we have attempted to utilize the findings of linguistic scholars in recent years and have made numerous and careful distinctions between formal and informal writing. Wherever pos-

Foreword

sible, we have avoided dogmatic assertions and frequently have included pointed comment on various levels of usage. Even so, we contend that college students are intellectually privileged and therefore should be trained to write and speak in ways appropriate to their opportunities and privileges. *The Harper Handbook* is filled with specific recommendations and definite suggestions; if some consider them to be rules and regulations, such may be the needs of students seeking positive answers. Our belief is that improvement in thinking and writing involves replacing bad habits with good, that learning composition—or any intellectual or social activity—is necessarily negative in part.

Experience suggests that there is no ideal plan of organization or order of assignments in freshman English. Any teacher will naturally follow the order of assignments which he has found most satisfactory and will vary this order from year to year according to the needs of his students. But since many students are weak in more than one division of writing, we recommend prompt assignment of the three prefatory chapters in this book dealing with communication, thinking, and early themes. The six major divisions of the text ("Grammar," "Punctuation and Mechanics," "The Whole Theme," "The Paragraph," "The Sentence," "The Word") may be taken up in any order. Perhaps the most common beginnings are a discussion of the whole theme and a review of grammar. The authors have each started at various times with every one of the six divisions save punctuation.

The Harper Handbook is designed for individual and classroom study and for easy reference in correcting themes. We have done everything we (and our colleagues and advisers) could do to make the book as easy to use, as sensibly comprehensive, as flexible, and as attractive as possible. If our efforts are successful, we owe much to those who have shared their professional experiences, to former teachers, and to former students from whom we have learned perhaps more than we have taught.

Particularly do we wish to express our hearty thanks to the gifted and experienced teachers who read the book while it was in proof form and made many helpful suggestions for addition, deletion, and emendation. Among these are William P. Albrecht, Uni-

Foreword

versity of New Mexico; Edna Anderson, Los Angeles City College; Paul W. Barrus, East Texas State Teachers College; Francis E. Bowman, Duke University; May Dulaney Bush, The Woman's College, University of North Carolina; Glenn Christensen, Lehigh University; Jane Dale, Oregon College of Education; C. Rexford Davis, Rutgers University; Ervin Gaines, Columbia University; Phil S. Grant, University of California; Kenneth W. Houp, Pennsylvania State College; Robert A. Hume, University of Nevada; Edith Layer, Western Reserve University; Ruth Middlebrook, New York University; R. V. Pence, University of Notre Dame; Paul M. Roberts, San Jose State College; Ernest Samuels, Northwestern University; Waters Turpin, Morgan State College; Carlton F. Wells, University of Michigan; R. A. Wells, Carnegie Institute of Technology; Norman Weyand, S.J., Loyola University (Chicago); and Philip R. Wikelund, Indiana University.

The present volume also contains ideas and suggestions offered by the late A. J. Bryan, Louisiana State University; E. B. Knowles, Jr., The Pratt Institute; and Philip Burnham, now of St. Paul's School, Concord, New Hampshire, formerly of the English A staff at Harvard University. To these teachers we acknowledge our indebtedness.

G. S. W.
H. S.

PART I

Getting Under Way

Chapter 1

You and the Process of Communication

Communication consists of two major divisions, each containing two closely related parts: (1) writing and reading, (2) speaking and listening.

The process of communication is similar to the use of telephone and radio: there are always a sender and a recipient. The writer writes for (sends to) a reader, the reader reads (receives) what the writer has "sent"; the speaker speaks for a listener, the listener receives what the speaker has transmitted. Between the sender and the receiver is, of course, the subject. When the recipient understands what the sender has wanted to convey, communication is completed. The more clearly and effectively the reader or listener understands the subject presented, the more successful communication is.

The process is illustrated by the following diagram:

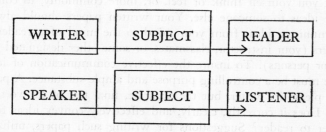

Through all parts of effective communication runs the thread of straight thinking—that is, of forward movement of thought, of a

3

clear, orderly plan and arrangement of ideas. In addition, there must be attention to methods of correct reasoning, so that conclusions or generalized statements are not based on faulty or insufficient evidence, so that good evidence is not misused to reach only seemingly correct conclusions. Writers and speakers are responsible for logical thinking in their parts of the communication process; when they become readers or listeners, their responsibility is to watch for illogical thinking in what they read or hear (see Chapter 2 for further discussion).

On the assumption that you are or come close to being an average adult, you spend 70 percent of your waking time in some form of communication, as follows: 11 percent of this communication time in writing activities; 32 percent in speaking; 15 percent in reading; and 42 percent in listening.[1]

You are, therefore, engaged in one of the four parts of communication when you write, or read, or speak, or listen. You can use each phase of the process to give yourself training and develop skills in any of the other parts. Obviously, a handbook of written composition is designed to further progress in writing, but your own writing achievement can be more easily and quickly attained, and more permanently *retained,* if you give adequate attention to your speaking, reading, and listening.

WRITING

The purpose of your writing is to express ideas, either to find out what you yourself think or feel, or, more commonly, to convey these ideas to someone else. Your written papers should always communicate ideas from your mind to the mind of a reader or readers (your instructor, classmates, or some other designated person or persons). To insure the effective communication of ideas there must be a controlling purpose and ample substance. A paper may please its writer, but the accurate, final test of its worth is this: Does it correctly, clearly, and effectively convey ideas from writer to reader? Suggestions for writing such papers, utilizing

---

[1] Paul T. Rankin, "The Importance of Listening Ability," *English Journal* (College Edition), XVII, 623–630.

the interrelated materials of words, sentences, paragraphs, and the whole composition, appear on virtually every page of this book.

Three essentials to the "good" theme or the well-written paper are correctness, clearness, effectiveness. If a theme lacks any one of these qualities, it is not a good theme; if it lacks more than one, or lacks any one to an unusual degree, it is a poor theme.

A well-written paper must be *correct* in its (1) grammar, (2) punctuation, (3) mechanics, and (4) spelling. It must be correct, clear, and effective in its (5) diction, (6) sentence structure, and (7) paragraph structure. It is quite possible for a paper to be *correct* in each of these seven elements and yet be neither clear nor effective. In fact, a paper which receives a passing grade is reasonably correct; but writing an excellent paper requires the added effort which contributes both clearness and effectiveness to the correctness that should, but cannot always, be assumed to be present in *formal* writing in university classes, or in formal or informal writing designed for readers beyond college boundaries.

Anyone who uses a handbook can learn to write correctly; the real achievement is to write clearly, vividly, effectively.

SPEAKING

The same general principles of correctness, clearness, and effectiveness apply to spoken communication. The same emphasis is needed on grammar, diction, sentence structure, paragraph structure (usually indicated in speaking by means of key words like "in the next place," "for example," "finally," etc.). The speaker does not worry, fortunately, about punctuation marks or misspellings; unlike the writer, however, he must be concerned about pronunciation, for it is as unforgivable for him to mispronounce words as it is for the writer to misspell.

The speaker, however, has one other heavy responsibility. The writer can expect—perhaps unreasonably—his reader to reread materials which he does not immediately understand or from which his attention has momentarily wandered. In listening, the communication is received but once, and unless it reaches the listener as the speaker desired it to do, communication fails. The

5

speaker has no opportunity, except in conversation, to repeat. He must therefore be *immediately* clear and effective.

Successful speaking, like successful writing, comes only through constant practice, but for the technical details of speaking (such as use of voice, posture, gestures, audience approach, type of speech, and the like) formal instruction is necessary through the aid of both teacher and textbook.

Can speaking help you in writing? Certainly. Since you speak many more times a day and on many more occasions than you write, habits of correct, clear, and effective speaking assist materially in correct, clear, and effective writing. On the negative side, watch your speaking (conversation, especially) for serious errors in grammar and word use. Such errors easily become habits and are frequently carried over into your writing.

READING

As a reader you move to the opposite end of the communication balance and "receive" what some other writer has sought to communicate. Your part in the process is not passive, unless of course you read merely to be entertained or to skim through for an idea here and there. Ordinarily, if you are reading for information and instruction, you will be an *active* reader and will have one of two major purposes, or both, in your reading: (I) to obtain as exactly as possible the ideas and content of the reading material; (II) to use the reading material for improving your own writing and speaking.

I. *In reading for information about ideas and content, use the following suggestions:*

1. Read and understand the title. Look also for any subtitle, prefatory note by the author, material about the author, any introductory summary, any footnotes giving additional information.

2. Determine the kind of reader (degree of education, occupation, age level, sex) for whom the author is writing. Determine also how well the author has adapted his material to this reader, and what the occasion or the circumstances were for his writing. Has the author anywhere stated his central purpose?

The Process of Communication

3. Look for mechanical aids that the author has used to help you: subheads; numbering of sections (I, II, III, etc.); blank spaces between sections; italicized words or sentences; paragraph divisions.

4. Read the entire article, chapter, or section rapidly, and then reread it paragraph by paragraph. Near the beginning look for a statement that gives the "theme" or central thought and the point of view to be used in developing it. Underline the topic sentence (or topic phrase or word) of each paragraph. Notice how these topics are developed within each paragraph (see pp. 311–326). Use pen or pencil to indicate which paragraphs belong together. Look for transitional devices (see pp. 338–340) which indicate how successive paragraphs are linked or change the direction of the discussion. Note the length of the paragraphs and try to account for those which are extremely short or extremely long.

5. As you read, underline the words whose meaning you do not know and whose meaning you cannot guess from the context. Look them up in a good dictionary, choose the definition which fits the context, and write it in the margin.

6. Make a formal outline (see pp. 223–229) of the material, using for your main heads and subheads the underlining and grouping which you have done according to Suggestion 4.

II. *In reading to help yourself write and speak correctly, clearly, and effectively, use the following suggestions:*

1. Occasionally underline a word or a group of words and identify it grammatically by definition and use. Assist your review of grammar by choosing various grammatical terms and looking for examples of these in your reading.

2. Look at the punctuation marks in three or four paragraphs. Do they follow the conventional principles of punctuation? If any marks are used in a striking or unconventional manner, give a reason for their use, the purpose that they serve.

3. Look on each page for three or four examples of words spelled according to rules and of words which are exceptions to the rules.

4. Underline a certain number of words which you know and which are effectively used. Underline a certain number of words

which you do not have in your active vocabulary but which you will hereupon add, through the aid of your dictionary.

5. Study a certain number of the sentences. Examine them for their use of phrases and clauses, of subordination and coördination. Determine which sentences are simple, complex, compound, compound-complex (see pp. 51–53). Which are loose or periodic (see pp. 53–54)? Which use inverted word order? What is the proportion of long and short sentences? Examine the ways in which sentences begin and end. Use all this material for a brief analysis of the author's style and compare it to that of your own written work.

6. Restudy the author's paragraphs according to Suggestion 4, p. 7. Apply to your own paragraphs whatever methods of effective paragraphing the author has used.

7. Study the author's use of title, of a "theme" statement, of a controlling purpose, of a point of view, and of a plan of organization. If these are clear and effective, adapt them to your own writing, where feasible.

LISTENING

Listening, the most commonly used form of communication (42 percent of an average adult's waking hours), is difficult to utilize effectively. Most people have only a haphazard and inaccurate idea of what they have heard, partly because memory is faulty and partly because they have but one opportunity to hear what is spoken. Therefore, aside from conversation and other informal talks for entertainment, some note taking is necessary when you listen to classroom lectures, formal speeches, radio addresses, forum and panel discussions, and the like.

To obtain the most from your listening, your notes should contain answers to the following questions:

1. What was the occasion for the speech? What were the circumstances under which it was given?

2. Was the address given before a miscellaneous group or a specialized one (college assembly, classroom lecture group, specific

The Process of Communication

society, etc.)? Was it appropriate or inappropriate for this specified audience?

3. What was the subject of the speech? Did the speaker give early a phrase or sentence stating his central theme?

4. What was the purpose of the speech: to entertain, inform, convince, persuade, or incite to action? Was the speaker consistent in using logical and intellectual materials or in using an emotional appeal?

5. What materials did the speaker use in support of his central theme? How did he organize them? How did he indicate his plan of organization? (Watch for such clues as "there are three reasons," "in the second place," "as an example," "by way of contrast," etc., and for other linking or transitional devices.)

6. How did the speech begin (challenging statement, personal experience, anecdote, quotation, historical incident, etc.)?

7. What devices to hold attention throughout the speech were used (specific examples, personal experiences, definitions, allusions, questions, humor, familiar or unusual materials, repetition, stories or anecdotes or incidents, etc.)?

8. How did the speech end (concise summary, repetition of central theme, quotation, appeal for belief or action, etc.)?

9. What striking or unusual words were used? Did the general tone seem impartial or were words used to "slant" the subject in a given direction? List some of these striking, unusual, or "slanting" words.

(For suggestions on taking notes on lectures as well as on your reading, see pp. 286–287.)

Two widely popular forms of listening are radio and television listening. Programs in these mediums of communication are extremely varied, most of them being primarily for entertainment. Some combine information and entertainment, but you will probably not take many notes, if any, on such programs (unless it be a formal radio address). There are, however, several useful listening hints, if your listening is to be active and critical, built on three basic questions: (1) What *kind* of program is it (news broadcast, news commentary, radio drama, dramatized biography, address, forum, quiz program, etc.)? (2) What is *the general purpose* (information, recreation, inspiration, argument, etc.)? (3) At what *general or specific class* of listeners is it aimed? If and when some of this information can be obtained *before* the time of listening, the listening process is facilitated and strengthened.

From our particular point of view (learning to write, speak, read, and listen effectively), the most useful and popular radio programs are news broadcasts, commentator programs, and radio dramas. Radio news broadcasts provide lessons in the selection of materials arousing and holding interest. News commentators can be listened to for similar material selection, for a differentiation of conjectures from facts, and for an attitude of partiality (see Item 9, above) or impartiality. Note also these devices: the use of short sentences, the placing of transitional devices at the beginning of sentences, the absence of difficult words, repetition to make ideas effective, and, in general, the use of a conversational tone.

In listening to radio drama, try to discover—either before or early in the broadcast—what kind of drama is being presented: light, serious, farcical, satirical, mystery, biographical, etc. Determine the central theme of the play and state it in a sentence or two. Note the contributions made by the announcer or commentator and by the different characters. How do what these say and the way they say it help to characterize them, make them definite and "picturable"? What sound effects are used and what specific purposes do they serve? Note also how music influences the mood or tone of the play, indicates passage of time or change of scene, and sometimes even replaces words.

Movie and television programs are also varied, but the major part of the first, and perhaps of the second, is the dramatic presentation. Note the similarities and differences between radio drama and movies or television. In these latter two note how sound and sight, hearing and seeing, complement each other: as an experiment close your eyes for part of the program and hold your ears shut for a part—how much is missed? Again, answer for yourself questions about the type of drama, subject matter, and the central theme. Also, since you are seeing as well as hearing, determine how well the speeches are adapted to or appropriate for each speaker. For the best critical and active listening to movie and television

The Process of Communication

programs, some advance preparation is essential, a preparation becoming increasingly easy through reviews and comments in newspapers and magazines. (For further discussion of "criticism" in general, see pp. 260–261.)

As outlined above, informal listening and careful formal listening with note taking can contribute to the clearness and effectiveness of your writing, for you can apply to it the methods used to enable you to listen effectively.

NOTE: The foregoing discussion of the process of communication is necessarily brief and introductory. By using the resources of the school library (see pp. 276–283), you will discover books and magazine articles of great help. For example, in addition to both general and specialized works on speaking and writing, you will find such books as Mortimer Adler's *How to Read a Book,* Edgar Dale's *How to Appreciate Motion Pictures* and *How to Read a Newspaper,* E. Wayne Marjarum's *How to Use a Book,* Luther Weaver's *How to Listen to the Radio,* and Edward A. Tenney and Ralph M. Wardle's *A Primer for Readers.*

Chapter 2

Clear Thinking

Clear, orderly thinking should be one of your primary aims in writing and speaking. Its presence in the writing and speaking of others should similarly be evident as you read and listen.

In narrative (storytelling), description (word painting), and some forms of exposition (explanation), you approximate clear thinking when your material follows a *clear, orderly* plan—each part leading logically on to the part that follows (see pp. 223–229).

But in other forms of exposition (such as fact finding and in accounts of experiments, in both of which a chain of reasoning is necessary to lead to a definite conclusion) and in argumentative writing or speaking (designed to convince or persuade of the truth or falsity of a proposal or statement), the process of clear thinking becomes more complicated than mere planning and arrangement.

Two common methods of clear thinking, used and violated every day, are *induction* and *deduction*.

Induction seeks to establish a general truth, a comprehensive principle, an all-embracing conclusion. The inductive process begins by using observation of a number of specific facts; it classifies these facts, looks for similarities among them, and guards against or watches for variations; and from a sufficient number of these facts or particulars it draws a conclusion or "leads into" a principle. Once the principle is stated, other particulars or examples are sought to support or verify it. The movement is always *from the particular to the general*.

Deduction seeks to establish a specific conclusion by showing how a particular statement is true because it conforms to or is part of or "leads down from" a general truth or principle. The move-

12

Clear Thinking

ment, implied or expressed, is always *from the general to the particular.*

As an illustration: numerous examples show that men do not live forever, that therefore *men are mortal* (general truth). John Smith is a man; therefore, in the light of the general truth, *John Smith is mortal* (particular truth). Through such reasoning, the "laws" (here meaning "principles" or "descriptive, generalized statements") of any science, such as medicine, biology, chemistry, physics, etc., have been arrived at and are being applied every day in particular situations. Similarly with the "laws" or "rules" (i.e., principles) of language. For example, in punctuation: you read several hundred lines or pages of prose and make note of every period that you see. From your data, you reach this principle of punctuation: "A period is used after abbreviations and after a declarative or mildly imperative sentence." If there is a small percentage of variation, then you insert "usually" or "commonly" in your general statement. This is *induction.* Now suppose you write a sentence and have to decide what mark of punctuation to place at the end. You check your *particular* sentence and are sure that it is a declarative sentence, a specific example of the general principle that you have already arrived at. Your mark of punctuation, therefore, is a period. This is *deduction.*

Errors in thinking often occur in fact-finding and experiment-describing exposition and in argumentative writing and speaking, especially when writer or speaker is concerned with establishing his "case" and yields to the temptation to ignore, twist, or even falsify the evidence. For clear and straight thinking, therefore, guard against the errors briefly discussed below when you write or speak. Train yourself to know what they are by looking for them in the writings and speeches of others. Happy hunting grounds for errors in thinking are magazines, newspapers, radio programs, motion pictures, and advertising.

1. *Not distinguishing fact from opinion* is an error that appears in much thinking. A fact is based on actuality and can be positively proved. Opinion, on the other hand, is merely a personal inference drawn from facts. That is, it is a belief, a notion, the value of which is determined by the facts which support it and the

judgment of the person holding or expressing it. In this sentence, the italicized phrase is opinion, the remainder is fact: Robert Louis Stevenson, *the world's greatest informal essayist,* was born in 1850. A favorite trick of politicians, advertising writers, and propagandists generally is to insert opinions in the wake of facts. Mingling fact and opinion is also a favorite device of those weak on facts but strong in feeling.

2. *Hasty generalization* is one of the greatest sins against clear thinking. Frequently we observe a few instances and illogically jump to a conclusion. But we should guard against drawing a general conclusion from a particular proposition (premise) or only a few. An elementary check for this error is to try to think of a dozen familiar examples whenever we see or hear an all-embracing statement. Suppose that you know an excellent athlete whose mental equipment is inferior. That he is an athlete and that he is stupid can be established. But a conclusion that *all* good athletes are mentally deficient is unwarranted, even if you know of ten or a hundred similar athletes, as perhaps you do. The generalization is unsound. Making hasty generalizations is probably the most prevalent logical flaw in theme writing. Here are a few other examples:

> I'm certain that money is unimportant because my father lived and died a poor but happy man.
> Because she came from a wealthy family and attended a fashionable school, she is quite unpopular at — College.
> He has a great respect for authority, because he was brought up in Europe.
> Doctors are not unselfish scientists; the ones in my home town live in the best houses.

3. The *it-does-not-follow error (non sequitur)* is common in deductive thinking just as hasty generalization is in inductive thinking. The *non sequitur* is an inference or conclusion that does not follow from the materials upon which it is apparently based. The example is not included in the expressed or implied *all* group of the generalized statement, and the conclusion, consequently, is not valid. Or if the generalized statement is not universally true, it does

14

not follow that this generalized statement necessarily fits a particular example. Each error is illustrated, respectively, in the following:

> All the women students on our campus are enrolled in the School of Chemistry, and since student X is taking chemistry, student X must be a woman student.
>
> Athletes are poor students, and since John is fond of playing tennis, he stands near the bottom of his class scholastically.

4. *Insufficient or biased or suppressed evidence* should be guarded against in any process of clear thinking. Evidence consists of facts which furnish ground for belief; they tend to prove or disprove an assumption or proposition. The use of insufficient evidence results in our making hasty generalizations; the use of biased evidence results in equally unwarranted and unproved assumptions which actually insult the intelligence of reader or listener; suppression of evidence—evidence in favor of the other side or casting some doubt on our own presentation—is completely dishonest, and flagrantly so when we are attempting to establish a general law or conclusion in the field of fact finding or experimental investigation.

To prove, for example, that agricultural income fluctuates too widely you should do more than cite figures for two years. These may have been unusual years, and your reader will immediately wonder what the figures over a five- or ten-year period would reveal. Similarly, the statistics of more than one organization should be cited; it may make considerable difference whether the figures come from an unbiased source, from a militant agricultural group, or from an association of consumers. Figures lie most easily when evidence is insufficient or biased or suppressed. ("Figures don't lie, but liars figure.") Much of the so-called truth about advertising, or national income, or the value of sports, or similar materials designed to impress the public comes from biased sources: paid propagandists and directly interested apologists. The testimony of a full-time secretary of a national fraternity is insufficient in itself to support a contention that fraternities are not snobbish; the evidence of a girl to whom no sorority ever paid any attention may be biased and is certainly insufficient to prove that sororities are

15

socially undesirable. A statement that all Joe's male ancestors were heroes, when you know that there were several "black sheep" among them, is an example of suppressed evidence.

5. *Begging the question* consists of taking an argument for granted before it is proved. Most superstitions and many folk sayings owe their existence to our willingness to accept what has not been proved. "He who hesitates is lost" is a commonly accepted statement, but the soundness of this advice has not been proved any oftener than that of "Look before you leap." For thousands of years many people have unhesitatingly accepted the statement that women are inferior to men. Had proof been demanded, we should long since have learned that women are superior to men in some respects, inferior in some, and equal in others. Jesus and Socrates, to mention only two names, were condemned to death by officials who begged the question, and their deaths were approved by many who never demanded proof of their guilt. We are prone to condemn people or groups or parties suspected of maliciousness or crime without demanding proof. How many times have you taken for granted some argument about democracy, or a political party, or socialism, or a college education without trying to get at the facts?

6. *Name calling,* the most prevalent and insidious form of "begging the question," deals with personalities rather than principles, seeking to discredit by emphasizing undesirable and often unproved characteristics. It appeals to prejudice and emotion, not to the intellect. Our minds are so quick to accept epithets that we fail to look behind the propaganda to the facts themselves. Frequently name calling appears as sarcasm and invective, which, like fireworks, are momentarily brilliant but without lasting effects. Examples: "this wolf in sheep's clothing," "fifth columnist," "this Don Juan among men," "a parlor pink," "a renegade statesman."

7. *"Slanting,"* a form both of "begging the question" and of "biased evidence," uses colored, unfairly suggestive words to create an emotional attitude for or against some person or movement. It is a favorite device of propagandists; its entire approach is one-sided, subtle, and cumulative. Examples: "this *undesirable* pro-

Clear Thinking

posal," "such a *sly* act," "an *unworkable* and *makeshift* substitute," "*dangerous* tendency."

Another form of "slanting" is using the same ambiguous word several times, with a shift in meaning that, it is hoped, will escape the reader or listener. You might write convincingly of sports and subtly shift your meaning to that of intercollegiate athletics. Both major political parties, for example, could use the following: "Preserve this great American democracy (republic) by voting the straight Democratic (Republican) ticket."

8. *Leaving gaps in thought* is as prevalent in argument as in exposition (see p. 241). But what is merely annoying in exposition will actually lose arguments. Such a statement as "John dislikes television, especially programs of popular songs" is illogical. The writer has first thought of television and then placed it and popular songs in the same class. The statement will be more coherent if it reads, "John dislikes televised musical programs, especially those of popular songs."

9. *Evading the issue* occurs most frequently in heated personal arguments but it is prevalent everywhere. It consists of ignoring the point of contact and making another statement which has no relevance. When you tell a classmate that his study habits are lax and he retorts that you don't handle your allowance properly, he has ignored the question. He may be quite right, but he has not won the argument; he may have quieted you, but his "argument" has no relevance. He has merely turned the talk against you, employed what logicians call *ad hominem* (against the person) argument. *Ad hominem* argument is especially common in political campaigns where issues are not met squarely. A candidate will attack the past record, character, and even family of his opponent without once confronting the issues themselves. His appeals to passion and prejudice may gain votes but they cannot be called sound argument, nor can they convince auditors who have trained themselves against the pitfalls of illogical thinking.

10. *Faulty analogy* occurs when we infer that because two objects or ideas are similar in one or more respects they must necessarily be similar in some further way. Analogy itself can be both accurate and effective; otherwise we could never make use of two rhetorical

17

devices based upon it: simile and metaphor. But all too frequently our use of analogy is faulty because stated points of similarity are not essential; they are either superficial or less important than the differences. We may, for example, argue that a certain law has operated well in Ohio; to infer that it will be equally effective in Texas or California or North Carolina is to argue by analogy, possibly faulty. To assume that what held true for the thirteen colonies in the eighteenth century also holds true for an industrial nation many times as large in the twentieth century is to use faulty analogy. Because a certain type of student government has worked well at — University, it does not necessarily follow that it will be ideally suited to — College.

Analogy is more effective in other forms of discourse than in closely reasoned writing. But in all writing and speaking it is effective only to the extent that it is illustrative, because in most analogies differences outweigh similarities.

From the foregoing paragraphs it is apparent that errors in thinking (technically, fallacies in logic) not only are common but overlap each other. The specific names of these fallacies and of others which could be mentioned are relatively unimportant. What is important is that we try to find and analyze evidence; that we do not permit emotional bias and prejudice to take the role of sound reason or let unsound reason corroborate our prejudices. In short, we should attempt to acquire honest habits of thought. Colleges may fall short of their goals in many other respects, but they do provide unlimited opportunities and training in this significant endeavor.

Chapter 3

Your First Themes

Regularly through your freshman year and occasionally in later college assignments you will be required to write papers of varying length. The chief purpose of this writing is to establish and confirm habits of correctness, clearness, and effectiveness in written work, so that in future years your writing will measure up to the standards expected of one with your degree of education.

"FRESHMAN ENGLISH"

Your college writing will begin in the first week or two of your freshman year with so-called formal training being given in freshman English. The aim of this course is to give you practice in the correct, clear, effective expression of your own ideas, emotions, reactions, thoughts. It is not a course designed for the training of professional writers. It makes no demands beyond the ability of the ordinary student. The instructor will grade your written work by marking all your major errors and many of your minor ones. Only as you eliminate these errors (and the more rapidly you do so, the better) will your writing conform to acceptable standards of Good English—written and spoken English used effectively in carrying on the business, professional, and social affairs of our country.

ATTAINING THE STANDARDS OF GOOD ENGLISH

To attain these standards of good English, you need constant practice in writing. You will get limited practice, once or twice a week, by writing papers in your freshman English course. But you cannot make much progress merely by letting your first draft be your final draft or by giving either first or last draft a hasty re-reading before calling it finished. Nor can you establish *satisfactory* habits by writing carefully only one or two papers a week for freshman English. Careful planning, composing, rereading, and checking—these you should apply to *everything* you write, even to the letters you send to relatives and friends. If you ignore this plan, you will always have so much trouble in writing that you will be afraid to write anything, and you will dread the task. If you follow this plan, you will be astonished at your progress, and you will soon find ease and pleasure in any writing that you do. Remember that any improvement in writing comes only through your own efforts, through the time, study, and care that you yourself devote. The best teacher and the best textbooks can only assist; they can never do the job for you.

It is impossible to state authoritatively how long you should spend in the preparation of a paper or theme. Subjects vary in difficulty. Students differ in their abilities: some write easily and rapidly; others write slowly and laboriously. However, *every student* should spend *at least two hours* on each 400- or 500-word assignment. If you have made any serious errors, work at them first. If you have few such errors, concentrate also on improving your sentences and word choice. Usually there is only one answer to that ubiquitous question, "How can I make my themes better?" It is the uninspired but eminently true "Take more time." Make this ironclad rule for yourself: *Always reread and revise every paper that you write: always proofread your final draft, pencil or pen in hand, pointing to every word and punctuation mark.* Reading aloud, when possible, will help, for it slows down proofreading speed. If you find that you are making several kinds of errors, reread each paper several times, looking during each reading for similar errors of a specific kind: that is, once for misspellings, once for errors in punctuation, once for errors in grammar—and the like.

AIDS IN ATTAINING STANDARDS OF GOOD ENGLISH

To help you attain standards of good English, your instructor will give during your freshman English course—in addition to new material—some review or memory-refreshing assignments in grammar, punctuation, spelling, diction, and sentence construction. Unfortunately, these assignments cannot be given simultaneously, nor can they always be given in the order in which you may need them. Your early writing, for example, may show errors in spelling, or diction, or punctuation, or grammar, while your assignments are dealing with the whole theme, choice of subject, planning, or paragraphing. You may feel aggrieved that your themes are being graded down for errors that you have not yet studied in your review assignments or classwork. When this happens, your task (and it is *your* task, no one else's—if you hope to improve) is as follows:

1. Utilize to the fullest extent any comment that your instructor makes on your themes. Note carefully the errors he marks and reference numbers indicating sections of this handbook. Through his aid you will find where your weaknesses lie, and you will be in a strategic position to make the necessary revisions and to avoid making the same errors in later themes.

2. As a part of this strategy, keep a record of your most common errors in writing (see chart on inside of cover) and consult it each time you have any writing to do.

3. Through the aid of the following pages (consult the Index, if necessary), immediately study and master the specific directions concerning the elimination of the error or errors that you are making. A worthy ideal is to try never to make the same mistake twice, or even the same kind of mistake.

4. An additional valuable aid is to make a "correction sheet" for every paper that is returned to you. A sample form, *filled out*, is given on the following page. In the left margin put the symbol and the handbook section number. In the left column copy the material from the theme exactly as it is; in the right column copy the same material but make *sufficient change* so that the error is corrected. Be sure to include enough in both columns so that both the error and the correction are immediately understandable (even weeks afterward) without further reference to the theme. Consult these correction sheets when you are assigned additional writing. As the

number of your correction sheets increases, you will have a personal guide to both the kinds of errors that you habitually make and the methods by which these errors can be corrected.

CORRECTIONS FOR THEME No. x

	Incorrect	*Correct*
sp 81e	admited	admitted
p 23a	a students first task	a student's first task
sp 81b	to many activities	too many activities
CS 18u	Many a freshman becomes a reporter for the student newspaper, this activity aids him in his writing.	Many a freshman becomes a reporter for the student newspaper; this activity aids him in his writing.
SF 61	Another activity that everyone needs involves physical exertion. If he wants to keep in good physical condition.	Another activity that everyone needs involves physical exertion, if he wants to keep in good physical condition.
gr 6b	The major activity of many students are in the field of athletics.	The major activity of many students is in the field of athletics.
gr 5c	An individual activity appeals to my roommate and I.	An individual activity appeals to my roommate and me.
FS 63	Such in brief are our extracurricular activities every student should choose one of them and take an active part.	Such in brief are our extracurricular activities; every student should choose one of them and take an active part.

SAMPLE FORM FOR "CORRECTION SHEET" FOR THEMES

SERIOUS ERRORS TO BE AVOIDED

As a short cut to more rapid improvement in writing, you should concentrate on avoiding all of the serious errors discussed below. (If any of these appear, consult immediately the pages listed.) You

Your First Themes

should answer satisfactorily each of the following questions about each of your early themes and continue applying the practice to all your written work.

1. IMPROPER CHOICE AND LIMITING OF SUBJECT.

Have I chosen a subject and narrowed it so that, in the number of words at my disposal, I have given my reader a clear and complete (not a vague, general, and rambling) account of what he expects to learn from my writing? (See pp. 207–210.)

2. FAULTY PLANNING.

Have I followed an orderly plan in the writing of my paper? (Always make a brief written or mental outline, dividing your subject into two, three, four, or more related parts and writing a paragraph on each part. See pp. 223–229.)

3. IMPROPER PARAGRAPHING.

Is each of my paragraphs an adequate treatment of one phase or division of the subject? Does it include material that belongs elsewhere in the paper? Does it omit material (or include it in some other paragraph) that is necessary to the clear development of the topic of this paragraph? Is any paragraph too long or detailed? Too short and concise? (See pp. 327–337.)

4. SENTENCE FRAGMENTS.

Have I written any unjustifiable sentence fragments? Remember that a sentence—to be clear, for most practical purposes, to your reader—must contain a subject and a predicate and must make sense by itself. When punctuated like a sentence, dependent clauses and various kinds of phrases—verb phrases, participial phrases, infinitive phrases, absolute phrases, appositive phrases, and prepositional phrases—serve in general only the undesirable purpose of confusing your reader. Such sentence fragments can usually be corrected (a) by attaching each to an independent statement or (b) by making each complete, with its own subject and predicate. (See pp. 350–351.)

Incorrect: I was a student for four years at Oriole High School. From which I was graduated in June, 1950. (Dependent clause.)

Correct: I was a student for four years at Oriole High School, from which I was graduated in June, 1950.

Incorrect: That night the river overflowed its banks. And flooded the lowlands. (Verb phrase.)

Correct: That night the river overflowed its banks and flooded the lowlands.

Incorrect: John thinks he is an experienced mechanic. Having worked in a garage for four years. (Participial phrase.)

Correct: John, having worked in a garage for four years, thinks he is an experienced mechanic.

Incorrect: Harry has two goals in life. To graduate from college and to establish himself in business. (Infinitive phrase.)

Correct: Harry has two goals in life: to graduate from college and to establish himself in business.

Incorrect: Winter having come early that year. The mountain passes were soon blocked by the snow. (Absolute phrase.)

Correct: Winter came early that year. Soon the mountain passes were blocked by the snow.

Incorrect: My mother spent her girlhood on a farm near Wildwood. A small town in southeastern Ohio. (Appositive phrase.)

Correct: My mother spent her girlhood on a farm near Wildwood, a small town in southeastern Ohio.

Incorrect: After a long hard day of classes and studying. I am ready to tumble into bed early. (Prepositional phrase.)

Correct: After a long hard day of classes and studying, I am ready to tumble into bed early.

5. FUSED SENTENCES.

Have I written two sentences together, with no mark of punctuation between, and thereby confused my reader by not indicating to him where one complete thought ends and another complete thought begins? (See p. 354.)

Incorrect: That night the river overflowed its banks and spread over the lowlands thousands of people were left homeless by the time the waters receded.

Correct: That night the river overflowed its banks and spread over the lowlands. Thousands of people were left homeless by the time the waters receded.

6. "COMMA SPLICES."

Have I avoided making any unjustifiable "comma splices"? (A "comma splice" results from using a comma to separate two complete sentences, or, in grammatical terms, using a comma between two independent clauses not joined by one of the simple conjunctions, *and, but, for, or, nor, neither, yet.*) If your rereading shows you an unjustifiable "comma splice," it is a very simple matter to correct: (a) replace the comma with a period or a semicolon; (b) use one of the simple conjunctions just mentioned immediately after the comma; or (c) change one of the independent clauses to a dependent clause or a phrase, and let the comma remain. See pp. 352–353.

Incorrect: There will be a meeting of the Science Club on Friday evening, several important matters are to be discussed.

Correct: There will be a meeting of the Science Club on Friday evening. Several important matters are to be discussed. (Use of period.)

There will be a meeting of the Science Club on Friday evening; several important matters are to be discussed. (Use of semicolon.)

There will be a meeting of the Science Club on Friday evening, for several important matters are to be discussed. (Simple conjunction inserted after comma.)

On Friday evening there will be a meeting of the Science Club, in order to discuss several important matters. (Changing one independent clause to a phrase.)

25

7. MISUSE OF SEMICOLON.

Have I misused the semicolon by using it to set off a dependent clause or a phrase? (Ordinarily, the semicolon serves the same purpose as the period: to indicate the end of one complete thought and the beginning of another; it is this "break" in thought that your reader expects when he sees a semicolon. One guide is this: no period, no semicolon. Setting off dependent clauses or phrases with semicolons leads to the same confusion in your reader's mind as is caused by the *sentence fragment*. See p. 160.

Incorrect: Smith has a good position waiting for him; as soon as he finishes college.
Correct: Smith has a good position waiting for him as soon as he finishes college.

Incorrect: If I were you; I should ask for a recount of the ballots.
Correct: If I were you, I should ask for a recount of the ballots.

Incorrect: Being careful to observe all traffic regulations; I am considered a good driver.
Correct: Being careful to observe all traffic regulations, I am considered a good driver.

8. SERIOUS ERRORS IN GRAMMAR.

Have I avoided making any serious errors in grammar that would distract my reader's attention from what I am saying to the way I am saying it?

a. *Have I made my subjects and predicates agree in number?* (This is a subtle principle more easily violated than observed, partly because of the position of the subject, or the way nouns form their plurals, or the way two or more members of a compound subject are connected. See pp. 64–68.)

Incorrect: More freshmen is needed for the football squad.
Correct: More freshmen are needed for the football squad.

Incorrect: In this house lives my sister, her husband, and their two children.

Your First Themes

Correct: In this house live my sister, her husband, and their two children.

Incorrect: Neither my sister nor her husband have a college education.

Correct: Neither my sister nor her husband has a college education.

b. *Have I used adjectives and adverbs correctly, and not used an adjective when I should have used an adverb, or vice versa?* (See pp. 106–108.)

Incorrect: Things are going *good* with me now.
Correct: Things are going *well* with me now.

Incorrect: I have never smelled anything so *fragrantly.*
Correct: I have never smelled anything so *fragrant.*

c. *Have I used the correct form of the verb?* (Serious errors in verb use, in addition to misusing singular-plural forms, are mistaking the past tense for the past participle, or vice versa, and confusing similar verbs like *lay—lie, sit—set, raise—rise.* See pp. 83–86.)

Incorrect: The cattle were laying on the grass.
Correct: The cattle were lying on the grass.

Incorrect: John seen the car coming and done his best to avoid the accident.
Correct: John saw the car coming and did his best to avoid the accident.

Incorrect: Father has ran for public office numerous times.
Correct: Father has run for public office numerous times.

d. *Have I used the correct case forms of pronouns when these are the objects of verbs or prepositions?* (See pp. 59–63.)

Incorrect: Did you telephone John or *I* last evening?
Correct: Did you telephone John or *me* last evening?

Incorrect: Your amusing letter to Harry and I was greatly enjoyed.
Correct: Your amusing letter to Harry and me was greatly enjoyed.

Incorrect: The purpose of we students now is to learn to write correctly.

Correct: The purpose of us students now is to learn to write correctly.

9. MISSPELLING.

Have I checked the spelling of all words about which I am in doubt? Have I carefully proofread once for any misspellings due to carelessness?

REMINDER: Only after a theme has been carefully planned, written, rewritten, checked for all kinds of errors, and proofread is it likely to be correct in all its details of grammar, punctuation, mechanics, spelling, diction (including idiom), and sentence and paragraph structure. Always study *systematically* and *conscientiously* the handbook sections dealing with your particular weaknesses so as to forestall making errors.

PART II

The Harper Handbook

Grammar

A Comprehensive Review

Grammar is the science that deals with words and their relationships to each other; it is a descriptive statement of the way a language works. Grammar includes a discussion of the forms of words, their use in phrases, clauses, and sentences, their tenses, cases, or other changes in form.

It is true that different levels of usage are appropriate to different levels of education, but a college student is expected to employ language as do others with his educational advantages. In carrying on his affairs, both private and public, in college and in later life, he should know and use the forms and constructions appropriate to English as it is spoken and written by educated people. Unfortunately, few college students, despite years of previous drill, do understand basic grammatical principles; many of them insist that grammar is "dull," "dry," "lifeless," "not worth studying." Such accusations reflect not facts so much as a method of teaching and an attitude of mind. Consider these points:

1. Grammar is "dull" and "dry" only when it is studied for its own sake, not when it is considered as a *means* toward correct, clear, and effective writing, which it definitely is. Actually, because grammar is a science, some people enjoy observing it, gathering facts, and classifying results just as do scientists in fields other than language. A linguist draws conclusions from his observations as does the chemist, the botanist, or the physicist. Most college students, however, are content with an understanding of basic principles evolved from the conclusions of linguists. All too often, they

are content with much less than this! Medical students do not ordinarily enjoy the study of anatomy, as such, but a knowledge of anatomy is necessary for both physician and surgeon. Many football players dislike drill in fundamentals, but games are won by players who have mastered blocking and tackling and are lost by those who have not. A study of anatomy, of football fundamentals, of grammar, is but a means to an end. Thus considered, none of these endeavors can be considered "dull" or "dry."

2. Grammar is far from "lifeless"; it is a kind of organism, always changing and developing. Grammar describes mutation. Language is not based upon grammar, for the latter is a study and record of speech habits. Grammar is not correctly considered as a list of rules imposed by authorities, a rigid set of *do's* and *do not's*. It is the scientific record of a series of observed language phenomena and is subject to constant fluctuations. Nothing can be more alive than grammar because nothing is more human. Many of the grammatical essentials discussed in the following pages may seem definite and unchangeable. This fixity is more apparent than real. Grammar is *descriptive* rather than *prescriptive,* and the statements which follow are quite different from those of fifty years ago. Presumably, because language and the grammar based upon it are both progressing and perfectible, the language used and grammar studied by our children and grandchildren may differ markedly from the comments which follow.

3. It is true that *what* we have to say is more interesting than a study of the language itself. Yet grammar is "worth studying" if only because, properly understood, it can help us to express our ideas correctly, clearly, and effectively. Obscurity and weakness in writing and incorrectness of sentence and paragraph structure are often directly traceable to an inadequate understanding of grammar. You do not need to know the principle of the combustion engine in order to drive an automobile, but you must know where to insert the ignition key, how to start the motor, how to shift gears, steer, and apply brakes. Some drivers are so proficient in these operations that they perform them almost automatically. Neither are skilled speakers and writers always consciously aware

of grammar. A professional writer might find it difficult to define an adjective, but if the phrase, "a night when the wind blew," came to mind, he might "instinctively" change it to the shorter and more effective "windy night." If you do not know what a clause and a phrase are, you will find it difficult to follow your instructor's suggestion to "reduce predication." But only a little knowledge of grammar will enable you to change the sentence "Diphtheria, which used to be a deadly disease, is now rare" to the more direct "Diphtheria, once a deadly disease, is now rare." Every good writer must have a working knowledge of words and their ways.

The study of grammar is of limited value in itself. To be able to say by rote, "A sentence is a group of words expressing a single, complete thought, or a group of very closely related thoughts" is of no help in constructing grammatically correct sentences unless the terms of the definition are thoroughly understood, unless comprehension of the *functions* of parts of speech, of various kinds of sentences, gives meaning to that definition. To learn the parts of speech, to distinguish simple, complex, and compound sentences—such additions to the store of memory represent wasted effort until you begin to relate them to the writing of real sentences, until you see such knowledge operating upon the sentences which you construct.

The following paragraphs are a review of the essential principles of grammar. Master them and *translate them into your own thought processes*. Make them serve you in your writing and your speaking.

Definitions of the grammatical terms used are listed alphabetically in the glossary, Section **15**, page 115. Refer to this glossary frequently as you study the following pages.

WORDS

1. A *word* is a concept, a combination of sounds forming an independent unit of thought. Since all writing and speaking consist of concepts, it is correct to say that our ideas can be no better than our vocabularies, our word supplies.

1a. Learn to identify each word as a part of speech.

Words are classified according to their use in larger units of thought, that is, sentences. This functional division results in the so-called *parts of speech*. A part of speech, therefore, is a word (sometimes a combination of words serving the purpose of one word) used in writing or speaking to express a definite idea, such use becoming definite only in relation to surrounding words. Every word must be one of the eight parts of speech: *noun, pronoun, adjective, verb, adverb, preposition, conjunction, interjection.*

Many words are always used in a certain way, as an unchanging part of speech; but since our language is constantly changing and since words also change in meaning, the function of words reflects such change. The word *iron*, at first thought, seems to be a noun only, as in *made of iron;* yet in *an iron bar* it is an adjective and in *to iron a shirt* it is a verb. A rather unusual extension is seen, for example, in the word *chair;* almost always a noun, it has been used as a verb. A. E. Housman tells of carrying a victorious athlete "shoulder-high" in a parade through his home town:

> The time you won your town the race
> We *chaired* you through the market-place.

1b. Distinguish carefully the purposes that words serve.

To determine what part of speech a given word is, see how the word is used in the sentence of which it is a part.

Words *name, assert, modify,* and *join.*

NAMING WORDS: NOUNS AND PRONOUNS

A *noun* names a person, place, or thing, a quality, idea, or action. Common nouns name all members of a common group: *man, officer, city, building, state.* Proper nouns name particular members of a group: *Mr. Ward, Jefferson Davis, Dallas, Parthenon, Arkansas.* Some common nouns are concrete: *book, candy, hammer, sweater*—names of objects which can be perceived by the senses of touch, sight, taste, hearing, or smell. Some are abstract nouns: *honesty, intelligence, grace, strength*—names of things which cannot be perceived by the senses. Some are collective nouns:

crew, family, assembly, union—names used for groups considered as units.

Nouns have *number,* singular or plural; *gender,* masculine, feminine, neuter, common (see **Gender** in the glossary, p. 121); and *case,* a common form (for both nominative and objective) and a possessive (genitive).

1c. Do not carelessly use the singular form of a noun for the plural.

Wrong: These *house* can be built rapidly.

Freshman and sophomores are seated in a special cheering section.

Some movie actors have three or four *wife* in rapid succession.

Plurals of nouns are formed as follows:

1. Most nouns form the plural by adding *-s* to the singular: dog, dogs.

2. Nouns ending in a sibilant sound *(ch, sh, ch, x, z)* add *-es:* church, churches; fox, foxes.

3. Nouns ending in *-y* preceded by a consonant ordinarily change *y* to *i* before adding *-es:* library, libraries; sky, skies. When the final *y* is preceded by a vowel, the *y* usually remains unchanged and only *s* is added: valley, valleys; key, keys.

4. Nouns ending in *-o* preceded by a vowel add *-s:* radio, radios. Some nouns ending in *-o* preceded by a consonant form their plurals with *-s:* piano, pianos; zero, zeros; others with *-es:* echo, echoes; potato, potatoes.

5. Nouns ending in *-f* are so variable that a dictionary should be consulted: chief, chiefs; loaf, loaves. Nouns ending in *-ff* add *-s:* sheriff, sheriffs. Most nouns ending in *-fe* change *-fe* to *-ve* and add *-s:* wife, wives.

6. Irregular plurals are numerous: man, men; child, children; foot, feet; sheep, sheep.

7. Compound nouns ordinarily form the plural by adding *-s* or *-es* to the important word in the compound: sons-in-law; passers-by. If the word elements are so closely related as to be

considered a single word, the *end* of the word is pluralized: hand-fuls.

8. Certain nouns of foreign origin retain the plural of the language from which they were borrowed: datum, data; hypothesis, hypotheses. Many borrowed words, however, have gradually assumed plurals with -s or es: area, areas; campus, campuses.

When in doubt concerning the spelling or the specific form of the singular or plural, consult your dictionary. The number of nouns when used as subjects of sentences is discussed further in Section **6,** page 64.

1d. Use the correct form of a particular noun in the possessive case.

Misuse of nouns in the possessive case is usually due to carelessness; many students write the plurals of nouns when these should be showing possession. Nouns form their possessive case as follows:

Singular nouns not ending in -s add -'s: a *boy's* game; a *dog's* life.

Singular nouns ending in -s add the apostrophe only; there being few s endings of common nouns in the singular using the apostrophe, this principle commonly applies to proper nouns, which may also add -'s: Mr. *Jones'* children or Mr. *Jones's* children.

Plural nouns ending in -s add the apostrophe only: *boys'* games; *girls'* dresses.

Plural nouns not ending in -s add -'s: *men's* hats; *women's* shoes; *children's* games.

For variety, for avoiding awkwardness, and with inanimate objects, possession is indicated by an *of* phrase: the home *of my parents* (my parents' home); the activities *of any student* (any student's activities).

Case of nouns is discussed further in Section **5,** page 59, and in Section **23,** page 170.

1e. Distinguish carefully the different kinds of pronouns and the purposes that they serve.

A *pronoun (pro,* literally *for* or *instead of)* substitutes for a noun or a noun equivalent. Every pronoun refers directly or by clear implication to a noun or noun equivalent (called the *antecedent* of

36

the pronoun) and agrees with that antecedent in person, number, and gender (but not necessarily in case): "Each boy present will please raise *his* hand."

Pronouns, which are used in all the grammatical functions of nouns (as object, subject, etc.), are of several kinds: *personal, relative, demonstrative, interrogative, reflexive* and *intensive, indefinite,* and *reciprocal.*

A *personal* pronoun is a direct substitute for a noun as subject or object: "Where did *you* buy it?" Like a noun, it has gender (some pronoun forms include all three genders; other forms show distinctive genders), number, and case, as shown by the following table.

	SINGULAR	
NOMINATIVE	POSSESSIVE	OBJECTIVE
1st person: I	my, mine	me
2nd person: you	your, yours	you
3rd person		
masculine: he	his	him
feminine: she	her, hers	her
neuter: it	its	it
	PLURAL	
1st person: we	our, ours	us
2nd person: you	your, yours	you
3rd person		
all genders: they	their, theirs	them

When there are two possessive forms of the personal pronoun, the first one given in the list above is followed by the noun it qualifies; the second is used alone.

My book is on the desk; *yours* is on the shelf.

The book on the desk is *mine.*

His appointment is at nine; *hers* is at ten o'clock.

Grammatical problems frequently arise from the fact that, unlike nouns, personal and relative pronouns (see below) have distinct forms for the nominative and objective cases. These problems are fully discussed in Section 5, page 59.

A *relative* pronoun relates or connects an adjective clause to the antecedent. It does have case but no forms distinctive of gender or number. However, the choice of a relative pronoun is determined in part by its antecedent: *who* is used to refer only to persons; *which* is used in reference to things (inanimate objects, animals) and may be used for a group of persons considered as a group; *that* may refer to either things or persons.

> The flyer *who* served in World War II is now an airline official.
> Radar equipment *which* is to be used for small ships must be installed carefully.
> The crew *which* won the race was excused from classes.
> The hat *that* I bought last summer is now out of fashion.
> The man *that* I saw was named Mortimer Taylor.

Of these three, *who* is the only one having case forms, as follows:

SINGULAR AND PLURAL

NOMINATIVE	POSSESSIVE	OBJECTIVE
who	whose	whom

That and *which* have no changes in form; the possessive of *which* is indicated by *of which*.

> My father, *who* is a doctor, lives in Seattle.
> John, *whose* ambition is to be a doctor, is in his third year of medical school.
> The students to *whom* we spoke are our classmates.
> The garment the color *of which* is faded must be redyed.

Who, which, and *that* are the most frequently used relative pronouns. *Whoever, whomever, whichever,* and *whatever* are less frequently employed compound forms; *whosoever, whichsoever,* and *whatsoever* have almost entirely gone out of current use.

A *demonstrative* pronoun points out and identifies. It has different forms for number but not for gender or case. The most important demonstrative pronouns are *this, that, these, those, such.*

> *This* is the way to kick a spiral.

That is my new television set.
These are your books; *those* on the desk are mine.

An *interrogative* pronoun (*who, which, what,* occasionally *whoever, whichever, whatever*) introduces a question.

Who shall demand that a pardon be granted?
Which is the route we should take from Hammond?
What do you have in mind?
Whom do you mean?

Like the relative pronouns, the interrogative *who,* only, has case forms, the same for both singular and plural: *who, whose, whom.*
A *reflexive* pronoun is used for simple reference to the subject; it usually follows the verb and directs or *reflects* its action back to the subject. It is composed of one of the personal pronouns plus *self* or *selves.* Most frequently employed reflexive pronouns are *myself, yourself, himself* (never *hisself*), *herself, itself, ourselves, yourselves, themselves.* These same forms, usually in an appositive position, when used to emphasize or *intensify* a noun are called *intensive* pronouns.

The cook accidentally scalded *herself.* (Reflexive use.)
They appointed *themselves* as cheer leaders. (Reflexive use.)
This barber always shaves *himself.* (Reflexive use.)
This barber *himself* shaves one hundred customers a day. (Intensive use.)
The nurse *herself* was at fault. (Intensive use.)
We students *ourselves* planned the program. (Intensive use.)

Indefinite pronouns are somewhat less exact in meaning than other pronouns. They are *pronouns* because they refer to antecedents; they are indefinite because the antecedents are not specifically named persons or things. Among the more frequently used indefinite pronouns are *another, any, anyone, anything, everybody, everyone, everything, few, many, nobody, none, one, several, some, someone,* and *something.* Compound forms built upon the pronoun *one* or the element *-body* have a possessive form ending in *-'s* (*anyone's, everybody's*). Indefinite pronouns involve grammatical problems which are discussed in Section **7,** page 69.

A *reciprocal* pronoun indicates an interchange of action suggested by the verb. This interchange may be seen in the following sentences involving the only two reciprocal pronouns in English:

The blonde and the brunette complemented *each other*.
The members of the exploring party shouted to *one another*.

ASSERTING WORDS: VERBS AND VERBALS

1f. Understand clearly the properties of verbs.

A *verb* asserts, or says, something; it may make a statement, give a command, or ask a question. A verb expresses action or a state of being.

They *fought* on the beachhead.
Is the corn ripe?
Be ready by eight o'clock.

Frequently, auxiliary (helping) verbs add particular shades of meaning—usually of time or voice—to the main verb. Such combinations are usually called verb phrases.

On one of the lawns in the outskirts of the village a woman *was cutting* the grass with a motorized lawn mower.
But the man of the soil *has been pushed* more and more out of the American picture.
A careful analysis of the oxygen content *should have been made* at the time.

Properties of the verb are voice (active and passive), mood (indicative, subjunctive, imperative), tense, number, and person. The last two of these properties are more concerned with the subject than with the verb itself; number and person are fully developed in Section 6, page 64. Tense, one of the most troublesome properties of a verb, is discussed in Section 10, page 87.

1g. Do not use a transitive verb for an intransitive verb, or an intransitive verb for a transitive verb.

Verbs are classified as either transitive or intransitive. A *transitive* verb is regularly accompanied by a direct object; this direct object completes the meaning of the verb: "They *accepted* his resignation." An *intransitive* verb requires no direct object: "He *will obey.*" Whether a verb is transitive or intransitive (the same verb may often be either) depends upon meaning, upon the idea which the writer wishes to show. In "He *will obey* our orders," the verb is transitive.

The most frequent misuse of transitive-intransitive verbs involves confusing *lie—lay, sit—set,* and *rise—raise.* The first verb in each of these pairs is intransitive, the second transitive (see the "Glossary of Faulty Diction," p. 459). If necessary, memorize the various forms of these verbs.

> A tree is *laying* across the road. (Verb should be *lying.*)
> I have *lain* my books on the desk. (Verb should be *laid.*)
> The old man *set* in the sun all afternoon. (Verb should be *sat.*)
> The kangaroo *raised* on its hind legs and ran away. (Verb should be *rose.*)
> The kangaroo *rose* itself on its hind legs and ran away. (Verb should be *raised.*)

Transitive verbs are further classified as to *voice—active* or *passive.* A verb is *active* when the subject is the performer of the action or is in the state or condition named.

> The engineers *threw* a bridge across the river.
> The lookout *sighted* the ship on the horizon.
> Tom *laid* the book on the table.

A verb is in the *passive* voice when its subject receives the action:

> A bridge *was thrown* across the river.
> The ship *was sighted* by the lookout.
> The book *was laid* on the table.

In the examples above, the point of view and the emphasis are quite different. The verbs which are active stress the doers of the action—engineers, lookout, and Tom; the verbs which are passive stress the recipients of the action—the bridge, the ship, and the book. Choice of active or passive voice depends upon context, upon relative importance of the doer and the recipient of the action. Since intransitive verbs rarely fulfill the conditions which make

41

1h

Words

verbs active or passive, only transitive verbs can have a passive voice. Voice is further discussed in Section 11, page 96.

The *mood* of a verb reveals how action is thought of: as a fact, a possibility, something desired, or a command. It is indicated by changes in verb form or through the use of auxiliary words. Problems of mood are discussed in Section 12, page 102; they largely concern the subjunctive, which is now less used than formerly. Differences between the indicative and subjunctive may be illustrated thus:

INDICATIVE	SUBJUNCTIVE
I take (am taken)	(if) I take (be taken)
you take (are taken)	(if) you take (be taken)
he, she, it takes (is taken)	(if) he, she, it take (be taken)
we take (are taken)	(if) we take (be taken)
I took (was taken)	(if) I took (were taken)

I am	we are	(if) I be	we be
you are	you are	(if) you be	you be
he is	they are	(if) he be	they be
I was	we were	(if) I were	we were

1h. Distinguish between finite verbs and verbals.

In English, verbs are finite and non-finite, depending on whether they are so formed and accompanied by another word as to make complete predications. Non-finite verb forms (words incapable of standing alone and making complete predications) are called *verbals*. The verbals are *participles, infinitives,* and *gerunds.*

Understanding the differences in form and function between finite verbs and verbals will help you avoid the most serious error in sentence construction, the half-sentence or fragment. Verbals cannot stand alone; if a group of words contains a verbal it must also include a finite verb in order to be a complete sentence.

A *participle* is a word which has the function of both verb and adjective. The *present participle* always ends in -*ing* (speaking, singing). The *past participle* has various forms (spoken, sung, walked, set); it is regularly in the passive voice. The *perfect participle* consists of *having* or *having been* plus the past participle (having spoken, having been sung); it is either active or passive in voice. The participle, since it is a form of the verb as well as an

42

adjective, can take an object and can be modified by an adverb. The participle resembles the adjective in that it can be modified by an adverb and can itself modify a noun or pronoun:

The ball *kicked* by the player went into the stands.
The boy expertly *riding* the horse is named John.
The tree *swaying* in the breeze is lovely.

An *infinitive* is a word which has the function of both verb and noun and which also may be employed as an adjectival or adverbial modifier. The infinitive is usually introduced by the sign *to* (to speak, to sing).

The *gerund* is a verbal noun ending in *-ing (speaking, singing)*. Because the gerund usually has the same form as the present participle, you must be careful to note the difference in their functions: the participle is a *verbal adjective;* the gerund is a *verbal noun*. Both an infinitive and a gerund can take an object and be modified by an adverb and, in their functions as nouns, can be the subject or object of a verb or the object of a preposition; gerunds can also be modified by adjectives.

Playing tennis is good exercise.   *participle*
To work intelligently is sometimes difficult.
He has plenty of time *to kill*.
All the campers enjoy *swimming*.   *gerund*
Steady *running* won the race for Henry.   *gerund*

MODIFYING WORDS: ADJECTIVES AND ADVERBS

1 i. For correct and exact meaning, understand the functions of adjectives and adverbs.

An *adjective* modifies a noun or pronoun by describing, limiting, or in some other closely related way making meaning more exact. An adjective may indicate quality or quantity, may identify or set limits. Consequently, adjectives are of three general types: descriptive (a *black* dress, an *easy* lesson, a *smashed* thumb); limiting (the *sixth* period, her *former* home, *several* times); proper (an *American* play, a *Colorado* melon).

The articles *(a, an, the)* may be classed as adjectives because

43

they possess limiting or specifying functions and always accompany a noun or, infrequently, a pronoun. *A* and *an* are indefinite articles; *the* is the definite article: *a* phonograph, *an* iconoclast, *the* physician. The initial sound of the following word determines the choice of *a* or *an*: *an* is used before words beginning with a vowel sound (including silent *h*); *a* is used before consonant sounds (except silent *h*) and before initial vowels that have both consonant and vowel sounds.

| an apple | an hour | a hero | a European visitor |

An adjective may modify a noun by preceding it, as do single adjectives or a series of single adjectives:

A *merry* laugh greeted us.
Red, green, and yellow lights are traffic signals.

Certain adjectives or adjective combinations may either precede or follow the noun; others, like restrictive adjective phrases and clauses, must follow.

The survivors, *tired, hungry, and emaciated,* moved feebly toward the ship. (Position optional.)
The boy *in the brown suit* is my brother.
The girl *rising to speak* is the valedictorian.

In sentences such as "The water felt *warm*" and "The corn is *green*," each adjective is related to the subject, the word it modifies, by a linking verb. (A linking verb has little meaning of its own; it functions primarily as a connection between subject and predicate noun or predicate adjective. In the sentences above, *warm* and *green* are called predicate adjectives or complements. See also Section 8, page 74.)

An *adverb* modifies or describes a verb, an adjective, or another adverb. In "A distant bugle sang *faintly*," the adverb modifies the verb *sang*. In "We were *almost* ready to start," the adverb modifies the adjective *ready*. And in "Open this jar *very* slowly," the adverb modifies the adverb *slowly* (which, in turn, modifies the verb *open*).

44

1j. Use the correct forms of adjectives and adverbs to indicate the three degrees of comparison.

Both adjectives and adverbs have changes in form or added modifiers to indicate *comparison*. If there is no comparison, the degree is *positive;* if two are compared, the degree is *comparative;* if three or more, the degree is *superlative*. The comparative and superlative degrees are formed, respectively, by adding *-er* and *-est* to adjectives and adverbs of one syllable and to some of two syllables; with other two-syllable adjectives and adverbs, if there is awkwardness, and with those of three or more syllables, the words *more* and *most* (upward comparison) and *less* and *least* (downward comparison) are used. (For further discussion, see the glossary, p. 118.)

Smith is a *tall* [*competent*] man. (Adjective, positive degree.)

Smith is a *taller* [*more competent*] man than I am. (Adjective, comparative degree.)

Smith is the *tallest* [*most competent*] man in our society. (Adjective, superlative degree.)

The Wabash River flows *fast* [*violently*] during the rainy season. (Adverb, positive degree.)

The Wabash River flows *faster* [*more violently*] in spring than in fall. (Adverb, comparative degree.)

The Wabash River flows *fastest* [*most violently*] in April, *least violently* in the winter months. (Adverbs, superlative degree.)

JOINING WORDS: PREPOSITIONS AND CONJUNCTIONS

1k. Distinguish between the functions of prepositions and conjunctions.

A *preposition* is a linking word used to show the relationship of a noun or pronoun to some other word in the sentence. Examples of frequently used prepositions are *at, with, to, from, in, into, of, before, after, through, except, by*. In common usage, certain prepositions are used with certain other parts of speech, forming idiomatic combinations:

comply with
independent of
blame you for it

entertain at dinner
plan on going
different from

These are only a few of hundreds of idioms in English, but they are among those most frequently misused. See Section **85**, pages 421–424, for a fuller discussion of idiom.

A *conjunction* is a linking word used to connect words or groups of words in a sentence. Conjunctions are of two main kinds: coördinating, which join words or groups of words of equal rank, such as *and, but, for, or, nor, neither, yet* (these seven are usually called pure or simple conjunctions); subordinating, which join dependent clauses to main clauses, such as *if, since, because, as, while, so that, although, unless,* etc.

Certain coördinating conjunctions used in pairs are called correlative conjunctions. Most frequently used of these are *both . . . and; either . . . or; neither . . . nor; so . . . as; whether . . . or.*

Another kind of conjunction is the conjunctive adverb, an adverb used as a connective. Examples are *accordingly, anyhow, indeed.* A discussion of the punctuation of conjunctive adverbs and an additional list of them are given in Section **19b**, page 157.

Conjunctions, particularly those which are to join clauses, must be chosen with care, for they always show logical relationships of ideas. Oftentimes a careless writer will use *and* where the relationship of clauses needs to be more accurately expressed, probably by use of subordination. Compare emphasis and meaning in these sentences:

> The search for the chemical formula has been rewarding, and further investigation will make the rewards even greater.
> Although the search for the chemical formula has been rewarding, further investigation will make the rewards even greater.

Common errors in the use of conjunctions are discussed in Section **14**, page 109.

These seven kinds of words—nouns, pronouns, verbs, adjectives, adverbs, prepositions, and conjunctions—are the principal parts of speech.

The eighth part of speech, the *interjection,* is simply an exclamatory word which has little connection with the remainder of the sentence: "*Oh,* must you go?" "And here, *alas,* our good fortune came to an abrupt end."

PHRASES

2. Identify phrases correctly, both for effectiveness in writing and for avoiding "sentence fragments."

A *phrase* is a group of related words not containing both a subject and a predicate. A phrase is used as a part of speech, the equivalent of a noun, adjective, adverb, or verb.

A phrase can be used in a sentence as a noun is used—as subject, object, etc.

Playing on top of the automobile was his special delight.

Used as a noun, the phrase is called a noun phrase. It functions in the sentence exactly as a single noun functions. In the example quoted, the noun phrase "playing on top of the automobile" serves as a name, a name for the particular activity which is a "special delight."

A phrase may modify a noun or pronoun, may function, that is, exactly as a single adjective functions; such a phrase is called an adjective (or adjectival) phrase.

The farmers *in the West* need rain.

Here the phrase describes "farmers"; for it the writer might well have used a single adjective: "The *western* farmers need rain."

Similarly, a phrase may modify a verb, adjective, or adverb, may function exactly like a single adverb; such a phrase is, of course, an adverb (or adverbial) phrase.

The woman fell *on the sidewalk.*

Here the phrase describes *where* the woman fell; it modifies "fell" even as a single adverb would modify it.

If a phrase is essential in order to explain or identify the word to which it refers, the phrase is called restrictive. If the phrase is not absolutely necessary, it is called nonrestrictive. Nonrestrictive phrases are always set off by commas from the remainder of the sentence.

The citizens' committee gains *in political stature.*

In this example the adverbial phrase is restrictive because it tells the particular way in which the committee gains.

The citizens' committee, *gaining in political stature,* began to demand reforms within the city government.

Here the adjective phrase is nonrestrictive because it is not essential to the writer's purpose in telling what the committee began to demand.

See Section **18m,** page 147, for further discussion and examples of punctuation for restrictive and nonrestrictive phrases.

A *verb phrase* consists of a group of words serving the function of a verb, such as an auxiliary verb with its main verb, or a verb with its modifiers.

By June your first college year *will have been completed.*
He *wrote legibly and carefully.*

Phrases may also be classified according to their initial or more important word. Four common divisions are the following:
Prepositional (used as adjectives or adverbs):

The house *on the corner* belongs to a fraternity.
The road winds *through the mountains.*

Participial:

Having completed my assignments, I went to bed.

Gerundive:

Going on a journey alone is not enjoyable.
After graduating from college, John went to New York.
(Prepositional-gerundive phrase.)

Infinitive:

To win games is the aim of every team.
He has worked hard *to achieve success.*

A peculiar kind of phrase is the *absolute phrase,* consisting usually of a noun followed and modified by a participle or participial phrase. It is a phrase because it cannot stand alone as a sentence; absolute, because it modifies no single word in the sentence of which it is a part.

Night coming, we ceased our work.

John went to bed, *his work being finished.*

The ability to identify and use prepositional, participial, gerundive, infinitive, and absolute phrases is necessary for correctness, clearness, and effectiveness in writing.

CLAUSES

A *clause* is a group of words which has both subject and predicate. Clauses are of two kinds: *independent* (or *main,* or *principal*) and *dependent* (or *subordinate*).

An *independent clause* makes a complete statement and may stand alone; that is, it makes reasonable sense if the remainder of the sentence is omitted.

I listened to the radio.

Although I should have been studying last night, *I listened to the radio.*

Sometimes there may be more than one independent clause in a sentence.

John studied, but *I listened to the radio.*

3. **Identify dependent clauses carefully, as a safeguard against writing sentence fragments and against incorrect punctuation.**

A *dependent clause* is not capable of standing alone; it depends upon the remainder of the sentence for its meaning, it is subordinate. Dependent clauses function as nouns, adjectives, or adverbs. Like an independent clause, a dependent clause contains a complete predication (subject and verb); but sometimes it shows dependence by the linking word which joins it to the independent clause.

What you paid was too much.

Here the dependent clause is used as a noun; the writer might have used a single noun as the subject of *was:* The *price* was too much.

49

He promised *that he would lend me the money.* (Noun clause used as the object of *promised.*)

I am fearful of *what he has in mind.* (Noun clause used as the object of the preposition *of.*)

His remark *that he hated college* surprised me. (Noun clause used as an *appositive;* see glossary, p. 117.)

His remarks usually were *whatever came to mind first.* (Noun clause used as a predicate complement; see **Complement,** p. 119.)

In the following examples the dependent clause is used as an adjective; each italicized clause functions exactly as would a single adjective:

The price *which he paid* was too much. (Clause modifies *price.*)

People *who rarely think* should say little. (Clause modifies *people.*)

You are the very person *whom I wanted.* (Clause modifies *person.*)

He is a boy *I never admired.* (Clause modifies *boy; whom* after *boy* is understood.)

Dependent clauses function as adverbs in the following sentences:

I shall pay the bill *when you send it.* (Clause modifies the verb *shall pay.*)

We are studying harder *than you are.* (Clause modifies the adverb *harder.*)

He was braver *than the other soldiers were.* (Clause modifies the adjective *braver.*)

If a dependent clause is essential in order to explain or identify the word to which it refers, the clause is called restrictive. If the dependent clause is not necessary, if it is in the nature of a parenthetical remark which could be removed from the sentence, leaving the essential meaning intact, it is called nonrestrictive. Nonrestrictive clauses are always set off from the remainder of the sentence by commas.

The man *who spoke at our Forum* is a member of the Commerce Commission.

The dependent clause is here restrictive, for it is necessary as a means of identifying the particular man. But in the following sentence the clause is nonrestrictive; the identification is made by the use of the proper name.

Captain Stiles, *who spoke at our Forum,* is a member of the Commerce Commission.

See Section **18m,** page 147, for further discussion of punctuation of clauses.

A special kind of clause is the *elliptical clause.* For practical purposes, it is a dependent clause; its subject and frequently part of its predicate are omitted because they are understood from the main clause. In the following pairs, the first example contains complete clauses, the second contains an elliptical clause.

Although I was ill, I insisted on attending class.
Although ill, I insisted on attending class.

When he was in New York, John went to the theater every night.
When in New York, John went to the theater every night.

While she was sewing, Mary listened to the radio.
While sewing, Mary listened to the radio.

Trouble arises when the omitted, understood parts are *not* those of the main clause.

When driving a car, the emergency brakes should be released.
When six years old, my mother married my stepfather.

SENTENCES

4. A *sentence* is a group of words containing a complete, independent thought or a group of closely related thoughts. A sentence must contain a *subject* and a *predicate*. The subject is the name of the person or thing about which the verb makes a statement. The predicate is what is said of the subject; it must contain a verb which can make a complete, independent statement. Such a verb is called a *finite* verb. REMEMBER: participles, infinitives, and gerunds are non-finite verb forms.

4a. Understand the grammatical classification of sentences to obtain variety.

Sentences may be classified according to grammatical structure as *simple, compound, complex,* or *compound-complex.*

A *simple sentence* contains only one subject and one predicate and expresses only one thought. But it may contain a compound subject (two or more nouns or pronouns joined by the proper conjunction) or a compound predicate (two or more finite verbs joined by the proper conjunction) or both.

> The street is paved. (Simple subject, simple predicate.)
> Peaches and plums are ripening on the trees. (Compound subject, simple predicate.)
> The girl arose and bowed. (Simple subject, compound predicate.)
> The boy and the girl talked and danced. (Compound subject, compound predicate.)
> Alumni, faculty, and students attended the game and cheered the team. (Compound subject, compound predicate.)

A *compound sentence* contains two or more independent clauses. The clauses of a compound sentence are grammatically capable of standing alone, but they are closely related parts of one main idea. (See "Clauses," p. 49.)

> The days are warm, but the nights are cool.
> She read, and I wrote letters.
> You may not win; nevertheless, you should try.

A *complex sentence* contains one independent clause and one or more dependent (subordinate) clauses.

> The student said that he had studied for over an hour.
> He is an athlete whose muscles are unusually supple.
> If the weather is fair, we shall go to the park.

A *compound-complex sentence* contains two or more independent clauses and one or more dependent clauses.

Sentences

4 b-c

Since the day was unpleasant, we stayed indoors; John studied, and I worked on my stamp collection.

4b. Understand the classification of sentences for the expression of meaning and purpose.

Sentences are also classified according to *meaning* and *purpose*. A *declarative sentence* states a fact or makes an assertion.

The house has twelve windows.

An *imperative sentence* expresses an entreaty or command.

Please come as soon as possible.

An *exclamatory sentence* expresses strong feeling.

Oh, if he were only here!

Thank goodness, you are here at last!

An *interrogative sentence* asks a question. Note that an interrogative sentence can be written in different ways:

By placing the subject after the auxiliary verb: *Are* you going? *Have* you bought any oranges? *Did* you study last night?

By using an interrogative pronoun or adverb: *Who* is it? *Which* is my book? *Where* did you find it? *How* are you?

By adding an interrogative statement to a declarative sentence: You have many visitors here, *haven't you?* You did study, *didn't you?*

By a question mark after a declarative statement: You're going home? You've been to the theater?

4c. Understand the arrangement of ideas in sentences for effectiveness.

Sentences are also classified according to the *arrangement* of their content. A sentence in which the words are so set down that the meaning is not completed until the end or near the end is called *periodic*. A sentence so constructed that the thought may be completed before the end is *loose*. Our conversation and informal writing contain many more loose sentences than periodic. Yet a periodic sentence does provide suspense and variety; it holds the attention of reader or listener and contributes to stylistic effectiveness. Although a natural form of expression, the periodic sentence

53

tends to become monotonous and forced and should not be over-used.

> Act quickly, or you will be too late to secure the bargain you want. (Loose.)
> He liked to play baseball and tennis but more than either he enjoyed dancing and ice skating. (Loose.)
> If you do not wish to go, please say so. (Periodic.)
> According to a former college president, to be at home in all lands and ages; to count Nature a familiar acquaintance and Art a familiar friend; to gain a standard for the appreciation of other men's work and the criticism of one's own; to make friends among men and women of one's own age who are to be the leaders in all walks of life; to lose one's self in generous enthusiasm and to coöperate with others for common ends; to learn manners from students who are gentlemen and gentle-women, and to form character under professors who are dedi-cated—these are the returns of a college for the best four years of one's life. (Periodic.)

A *balanced sentence* is so constructed that similar or opposing thoughts have similar structure. Such a sentence is sometimes used to make a statement especially emphatic and for comparisons and contrasts.

> Time is money; money is important.
> You can take a man out of the country; you can't take the "country" out of a man.
> You may call him the man who invented sin, but I would say he is the man whom sin invented.

For further discussion of the sentence see "The Sentence," pages 348–398.

SUMMARY

The sentence is the thought unit of composition. Themes can be no better than their individual sentences, and the ordinary writer cannot phrase good sentences without an understanding of the grammatical principles just discussed. Learn carefully the definitions and functions of the various terms mentioned. They are the *elements* of sentences, the words and groups of words which constitute sentences, the basic units of thought. But remember that the study of these definitions and functions is of little value in itself; only as the knowledge gained is used in avoiding errors, in building more concise, clear, and effective sentences does such study become worth while. A writer must understand words and their ways in order to control them, to work with them most efficiently. After you have mastered these fundamentals, you may profitably study the sections which follow.

EXERCISES

A. In the blank space following each italicized word write the part of speech of that word, using the abbreviations given (**N**—noun; **V**—verb; **Adj**—adjective; **Con**—conjunction; **Pro**—pronoun; **Adv**—adverb; **Prep**—preposition; **Int**—interjection):

Many (......) students *attend* (..V....) football *games* (......) *every* (......) week *during* (......) the season, *whereas* (......) *we* (......) notice that *some* (......) *work* (......) *busily* (......) in the library even while *the* (......) games are *in* (......) progress.

B. In the space provided write the part of speech of each italicized word in the following sentences:

1. It was a *very* warm day. ......
2. Susan was a most *intelligent* child. ......
3. He *caught* the book as it fell. ......
4. The *suit* will cost too much money. ......
5. He is sitting *by* a roaring fire. ......
6. They cannot go *because* it has rained. ......
7. This is the magazine of *which* you spoke. ......
8. He bought his books and *a* writing tablet. ......
9. "*Goodness!*" she said; "I'm an hour late already." ......
10. It seems to me that he *talks* too much. ......

C. Name the parts of speech of the italicized words, using the abbreviations given in Exercise A.

1. Fuchsias *and sunflowers make* an ugly bouquet.

2. *What!* six *hot* dogs in *one* afternoon!
3. The edge of the *razor* blade *resembled* a saw.
4. The drift *crept* imperceptibly *but relentlessly* on.
5. The rusty, *worn* old *chain* snapped in an instant.
6. The extent of the storm is *difficult* of prognostication.
7. *Her* slant on life is a *hard* one to *explain*.
8. *Who* wrote the note is *his* problem, not *mine*.
9. *Come,* Harry, can't you hurry up *quietly?*
10. *For* the life of *me,* I could *not* solve the problem.

D. In the following sentences underline each verbal and write above it an identifying letter: **P**—participle; **G**—gerund; **I**—infinitive.

1. He liked to swim and dance with me, but I always felt that he would rather read than do either.
2. He is constantly striving to better himself by taking courses in adult education.
3. Bathing, shaving, and dressing are unfortunately necessary preliminaries to eating breakfast.
4. The man buying his ticket is a merchant from a nearby city.
5. The game already having been won, we decided to leave soon after the intermission.
6. I tried to admire and respect him, and yet all I could do was to look upon him with loathing.
7. "What I want to know," asked one woman, "is whether to give my son a key and let him stay out as long as he likes. Isn't a boy given that much freedom likely to get into trouble, riding around at all hours of the night?"
8. His tackling and running are excellent, but I don't believe that he will ever learn to punt or catch passes.
9. As I had thought that talking and real conversation were the same thing, I was in no position to enjoy the elegant badinage to be heard at the captain's table.
10. He was a person who had enjoyed rowing for years—since reaching his sixth birthday, in fact—but now in this moment of peril to move an oar seemed impossible.
11. When some sniveling courtier asked the duke how one should enter a ballroom properly, he whipped out a folded handkerchief and flicked the man's cringing face.
12. Spoken words are naturally kept in mind with much more difficulty

than those one reads, but a well-trained spy can retain amazing amounts of conversation that he has heard.

13. As it flowed down the gray rock wall, the swiftly falling water seemed to have lost its liquid quality; it looked like a smooth and solidified pillar of green.

14. For a skater to fall occasionally is no more of a calamity than occurs to a speeding hurdler when he topples over a hurdle, but I fell times past counting.

15. Having opened the door before she looked through the peephole, she was startled to see an officer before her.

E. In the following sentences underline each phrase and write above it its identification, using the abbreviations: **Prep**—prepositional; **Part**—participial; **Ger**—gerundive; **Inf**—infinitive; **Abs**—absolute.

1. Through the night the train roared on to its destination.
2. To get along well with people, you must learn to share their interests.
3. In the spring, according to the poet, a young man's fancy lightly turns to thoughts of love.
4. Having reached the age of nineteen, I have no desire ever to fall in love again.
5. A motion for adjournment having been made, the meeting disbanded.
6. Traveling by airplane is our swiftest mode of travel; traveling by oxcart is the slowest.
7. Your teacher has no objection to your turning in well-written themes.
8. John wrote to a friend in Chicago to inquire about obtaining employment for the summer.
9. Smith being pretty well battered, the coach sent in Jones to replace him at tackle.
10. Seen from a distance, the night train, creeping up the mountain grade, looked like an animated glowworm.
11. A motion was made to close the nominations, no other names being proposed.
12. After opening and reading your letter, I understood your not receiving my invitation in time to accept.
13. To get experience and not to make money was his goal in seeking a summer job.

4 **Exercises**

14. Having been unanimously elected president, I expressed my gratitude for the honor bestowed upon me.
15. In catching fifteen trout, we had a good day of fishing, the legal limit being twenty.

F. Underline each phrase and clause in the following sentences. Above each phrase and clause indicate by these abbreviations its function in the sentence: **N**—noun; **Adv**—adverb; **Adj**—adjective; **Ind**—independent.

1. Although he may be too ill to go, I think that we should ask him to accompany us anyway.
2. I thought that he had gone to his room, but evidently he went to the cafeteria.
3. The people in that section have been marketing a great quantity of vegetables in the city this summer.
4. The task which he has set himself is too heavy for his limited ability. He has been trying to recover his health, catch up with the class, and do the current assignments all at the same time.
5. While you start the fire I'll try to get the tent put up.
6. Now that he has made a fortune, he is expected to start for Europe within the month.
7. He jumped up and down, he shouted and yelled; and yet, for some strange reason, none paid him the slightest attention.
8. When you have time, please help me translate this passage from Goethe. I have been trying for an hour to find out what he means.
9. The men who have been working in the experiment station are trying to develop a plant that will grow in any kind of soil.
10. If you come over tonight, we might listen to the new records in my collection.

G. In the blanks to the left indicate the kinds of sentences by writing the proper symbol: **S**—simple; **Cp**—compound; **Cx**—complex; **Cc**—compound-complex.

...... 1. Every street in the village is paved with wood blocks.
...... 2. Whenever the postman rings twice, my sister knows that he has a letter for her from Jack.
...... 3. The snow covered the roads to a depth of eight inches, but we had no difficulty in rolling right along.

Case

...... 4. If the gun jams easily, you should notify the corporal, and he will provide you with a new one.

...... 5. Twelve hours is a long while to sleep, but our bodies need such a rest occasionally because we regularly overwork them.

...... 6. Joan and Patricia, eager to make a real contribution to the bazaar, worked from early morning until after midnight.

...... 7. Cheap cars soon begin to consume a great deal of oil, and I know of no inexpensive way to remedy the fault.

...... 8. Literature is often difficult for engineers, it seems to me, because they have spent their youth working with gadgets instead of reading books.

...... 9. Since red-shouldered hawks rarely utter a call, the bird you heard screaming must have been a red-tailed hawk.

...... 10. I will go because you have invited me, but if the orchestra is poor and the girls are stupid, I won't stay late.

...... 11. Why don't we get all the interested men, women, and children of the towns around Midvale to contribute toward the pool?

...... 12. The folly of such wild spending ought to be patent enough, even to people of little education.

...... 13. When I told about my plans, she agreed at once, and so did he.

...... 14. A tornado is a cyclone which has small diameter but great intensity.

...... 15. Hard work seems to have more than personal or social advantages.

CASE

5. Case is one of the forms that a noun or pronoun takes to indicate its relation to other words in a sentence. There are only three cases in English: nominative (subjective); possessive (genitive); and objective (accusative).

In English, case is a less important grammatical factor than in other languages you may be studying. For example, English nouns are not inflected to show the difference between nominative and objective case; in German and Latin, nouns are declined to show

59

endings for the nominative, possessive, dative (indirect object), and objective cases. In addition, Latin nouns have an ablative case. In these two languages adjectives also are fully declined, but English adjectives take no endings.

The following rules for the use of the nominative and objective really deal only with pronouns.

NOMINATIVE CASE *appositive] Rev. Green, the minister*

5a. The subject of a finite verb is in the nominative case.

I should like to accompany you.
She is an excellent cook.

5b. A predicate complement is in the nominative case. (See Complement, Section 15.)

It was *they*. (not *them*)
Is it *she* who is going?
That is *he*.

NOTE: *It is me* and *it's me* are acceptable in colloquial speech and informal writing. *It is I* (*it's I*) is employed by unusually careful speakers and writers.

OBJECTIVE CASE

5c. The object of a verb or preposition is in the objective case.

The teacher blamed *her*.
Whom did she see?
This was bad news for *them*.
A group of *us* protested the decision.
There is no disagreement between *him and me*.

5d. The indirect object of a verb is in the objective case.

Give *us* this day our daily bread.
Write *me* a letter about your plans.

5e. The subject, object, or objective complement of an infinitive is in the objective case.

Whom did you take *her* to be? (*Her* is the subject of *to be*; *whom* is an objective complement.)

5f

John made *him* do that. (Subject of {*to*] *do*.)
His desire to please *her* was great. (Object.)
Did you think her to be *me?* (Objective complement.)

NOMINATIVE OR OBJECTIVE CASE

5f. Who and whoever are used as subjects, whom and whomever as objects of verbs and prepositions.

Many errors arise from misunderstanding the *function* of the pronoun, particularly with *who* or *whom* and with *whoever* or *whomever*. In the following sentences, *who* and *whoever*, nominative forms, are correct because they act as subjects of the verbs in the dependent clauses:

I demand membership for *whoever* wishes it!

The question of *who* can ask for membership should not arise.

In the first sentence, *whoever* is a part of the dependent clause; it functions as the subject of the finite verb *wishes*. The whole clause is the object of the preposition "for." Similarly, in the second sentence, *who* is the subject of the finite verb *can ask*.

These sentences illustrate proper use of *whom* and *whomever*, objective forms:

This is the same man *whom* I saw at Oak Bluffs last summer.

The first person *whom* I met was Martin Henderson.

He asked *whomever* he knew.

He told the same old story to *whomever* he met.

In these four sentences, the pronouns function in the dependent clauses as objects of the verbs. In the last sentence, notice that the whole clause is the object of the preposition "to."

The nominative and objective cases are frequently confused because of intervening words. The case of a pronoun depends upon its syntax and must not be influenced by words which come between the pronoun and its antecedent.

He asked me *who* I thought would be chosen.

Who do you suppose drew up these plans?

She asked the question of the one student in the whole class *who* had not prepared the assignment.

61

5g. An appositive should be in the same case as the noun or pronoun it explains (antecedent).

We, *you* and *I*, must leave at once. (Nominative.)
The man laughed at us, *you* and *me*. (Objective.)

5h. An elliptical clause of comparison, preceded by than or as, requires the case called for by the expanded construction.

He is much taller than *I* (am). (Nominative.)
He is as strong as *I* (am). (Nominative.)
He terrified her as well as (he terrified) *me*. (Objective.)
The clown amused her as much as (he amused) *me*. (Objective.)

POSSESSIVE CASE

5i. A noun or pronoun linked with a gerund should preferably be in the possessive case.

He resents *your* having more than he.
John sent the money without *my* asking him.
She objected to the *coach's* being there.

NOTE: 1. This rule is not invariably followed by all good speakers and writers. The *best* usage requires the possessive case with a gerund, however, because it is always clear, whereas the objective is not. When the use of a possessive with a gerund causes awkwardness, recast the sentence.

2. Do not confuse the possessive-with-gerund and noun-with-participle constructions.

I heard of the coach's *appealing* for more spirit. (Gerund.)
I heard the coach *appealing* for more spirit. (Participle.)

5j. Do not attribute possession to an inanimate object; use an of phrase.

Awkward: The *house's* roof was on fire.
Better: The roof *of the house* was on fire.

NOTE: Do not follow this rule implicitly if it violates good idiomatic usage. Such expressions as these—using the possessive case to indicate measure, extent of time, and the like—are permissible and desirable: *a day's work; an hour's time; three years' experience; a dollar's worth; a stone's throw; at his wit's end; the law's delay; tomorrow's weather report.*

EXERCISES

A. Correct the errors in case which occur in the following sentences:

1. He strongly desires *your* you being chosen to go.
2. *We* Us two had a good time on our last hunting trip.
3. He studies much longer than *I* me.
4. "It's *they* them—it's *they* them at last," he cried jubilantly.
5. Give it to the janitor, or the porter, or whomever comes by first.
6. The road's surface *of the road* is very slippery in wet weather.
7. Did she think he was *I* me?
8. The bull frightened John as well as *me* I.
9. "Is that *she* her?" he asked scornfully.
10. "Don't let anybody come between you and *me* I," he cautioned me.
11. She had become a person who, two years ago, she would have despised.
12. It was *she* her who you saw, but I object to your mentioning it.
13. I paid careful attention to *him* his studying the lesson.
14. The speech should be made by whomever knows most about the subject.
15. The *state* governor raised the question as to *who* whom should be extradited.

B. In each of the following sentences underline or draw a circle around the correct form of the italicized pronoun or noun.

1. I don't care *who whom* is going to speak; I won't go to the lecture.
2. He knew it was *us we* as soon as he arrived.
3. The *book's cover cover of the book* is badly stained.
4. *My me* passing the course depends upon *his him* helping me study.
5. I dislike speaking to people *who whom* I have never met formally.
6. The acrobat amused Jane as well as *I me.*
7. Please see that *them those* clothes are sent to the laundry today.
8. She is prettier than any other girl *who whom* I have ever seen.

9. Mrs. Smith did not know about the *doctor doctor's* coming here last night.
10. The part should be given to *whoever whomever* is the best actor.
11. He heated the *runners of the sled the sled's runners* with a blowtorch, which made *him his* winning the race a certainty.
12. With never a glance at Grace and *myself I me,* he bowed to *them those* having the box seats.
13. This is the child *whom who* they reported for shooting kittens.
14. Jack and his sister are good enough bridge players to defeat any couple *who whom which* opposes them.
15. It happens that I have been informed already about *you your* hitting the policeman.

C. In the following sentences underline the pronouns which are in the wrong case. Name the correct form.

1. No one expected him to make an issue of whom was to be appointed, since Gus and me had volunteered to go.
2. At any other time I would have known it was them.
3. Him having to stay in bed upset our whole camping trip.
4. Artificial respiration should be attempted only by whomever is a trained practitioner, not by we amateurs.
5. In the bus us girls giggled and giggled at the boys.
6. Because of our height he has often been mistaken for I.
7. It was the boy who we expected to see.
8. The child would have given the ring to whomever asked for it first; my brother and myself happened to be the ones.
9. The freshmen quickly volunteered theirselves.
10. After all, how do you know it was her?
11. My dad never lets anything stand between him and I.
12. We did not enjoy him being with us even for a minute.
13. Politeness forbids you repeating the story.
14. As it happens, there is no way to choose between I and him, for it was us alone who made 100.
15. With a deep bow he presented the prizes to Mary and I.

AGREEMENT OF SUBJECT AND VERB

6. Agreement means being in unison or concord. Thus when a subject *agrees* with its verb, they are alike in having the same *person* (first, second, or third) and *number* (singular or plural).

Agreement of Subject and Verb

Few problems in agreement arise because English verbs (except *to be*) have one form for singular and plural and for all persons except the third person singular present. But the errors which do occur are important. Usually they appear when a writer or speaker is confused over the number of the subject because of other words or when he uses a verb to agree not with the grammatical form of a subject but with its meaning. In short, you need to know what the subject is and whether it is singular or plural.

Most nouns and verbs form their plurals in directly opposite ways. Except for special groups, nouns form their *plurals* by adding *-s, -es, -ies:* desk, desks; glass, glasses; lady, ladies. (See Section 1c, p. 35.) Most verbs add an *s* in the third person *singular:* he walks, they walk; she speaks, the men speak. Remember that for most nouns and verbs, the procedure is vice versa.

6a. A verb must agree with its subject in person and number.

The *men speak* too rapidly. (*Men* and *speak* are in the third person and are plural in number.)

I agree to your proposal. (*I* and *agree* are in the first person and are singular in number.)

He agrees to your proposal. (*He* and *agrees* are in the third person and are singular in number.)

Section **6a** states the general rule; however, study the following subsections to avoid errors.

6b. A verb should not agree with a noun which intervenes between it and the subject, when such noun is an appositive or the object in a phrase.

Correct: The *cause* for all the requests and demands *was* not apparent.

I, the delegate, *am* the one to determine that.

I, together with John and Mary, *am* going.

The *boy*, as well as all the members of his family, *was* determined to stay.

6c. Singular pronouns require singular verbs. These pronouns are singular: each, everyone, everybody, anyone, anybody, someone, somebody, no one, nobody, one, many a one, another, anything, either, neither.

65

Each *has* his own money.
Someone *is* speaking now.
One of you *has* made a mistake.
No one *skates* better than Margaret.

NOTE: *None* (literally *no one,* but frequently meaning *not any*) may be followed by either a singular or a plural verb. Studies of the use of *none* by good writers have revealed that it is as frequently followed by a plural as by a singular verb, especially when the phrase which modifies *none* contains a plural noun.

6d. For nouns plural in form but singular in meaning, use a singular verb.

NOTE: 1. Authorities differ in their opinions about the number of many such nouns. A good rule, according to usage, is: When in doubt use a singular verb. The following are nearly always used with singular verbs: *physics, economics, mathematics, news, politics, whereabouts, mechanics, ethics, mumps,* and *stamina.*

Physics, they were told, *is* the study of heat, light, sound, mechanics, and electricity.

2. Subjects plural in form, which describe a quantity or number, require a singular verb when the subject is regarded as a unit.

Ten miles *is* too far to walk.
Two from five *leaves* three.
Five dollars *was* asked for the lamp.
Three-fourths of a bushel *does* not seem enough.

6e. Use a plural verb with two or more nouns or pronouns joined by and.

Both the house and the automobile *were* painted green.
Behind the wall *stand* a house and a garden.

NOTE: When the two subjects form a single thought or have a very closely related meaning, a singular verb is frequently used by good writers.

My comrade and friend *was* present.
The sum and substance of his remarks *is* clear.

Agreement of Subject and Verb

6 f-i

6f. Two or more singular subjects joined by <u>or</u> or <u>nor</u> require a singular verb.

Neither John nor Henry *was* able to leave.
Either Mark or Peter *is* certain to be there.

NOTE: If the subjects differ in number or person, the verb agrees with the nearer.

Neither Jack nor the other boys *know*.
Either they or I *am* at fault.

6g. Relative pronouns referring to plural antecedents require plural verbs.

Each of those who *are* there should play well.
He is one of the most able men who *have* ever been in the Senate.

NOTE: If *only* or some similar qualifying word precedes *one,* the verb in the subordinate clause is singular.

He is the *only one* of those present who *plays* well.

6h. A verb does not agree with a predicate noun.

The best part of the meal *is* the coffee and cigars.
Coffee and cigars *are* the best part of the meal.

6i. After the expletive <u>there</u> the verb is singular or plural according to the number of the subject that follows.

Fortunately, there *exist* (not *exists*) forces which can help us.
There *were* (not *was*) baseball, tennis, and swimming.
In the meadow there *stands* (not *stand*) a towering tree.

NOTE: Always use a singular verb after the expletive *it.* (See **Expletive,** Section 15.)

It *is* (not *are*) the girls who must decide.

6j. A collective noun takes a singular verb when the group is regarded as a unit, a plural verb when the individuals of the group are regarded separately.

The crew *has asked* him to appear at the meeting.
The crew *are coming* on board in a few hours.

67

The family *was named* Brown.
The family *were seated* on the lawn.

EXERCISES

A. Correct the lack of agreement between subject and predicate in the following sentences:

1. The reason for their protests were easily discovered.
2. There goes the man and his wife.
3. The criminal's whereabouts were not known.
4. The coroner's jury were rendering a verdict as he entered.
5. Neither the professor nor his wife were at home.
6. John, with Henry's brothers, are picking apples.
7. Twenty months are a long period of time.
8. The decision of the three officials were announced at noon.
9. The larger part of these books are the vocabularies.
10. This is one of the best flowering shrubs that has been developed in years.
11. There is good business prospects in our town for an ambitious person.
12. Each of you are to be congratulated.
13. It were those little errors that caused most of my trouble.
14. The most exciting part of a football game are the long runs.
15. Even the remaining resources of the land is being used inefficiently.

B. Directions given in Exercise A.

1. The raising of purebred registered dogs are what these kennels are famous for.
2. Many business have gone bankrupt trying to get started in our town.
3. Some students think a college instructor don't care whether his students learn anything or not.
4. There wasn't many cars parked in front of City Hall that day.
5. Freight shipments from Cleveland to our city takes only a few hours.
6. A combination of teaching and farming seem to be a good idea.
7. The reasons for Andrew Carnegie's financial success is numerous.
8. Of the new employees, John is the only one who show any initiative.
9. Your chances of getting a job during Christmas vacation isn't very good.

10. Ellen, along with two or three of her friends, plan to tour the Southwest this summer.
11. Every one of these books are well worth reading.
12. Coming down the aisle is the bride and her father.
13. Neither the other students nor the instructor were surprised when I came in late.
14. Elmwood is one of the few towns that does not have a chamber of commerce.
15. Charles Dickens' greatest achievement are the novels that he wrote.

C. Underline all verbs in the following sentences which are not in agreement with the subjects. Name the correct form.

1. We live in one of those three-story houses that fronts on Moreland Drive and rents for $1800 a year.
2. The weakest section in student themes are the conclusion.
3. Five years are certainly a long time to wait for a girl.
4. The sprinter, with two half-milers, were warming up.
5. You may remember the three basic principles on which our earlier experiments and today's experiment depends.
6. I found that neither Helen nor her sister were at home.
7. There is a man and his wife to be located yet.
8. The fields, the sky, the warm air—all combines to make me happy, even though none is unusual for a day in June.
9. When he entered, the executive committee was in session.
10. That cake's too sweet; it don't agree with me at all.
11. Bill whispered that either Peg or Jill are to recite.
12. The only part I enjoy are physics and chemistry.
13. The brown puppy, as well as the black and the white ones, were badly in need of food.
14. What will you say to the customer when everybody refuse to exchange the goods and insist on keeping them?
15. I am convinced that either the teacher or the boys is mistaken, but each of us were ordered to say nothing.

PRONOUN AND ANTECEDENT

7. A pronoun does not necessarily agree with its antecedent in case (its use in the sentence determines the correct case), but it does agree in *gender, number,* and *person.* Since a pronoun is a word used instead of a noun or noun equivalent, such noun or noun equivalent must be unmistakably clear as the antecedent of the pronoun.

> The *woman* put on *her* hat.
> The *women* put on *their* hats.
> The *boy* misplaced *his* tickets.
> The *boys* misplaced *their* tickets.

7a. Singular pronouns refer to singular antecedents. (See Section 6c.)

> Each person present will please raise *his* hand.
> Everybody is expected to contribute *his* share.

NOTE: In the sentence immediately above, *everybody* may refer to men and women. Only in colloquial English could you say "Everybody is expected to contribute *their* share." You may write "Everybody is expected to contribute *his or her* share," although this construction sounds somewhat artificial, even awkward. In grammar—and perhaps in few other situations and places—men are more important than women.

7b. A pronoun agrees with the nearer of two antecedents.

> He loves anything and everybody *who* is connected with his work.
> He loves anybody and anything *which* is connected with his work.
> Either the plant or the flowers will lose *their* freshness.

7c. A collective noun used as an antecedent takes either a singular or plural pronoun, depending upon the sense of the sentence. (See Section 6j.)

> The crowd of men took off *their* hats. (The crowd acted as individuals.)
> The crowd of men was cheering *its* loudest. (The group acted as a unit.)

NOTE: Be consistent in the use of collective nouns with singular or plural predicates and with singular or plural pronouns.

Inconsistent: The class *was* unanimous in *their* choice of a president.

Consistent: The class *was* unanimous in *its* choice of a president.

7d. Do not confuse the relative pronouns who, which, and that.

Who usually refers only to persons.
Which usually refers only to things.
That refers to persons or things.

Wrong: The horse *who* stands there is a stallion.

The person *which* you mentioned is away from the city.

7e. Avoid vague reference for a pronoun. (See Section 70.)

Every pronoun (and especially *this, that, which, it*) should refer clearly to its antecedent or should be made clear by some other statement in the sentence.

His attitude gave me *that* sinking feeling.

Better: His attitude gave me a sinking feeling (or, His attitude depressed me).

In this magazine article *it* states that war is not inevitable.

Better: This magazine article states that, etc.

They say that China is a potentially wealthy nation.

Better: It is said that China is, etc.

This book is so written that the reader may study any one section and so that *it* may be studied as a unit.

Better: This book is so written that the reader may study any one section or this section may be studied as a unit.

When a salesman hands over an article to a customer, *he* is not always certain of its worth.

Better: A salesman is not always certain of the worth of an article when, etc.

7f. Avoid the use of you and they as indefinite pronouns.

This suggestion is closely related to 7e, but the usage causes sufficient difficulty to merit separate discussion. In colloquial or informal speech and writing, an expression such as "You can see how important money is" is permissible even though *you* may refer to no particular person or group. Formal English requires the use of *one* or *anyone* in such a statement. See also Section **70c, d.**

Colloquial: In South America *they* raise more cattle than in Europe.

Preferable: South Americans raise more cattle than Europeans.

Colloquial: *They* don't have much money in that country.

Preferable: People in that country have little money (or, There is little money in that country).

Dubious: In high school *you* should have to do more theme writing.

Preferable: In high school the student should have to do more theme writing.

7g. Do not use <u>myself</u>, <u>himself</u>, etc., unless an intensive or reflexive idea is present. (See Section 1e.)

Incorrect: John and myself can carry it.
Correct: John and I can carry it.
            John himself can carry it.

Incorrect: This is a matter that concerns only you and myself.
Correct: This is a matter that concerns only you and me.

Incorrect: This is a matter that concerns only you and himself.
Correct: This is a matter that concerns only you and him.

EXERCISES

A. Correct the lack of agreement between pronoun and antecedent in the following sentences:

1. Everybody should be correct in their diction.
2. Either the girl or the women will miss her train.
3. He told me about the places and the people which he liked.
4. Everyone should remember what they hear at this lecture.
5. Each man or woman will have a chance to cast their vote.
6. The audience cheered and cheered for their hero.

7. Every runner must be on their line before the signal.
8. Some man would do this, or would if they knew about it.
9. To care for their own animals is the joy of every dog lover.
10. Not one of this sort of bats can manipulate their toes.
11. Sentimental Sue adores anybody and anything who comes to her.
12. The guards are each presumed to account for their opponent.
13. It would surprise me if either a junior or senior could get their story credited after what happened last night.
14. During this maneuver nobody can let their attention wander.
15. Any one of this fifteen pages is enough to drive you mad.

B. Correct the misuse of pronouns in the following sentences:
1. They have six theaters in this city.
2. I did not see the people which you wrote me were your friends.
3. I see in the newspaper where it says that Brown was elected.
4. He called for aid to one of the men which stood on the shore.
5. When I write a letter to you it never says what I mean.
6. It was one of those beautiful dresses.
7. The crowd, which was all men, shouted and cheered.
8. In this book it says that Jackson was a great general that never made a tactical mistake.
9. I discovered glaring contradictions in the story. This spoiled my pleasure.
10. He was a businessman, and all his life he tried to make his son like it, too.
11. I saw the movie whom you mentioned.
12. They don't seem to do anything in this town but play bridge.
13. He took an instrument from the table which looked broken.
14. In this editorial it says that war never accomplishes any really satisfactory purpose.
15. When Flora invited her to the party she declined, which was just the chance she was waiting for.

C. Underline any incorrectly used pronouns in the following sentences. Make necessary corrections.

1. Most people consider the Pekinese a useless animal, but I have found that they are of real, practical value.
2. She longed to be one of those tall, statuesque girls.
3. My father was for Wilson because he appreciated his sincerity.
4. The elephant we always feed is the one who stands at the end.

5. In Idaho they pay much less for potatoes than we do here.
6. You should expect little imagination from men which are past sixty; it says that in my new psychology book.
7. The sonnets were usually directed to a woman they were madly in love with, according to our teacher.
8. Not every book need announce its source, but it should be based upon it.
9. When Mother returned with Ellen, I could see that she was delighted with her performance.
10. A horse who has served as faithfully as ours deserves a vacation.

D. In each of the following sentences draw a circle around the correct form of the italicized verb or pronoun.

1. The reason for all the cries and explanations *was were* not apparent to us.
2. He says that athletics *are is* more important than studies.
3. Has the school declared a holiday for *their its* students?
4. Four pages *are is* too long an assignment in Latin.
5. Anyone who wishes may bring *his their* own camera.
6. He is one of the best teachers who *have has* ever been at this school.
7. It is this type of student who complains loudest when *his their* marks are low.
8. Each of those who *are is* present should applaud vigorously.
9. Mr. Buck talked about the animals *which who* were most fierce.
10. Each member of the family is agreed upon *their his* own plans for the evening.

LINKING AND AUXILIARY VERBS

8. In order to write correctly, clearly, and effectively, as well as to read satisfactorily, you need an adequate understanding of linking and auxiliary verbs. Such verbs are basic in many foreign languages; they are basic in English.

LINKING VERBS

Most verbs assert action, but a few express a static condition or state of being (no action). These are *linking* (or *joining* or *copulative*) verbs. They serve the purpose of coming between, or *coupling,* two substantives or a substantive and an adjective.

74

Linking and Auxiliary Verbs   **8 a-b**

The substantive following the linking verb is a *predicate noun* or *predicate pronoun* (never a direct object). An adjective following the linking verb is a *predicate adjective,* for it modifies the subject, not the predicate.

The most common linking verb is *to be,* in its various forms of number, person, tense, and mood (for a table of these forms, see p. 76; for the meaning of tense, see p. 132; for the meaning of mood, see p. 125). Other common linking verbs are *seem, appear, taste, smell, sound, look, feel, become, grow, prove,* and *turn.* Some of these may also imply or express action occasionally; you can tell when they are linking verbs if you can substitute some form of *to be* (*are, is, was, were,* especially) for them. Examples of linking verbs:

My name *is* John.
That *was* he who just spoke.
The weather *is* cold today; tomorrow it may *become (grow)* colder.
The excitement *seemed (grew)* greater as the game progressed.
Those clouds *appear* salmon-colored.

8a. Do not confuse a linking verb with a verb expressing action.

Distinguish carefully between the meanings of the same verb word when it asserts action of the subject in one meaning and does not assert action in another; in the latter sense only is it a linking verb. Observe differences in the following:

The river *looks* muddy this morning. (Linking.)
John *looked* steadily at the scene before him. (Action.)
Oranges *taste* sweet. (Linking.)
Mary carefully *tasted* the salad. (Action.)
We do not *feel* bad about our defeat. (Linking.)
In the dark John stumbled against the furniture and *felt* his way carefully across the room. (Action.)

8b. Use the correct number in a linking verb, the correct pronoun case after it, and, as predicate complement, an adjective, not an adverb.

For correct number, see Section 6; for correct case, see Section

TABLE I. LINKING AND AUXILIARY VERBS

	TO BE	TO HAVE	TO DO
Principal Parts	be was been	have had had	do did done

INDICATIVE MOOD

Present Tense

	TO BE Singular	TO BE Plural	TO HAVE Singular	TO HAVE Plural	TO DO Singular	TO DO Plural
1st person	I am	we ⎫	I have	we ⎫	I do	we ⎫
2nd person	you are	you ⎬ are	you have	you ⎬ have	you do	you ⎬ do
3rd person	he is (she, it)	they ⎭	he has (she, it)	they ⎭	he does (she, it)	they ⎭

Past Tense

	TO BE Singular	TO BE Plural	TO HAVE Singular	TO HAVE Plural	TO DO Singular	TO DO Plural
1st person	I was	we ⎫	I ⎫	we ⎫	I ⎫	we ⎫
2nd person	you were	you ⎬ were	you ⎬ had	you ⎬ had	you ⎬ did	you ⎬ did
3rd person	he was	they ⎭	he ⎭	they ⎭	he ⎭	they ⎭

Future Tense

	TO BE Singular	TO BE Plural	TO HAVE Singular	TO HAVE Plural
1st person	I shall be	we shall be	I shall have	we shall have
2nd person	you will be	you will be	you will have	you will have
3rd person	he will be	they will be	he will have	they will have

Present Perfect Tense

	TO BE Singular	TO BE Plural	TO HAVE
1st person	I have been	we ⎫	we ⎫
2nd person	you have been	you ⎬ have been	you ⎬ have
3rd person	he has been	they ⎭	

Past Perfect Tense

	TO BE Singular	TO HAVE
1st person	I ⎫ had been	we ⎫ had been
2nd person	you ⎬ had been	you ⎬ had been

NOTE: The present perfect, past perfect, and future perfect tenses of *have* and *do* are rarely, if ever, used as *auxiliary* verb forms. As *main* verbs, they form these tenses as does any other main verb. See pp. 83–93.

	Singular		Plural
1st person	I shall have been		we shall have been
2nd person	you will have been		you will have been
3rd person	he will have been		they will have been

SUBJUNCTIVE MOOD

Present Tense

	Singular		Plural		Singular		Plural	
1st person	(if) I	} be	(if) we	} be	(if) I	} have	(if) we	} have
2nd person	(if) you		(if) you		(if) you		(if) you	
3rd person	(if) he (she, it)		(if) they		(if) he (he, she)		(if) they	

	Singular		Plural	
1st person	(if) I	} do	(if) we	} do
2nd person	(if) you		(if) you	
3rd person	(if) he (he, she)		(if) they	

Past Tense

	Singular		Plural	
1st person	(if) I	} were	(if) we	} were
2nd person	(if) you		(if) you	
3rd person	(if) he		(if) they	

NOTE: The other tense forms, in the subjunctive mood, of *to be, to have, to do* are identical to the corresponding tense forms of the indicative mood.

Verbals (Non-finite Verb Forms)

Present infinitive:	to be
Perfect infinitive:	to have been
Present participle:	being
Past participle:	been
Perfect participle:	having been
Present gerund:	being
Perfect gerund:	having been

Present infinitive:	to have
Perfect infinitive:	to have had
Present participle:	having
Past participle:	had
Perfect participle:	having had
Present gerund:	having
Perfect gerund:	having had

NOTE: Gerunds have the same form as participles, except that there is no past gerund.

5; for adjective-adverb use, see Section 13. Remember that when the linking verb is specifically described, an adverb is used; when the subject is described, an adjective is used.

AUXILIARY VERBS

8c. Use the correct form of the auxiliary verb with a main verb.

An auxiliary verb is one that "helps out" a main verb; that is, it helps to form the tense and tone (see Section 10), the mood (see Section 12), and the voice (see Section 11) of the main verb. Sometimes it has little meaning of its own; sometimes it changes the meaning of the main verb, which of course contains the central or "key" meaning of the verb phrase. In the following sentences, the italicized form is an auxiliary verb, the black-type form is the main verb.

> John *has* **gone** home.
> The furniture *will be* **shipped** by express.
> As we *were* **coming** home, we *were* **stopped** by a policeman.
> I *did* **mail** your letters.

The most common auxiliary verbs are forms of *to be, to have, and to do*. A table showing the various forms of these as auxiliary verbs is given on page 76. The other common auxiliary verbs are *shall, should, will, would, may, might, can, could, must, ought,* and *let*.

NOTE: Never use *of* as a substitute for the auxiliary *have*. The error is frequently made after *shall, will, should, would, may, might, could,* and *must*.

> Wrong: You should *of* informed me sooner.
> Wrong: I could *of* gone yesterday.
> Wrong: Mary must *of* paid this bill, for she has a receipt.

8d. Use the correct form of the main verb with the auxiliary verb.

Given the principal parts of the main verb (see Section 9) and knowing the auxiliaries, you can form any desired tense, tone, mood, and voice, if such exist in good English usage. The present infinitive (with or without the sign *to*), the past participle, and the present participle ending in *-ing* are the parts of the main verb

78

used with auxiliaries. (See Sections 1h and 15, and tables on pp. 76–77, 88–89.)

8e. Distinguish between a verb form used as an auxiliary and a verb form used as a main verb.

At least three specific verbs, dependent upon purpose, may be either auxiliary verbs or main verbs. *To be* may be a linking (and therefore main) verb, or it may help to express the progressive tone or the passive voice; *to have* (the auxiliary in the perfect tenses) and *to do* (expressing emphasis in the present and past tenses) are also used as main verbs. Notice the differences in the following:

His name *was* John. (Main verb.)
He *was* named John. (Auxiliary verb.)
He *was* telephoning when I came. (Auxiliary verb.)
I *have* no money. (Main verb.)
I *have* lost my money. (Auxiliary verb.)
She *does* her work well. (Main verb.)
She *does* spend her money foolishly. (Auxiliary verb.)

For the various meanings of *have* and *do* as main verbs, see your dictionary.

NOTE: Do not use the same verb form to serve as both auxiliary and main verb.

Incorrect: His name was John and given him by his grandfather.
Incorrect: She does her work well but spend money foolishly.

8f. Use the correct auxiliary verb.

The common auxiliary verbs are as follows:
1. *to be*—
used in all tenses in forming the progressive tone and the passive voice.
2. *to have*—
used in the present perfect, past perfect, and future perfect tenses.
3. *to do*—
used to express emphasis (emphatic tone) in the present and past tenses.

79

used to avoid repetition of a verb or full verb expression: "John slept as soundly as I *did*." "I shall go when you *do*."

4. *shall*—

used as the precise auxiliary for the first person, future and future perfect tenses (but see p. 467).

used in the second and third persons to express command or determination: "You *shall* not fool me again."

5. *will*—

used as the precise auxiliary for the second and third persons, future and future perfect tenses (but see p. 467).

used in all three persons to express willingness or consent: "I *will* write you tomorrow."

used in the first person to indicate determination or resolution: "We *will* rush your order immediately."

6. *should*—

used as a kind of "past" tense of *shall,* in the first person, but weaker in emphasis: "I *should* prefer not to come." "I *should* not judge him harshly."

used frequently in a subjunctive (conditional) meaning: "If I *should* decide, I shall let you know." "If John *should* call, tell him to leave a message."

used in all three persons to express duty or propriety or necessity: "You *should* attend class regularly." "He *should* be ashamed of himself."

used in all three persons to express expectation: "By dusk we *should* be halfway to St. Louis." "Mary *should* arrive home by noon if she left early this morning."

7. *would*—

used as a kind of "past" tense of *will,* in the second and third persons, but less strong in meaning: "You *would* not recognize him."

used frequently in a subjunctive (conditional) meaning, or after a conditional clause: "If you *would* consent, everyone would be happy." "If the weather were good, he *would* walk in the park."

used to express determination: "He *would* do it, no matter how much we protested."

used in all three persons to express repeated or habitual action: "Last summer I *would* read three books every week."

used to express wish or desire: *"Would* that I had gone with you!"

NOTE: If the governing verb is in the past tense, use *would* to express futurity; if the governing verb is in the present tense, use *will:* "Henry *said* that he *would* go." "Henry *says* that he *will* go."

8. *may*—

used to express permission, probability, or a wish: "You *may* have my book." "It *may* rain tomorrow." "If I *may* say so, the idea is absurd." *"May* the better team win!"

9. *might*—

used as a kind of "past" tense of *may* to express the same ideas of possibility or probability in a weaker manner: "You *might* find the address in the telephone directory."

10. *can*—

used to express ability or power or the idea of "being able to": "I *can* come at six o'clock." "He *can* do anything that you *can.*"

11. *could*—

used as a kind of "past" tense of *can* to express the same ideas in a weaker manner: "John *could* not do all the assigned work."

12. *let*—

used to express the ideas of "allowing," "permitting," "suggesting," "ordering": *"Let's* go to the movies."

13. *must*—

used to express obligation, compulsion, or reasonable certainty: "Every man *must* do his duty." "You *must* have your report in by next week." "John left for Louisville this morning, and he *must* be there now."

14. *ought*—

used to express duty or obligation, one of the few auxiliary verbs followed by the sign of the infinitive *(to)* with the main verb: "You *ought* to write letters to your friends more frequently." "Everyone *ought* to pay his bills promptly."

NOTE: *Have* and *had* are never used before *ought* or *must*. Wrong: "I *had ought* to start studying."

EXERCISES

A. In the following sentences, indicate which verbs are linking verbs and which express action:

1. The runner seemed stronger at the finish than at the beginning.
2. The dog smelled the bone indifferently.
3. When you have a cold, you certainly feel bad.
4. You have misspelled five words; you are becoming careless.
5. As a good chef Henry tasted the unsavory mess wryly.
6. You surely look good to me.
7. When you lose an argument, you feel certain that you are miserable.
8. Put the dog outside; he smells.
9. The fighter looked sure of himself after the first round.
10. On a cold day a cup of hot coffee smells good and tastes better.

B. In the following sentences, underline all the linking and auxiliary verbs. If the verb underlined is an auxiliary verb, indicate the purpose that it serves.

1. Must you go? You have not been here long.
2. We should have won the relay race; in fact, we might have won it if our anchor man had not stumbled on the last lap.
3. You may borrow my car, but can you drive it?
4. The roses are fresh and fragrant today, but by next week they will be wilted.
5. I will never permit a friend of mine to be without money.
6. Some people should buy a book of etiquette; they could certainly profit by reading it.
7. When I was a boy, Mother would serve us fried chicken at least once a week.
8. Have you tried hot lemonade? It might help you.
9. I shall be bowling this evening, but I can help you with your chemistry tomorrow morning.
10. One ought to obey traffic regulations; otherwise, he may find himself involved with an officer of the law.

PRINCIPAL PARTS OF VERBS

9. Errors in tense and voice (see below, pp. 87–101) are often
due to insufficient knowledge of the principal parts of verbs. It is
important to know the principal parts of verbs you are using, for
with them and with auxiliary verbs (see pp. 74–82) you can form
any tense in both the active and the passive voice.

The principal parts of an English verb are the *present tense*
(present infinitive), the *past tense,* and the *past participle* (see,
saw, seen). An excellent way to recall these parts of a verb is to
put the verb in these expressions:

I *see* today.

I *saw* yesterday.

I *have seen* every day this week.

The formation of principal parts varies with "weak" and "strong"
verbs.

Weak verbs (the great majority of verbs in English, including
all those added to the language in the past several centuries) form
the past tense and past participle by adding *-ed, -d,* or *-t* to the
infinitive. The past tense and past participial forms are usually
identical. *Walk, walked, walked; move, moved, moved; mean,
meant, meant.*

Strong verbs, usually called irregular verbs in current English,
form the past tense and past participle by a vowel change within
the verb as well as by the occasional addition of an ending. A few
make no change from the infinitive. *Throw, threw, thrown; steal,
stole, stolen; give, gave, given; stand, stood, stood; sleep, slept,
slept; cut, cut, cut; hurt, hurt, hurt.*

Your safest guide to the principal parts of verbs is your dictionary. If no additional forms there follow a main entry, principal
parts are those of a weak verb. Otherwise, the past tense and past
participle (and even the present participle) will be given immediately after the verb.

A necessary verb form, although not a principal part, is the
present participle, easily formed by adding the ending *-ing* to the

present infinitive: *seeing, talking, speaking*. This participial form has constant use both as part of the predicate and as an adjective (see Section 1h, p. 42).

9a. Do not misuse the past tense and past participle:

> Wrong: I swum the lake yesterday.
> He drunk the whole bottle.
> The rain has fell all day.

The confusion of the past tense with the past participle is a serious blunder. You can avoid it only by memorizing the principal parts of all verbs used, or by looking them up in a dictionary.

9b. Do not carelessly omit the ending of a weak verb, especially in the past participle.

> Wrong: I have been *ask* to say a few words.
> No one is *suppose* to do more than he is able to do.
> The city will be *attack* by land, sea, and air.

9c. Do not confuse a strong verb with a weak verb.

Confusion may cause you to add weak-verb endings to strong or irregular verbs or to treat an occasional weak verb like a strong verb.

> Wrong: I was *borned* on a small farm in Ohio.
> He *drawed* a plan of the building.
> The cloth has *shrinked* too much.
> My parents have *moven* to California.

The following verbs are troublesome. Study them carefully; put them into the three expressions mentioned above on page 83.

arise	arose	arisen
bear	bore	borne (born—given birth to)
begin	began	begun
bid	bid	bid (as in an auction)
bid	bade	bidden (as in a command)
bite	bit	bitten (bit)
blow	blew	blown
break	broke	broken

Principal Parts of Verbs

burst	burst	burst
catch	caught	caught
choose	chose	chosen
come	came	come
deal	dealt	dealt
dig	dug	dug
dive	dived	dived
do	did	done
draw	drew	drawn
drink	drank	drunk
drown	drowned	drowned
eat	ate	eaten
fall	fell	fallen
flow	flowed	flowed
fly	flew	flown
forget	forgot	forgotten (forgot)
freeze	froze	frozen
get	got	got (gotten)
go	went	gone
hang	hung	hung (object)
hang	hanged	hanged (person)
know	knew	known
lay	laid	laid
lead	led	led
lend	lent	lent
lie	lay	lain (recline)
lie	lied	lied (falsehood)
loose	loosed	loosed
lose	lost	lost
pay	paid	paid
prove	proved	proved
raise	raised	raised
ride	rode	ridden
rise	rose	risen
run	ran	run
set	set	set
sing	sang	sung
sit	sat	sat
speak	spoke	spoken
swim	swam	swum

take	took	taken
tear	tore	torn
wake	waked (woke)	waked (woke)
wear	wore	worn
wring	wrung	wrung
write	wrote	written

EXERCISES

A. In each of the following sentences draw a circle around the correct form of the verb.

1. He was very much embarrassed because his trousers were *tore torn*.
2. Our team was *beaten beat* badly last Saturday.
3. The bread was *cast casted* to the fish.
4. Before the teacher had *spoken spoke* a word, he drank a glass of water.
5. The man was sentenced to be *hung hanged* on October 15.
6. Clark pulled off his clothes and *dived dove* into the icy water.
7. The teacher saw immediately that I had not *got gotten* the prescribed book.
8. I have *swum swam* across the lake nine times this summer.
9. She was so exhausted that she *laid lay* down to rest.
10. After a little while it *began begun* to rain.
11. The bell for assembly has already *rang rung* twice.
12. He *sprung sprang* into the saddle and galloped away.
13. Our captain has *drawn drew* the pole position.
14. He struck a blow that would have *felled fallen* a heavyweight boxer.
15. *Set sit* the book on the table and *set sit* down.

B. Give the correct forms of the verbs that appear in parenthesis in the following sentences.

1. I refuse to have that book (bite) by your puppy.
2. He wasn't sure when he should have (sow) the wheat.
3. He (lead) me a dog's life.
4. The teacher should have (know) the answer.
5. It is not easy to remember just when one has (give) money to people who have (come) to the door.
6. No one wants to be (catch) in his company.
7. Let's forget that he (steal) that loaf of bread.

8. In my youth I could have (spring) to my saddle easily.
9. The twins were (bear) last Sunday at ten o'clock.
10. Children like to have lots of pictures (hang) on the walls of their rooms.
11. His suit had (shrink) to the point of being almost unwearable.
12. She never (bear) her share of the responsibilities.
13. Crowds used to come to watch a man get (hang).
14. He knew then that he had (dive) too deep.
15. I don't care if you (lend) him all you had yesterday afternoon.

TENSE AND TONE

10. *Tense* indicates the *time* of the action or state expressed by a verb. The three divisions of time—past, present, and future—are shown by six tenses in English.

The three primary, or simple, tenses are the *present tense,* the *past tense,* and the *future tense.* The other three are secondary, or compound, tenses: the *present perfect,* the *past perfect,* and the *future perfect.*

English, unlike a highly inflected language such as German, has few tense *forms.* Verbs reveal change in tense only by inflection, or by the addition of auxiliary words. (See Section 8.)

Within some tenses, verbs also have certain "tones" which express precisely what the writer wishes to say. These are the "simple" tone, the "progressive" tone, and the "emphatic" tone. Consider the differences in the following:

> I *read* three magazines a week. (Simple tone.)
>
> Right now I *am reading* my history assignment. (Progressive tone.)
>
> I *do read* my assignments two or three times. (Emphatic tone.)

The "simple" tone is a concise statement, a kind of snapshot picture. The "progressive" tone indicates a kind of moving picture, a continuing action within the tense limit. The "emphatic" tone serves both to emphasize a statement and, using inverted order, commonly to ask a question.

Students frequently have difficulty in tense usage, but such diffi-

TABLE II. **To See, INDICATIVE MOOD, ACTIVE VOICE**

Principal Parts: see saw seen

Present Tense

	Singular		Plural	
	Simple	Progressive	Simple	Progressive
1st person	I see	am seeing	we ⎫	are seeing
2nd person	you see	are seeing	you ⎬ see	
3rd person	he sees (she, it)	is seeing	they ⎭	

Past Tense

	Singular		Plural	
	Simple	Progressive	Simple	Progressive
1st person	I ⎫	was seeing	we ⎫	were seeing
2nd person	you ⎬ saw	were seeing	you ⎬ saw	
3rd person	he ⎭	was seeing	they ⎭	

Future Tense

	Singular		Plural	
	Simple	Progressive	Simple	Progressive
1st person	I shall see	shall be seeing	we shall see	shall be seeing
2nd person	you will see	will be seeing	you will see	will be seeing
3rd person	he will see	will be seeing	they will see	will be seeing

Present Perfect Tense

	Singular		Plural	
	Simple	Progressive	Simple	Progressive
1st person	I have seen	have been seeing	we ⎫	have been seeing
2nd person	you have seen	have been seeing	you ⎬ have seen	
3rd person	he has seen	has been seeing	they ⎭	

Past Perfect Tense

1st person	I	} had seen	had been seeing	we	} had seen	had been seeing
2nd person	you			you		
3rd person	he			they		

Future Perfect Tense

1st person	I shall have seen	shall have been seeing	we shall have seen	shall have been seeing
2nd person	you will have seen	will have been seeing	you will have seen	will have been seeing
3rd person	he will have seen	will have been seeing	they will have seen	will have been seeing

Verbals (Non-finite Verb Forms)

	Simple	Progressive
Present infinitive:	to see	to be seeing
Perfect infinitive:	to have seen	to have been seeing
Present participle:	seeing	(none)
Past participle:	seen	(none)
Perfect participle:	having seen	having been seeing
Present gerund:	seeing	(none)
Perfect gerund:	having seen	having been seeing

NOTE: Gerunds have the same form as participles, except that there is no past gerund.

culty is caused by ignorance of the functions of the six tenses, or by the writer's not having thought out carefully the *time* expressed in his ideas. The time idea is unmistakable, and if you will make sure of it, you can then find the proper tense form and tone form for it.

Study carefully the following comments on each tense and on the formation of tenses and tones. Study also Table II, page 88.

1. *Present* tense indicates that the action or condition is going on or exists *now*.

> Mary *watches* the experiment carefully.
> John *is working* in his garden today.

2. *Past* tense indicates that an action or condition took place or existed at some definite time in the past (before now).

> I *saw* the salesman yesterday.
> He *was traveling* south on Main Street.

3. *Future* tense indicates that an action will take place, or that a certain condition will exist, in the future (i.e., after the present).

> She *will go* with you to the dance.
> We *shall have* warmer weather next month.
> Mother *will be expecting* you this evening.

NOTE: Future time may be indicated by the present tense accompanied by an adverb (or adverbial phrase) of time or by the use of expressions like "going to." Such constructions as the following are common:

> The new students arrive tomorrow.
> I am taking my entrance examinations next week.
> This Thursday the team leaves for Denver.
> I am going to send my check soon.

4. *Present perfect* tense indicates that an action or condition was begun in the past and is completed at the present time. The time is past but it is connected with the present, and the action or condition may necessarily still be going on. The present perfect tense presupposes something in the present.

You *have been* very ill.

The ice on the lake *has melted.*

The class *has been writing* steadily for an hour.

5. *Past perfect* tense indicates that an action or condition was completed at a time now past. It indicates action "two steps back." That is, the past perfect tense presupposes some action or condition expressed in the past tense, to which it is related.

The roads were impassable because the snow *had fallen* fast.

He worked in a grocery store; he *had been* there a year.

6. *Future perfect* tense indicates that an action or condition will be completed at a future time, stated or implied.

I *shall have gone* by that time.

The snow *will have melted* before you arrive.

By June I *shall have been working* for my present employer almost ten years.

NOTE: The three secondary, or compound, tenses usually indicate *completed* action, whether it be in the present (present perfect tense), in the past (past perfect tense), or in the future (future perfect tense).

FORMATION OF TENSES AND TONES

10a. Use the correct tense form and tone form to express precise meaning.

In the active voice (for a discussion of *voice* and of the formation of verbs in the passive voice, see Section 11), tense and tone are formed as follows (compare with Table I on p. 76):

Simple Tone

Present—uses the first principal part of the verb. Only the third person singular, by adding *-s* or *-es,* varies from the singular and plural forms, which are identical.

Past—uses the second principal part of the verb.

Future—formed by the auxiliaries *shall* (in the first person) and *will* (in the second and third persons) with the present infinitive.

I *shall* come tomorrow.

He *will* arrive in time for the meeting.

NOTE: Careful writers and speakers still observe the distinctions between *shall* and *will* as auxiliaries in the future tense; but the distinction is breaking down in current use, partly because it does not seem important, partly because *will* suggests the idea of willingness, as in *I will speak* (i.e., *am willing to speak*) *before your group.* However, *shall* in the second and third persons is used only to express determination on the part of the speaker: "You *shall* not borrow my clothes, and your friends *shall* not play that trick on me again." So, too, *will* in the first person can express determination or emphasis: "I *will* speak."

Present perfect—uses the auxiliary *have (has)* with the past participle.

Past perfect—uses the auxiliary *had* with the past participle.

Future perfect—uses the simple future of *have (shall have, will have)* with the past participle.

For verbals (or non-finite verb forms) the formation is as follows:

Present infinitive—given as the first principal part of the verb: *to see.*

Perfect infinitive—formed by the present infinitive, *to have,* with the past participle: *to have seen.*

Present participle—formed by adding *-ing* to the present tense form: *seeing.*

Past participle—given as the third principal part of the verb.

Perfect participle—formed by the present participle, *having,* and the past participle: *having seen.*

Progressive Tone

The progressive-tone forms in each tense are built by using the proper tense forms of the auxiliary verb *to be* (see p. 76) with the present participle of the main verb: *am coming, were coming, have been coming,* etc. (See Table II on p. 88.)

Emphatic Tone

The emphatic tone is used only in the present and past tenses, indicative mood, active voice, and is formed by the auxiliary verb forms of *do* with the present infinitive of the main verb.

PRESENT		PAST	
SINGULAR	PLURAL	SINGULAR	PLURAL
I do see	we do see	I did see	we did see
you do see	you do see	you did see	you did see
he does see	they do see	he did see	they did see

With the foregoing information mastered, you should have little difficulty in using the correct tense and tone form for any given time of action. However, when more than two verbs occur in a sentence, it is sometimes difficult to determine the proper *sequence* of tenses. The following rules may be helpful.

SEQUENCE OF TENSES —*verbals*

The tense of the verb in a subordinate clause depends on the tense of the verb in the main clause.

10b. The present tense is used in a dependent clause to express a general truth.

Some people did not believe that the earth *is* a planet.

NOTE: 1. The present tense is used alone to express a "timeless" truth: "Water *is* wet." "Thought *makes* the whole dignity of man."

2. Do not allow the tense of a verb to be attracted into the past when it should be present: "Last summer, I visited a small town in Utah. The houses *were* old and picturesque." (It is conceivable that the town has been wiped out, but is that what is meant?)

3. Passages in some short stories and novels are written in the present tense although the action occurred in time which is past. This use of what is called the historical present sometimes makes narrative more vivid, but it quickly becomes monotonous.

10c. Use a present infinitive except when the infinitive represents action completed before the time of the governing verb.

I intended to *see* (not to *have seen*) you about it.

10d. A present participle indicates action at the time expressed by the verb; a past participle indicates action before that of the verb.

Being wealthy, he *is* able to satisfy his whims.

Having been a good student, he *was* able to get many letters of recommendation.

10e. When narration in the past tense is interrupted for reference to a preceding event, use the past perfect tense.

In April they *repaired* the streets which *had been damaged* by cold weather.

The book which he *was reading had been published* in Philadelphia.

CAUTION: 1. Use tenses consistently and logically. Do not needlessly shift tense (see Section **75**).

2. The tense of a verb in a dependent clause always depends on the tense of the main verb.

These two formulas for the sequence of tenses may help:

1. PAST ⟵ PRESENT ⟶ FUTURE
2. PAST PERFECT ⟵ PAST ⟶ FUTURE

Explanation: The present or the past is the principal tense. Each becomes the norm, as it were, for other tenses, as is indicated above. Thus:

1. He *tells* me that he *was* here yesterday and that he *will be* here tomorrow.

2. He *told* me that he *had been* here yesterday and that he *would be* here tomorrow.

EXERCISES

A. Underline all the verbs and verb phrases in the following sentences, and name the tense and tone of each.

1. When I have finished writing my theme, I shall begin to prepare my history assignment.

2. Father and Mother will celebrate their silver wedding anniversary next month; they do not plan a celebration.

3. Mary has been sending out letters of application, but by last evening she had not received any replies.

4. Our leaders said that they saw that war was inevitably coming.

Exercises

5. You do believe, don't you, that to see a football game is better than to read about it in the Sunday newspaper?
6. Whenever John leaves me, he always says, "I'll be seeing you."
7. Having flown on numerous trips, I am wondering whether I shall have the patience ever to travel by automobile again.
8. Henry had never heard of our product before I mentioned it to him; now he is using it continuously.
9. I heard a new radio program last evening; I had never heard it before and I most certainly shall not listen again.
10. My family is going to travel abroad this summer, and when my summer school is over, I am flying over to join them.
11. If you live until January 1, 2000, you will have seen the birth of a new century.
12. Did you wonder what had happened to us when we did not meet you as we had planned?
13. Professor Jones does not know why Mary failed; she did study, she said, and he believes her.
14. When you reach the top of the hill, you will see an abandoned building on the left.
15. The outfielder ran back to the fence and caught the ball, but he did succeed only after a hard run.

B. Correct the errors in tense in the following sentences:

1. Did you receive the letter yet?
2. He stated that lead was heavier than tin.
3. He was reported to be in New York yesterday.
4. Since May there were two heavy rains on our farm.
5. I would not have done that if I had thought it would have caused all this trouble.
6. The apple he bought was picked days before.
7. He has been in California many years, going there in 1937.
8. I proposed to have called this to your attention tomorrow.
9. When we entered our cabin, we found out some thief made off with our supplies.
10. He has completed the course last June.

C. Directions given in Exercise B:

1. James and Marie corresponded with each other ever since the latter went to Omaha.

2. The credit manager explained to her that he already wrote her twice.
3. I accepted the invitation because I knew that Shirley would have wished me to have been there.
4. Did you get the check your father was to send yet?
5. Walking slowly up the stairs, he was entering the room quietly.
6. She wouldn't have dreaded to have gone to the dance if she had not been afraid no one asked her to dance.
7. The speaker was so vigorously applauded that he seems to be liked.
8. He lives in New Mexico now; he was there for nearly two years.
9. Frank did not intend to have been rude, but he forgot his manners.
10. The novel revealed clearly the scenes about which the author is writing.

D. In the following sentences cross out all incorrect tense forms and name the correct forms.

1. The old dog lay on his grave for days because it knew its master would have wanted it to have stayed there.
2. He lengthened his stride to the point where he has to take only three steps between hurdles instead of four.
3. Her book lays bare the many tragedies that occurred in her family in the four generations since her ancestor had landed in Boston.
4. If Gertrude would have put on less lipstick, her face will have seemed less tough looking.
5. Did Bill Omwake get his football letter yet?
6. How could you ever forget that salt was soluble in water?
7. Since my twelfth birthday I was able to save an average of four dollars a month.
8. Finishing the tower on the first of last June, the contractors were able to have had the chimes rung on the Fourth of July.
9. My trip to the circus was exciting, but it may have been forgotten if I did not bring home those souvenirs.
10. Having seen the broken rail, the little girl runs to the station and tells the agent.

VOICE

11. In the study of grammar, when you hear or use *voice,* think of verbs and of A and P (active and passive). Voice is the grammatical term indicating whether the subject of the verb is acting or being acted upon. In the active voice, the subject (person or thing) is literally the actor; in the passive voice, the subject does nothing, is literally passive or inactive, and has something done to it. Study these applications:

> John *wrote* a short story. (Active voice.)
> A short story *was written* by John. (Passive voice.)
>
> Every day I *ride* my horse, Bulger. (Active voice.)
> My horse, Bulger, *is ridden* every day. (Passive voice.)
>
> Father *has changed* his place of residence three times in five years. (Active voice.)
> His place of residence *has been changed* by Father three times in five years. (Passive voice.)

11a. Use correct forms of the auxiliary and main verbs in forming the passive voice.

Like verbs in the active voice, verbs in the passive also have tense (time) and tone. To form the passive voice, use the auxiliary verb *to be* in its various forms and the past participle of the main verb. Study the forms of this auxiliary verb (Table I, p. 76), and then study Table III (p. 98), noting how auxiliary forms are applied.

Note also that in *tone* the passive voice has all the forms in the simple tone; it has none in the emphatic tone; and it uses, commonly, in the progressive tone the present, past, and future tenses only. The compound tenses (present perfect, past perfect, future perfect) in the progressive can be formed, but they are cumbersome, awkward, and uneuphonious. The ideas in the perfect progressive tenses *(have been being seen, had been being seen, shall have been being seen)* are more easily and effectively expressed by the simple tone of these tenses *(have been seen, had been seen, shall have been seen).*

11b. Do not use intransitive verb forms in a passive-voice construction.

With a transitive verb, you recall (see p. 40), there is a direct object which receives the action of the verb; with an intransitive

TABLE III. To See, INDICATIVE MOOD, PASSIVE VOICE

Principal Parts: see saw seen

	Singular		Plural	
	Simple	Progressive	Simple	Progressive
Present Tense				
1st person	I am seen	am being seen	we ⎫	
2nd person	you are seen	are being seen	you ⎬ are seen	are being seen
3rd person	he is seen (she, it)	is being seen	they ⎭	
Past Tense				
1st person	I was seen	was being seen	we ⎫	
2nd person	you were seen	were being seen	you ⎬ were seen	were being seen
3rd person	he was seen	was being seen	they ⎭	
Future Tense				
1st person	I shall be seen	shall be being seen	we shall be seen	shall be being seen
2nd person	you will be seen	will be being seen	you will be seen	will be being seen
3rd person	he will be seen	will be being seen	they will be seen	will be being seen
Present Perfect Tense				
1st person	I have been seen		we ⎫	
2nd person	you have been seen		you ⎬ have been seen	
3rd person	he has been seen		they ⎭	

Past Perfect Tense

1st person	I	
2nd person	you	} had been seen
3rd person	he	

1st person	we	
2nd person	you	} had been seen
3rd person	they	

Future Perfect Tense

1st person	I shall have been seen
2nd person	you will have been seen
3rd person	he will have been seen

1st person	we shall have been seen
2nd person	you will have been seen
3rd person	they will have been seen

Verbals (Non-finite Verb Forms)

Simple

Present infinitive:	to be seen
Perfect infinitive:	to have been seen
Present participle:	being seen
Past participle:	(none)
Perfect participle:	having been seen
Present gerund:	being seen
Perfect gerund:	having been seen

NOTE: Gerunds have the same form as participles, except that there is no past gerund.

verb there is no such object. Only transitive verbs, therefore, can be used in the passive voice. In this process, the direct object of the transitive verb is shifted in front of the verb and becomes the subject, and the subject of the transitive active verb becomes the expressed agent (preceded by the preposition *by*) or the implied agent.

> John Brown writes novels. (Active voice, transitive verb.)
> Novels are written by John Brown. (Passive voice.)
> Our class has performed many experiments dealing with moisture condensation. (Active voice, transitive verb.)
> Many experiments dealing with moisture condensation have been performed. (Passive voice; "by our class," the agent, is implied.)

A passive-voice construction is sometimes used when an indirect object in one sentence is made the "passive" subject in a rephrased sentence.

> Father gave me some money. (Active voice.)
> I was given some money by Father. (Passive voice.)
> or
> Some money was given me by Father.

> His company granted John a month's vacation. (Active voice.)
> John was granted a month's vacation by his company. (Passive voice.)
> or
> A month's vacation was granted John by his company.

Verbs with an intransitive meaning cannot be used in the passive voice.

> Incorrect: The river has been risen because of the recent rains.
> Correct: The river has risen because of the recent rains.

> Incorrect: The dog was sat on the chair.
> Correct: The dog was made to sit on the chair.

> Incorrect: Your letters have been lain on your desk.
> Correct: Your letters have been laid on your desk.

NOTE: Idiomatic usage permits an *apparent* passive construction of a few intransitive verbs: Jesus is risen; Mary is gone; I am come to tell you the plans.

11c. Do not shift needlessly from active voice to passive voice.

Use the passive voice when it is effectively appropriate, that is, when the point of the sentence is to represent the subject as acted upon. Use verbs in the active voice wherever you express or imply action, mental or physical. But do not shift needlessly from active to passive, since such shift confounds sense: "I started up and a scream was heard." No reader can tell who screamed, who heard, whether the scream was involuntary or took the speaker by surprise.

11d. Use the passive voice in impersonal writing.

Writing is impersonal when it avoids use of personal pronouns; it is completely impersonal when it avoids even the use of the indefinite pronouns, *one, someone, everybody,* and the like. In certain kinds of writing, as in the recording of experiments, completely impersonal expression may be desirable and is obtained by using the passive. (See also Section **79b.**)

> The experiment was performed in order to . . .
> The following facts were obtained . . .
> The results were tabulated, and from them the following conclusions were reached . . .
> On the basis of these conclusions, the following changes are recommended . . .

EXERCISES

A. Underline all the verbs and verb phrases in the following sentences. Name the voice, tense, and tone which each illustrates.

1. The work will be done, even if one hundred men are needed for the job.
2. I am being considered as a candidate for class president.
3. Heavy-duty trucks are used in long-distance hauling; light trucks are utilized for local deliveries.
4. The subject of the address was not announced until the guests of honor had been ushered to their seats.

5. Five recommendations were proposed on the basis of the facts that had been established.
6. A famous movie star in person will be being seen all next week at the Acme Theater.
7. My having been elected vice-president last year was a stepping stone to my being chosen president this year.
8. To be forced from your home by floods is as tragic as to be driven from your home by fire.
9. Although the fact was not known to you, you were being heard on the radio by thousands of unseen listeners.
10. Old jokes have been told so often that script writers are hard pressed for material.

B. Change all passive-voice verb forms in the following sentences to the active voice.

1. The letter was written by me to Mother.
2. When the question was asked by Mary, it was considered too difficult to be answered by the lecturer.
3. The chair was sprung from by the woman, and a piercing shriek was uttered by her.
4. The vegetables are being cooked by the women, and the dessert is being bought by the men.
5. Over a hundred speeches will have been given by the candidate before the ballots are cast by the voters.
6. The grass has been mowed by John, but the hedge has been trimmed by Henry.
7. Being seen in public for the first time in weeks, John was asked by us how his illness had been overcome.
8. "Aye" was shouted by the majority, and a few "No's" were uttered by the minority.
9. When your theme has been written, your paper is to be folded and handed in.
10. The house will be painted by George, if he can be persuaded by me that the job should be undertaken by him.

MOOD

12. The mood (mode) of a verb indicates the manner in which a statement is made. Thus, if we wish to express a fact or what seems to be a fact, or if we ask a question of fact, we use the *indicative* mood:

> The maple tree *is* tall. (Statement of fact.)
> *Is* the maple tree tall? (Question.)

If we wish to express a condition contrary to fact, or a desire, we use the *subjunctive* mood:

> If I *were* rich, I should give you the money. (Contrary to fact.)

> Oh, how I wish I *were* rich! (Desire.)

If we wish to give a command, we use the *imperative* mood:

> *Close* the door, please.

The indicative mood is not troublesome (see Tables II and III, pp. 88, 98), nor is the imperative mood, which has only one form, the same as the present infinitive without *to: come, go, speak, do, be.*

The use of distinctive subjunctive verb forms has largely disappeared in current English in favor of indicative verb forms.

> Former use: If it *be* possible, I shall come.
> A student, if he *write* well, will receive a high grade.
> Current use: If it *is* possible, I shall come.
> A student, if he *writes* well, will receive a high grade.

The verb *to be* (both as linking and as auxiliary verb) has only two distinct subjunctive forms now in occasional use: the form *be* for all persons in the singular and plural, present tense, and the form *were* for all persons in the singular and plural, past tense (see p. 77).

For all other verb forms, the only subjunctive form different from the indicative is the third person singular present, which, by dropping the -s ending, becomes exactly like the other forms: *I do,*

103

you do, he do; I have, you have, he have; I come, you come, he come.

But only rarely can you find such main-verb subjunctive forms, third person singular present, in current writing. Instead, subjunctive ideas are expressed by the use of auxiliary verbs: *should, would, can, could, may, might* (see Section 8f).

> Rare: If he *write* me, I shall reply.
> Common: If he *should write* me, I shall reply.

Our speech still retains numerous subjunctive forms, however, in sayings handed down from times when this mood was more widely used: *Heaven forbid, if need be, suffice it to say, come what may,* etc. Also, careful speakers and writers employ the subjunctive to express the precise manner in which they make their statements, when the indicative would not serve.

12a. Use the subjunctive mood, not the indicative, to express a condition contrary to fact.

> If I *were* the king, I would have you decorated. -
> If she *were* I, would she succeed in doing better?
> He worked as if he *were* never going to have another chance.

NOTE: 1. The subjunctive is used in expressions of *supposition* and to indicate that a condition is *highly improbable* even though not completely contrary to fact.

> Suppose he *were* to ask you a question!
> If I *should be* too talkative, let me know.

2. Use the subjunctive in clauses introduced by *as though* or *as if* to express doubt or uncertainty.

> He talks as if he *were* the only intelligent person in the group.
> As though he *were* any smarter himself!

3. Use the subjunctive in *that* clauses expressing necessity or a parliamentary motion.

> It is essential that he *appear* at the meeting of the committee.
> I insisted that she *come* to my office.

It is expected that every man *pay* his own way.

I move that the chairman *be authorized* to proceed.

12b. Use the subjunctive mood to express a desire. (Wish, volition.)

She wishes that she *were* going to meet him.

I desire that you *be* rewarded.

12c. In parallel constructions do not shift the mood of verbs.

Wrong: If I *were* in your position and *was* not prevented, I
should certainly go. (Change *was* to *were*.)

EXERCISES

A. Choose between the subjunctive and indicative forms in the
following sentences and account for your choice:

1. I wish that I (<u>were</u>, was) you! *contrary to fact*
2. If this (<u>were</u>, was) December, I could pay you what I owe. *contrary to fact.*
3. If she (<u>were</u>, was) pretty, he might love her more. *contrary to fact.*
4. I wonder if the doctor (be, <u>is</u>) willing to operate.
5. If only he (<u>were</u>, was) in Detroit, and I (were, was) at Ann Arbor! *contrary to fact*
6. If I (<u>were</u>, was) going, I should begin to make preparations. *fact fact*
7. I wondered whether this (were, <u>was</u>) an intentional error.
8. Although every precaution (be, <u>is</u>) taken, the expedition will be
   hazardous.
9. If this (be, is) what you mean, you are in error.
10. If you (<u>were</u>, was) to meet him, what would you say?

B. In the following sentences underline the italicized form that
you prefer. If you choose the subjunctive form, state whether you
are following rule **12a, 12b,** or **12c.**

1. It made no difference to me if he *were was* coming or not.
2. If I *was were* thirty instead of twenty, I'd know what to do.
3. I strongly advocate that a vote of censure *be is* ordered.
4. It is imperative that there *is be* not the slightest delay.
5. We shall all suffer if the country *be is* invaded.
6. Even though extreme measures for our safety *are be* taken, the
   consequences are dubious.
7. My, how he wished he *was were* a few inches taller.
8. If the President were given a free hand and *were was* sent to nego-
   tiate, we would see some action.

9. It hardly seems possible that the doctor *is would be* willing to give that anesthetic to a baby.
10. You can be sure the corporal wished he *was were* miles away.

ADJECTIVES AND ADVERBS

13. Ordinarily, it is not difficult to determine when an adjective or adverb should be used. An *adjective* modifies only a noun or pronoun; an *adverb* modifies only a verb, adjective, or another adverb. This rule is simple enough, and yet misuse of adjectives and adverbs is frequent. A part of the confusion is caused by the fact that idiomatic usage frequently violates this fundamental precept.

Still more confusion comes from the fact that the form of a word does not always reveal whether it is an adjective or adverb; most words ending in *-ly* are adverbs, but *womanly* and *holy*, for example, are not. Again, some adjectives and adverbs have identical form (*quick, little, early*), but these cause no trouble until you are called on to tell which is which. Finally, a few adverbs have two forms which differ in meaning (*sharp, sharply; late, lately*, etc.).

In formal writing, remember that if the term about which you are in doubt primarily modifies a noun or pronoun, the chances are that it should be an adjective. But if the term modifies or even loosely applies to the verb, it should be an adverb. (For further discussion, see p. 43.)

13a. Do not use an adjective to modify a verb.

Wrong: He talks too *rapid*. (*Rapidly* modifies the verb *talks*.)
He takes himself too *serious*.
She dresses *neat* when he comes.

13b. Do not use an adjective to modify another adjective.

Wrong: He is a *real* good player.
That is a *strong* made box.

13c. After such verbs as <u>appear</u>, <u>be</u>, <u>become</u>, <u>feel</u>, <u>look</u>, <u>seem</u>, <u>smell</u>, <u>taste</u>, etc., the modifier should be an adjective if it refers to the subject, an adverb if it describes or defines the verb.

Correct: The cake tastes *good*. (Adjective.)
The girl looked *beautiful*. (Adjective.)
She looked at him *angrily*. (Adverb.)
She feels *strongly* that she was cheated. (Adverb.)

The first two italicized modifiers are adjectives because they refer to the *subjects* of the sentences. The last two are adverbs because they modify *verbs*. (See Sections 8a, 8b.)

He looks *careful*. (Adjective: he appears to be a person who is careful.)
He looks *carefully*. (Adverb: descriptive of the verb *looks*.)

13d. Be accurate in the use of words that may be either adjectives or adverbs, and of adjectives that end in -ly.

Cheap, deep, far, fast, wrong, etc., are both adjectives and adverbs. Further, *cheap, deep*, and *wrong* also have *-ly* forms. Words such as *lovely, timely, manly, kindly, goodly*, etc., are adjectives. Consult a dictionary when in doubt.

Correct: This is a *fast* color. (Adjective.)
He ran very *fast*. (Adverb.)
Wrong: He acted *manly*.
Correct: He acted *in a manly fashion*.

13e. Be accurate in the use of comparatives and superlatives.

Both adjectives and adverbs may be changed in form to show a greater or lesser degree of the quality they indicate: *large, larger, largest; good, better, best; slowly, less slowly, least slowly*. (For further discussion, see p. 45 and the glossary, p. 118.)

NOTE: 1. Some adjectives are logically incapable of comparison because their meaning is absolute: *perpendicular, unique, excellent*, etc. Only in informal speech and writing can something be *more impossible* or *more final* or *more fatal* or *more round*.

2. Avoid including the subject compared if the subject is part of the group with which it is compared.

She is older than any girl in her class.
Preferable: She is older than any other girl in her class.

3. Do not use the word *other* when the superlative degree indicates that the subject compared is part of the group.

> Incorrect: He is the most alert of all the other students in the class.
>
> Correct: He is the most alert of all the students in the class.

4. Use the comparative degree with two, the superlative with more than two. In informal usage we hear such a statement as "Navy's team is the *best*" when only two teams are being compared. Careful speakers and writers would use *better* in such a sentence.

> Bring me the *better* of those knives. (Two knives concerned.)
> Bring me the *best* of those knives. (Three or more knives concerned.)

5. In informal and colloquial English the superlative is sometimes used when no particular comparison is intended: "You are *most* generous." Such a use of *most* is understandably rare in formal writing.

6. Avoid the trap of the double comparative or double superlative: "This test was *more harder* than the other." "You will find him the *most kindest* person on the campus." Such expressions are not permissible even in informal usage.

EXERCISES

A. Correct the misuse of adjectives and adverbs in the following sentences:

1. He mowed the lawn real good.
2. The orator spoke timely enough.
3. This roast sure does smell well.
4. The letter was slipped silent under the door.
5. This is a pure heroic notion that he has.
6. I feel badly. (That is, in bad health.)
7. The plow cut the furrow deeply.
8. This automobile runs good. *well*
9. She walked too rapid for me to keep up.
10. Mary and Edna are both smart, but Edna is the *better* best student.

B. In each of the following sentences draw a circle around the correct italicized form:

1. Things looked very *different differently* to me after I returned to college.
2. Come *quick quickly,* or your mother will be angry.
3. The instructor did not meet the class that day because he felt *bad badly.*
4. My strength has improved *some somewhat* since I last saw you.
5. The water tasted *bitterly bitter* to me.
6. He performed the operation as *skillful skillfully* as he could, I suppose.
7. Miriam swims much more *able ably* than I do.
8. His habits have improved *considerably considerable* during his stay in camp.
9. She looks very *queerly queer* to me.
10. He must have felt *bad badly* when the rookie outhit him that year.

C. In the following sentences underline the words which are modified by the italicized words. If the italicized word is incorrect, give the correct form.

1. He tried for years before he parted his hair *straight.*
2. Except for your hoarseness, you spoke *good* today.
3. Our town has a *municipal*-owned bowling alley.
4. It takes more than education to make us *real* happy.
5. It must have been the crab meat; I feel *badly.*
6. An owl sees much *clearer* at night than a hawk does.
7. The fall stretched the tendons *some* in his ankle.
8. You could improve your tones *considerable* by practice.
9. I was never in a more *smooth*-riding car.
10. He has written a *good* book, in spite of himself.

CONJUNCTIONS

14. A *conjunction* is a word used to join words, phrases, clauses, and, occasionally, sentences. It is a *joining* or *connecting* word and has no other function than to couple two elements.

You should know the various kinds of conjunctions in order to be able to write clearly and correctly. Conjunctions are divided into two main groups: (1) *coördinate,* and (2) *subordinate.* A coördinate conjunction (such as *and, but, for*) joins words (phrases, etc.) of equal rank, that is, elements not dependent in any way upon one another. A subordinate conjunction (such as *although, because, if, while, unless*) joins clauses of unequal rank, that is, elements of which one depends upon the other.

Coördinate conjunctions rarely cause the writer trouble, but subordinate conjunctions are numerous and have to be used carefully. There are many different kinds of subordinate conjunctions, but the following four are perhaps most frequently used:

1. A *causal* subordinate conjunction indicates reason, result, condition, etc.: *because, so that, whereas, lest,* etc.

The grass was wet *because* it had rained.

2. A *temporal* conjunction indicates time: *after, before, until, when, while.*

I shall not leave *before* you arrive.

3. A *local,* or spatial, conjunction indicates position: *where, whence, whither,* etc.

It is on the table *where* I left it.

4. A subordinating conjunction of *concession* indicates acknowledgment or admission: *although, notwithstanding, though,* etc.

Although I was feeling ill, I should have made an effort to come.

14a. Do not misuse simple coördinating conjunctions. (See Section 76.)

Wrong: I had hoped you would go, *but* you did.
The book may have been excellent in your opinion, *and* it was not in mine.
(Interchange the conjunctions.)

14b. Avoid using conjunctive adverbs to join words or phrases. (See Section 1k.)

Wrong: John studied for several hours, then went to bed.

Conjunctions

14 c-e

> John, also Henry, will be at the meeting.
> At last reports the channel swimmer had swum for twelve hours; still was going strong.

In constructions such as these, a pure coördinating conjunction should be used before the adverb, which becomes weakly parenthetic.

14c. Do not misuse subordinate conjunctions. (See 14.)

> Wrong: I do not know *as how* I trust him.
> He told me *how that* he went fishing.
> I hear *where* he has broken another record.

Each of these sentences may be corrected by substituting *that* for the italicized word or phrase.

14d. Avoid the use of like as a conjunction.

In recent years *like* has been increasingly employed as a conjunction, especially in public addresses, on the radio, and in the dialogue of novels and short stories. Careful speakers, writers, and editors still consider *like* a preposition and use *as* or *as if,* proper subordinate conjunctions, in constructions such as the following:

> I did it exactly like you told me to.
> It looks like it might snow.

If *like* is followed by a noun or pronoun without a verb it may correctly be used as a preposition:

> He looks *like* his mother.

14e. Do not use while to express contrast.

While is a subordinate conjunction which most exactly indicates time. Somewhat less clearly it expresses concession (though, although, etc.). Its use in expressions of contrast is considered incorrect or, at most, quite informal.

> Wrong: Henry played well *while* Bob did not. (Use *whereas, although,* etc.)
> Right: I watered the lawn *while* you were away. (Idea of time.)

111

Permissible: *While* I admit its intrinsic worth, I still think the price is too high. (Concession.)

EXERCISES

Correct all the errors in the use of conjunctions in the following sentences:

1. He cannot pitch well except [*unless*] he warms up thoroughly.
2. You may have thought it an excellent program, and [*but*] it was not.
3. John overslept his eight-o'clock class, so [*and*] had no good excuse.
4. He acts like [*as if*] he knew exactly what to do under all circumstances.
5. He never answers without [*unless*] he first knows what Louise is going to say.
6. I read my day's assignments carefully, then [*and*] made notes on my reading.
7. I don't know as [*that*] they have any right to enforce this regulation.
8. I read where [*that*] another swimming record was broken at a recent meet.
9. Mary's luncheon consists mainly of salads, also [*and*] light desserts.
10. I went to my room early that evening, as [*since*] I had much work to do.
11. Did you have my suit cleaned like [*as*] I told you to?
12. Father telegraphed that he had missed the last train; therefore [*he*] will come home tomorrow.
13. The grass was very wet; nevertheless, [*since*] it had rained hard during the night.
14. Fred engaged in all types of athletics, while [*and*] Bill went to dances almost every afternoon and night.
15. Henry received the majority of the votes; thus [*and*] was declared elected.

GENERAL EXERCISES: GRAMMAR

A. Correct all the grammatical errors in the following sentences. If necessary, refer frequently to Sections 1–14.

1. He has been speaking loud [*loudly*] for a long time. Talking [*He talked*] for at least an hour.
2. It was her [*she*] whom you saw laying [*lying*] there.
3. He has [*had*] completed his college course last June, while I have two more years to go, which are [*is*] a long time.
4. I wrang [*wrung*] out my wet clothes as good [*well*] as I could, like [*as*] you suggested.
5. There is [*are*] at least two hundred people in the audience, and [*but*] I don't mind facing them at all.
6. He said how [*that*] he would go, if he was I, but I have chose [*chosen*] different.

112

General Exercises

7. Neither Mr. nor Mrs. Black were at home, but I laid the package on the porch.
8. This is, despite what you say, not the man whom you thought it was.
9. They had past my house just after I finished mowing the lawn real good.
10. I have forgot whether Max or Frank said they would attend to it.

B. Directions given in Exercise A.

1. She recited the poem beautiful, but everyone of us were certain she didn't really understand it.
2. Suppose you were in my position and was my age, would you raise the question as to whom should be selected?
3. The radio's tubes were burned out, but nobody has the money to buy a new one.
4. Neither John or Henry were dressed for the occasion, and I was.
5. He sure proved that the earth rotated on its axis.
6. The news are broadcast every fifteen minutes, which is too short an interval to be born by most listeners.
7. The real sound reason for him not going is that he loaned all his money to someone else.
8. He did good in all sports. Such as football, swimming, and tennis.
9. When I was told about me being elected, I said that every man in the troop should do their best to help me.
10. He tells me that he had practiced an hour yesterday and would do so again tomorrow.

C. Name the errors that you find in these sentences. Write each sentence correctly.

1. None of us were positive of the question because the teacher spoke very soft—like he'd lost his voice.
2. I should learn my brother to play the piano real well, he then could teach himself how to play the other instruments. Like the saxophone or trombone.
3. The sergeant pointed to Jack and I and saying something about being sorry to caught us out of step again.
4. The men behind we two snickered, because they knew it was them who had not kept in step good.
5. If he would have got his bonus, like he was promised, you would never of heard of him borrowing from his friends.

113

6. Ever since my operation last June I enjoyed the best of health, and I aims to keep fit in the future. By exercising regular and sleep nine hours a day.
7. Just imagine what a foreigner would do if they were in my position last night and have been ordered to recite the *Gettysburg Address* to them!
8. Being that I am a sociable person, I'll speak to whoever I meet without them introducing themselves.
9. When the coach was waiting with Butch for the bus, he explained to him why he was leaving. In spite of his many friends and general happy situation here.
10. As The Ripper lay his razor on the table, I would have liked to have been far, far away, while Jack, who is one of those steady fellows, seems as calm as if nothing is wrong.

D. The following article was printed in a fraternity magazine and is here reprinted verbatim except for changes of names. It is filled with errors in grammar, punctuation, etc. Rewrite the article, correcting all errors.

Hovey College has always been recognized as one of the most active colleges in the west, not only in their selection of the finest boys but also in its social life. Every year we, the school, give six sets of dances that are held in the Caldwell Armory Auditorium. For every one of these dances the Pan Hellenic Council selects the best dance orchestra available. For an example, at Mid Winters they provided Johnnie Swyles and his orchestra that was accepted by everyone with great enthusiasm. Every orchestra billed for a Hovey dance is of the better class and supplies the best of music.

Last year we Psi Etas held a banquet at every one of the dances that could not be surpassed by any other organization on the campus. They were held in Caldwell's new T & H Cafeteria, on Saturday evening between the tea dance and the evening dance. At each banquet a chosen master of ceremonies presented what one would call an organized program with different brothers taking parts that gave great amusement. Our private banquet room is very cleverly decorated each time according to the dance and our fraternity colors of maize and white. The brothers always have "Piles" of "girls" at these banquets and dances which always lend a most pleasing air to the entire affair.

During the rushing period we have our parties very frequently as you have probably noticed already according to the schedule. This is to enable the boys to learn each other and to acquire the well known "Hovey Air." After rushing season is over and all of the boys have made their decisions, everyone settles down to earth to begin their work with the school. Perhaps one thinks that from then until the end of school, except for a dance occasionally, we keep our noses buried in the books, never to get them aired. This is all a misconception. Quite often we have a party with girls and practically every Sunday night we have a feed at the house after church services, so that the brothers will get together in one group and air out each others "wind-bags." This, by no means, interferes with the work of a Brother as it is just a little carefree moment which the chapter has only on weekends, in order that the brothers may learn each other better.

A Psi Eta does not have to worry about having a girl up to the dances. After she has accepted his invitation he turns her name over to the social committee who secures a room for her in the private home of some Hovey citizen who has an unbendable reputation, and will take care of her as if she were his own. For this reason the Psi Etas have the largest and best set of girls on the campus during every social function.

Just before the final examinations begin, each fraternity gives its social of the year. This party is called the annual May Frolic. For several years Psi Eta has been noted for giving the most original and entertaining social presented on the campus. Last year the chapter surpassed its own record by giving a dance in the Caldwell Woman's Club. With Hub Brande and his orchestra, attractive refreshments, and an excellent group of girls, the brothers and numerous visitors enjoyed an exceptional evening. The whole chapter is eagerly awaiting the May Frolics which will uphold the high standard already set.

GRAMMATICAL TERMS

15. Many writers have partially or entirely forgotten the definitions of most grammatical terms. This is unfortunate only when a lack of knowledge of the meaning of terms causes a writer to phrase his ideas incorrectly, obscurely, or awkwardly. The following list defines and briefly discusses some of the elements of grammar which you will have most need for and have possibly forgotten. Refer to this glossary whenever you are in doubt about the definition of a grammatical term as you study the sections on grammar (1–14), punctuation (16–30), and the sentence (61–80).

15   Grammatical Terms

1. **Absolute expression.** An "absolute" expression is one which has a thought relationship, but no grammatical relationship, with the remainder of the sentence in which it occurs. An absolute expression is usually composed of a noun or pronoun followed by a participle:

> *The tire being flat,* we decided to pump it up.
> *Two hours having elapsed,* we again set forward.
> We left immediately, *our mission having been accomplished.*

2. **Abstract noun.** The name of a thing not evident to the senses, like a quality: *beauty, honor, duty, sadness.*

3. **Accusative.** A *case* name meaning the same as the *objective* (which see).

4. **Active voice.** The form of the verb in which the subject does or performs the action. (See **Voice,** below.)

5. **Adjective.** A part of speech modifying a noun or pronoun by limiting or describing: *red* shoes, *happy* children, *six* eggs. Errors in the use of adjectives are discussed in Section **13**.

6. **Adjective clause.** A dependent clause used to modify a noun or pronoun.

> The hat *which I bought* was not expensive.
> This is Mr. Brown, *who will speak to us this evening.*

7. **Adverb.** A part of speech modifying a verb (he runs *swiftly*), an adjective (an *extremely* good dinner), or another adverb (she spoke *very* rapidly). Errors in the use of adverbs are discussed in Section **13**.

8. **Adverbial clause.** A dependent clause used to modify a verb, an adjective, or an adverb.

> John works part-time *because he needs the money.* (Modifies verb *works.*) This is better *than I usually do.* (Modifies adjective *better.*) Do you work more rapidly *than I do?* (Modifies adverb *more rapidly.*)

9. **Agreement.** Correspondence in number, gender, and person. Subjects and predicates *agree* in number (both are singular or both are plural):

> John *is* my brother.
> John and Harry *are* my brothers.

Pronouns agree with their antecedents in having the same gender, person, and number:

> Many a *man* attains *his* goal in life.
> She is one of *those girls who are* always giggling.

10. Antecedent (literally, *placed before*). The substantive (noun, pronoun, or noun equivalent) to which a pronoun refers. See Section 7.

> The *girl* has lost *her* gloves. (*Girl* is the antecedent of *her*.)
> *Men* were willing to stake *their* lives on the issue. (*Men* is the antecedent of *their*.)
> Remember that *pronouns* agree with *their* antecedents in gender, number, and person. (*Pronouns* is the antecedent of *their*.)

11. Appositive. A substantive added to another substantive to identify or explain it. The appositive signifies the same thing and is said to be in apposition.

> One important product, *rubber*, this country had to import. (*Rubber* is in apposition with *product*.)
> More hardy than wheat are these grains—*rye, oats*, and *barley*. (*Rye, oats,* and *barley* are in apposition with *grains*.)

An appositive agrees with its substantive in number and case; it is set off by commas if its relationship is loose (nonrestrictive) and is used without punctuation if the relationship is close (restrictive). See page 147.

12. Articles. The *indefinite* articles *a* and *an*, and the *definite* article *the* are adjectives since they always accompany nouns.

13. Auxiliary. A verb used to "help" another verb in the formation of tenses, voice, etc. *Be, can, do, have, may, must, ought, shall, will* are examples. See Section 8.

> He *has* gone away for a visit.
> You *will* please turn out the light!
> We *should have been* working with the stevedores on the dock.

14. Balanced sentence. A sentence so constructed that like or unlike thoughts have similar structure for purposes of comparison, contrast, or emphasis.

To hate is human; to forgive is divine.

We fought our enemy in the streets; they fought us from the housetops.

15. Case. A term referring to the forms that nouns or pronouns have (nominative, possessive, objective) to indicate their relation to other words in the sentence. See Section 5.

16. Clause. A group of words containing a subject and predicate and forming part of a sentence.

Knowledge is wisdom, and wisdom is power. (Two independent clauses.)

When I arrive, I shall telephone you. (One dependent clause; one independent.)

Those who strive usually succeed. (One dependent clause; one independent.)

17. Collective noun. The name of a group composed of individuals but considered as a unit: *team, class, audience, jury.*

18. Common noun. A noun naming a member or members of a common or general group: *street, dog, coat.*

19. Comparative degree. The form of an adjective or adverb comparing two objects. See **Comparison,** below.

20. Comparison. The change in the form of an *adjective* or *adverb* to indicate greater or smaller degrees of quantity, quality, or manner. The three degrees of comparison are *positive, comparative,* and *superlative:*

small	smaller	smallest
little	less	least
wisely	more wisely	most wisely
quickly	less quickly	least quickly

Comparative degree is used to show relationship between two persons, objects, or ideas:

Fred is taller than I.

This box is less full than the other one.

Superlative degree is used to show relationships among three or more:

Alan is the tallest one in his family.

This sewing kit is the fullest of the six available.

For further discussion of comparison, see page 45.

21. **Complement.** A word or expression used to complete the idea indicated by another word or expression. A *predicate complement* describes or identifies the subject of a linking verb: "That tree is a *maple.*" An *objective complement* completes the meaning of the direct object of a verb: "They called the dog *Peter.*"

22. **Complex sentence.** A sentence containing one independent clause and one or more dependent clauses.

> When I arrived, my father was already there.

23. **Compound object.** See **Object,** below.

24. **Compound sentence.** A sentence containing two or more independent clauses.

> Give willingly; give quickly; give abundantly.

25. **Compound-complex sentence.** A sentence containing two or more independent clauses and one or more dependent clauses.

> I like to read, but my brother, who is mechanically inclined, rarely opens a book.

26. **Compound predicate.** See **Predicate,** below.

27. **Compound subject.** See **Subject,** below.

28. **Concord.** A grammatical term meaning the same as **Agreement** (which see).

29. **Concrete noun.** A noun naming an object evident to one of the senses of sight, hearing, touch, taste, smell: *shoe, song, skin, coffee, perfume.*

30. **Conjugation.** The changes in a verb to show mood, tense, number, person, and voice. See these terms and also Sections **9, 10, 11, 12.**

31. **Conjunction.** A linking word (part of speech) used to connect words or groups of words: *and, or, if, when, nevertheless,* etc.

32. **Conjunctive adverb.** A certain kind of adverb which can be used as a conjunction coördinating two independent clauses: *also, furthermore, nevertheless, besides, however, therefore, thus, so, consequently, hence, likewise, still, then, moreover,* etc. See page 157.

33. **Construction.** The *arrangement* and *connection* of two or more words or forms making up a grammatical unit within a sentence.

34. **Coördinating conjunction.** A conjunction (which see) relating

words or phrases or clauses of equal value (*coördinate* means *of equal rank*).

35. **Copula.** The verbs *to be, look, seem, smell,* etc., are copulative, or linking, verbs which express the relation between subject and complement. See Section 8.

> The other man *was* his nephew.
> That *seems* inexpensive.

36. **Correlative conjunctions.** Coördinating conjunctions used in pairs. The most common are: *neither . . . nor, either . . . or, both . . . and, not only . . . but also.* Each member of the pair is followed by the same grammatical construction.

> *Both* Father *and* Mother are natives of Kansas. (Nouns corelated.)
> I could find my books *neither* at home *nor* at school. (Prepositional phrases corelated.)

37. **Declension.** The changes in the form of a noun or pronoun to indicate case, number, and person. "To decline" grammatically means to give these changes. See pages 37–38.

38. **Decline.** See **Declension.**

39. **Demonstrative pronoun.** A pronoun pointing to or pointing out: *this, that, these, those, such.*

40. **Dependent clause** (or subordinate clause). A *clause* (which see) that does not provide complete meaning in itself, that "depends" on an independent clause. There are three kinds of dependent clauses: noun clause, adjective clause, and adverbial clause (which see).

41. **Direct address.** The substantive showing to whom speech is addressed (also called the vocative):

> *John,* where are you?
> When we finish rolling the court, *Fred,* we'll still have time for two sets of tennis.

42. **Ellipsis.** The omission of a word or words necessary to the grammatical completeness of a clause or sentence. The words shown in brackets are often omitted in speaking and writing; without such words the sentences are called elliptical:

120

Some of the patriots carried guns, others [carried] swords, still others [carried] clubs and sticks.

While [we were] drifting downstream, we grounded on a sand bar.

He was eighteen years of age, his brother [was] twelve [years of age].

43. **Elliptical clause.** Usually a dependent clause with its subject and part of its predicate omitted, since these are understood from the main clause. For examples, see **Ellipsis**, above.

44. **Emphatic verb form.** Present or past tenses using an auxiliary verb: *do, does, did*.

Though I *did* work and still *do* work, I make no progress.

45. **Exclamatory sentence.** A sentence or "sentence fragment" expressing surprise or strong feeling: *What a day! We're there!*

46. **Expletive.** An expletive is a word or phrase added either to fill out a sentence or to provide emphasis. This latter function is performed by expressions which are exclamatory or profane. The more frequently employed function of the expletive is complementary, however; in this sense, *surely, indeed, why, yes,* etc., may be considered expletives. *It* and *there* are commonly used as expletives:

It was Alice sitting on the porch.
It is a truism that men love freedom.
There are four hundred people present.

47. **Finite verb.** A verb that is capable of making a complete and independent assertion. Verbals are not finite verbs. If this distinction is not clear, see pages 42–43.

48. **Future perfect tense.** The time of the action of a verb beginning in the present and ending at some point in the future. See page 91.

49. **Future tense.** The time of a verb expressing "after now" or "after the present." See page 90.

50. **Gender.** The classification of substantives according to sex. There are four genders: masculine, feminine, neuter, and common (either masculine or feminine): *boy, girl, it, individual.* In modern English, nearly all traces of grammatical gender have disappeared.

51. Genitive. A *case* name meaning the same as *possessive* (which see).

52. Gerund. A verbal noun ending in *-ing*. A gerund has the same form as the present or perfect participle. See page 42.

53. Gerundive phrase. A phrase introduced by a gerund. If begun by a preposition, the phrase is prepositional-gerundive.

> *Memorizing poetry* is a pleasant occupation. (Gerundive phrase.)
> *Upon achieving my first goal,* I aimed *at achieving my second.* (Prepositional-gerundive phrases.)

54. Grammar. The science which deals with words and their relationships to each other. *Rhetoric* deals with the art of expressive speech and writing, with the laws of clear, effective writing; *grammar* is concerned with a consideration and account of the features of a language and with speech and writing according to various standards of usage.

55. Idiom (idiomatic usage). The manner of expression characteristic of a language. See Section 85.

56. Imperative. The mood (or mode) of a verb expressing a command or a request. See **Mood** and page 42.

> *Send* the enclosed card immediately.
> *Give* generously if you can.

57. Imperative sentence. A sentence expressing a command or a request. See **Imperative** for examples.

58. Impersonal construction. A method of phrasing in which pronouns or persons as nouns are not stated as the actor. The passive voice is used, or the expletives *it* or *there.*

> I have three reasons for my choice. (Personal.)
> There are three reasons for this choice. (Impersonal.)
> We must consider three proposals. (Personal.)
> It is necessary to consider three proposals. (Impersonal.)
> Three proposals must be considered. (Impersonal.)

59. Indefinite pronoun. A pronoun implying an antecedent but referring to no specific person, place, or thing: *one, someone, everybody, each, none, nobody, everything, nothing,* etc.

60. Independent clause. A clause (which see) that makes complete sense, that gives complete meaning (it could stand as a single sentence).

Harry plans to be a chemist, but John will become a doctor.
(Each clause here makes a complete statement.)
If he is admitted, John will enter medical school this autumn.
(The first clause is dependent; the second one is independent.)

61. Indicative. The mood (or mode) of the verb expressing a fact or what seems to be a fact. See **Mood** and page 42.

We sell books here.
I think that today is Tuesday.

62. Indirect object. An object preceding the direct object and before which the word *to* or *for* is understood. When such an object follows the direct object, *to* or *for* is used.

He wrote *me* a letter.
(He wrote a letter *to me*.)
Mother bought *Mary* a new dress.
(Mother bought a new dress *for Mary*.)

63. Indirect question. Statement by one person of a direct question asked by another (see **Interrogative sentence,** below).

Direct: When will you arrive?
Indirect: Jane asked when I would arrive.

64. Infinitive. A verb form which is the first of the three principal parts, having the function of verb (part of predicate), noun, adjective, or adverb. In the last three uses, it is preceded by the sign *to,* stated or implied.

I should *study* tonight. (Infinitive as part of predicate.)
Will you *telegraph* me immediately? (Infinitive as part of predicate.)
To succeed in life is my ambition. (Infinitive as noun.)
The candidate *to elect* is the present president. (Infinitive as adjective.)
John came in *to tell* me of his success. (Infinitive as adverb.)

65. Infinitive phrase. A phrase introduced by an infinitive: *to study mathematics.* For other examples, see **Infinitive,** above.

66. Inflection. A change in the form of a word to show a change in meaning. *Comparison, conjugation,* and *declension* are inflections of various parts of speech. See these terms, and also pages 45, 59.

67. Intensive pronoun. A pronoun having the same form as the reflexive pronoun (which see) and usually used immediately after its antecedent for emphasis.

> Mary *herself* baked the cake.
> I *myself* turned in the money.
> At this meeting the students *themselves* assumed full charge.

68. Interjection. An exclamatory word, expressing strong feeling or surprise, which has little connection with the remainder of the sentence.

> *Oh,* so that's how it was.
> *Hurrah!* We've won!

69. Interrogative adverb. An adverb used in asking a question: *where, when, how.*

> *Where* is University Hall? *When* was it built? *How* large is it?

70. Interrogative pronoun. A pronoun used in asking a question: *who, which, what.*

> *Who* is arriving tonight? On *which* train? *What* is he coming for?

71. Interrogative sentence. A sentence asking a question and followed by a question mark.

> You're planning to go tonight, aren't you?
> You say you've not paid your insurance premium yet?

For other examples, see **Interrogative adverb** and **Interrogative pronoun,** above, and page 53.

72. Intransitive verb. A verb that does not require a direct object to complete its meaning (ends in itself and cannot take a direct object). See page 41.

> The night plane *has arrived.*
> He *mused* for an hour.

73. Inverted order. Arrangement of the words in a sentence so that the whole or part of the predicate precedes the subject.

> In God we trust.
> Down from the hills came the roving outlaw bands.

Grammatical Terms

74. Irregular verbs.   See **Strong verbs,** below.

75. Linking verb.   See **Copula** above.

76. Loose sentence.   A sentence so constructed that its meaning is clear prior to the end. See page 53.

> I shall be in Chicago early next month, and I shall hope to see you then.

77. Mode.   A term meaning the same as **Mood,** which see.

78. Modify.   Adjectives used with nouns or pronouns and adverbs used with verbs, adjectives, or other adverbs *modify* when they describe, limit, or make meaning more exact in some other closely related way.

79. Mood.   A characteristic of verbs, revealing how action is thought of: as a fact (indicative mood), as a possibility or something desired (subjunctive mood), or as a command or request (imperative mood). See Section 12.

80. Nominative.   The *case* form of nouns or pronouns used as grammatical subject or predicate complement. See Section 5.

81. Non-finite verb.   A verb form (gerund, infinitive, participle) that does not have "person" or "number" and cannot, therefore, be used as a predicate. See **Verbals,** below.

82. Nonrestrictive.   A modifier that does not limit but describes or adds information. The term is ordinarily used with phrases and dependent clauses.

> Professor Brown, *having given out the test questions,* told us to begin.
>
> This hat, *which I borrowed from John,* does not fit me.

83. Noun.   A word naming a person, place, thing, quality, idea, or action: *John, meadow, paper, beauty, realism, walking.* See page 34.

84. Noun clause.   A dependent clause serving the function of a single noun.

> *What I do* is important to me. (Noun clause as subject of sentence.)
>
> John wrote *that he would come on Tuesday.* (Noun clause as object of verb.)

85. Number.   The change in the form of a substantive or verb to show whether one or more than one is indicated. The formation of the plural of nouns is discussed on page 35.

Plurals of verbs are relatively simple. Main verbs have the same form for singular and plural except in the third person singular, present tense, which ends in -s (*sees, moves, thinks,* etc.) or occasionally -es (goes).

Of the verb *to be:* in the present tense, *am* and *is* are singular, *are* is plural; in the past tense, *was* is singular, *were* is plural.

Of the verb *to have, has* is the third person singular, present tense form. Of the verb *to do, does* is the third person singular, present tense form.

Use your dictionary when you are in doubt concerning the singular or plural form of a noun, pronoun, or verb. The following examples may help to fix a few basic principles in mind:

Singular: man, boy, lady, knife, he, this, talks, was.
Plural: men, boys, ladies, knives, they, these, talk, were.

86. Object. The substantive following a preposition, or the word, phrase or clause indicating the thing or person affected by a transitive verb.

He is in the *room.*
The carpenters built a *house.*
He said *that he would go.*

A *simple object* is the substantive alone. A *complete object* is a simple object together with its modifiers. A *compound object* consists of two or more substantives.

The Duanes built the large green *house* on the hill. (Simple.)
The Duanes built *the large green house on the hill.* (Complete.)
The Duanes built *the house and the barn.* (Compound object of verb.)
You should speak courteously to *your father and your mother.* (Compound object of preposition.)

87. Object complement. A word used after the direct object of certain verbs to complete the meaning.

They elected John *captain.*
We painted our house *white.*

88. Objective. The *case* form of nouns or pronouns used as "objects" of prepositions or as direct or indirect "objects" of verbs. See **Object**, above, and page 60.

89. **Parallelism.** The use of the same structural form for ideas of equal value. See Section **74** and page 54.

90. **Parenthetical material.** Any expression which is not necessary for the grammatical completeness of the sentence in which it occurs. See Section **18n**.

91. **Participial phrase.** A phrase introduced by a participle.

> *Writing steadily,* I soon finished my theme.
> *Having finished my theme,* I signed my name and turned in my paper.

92. **Participle.** A verb form having the function of either a verb (used as part of the predicate) or an adjective. See page 42.

> I have *finished* my theme. (Part of predicate.)
> A *driving* rain delayed our progress. (Used as adjective.)

93. **Parts of speech.** The classifications to one of which every word must belong: *noun, pronoun, adjective, verb, adverb, preposition, conjunction, interjection.* See each of these terms in this glossary; see also page 34.

94. **Passive voice.** The form of the verb in which the subject does not act but is acted upon. Literally, the subject is *passive.* See **Voice**, below.

95. **Past participle.** The third principal part of a verb, used as an adjective or as part of the predicate. Unless it is formed simply by adding -*d* or -*ed* or *t*, you will find the correct form given in your dictionary.

96. **Past perfect tense.** The time of the action of a verb beginning at a point in the past and ending at a later point in the past. See page 91.

> By last September I *had earned* three hundred dollars.

97. **Past tense.** The time of a verb which expresses a before-now action. It is the second principal part of verbs, and unless it is formed simply by adding -*d* or -*ed* or *t*, you will find the correct form given in your dictionary.

98. **Perfect infinitive.** Formed by the auxiliary *to have* plus the past participle: *to have seen, to have worked.*

99. **Perfect participle.** Formed by the auxiliary verb *having* plus the past participle: *having seen, having worked.*

100. Periodic sentence. A sentence so constructed that its meaning is not complete or clear until the end is reached or nearly reached. See page 53.

> When I received the telegram, I knew that I had won.

101. Person. The modification of the form of a pronoun or verb to indicate whether the person is speaking (*first person*), is spoken to (*second person*), or is spoken about (*third person*).

> *I read, you read, he reads.*

102. Personal pronoun (see **Person,** above). A pronoun referring to the speaker (first person, *I, we*), the person spoken to (second person, *you*), or the person spoken of (third person, *he, she, it, they, them*). See page 37.

103. Phrase. A group of related words not containing a subject and a predicate. See page 47.

104. Plural. A classification of nouns, pronouns, subjects, and predicates, to indicate two or more units or members. Note that two or more singulars joined by *and* become a plural.

105. Positive degree. The simple form of an adjective or adverb in which no comparison is expressed: *red, tall, rapid, beautiful.* See **Comparison,** above.

106. Possessive. The *case* form of nouns or pronouns indicating ownership or some idiomatic use: *the man's hat, my job, children's toys, a minute's notice.* See page 62.

107. Predicate. The part of a sentence which makes an assertion about the subject. A *simple predicate* is the finite verb (or verb phrase) alone; a *complete predicate* consists of the finite verb with all its modifiers; a *compound predicate* consists of two or more finite verbs.

> Mr. Tyler drove the ball nearly two hundred yards. (*Drove* is the simple predicate; *drove the ball nearly two hundred yards* is the complete predicate.)
>
> I *wrote* the letter that night *and mailed* it this morning. (Compound predicate.)

108. Predicate adjective. An adjective used in the predicate after a linking or copulative verb and modifying the subject.

> This task is *difficult.*

Today seems *colder* than yesterday.
The team appears *ready* for the game.

109. Predicate complement. A predicate noun or pronoun, or a predicate adjective. See these terms.

110. Predicate noun or pronoun. A noun or pronoun used in the predicate after a linking or copulative verb.

This is *he* speaking.
That is *the last theme* I wrote.

111. Preposition. (Literally, *placed before.*) A part of speech showing the relationship of a noun or pronoun (the object of the preposition) to some other word: *at* home, *to* school, *from* a book, *through* the tunnel.

112. Prepositional phrase. A phrase introduced by a preposition. For examples, see under **Preposition.**

113. Present participle. A verb form (verbal) ending in *-ing* and used as an adjective or as part of the predicate. A *thriving* business (adjective use). We are *coming* (part of predicate).

114. Present perfect tense. The time of the action of a verb beginning in the past and just ending or still going on in the present.

I *have studied* for the last two hours.

115. Present tense. The "now" time of a verb: *I work, I am working, I do work.*

116. Principal parts. The three parts of a verb (present infinitive, past tense, and past participle) from which all other functions of verbs (tense, mood, voice) can be formed. In learning the principal parts of unfamiliar verbs, consult your dictionary. See **Strong verbs** and **Weak verbs,** below, and also page 83.

117. Progressive verb form. A statement of continuing action within a tense, formed by the correct forms of the auxiliary *to be* plus the present participle.

We *are writing* our themes today.
John *was studying* when I arrived.
I *shall be leaving* at six o'clock.

118. Pronoun (literally, *pro,* for, plus *noun,* name). A word which substitutes for a noun or a noun equivalent: *I, you, he, they, whom,* etc. See page 37.

119. **Proper noun.** A noun naming a particular or individual member of a group: *Harry, Mexico, Mrs. Jane Wilson.* Note that proper nouns are always capitalized.

120. **Pure conjunction.** A short or simple commonly used coördinating conjunction: *and, but, for, or, nor, neither, yet.*

121. **Quotation.** Words written or said by someone. If these are given exactly as written or spoken, the quotation is *direct;* if they are given in the words of another person, the quotation is *indirect.* Note the differences in punctuation.

> Direct: Henry said, "I have finished my work."
> Indirect: Henry said that he had finished his work.

122. **Reciprocal pronoun.** A pronoun indicating interchange of action. There are only two in English: *each other, one another.*

123. **Reference.** An act of direction used with pronouns and their antecedents, the latter being indicated or *referred* to by the pronouns.

124. **Reflexive pronoun.** A combination of *self* or *selves* with one of the forms of personal pronouns, usually placed after a verb or preposition and referring or reflecting back to the subject: *myself, yourself, himself, herself, itself, ourselves, yourselves, themselves, oneself.*

> We asked *ourselves* these questions.
> He sometimes whispers nonsense to *himself.*

125. **Relative pronoun.** A pronoun *relating* or connecting an adjective clause to its antecedent: *who, which, that.*

> The man *whom* we met lives in the house *that* we just passed.

126. **Restrictive.** A modifier that limits or identifies the word modified.

> A man *who works hard* should succeed.
> The hat *on the table* is mine.

127. **Sentence.** A group of words containing a complete, independent thought or a group of closely related thoughts. For fuller discussion, see Section 4.

128. **Sentence fragment.** A group of words, usually a phrase or a dependent clause, not expressing a complete thought. Exclamatory "sentences," answers to questions, and broken conversation are allowable and frequently used sentence fragments. But complete sentences are necessary in most writing where clearness is the aim.

130

129. Sequence of tenses. The logical order of time in verb forms when there are two or more clauses. See page 93.

130. Sign of the infinitive. The word *to* accompanying the infinitive verb: *to* go, *to* see, *to* arrive. In certain expressions it is omitted: He can *go;* I do *see.*

131. Simple sentence. A sentence containing one subject (simple or compound) and one predicate (simple or compound). See page 52.

> Weather conditions were perfect for flying.
> Books and magazines are read by some and are studied by others.

132. Simple verb form. Usually a statement of a "snapshot" or instantaneous action of a verb. (Compare with **Emphatic verb form** and **Progressive verb form,** above.)

> He *won* the race.
> I *have written* the letter.

133. Singular. The number category used of nouns, pronouns, subjects, and predicates to indicate one: *Boy, I, was, has.*

134. Strong verbs. Sometimes called *irregular,* strong verbs do not follow a regular system in forming their principal parts, which instead are formed by a change in the root vowel: *see, saw, seen; drive, drove, driven; choose, chose, chosen.* See page 83.

135. Subject. A substantive naming the person or thing about which an assertion is made. A *simple subject* is a substantive alone. A *complete subject* is a simple subject together with its modifiers. A *compound subject* consists of two or more substantives.

> The green *house* is for sale. (Simple.)
> *The green house* is for sale. (Complete.)
> *The green house and two acres of land* are for sale. (Compound.)

136. Subjunctive. The mood (or mode) of a verb expressing possibility, desire, or a condition contrary to fact. See Section **12.**

> I wish I *were* there.
> If I *had gone,* I should have regretted it.

137. Subordinate clause. Another name for **Dependent clause** (which see).

138. Subordinating conjunction. A conjunction joining a dependent (noun or adverbial) clause to its independent clause: *when, if, since, because, that,* etc.

> Dues were increased *because* there was no money in the treasury.
> He thinks *that* he will come.

139. Substantive. An inclusive term for a noun and all noun equivalents. Pronouns, infinitives, noun phrases, and noun clauses are noun equivalents. The following italicized words are substantives:

> The *dog* was three years old.
> *They* are coming tomorrow.
> *From New Orleans to Chicago* is a long distance.
> Are you positive *that he was here yesterday?*

140. Superlative degree. The form of an adjective or adverb comparing three or more objects. See **Comparison** above.

> Of the three brothers, John is the *tallest.*
> In our family, Mother is the one who drives *most carefully.*

141. Syntax. Construction; the grammatical relations between words in sentences.

142. Tense. The time of the action or of the state of being expressed by the verb: present, past, future, present perfect, past perfect, future perfect. The first three of these six are sometimes named the *simple* or *primary* tenses; the last three are sometimes named the *compound* or *secondary* or *perfect* tenses. See pages 87–94.

143. Tone. A characteristic of tenses of verbs, indicating within any one time limit *emphasis* or *progress,* or neither. See **Emphatic verb form, Progressive verb form, Simple verb form** (above).

144. Transitive verb. A verb accompanied by a direct object which completes its meaning. See page 40.

> The player *hit* the ball.
> My brother *studied* the assignment.

145. Verb. A word (part of speech) expressing action or a state of being (static condition).

> The river *flows* slowly.
> My name *is* John.
> Yesterday *seemed* warm.

146. Verb phrase. A verb together with an auxiliary: *is going, was finished, shall take, shall have taken, will have been taken,* etc. Distinguish between a verb phrase and a *verbal* (participle, infinitive, gerund). See page 42.

147. Verbals. Non-finite verb forms: participles, gerunds, infinitives (which see.) One or more of these serve at times as adjectives, adverbs, nouns, parts of the predicate—but *never* as the predicate alone.

148. Vocative. See **Direct address,** above.

149. Voice. The change in the form of a verb to indicate whether the subject is the performer of the action (active voice) or is acted upon (passive voice). In the formation of the latter, some form of the auxiliary *to be* is used with the past participle. See Section 11.

> Active: The coupled *danced* a rumba.
> Passive: A rumba *was danced* by the couple.

150. Weak verbs. The most common verbs in English, also called *regular* verbs because they usually form their past tense and past participle by adding *-d, -ed* or *-t* to the present infinitive form: *move, moved, moved; walk, walked, walked; mean, meant, meant.*

Punctuation and Mechanics

Punctuation is a system or method by which, through the use of certain mechanical marks, the meaning of written or printed communication is made clear. Proper punctuation is, therefore, an indispensable aid to correct, clear, effective writing because it helps to express thoughts and the relationships of thoughts. It developed originally because, without it, written language was unable to indicate or reproduce certain qualities of speech. In speaking, a pause or a rising inflection, for example, conveys meaning. These and other qualities of speech are reproduced in writing by certain marks of punctuation. Similarly, the relationship between parts in a sentence is revealed by word order. But modern English is not a highly inflected language, and word order is flexible. In written English, the various marks of punctuation suggest and indicate the grouping and relationship required to convey meaning clearly.

Punctuation, therefore, is an *organic* part of writing; it is not mechanical or arbitrary. Usage does vary with individual writers, but fundamental principles remain the same. These fundamental principles, or descriptive "rules," are drawn from thousands of examples of punctuation as applied in writing and printing by authors, printers, editors, and others whose knowledge and practice we respect. When there are enough examples of one use of a certain punctuation mark, we state this as a general principle or rule, beginning it thus: "Use the . . ." or *"Always* use the . . . ." When most of our examples agree: "The [mark] is *usually* used . . ."; when there are not enough examples to make a generalization: "The [mark] is *occasionally* used . . . ." Correct punctuation

134

Punctuation and Mechanics

permits individuality only to the extent that communication of ideas from writer to reader is aided, not impeded.

The most important marks of punctuation are:

.	Period	—	Dash
?	Question mark	-	Hyphen
!	Exclamation point	'	Apostrophe
,	Comma	" "	Double quotation marks
;	Semicolon	' '	Single quotation marks
:	Colon	( )	Parentheses

Less commonly used marks of punctuation are:

[ ]	Brackets	∧	Caret
. . .	Ellipsis periods	¨	Dieresis marks
* * *	Asterisks	´ ` ^	Accent marks

(handwritten margin notes: also, tilde, Cadilla, ténar, when you have a double letter coöperate)

The Four Purposes of Punctuation

Ordinarily you will apply a principle or specific "rule" of punctuation to a specific instance or sentence element. But you may be helped in such application by remembering that punctuation usually serves one of four purposes:

1. To *end* or *terminate* a statement (use period, question mark, or exclamation point).

   > Little progress was reported.
   > Are you going home?
   > What an occasion!

2. To *introduce* (use comma, colon, or dash).

   > Only one quality is needed, perseverance.
   > My purpose is simple: to succeed in life.
   > My goal in life is simple—success.

3. To *separate* parts of a sentence or word (use comma, semicolon, dash, hyphen, or apostrophe).

   > If you have any influence at all, try to have me excused.
   > Some people prefer dinner at noon; others prefer it in the evening.

16 a-b The Period

Commas, periods, semicolons, and colons—these are common marks of punctuation.

Mr. Brown was elected secretary-treasurer.

It isn't nine o'clock yet.

4. To *enclose* parts of a sentence or a whole sentence (use commas, dashes, quotation marks, single quotation marks, parentheses, brackets). *Enclosure marks are used in pairs, except when the capital letter at the beginning of a sentence takes the place of the first or when a terminating mark at the end takes the place of the second.*

You are, my dear Henry, the first one I've asked.

My dear Henry, you are the first one I've asked.

You are not—and everyone knows this—a very careful driver.

You are not a very careful driver—and everyone knows this.

"The word 'lousy' is not in reputable use as a term in literary criticism," said the lecturer.

You are referred to the United States Constitution (see especially Article VIII).

NOTE: Different marks to indicate these four principal purposes are, obviously, not necessarily interchangeable. The comma and the dash, for example, can serve three of the purposes, but the writer must choose which mark will best serve overall clearness and effectiveness.

THE PERIOD

16a. Use a period at the end of a complete declarative sentence.

When autumn comes, birds begin flying south.

Some people read two or three newspapers a day.

Grandfather spends his winters in Florida; Father spends his in Maine.

16b. Use a period after a mildly imperative sentence (a command or a polite request).

Never leap before you look.

Write all your business letters on business stationery.

136

The Period

16 c-g

16c. Use a period after an indirect question.

Mr. Brown asked when I could report for work.
Tell me what he said.

16d. Use a period after a standard abbreviation.

Mr. and Mrs. James Brown
Henry Smith, M.D. (b. 1900; d. 1950)
Sept. 15; lbs.; n.b.; ff.; q.v.; a.m.

See Section **28c** for exceptions.

NOTE: 1. If a declarative sentence ends with an abbreviation, one period only is used. If the sentence is interrogative or exclamatory, a question mark or exclamation point follows the abbreviation period. Inside the sentence, the period is followed by any logical punctuation which would have been used regardless of the period. Note the semicolons in the third line of examples, above.

2. *For the use of ellipsis periods* see Section **24g**.

16e. Use a period before a decimal, to separate dollars and cents, and to precede cents written alone.

4.25 percent $5.75 $.52

16f. Do not punctuate sentence fragments as complete units of thought unless they obviously stand for complete expressions. (See Section 61.)

Correct: "Where have you been?"
                 "At the library."
                 "What were you doing?"
                 "Reading a magazine."

Incorrect: Part of every afternoon I spend at the library. *Reading a magazine or anything else that looks interesting.*

We sat in the first balcony. *Although there were still a few seats available downstairs.*

16g. Do not use a period at the end of a title or after a centered or side subhead in the body of a manuscript.

137

16h. Do <u>not</u> use a period after a quotation mark that is preceded by a period.

> Wrong: He said, "Stop at the next corner.".
> Right: He said, "Stop at the next corner."

EXCLAMATION POINTS AND QUESTION MARKS

17. Like the period, the exclamation point and the question mark are usually marks of termination.

17a. Use the exclamation point to terminate a forceful interjection, or to express surprise, emphasis, strong emotion, or command (i.e., a vigorously imperative sentence).

> Oh, what a remark to make!
> Help! Help!
> What! You didn't see the stop sign!
> Come at once!

An exclamation point also may be used after a phrase or sentence to express irony. Often the exclamation used for this purpose is put in parentheses.

> Is the coach to be the slave of the alumni!
> She said that she might possibly condescend (!) to write.

CAUTION: Do not overuse the exclamation point. The emotion must be strong, the surprise genuine, the command really imperative to call for the use of this punctuation. Too frequent use of the exclamation point weakens its effectiveness. Notice that a comma, not an exclamation point, is used above after the mild interjection *oh*.

17b. Use a question mark at the end of every direct question.

> Do you really know?
> You really do know?
> Why are you so eager to go?
> You're going home next week, aren't you?
> Who said, "What is Man?" (Note single question mark.)

CAUTION: Do not use the question mark after an indirect question.

> Wrong: I was asked if I wanted to go?
> Right: I was asked if I wanted to go.

17c. Use question marks to indicate a series of queries in the same sentence.

> Will you be there? or your brother? or your parents?
> Also: Will you be there—or your brother—or your parents?
> Will you be there, or your brother, or your parents?

17d. Use a question mark, enclosed in parentheses, to express doubt or uncertainty.

> This is a genuine (?) leather bag.
> Richardson was born in 1900 (?) in Selma.

CAUTION: Do not overuse the question mark for this purpose. If it is impossible for you to find the exact information needed, you may use the question mark. But do not use it as a substitute for research.

17e. Do not use a question mark in parentheses to indicate an ironical or humorous meaning.

> Undesirable: The ambitious candidate sang his own praises in a modest (?) way and never raised his voice above a gentle (?) roar.

EXERCISES (Sections 16, 17)

A. Copy a paragraph of 100–300 words from a book or magazine, omitting all terminal punctuation marks and changing all sentence beginnings to small letters. Give it to a classmate for recapitalization and for reinsertion of terminal marks.

B. Underline all the periods, question marks, and exclamation points on any page of a magazine story you have just read. Account for the use of each mark by careful reference to one of the rules cited in Sections **16, 17.**

C. Use the period, exclamation point, and question mark correctly in the following sentences. Note that their use is called for in other places than the ends of the sentences.

1. Milton Johnson, J D, was one of the best lawyers in Barton, Nev
2. May I go with you Yes Oh, that will be wonderful
3. He asked Mary, Alice, Sidney, et al, if they would go
4. How feverish you seem Are you certain you are all right Shall I call Dr Jones You must be ill
5. What is your opinion of his capacity his character his will
6. Ouch Watch where you are going
7. "Why is he leaving Any particular reason"
8. "I am going blind How can I ever be happy again Oh, can't you do something for me I shall go insane"
9. "Please stop that You know crying only makes you feel worse Hush"
10. He asked John if he would go John emphatically said, "Never"

   D. Directions given in Exercise C.

1. "Oh so you thought you could get away with that trick, did you"
2. Are you quite certain that he is a recognized M D
3. Fifty percent of the boys left for the holidays on Dec 20; the others left on Dec 22
4. Evidently no one heard her, for she says that she shouted Help Help for hours
5. Isn't it strange that Prof and Mrs Browne were both born on Dec 11, 1898
6. The 1st, 2nd, and 3rd speakers argued that Edw VIII should not have abdicated
7. The advt announced the price as one dollar a yard, but the statement I have rec'd indicates the charge is $105 a yd What is the explanation
8. T Woodrow Wilson, 28th pres of the U S (b 1856; d 1924), served from 1913 to 1921
9. If only I could relive my college days How differently I would act
10. Bob is in his 4th year at the Univ of Minn, but he is still not quite certain whether, after college, he will work for his father or try to earn a degree of D D S

THE COMMA

18. The comma serves the purpose of introducing, separating, or (with another comma) enclosing. Because it has varied and distinct uses, it is the most troublesome of all marks of punctuation. Always used within the sentence, it differs from terminal marks (the period, question mark, exclamation point) in *degree;* it shows a brief pause, less complete separation than the full stops.

Note also that the comma, the semicolon, and the period form a series in which the members have a relative and increasing strength. The *comma* is the weakest mark of the three, for it separates short groups within the sentence and indicates comparatively close connection. The *semicolon* is used between longer and more important groups within the sentence, or between those which have a comparatively remote connection in thought. The *period* is the strongest mark of the three: it points out the most important division of thought, the sentence; it also indicates the greatest remoteness in thought.

COMMAS TO INTRODUCE

18a. Use a comma to introduce a word, a phrase, or, occasionally, a clause.

My aim in this course is easily stated, a high grade.
There is only one other possibility, to travel by air.
Our next problem is, where do we go from here?

18b. Use a comma to introduce a short quotation.

John said, "I'll never do that again."

NOTE: 1. If the equivalent of "he said" follows, it is separated by a comma; if it is inserted within the quotation, it is enclosed by commas.

"I'll never do that again," said John.
"I'll never do that again," said John, "unless I lose my temper."

2. Before a long or formal quotation, use a colon. (See Section 20d.)

3. Make a careful distinction between quotations which are really quotations of speaking or writing and quoted material which is the subject or object of a verb. Study the punctuation of the following:

18c-d

The usual remark is "May the better man win."
"Make haste slowly" came to my mind at once.
When Patrick Henry thundered "Give me liberty or give me death," he contributed a great catch phrase to the world.

18c. Use a comma after the salutation to introduce a friendly or social letter. (See Section 20e.)

Dear John,　　　　Dear Father,　　　　Dear Mr. Brown,

COMMAS TO SEPARATE

18d. Use a comma to separate independent clauses joined by one of the pure or simple coördinating conjunctions: and, but, for, nor, or, neither, yet.

I have not seen John recently, nor has anyone else seen him.
Commas are important marks of punctuation, and you will do well to master their use.
I tried to show him the error of his argument, but he would not be convinced.

NOTE: 1. The contrasting word *but* and the word *for,* as pure conjunctions joining independent clauses, invariably demand commas. Without the comma, the reader is led to believe, rightly, that *for* is a preposition.

I went home early last evening, *for* my parents did not wish to be alone.
I went home early last evening *for* the purpose of getting a good night's sleep.

2. If the independent clauses are short, the comma may be omitted before the pure conjunction. This statement, however, immediately brings up the question, "How short is short?" If the independent clauses consist of only subject and predicate, or of three or four words each, then they are obviously short and the comma may be omitted. Examples:

The rains came and the rivers rose.
I read awhile and then I studied.

Sometimes lack of punctuation between short clauses may cause momentary misreading, and a comma is necessary.

We ate *bacon and the hired man* ate eggs.

3. Fairly long clauses are sometimes written without a comma between them if their connection in thought is particularly close, that is, if the subject of the two separated predicates is the same.

I read the assignment over hurriedly and then I began a more careful rereading of it.

When the subject of the second clause is omitted, the sentence has merely a compound predicate and does not contain a comma before the conjunction, unless the members are unusually long.

He came hurriedly into the house and called excitedly to his mother.

The last person spoke clearly and made a favorable impression upon the audience.

4. Always use commas between clauses to which you wish to give special emphasis.

You must pay promptly, or you will be penalized.

5. Long independent clauses—but be sure they are *long*—which contain complicated internal punctuation (a sprinkling of three, four, or five commas) should be separated by a semicolon before the conjunction (see Section **19c**).

18e. Use a comma to separate dependent contrasting clauses.

Such clauses, although in good use, are peculiar, for each one alone is dependent and does not make complete sense, but taken together the two form a complete statement.

The higher we go into the air, the more rarefied the atmosphere becomes.

The more tired the team became, the better it played.

The less haste some people make, the more progress they achieve.

18f. Use a comma to separate an introductory adverbial clause from the independent clause.

> When you have finished the examination, sign your name and turn in your paper.
> Before John started on his trip, he made a careful plan of his itinerary.
> If I arrive first, I'll wait for you in the library.

NOTE: 1. When the adverbial clause follows the independent clause:

a. Omit the comma if the adverbial clause is necessary to complete (i.e., if it restricts) the meaning of the sentence.

> The accident occurred as I turned into Tenth Street.
> John works because he has no other way to live.

b. Use a comma if the clauses are fairly long, or if a slight pause is desired; omit it if the clauses are short.

> I'm quite willing to be a delegate to the convention, although there are others more capable than I.
> I'll go, if I have to go.
> I'll go if I have to go.

2. An introductory noun clause is not set off by a comma.

> What you say is true.
> That your theme was turned in late is unfortunate.

18g. Use a comma to set off an introductory phrase containing a verb form.

> Half-concealed in the bushes, the dog watched us go by.
> In order to play a vigorous game, you should be in good physical condition.
> By studying slowly and carefully, John mastered the subject.
> Because of his hidden fear of water, he refused to go swimming.

NOTE: Unless an introductory phrase without a verb form is fairly long, it is not set off by a comma.

144

Without fail I'll be there.

Because of lack of money John had to drop out of school.

18h. Use commas to separate words, phrases, or clauses in a series.

I have brought my textbook, my notebook, and some theme paper with me.

You will find Henry around somewhere: in the living room, in the basement, or out in the garden.

He whispered, he muttered, and finally he shouted.

NOTE: 1. Punctuation of a series (three or more) may be represented by A, B, and C. Some writers omit the comma before the conjunction and use A, B and C. But greater clearness is frequently obtained by the use of the comma before the conjunction, a practice which is advocated by the United States Government Printing Office *Style Manual* and the University of Chicago's *A Manual of Style*.

2. Do not use commas separating members of a series (unless emphasis is desired) when a conjunction is used to join each pair.

I have read nothing by Spenser or Milton or Wordsworth.

John says he is going to have ice cream and cake and pie and pudding for his dessert.

18i. Use a comma to separate two or more adjectives when they modify, equally and coördinately, the same noun.

I bought an old, dilapidated chair and a new, ugly, badly faded rug.

The building is surmounted by a tall, stately, ivy-covered tower.

NOTE: When the adjectives are not coördinate, commas are omitted.

A heavy steel cable spans the rugged green ravine.

One way of testing is to use *and* between the adjectives. If the *and* fits naturally, but is omitted, use a comma; otherwise, not. Sometimes there may be doubt as in "an old, dilapidated chair" above; then the writer should choose his course and justify it.

18 j-l

 The Comma

Notice that a comma is *never* used to separate the last adjective from the noun.

18j. Use a comma to separate contrasted coördinate elements.

> Psmith begins his name with a P, not an S.
> Your misspelling is due to carelessness, not ignorance.
> The pitcher threw slowly, but effectively.
> This garden spray is effective, yet safe.

18k. Use a comma to separate words or other sentence elements that might be misread.

> Misleading: The day after a salesman called with the same product.
> Outside the house needs a coat of paint; inside the walls need replastering.
> Instead of a hundred thousands came.
> In 1949 800 freshmen appeared on our campus.
> Last week I was in bed with a cold and my mother took care of me.
>
> Improved: The day after, a salesman called with the same product.
> Outside, the house needs a coat of paint; inside, the walls need replastering.
> Instead of a hundred, thousands came.
> In 1949, 800 freshmen appeared on our campus.
> Last week I was in bed with a cold, and my mother took care of me.

NOTE: Constructions in which commas are needed to prevent misreading are usually questionable or faulty. If possible, rephrase such sentences to eliminate awkwardness and to increase clearness:

> Instead of the hundred people expected, thousands came.
> Last week, when I was in bed with a cold, my mother took care of me.

18l. Use the comma to separate thousands, millions, etc. (i.e., numbers of four or more digits except numbers indicating years and telephone numbers).

146

18 m

In the fall of 1949 our freshman class numbered exactly 1,949 students.

In this contest 5,612 entries have been received.

If you telephone Prospect 1452, you will learn that the population of our city is now 312,456.

The government deficit may reach $5,565,000,000 this year.

COMMAS TO ENCLOSE

18m. Use commas to enclose <u>nonrestrictive</u> clauses and phrases within the sentence.

Clauses and phrases (usually when used as adjectives) are nonrestrictive when they do not restrict or limit the meaning of the sentence. Clauses and phrases are restrictive when they limit the word or words modified. Study these examples:

1. The *Queen Mary,* which is a large ship, was built in Scotland.
2. The ship which arrived yesterday is named the *Queen Mary.*

In the first sentence above, the omission of *which is a large ship* does not materially change the meaning of the sentence; its purpose is to give added information. In the second sentence, the clause *which arrived yesterday* is necessary for the complete expression of the idea. That is, it tells which ship *is* the *Queen Mary.* The clause in the first sentence is nonrestrictive, and it is thus enclosed, or set off from the remainder of the sentence, by commas; the clause in the second sentence is restrictive; it is not enclosed. Note also the labels attached to the following:

Chapter 10, *which tells of the rescue,* is well written. (Nonrestrictive or nonlimiting clause.)

The chapter *which tells of the rescue* is well written. (Restrictive or limiting clause.)

The book *lying on the living-room table* is dog-eared and dirty. (Restrictive or limiting phrase.)

Mark Twain's *Huckleberry Finn, lying on the living-room table,* is dog-eared and dirty. (Nonrestrictive or nonlimiting phrase.)

147

> John Jones, *who is our postman,* is a World War II veteran. (Nonrestrictive or nonlimiting clause.)
>
> The man who is our postman is a World War II veteran. (Restrictive or limiting clause.)

Preceding sentences show that the modifier (clause or phrase) may be either restrictive or nonrestrictive, depending upon the intended purpose. Restrictive phrases and clauses may therefore be explained as those necessary to identify the word or words they modify. They answer such questions about the word or words as *who? which one?* Each of the restrictive modifiers above serves to identify the word it modifies.

. The *context* sometimes determines whether a clause or phrase is restrictive or nonrestrictive. If the word or words are already identified by a phrase or clause, an additional modifier is likely to be nonrestrictive.

> The man who sharpens our lawn mower every summer is a genius.
>
> We were fortunate in finding a little shop full of all kinds of mechanical gadgets and kept by a thin, undersized little old man. We have no doubt that the man, who sharpens our lawn mower every summer, is a genius.

(In the first example, *who sharpens our lawn mower every summer* is restrictive, for it identifies. But in the second example, the man is identified in the sentence discussing the shop, and the clause *who sharpens our lawn mower every summer* is nonrestrictive.) Similarly:

> The man *sitting across the aisle from us* was going to Cincinnati. (Restrictive.)
>
> The man in the blue serge suit and wearing a brown straw hat, *sitting across the aisle from us,* was going to Cincinnati. (Nonrestrictive.)

Usually proper names are modified by nonrestrictive phrases or clauses. But occasionally they too need identification.

> The John Jones who is our postman is not the John Jones who lives on University Avenue. (Restrictive.)

148

The President Roosevelt who initiated the New Deal was not the President Roosevelt who once led the Bull Moose ticket. (Restrictive.)

18n. Use commas to enclose parenthetical words, phrases, or clauses.

A fairly adequate test is this: an expression is parenthetical if it may be omitted without materially affecting the meaning of the sentence; frequently, too, its position in the sentence may be shifted.

> *However,* we do not disagree too much.
> We do not, *however,* disagree too much.
> We do not disagree too much, *however.*
> We must, *on the other hand,* discuss every aspect of the problem.
> I believe, *if anyone should ask my opinion,* that action should be postponed.

NOTE: 1. Parenthetic elements vary in intensity, and the writer shows by punctuation their relative strength. Many words and phrases are so weak that they require no punctuation.

> I *also* believe in progress.
> *In fact* I am inclined to agree.

Other words and phrases, and dependent clauses, require commas.

> This problem, *as I said,* is difficult to solve.

Independent clauses—as well as some phrases and dependent clauses used emphatically—are so strong, parenthetically, that the enclosure marks should be dashes or parentheses. (See Sections 21e and 24a.)

> There is no reason—*no good reason, that is*—for spending so much money now.
> The lovely little town of Kickapoo Falls—*I was born there, you know*—hasn't changed much since I was a boy.
> My father has been a physician (*he received his training at the University of Louisville*) in Kickapoo Falls for thirty years.

2. *Inserted sentence elements* such as emphatic, suspended, or transposed expressions are somewhat similar to parenthetical words, phrases, and clauses, and are also enclosed by commas. Such inserted expressions are frequently more essential to the thought of the sentence than purely parenthetical material, but they are non-restrictive in function.

Emphatic insertion:	He did not make that statement, *as you will see if you read more carefully,* and I am certain that he did not mean it.
Suspended:	This is a good novel, *not only because it contains plenty of action,* but because it fully develops three characters.
Transposed:	Action, *I believe,* should be postponed. (Not transposed: I believe action should be postponed.)
Transposed:	On that night, *it seems,* there is to be a full moon. (Not transposed: It seems on that night there is to be a full moon.)

18o. Use commas to enclose absolute phrases.

An absolute phrase is a group of words that has no grammatical relation to any word in the sentence; it consists of a noun and a participial modifier (the latter sometimes omitted, but understood).

The task being finished, we started on our return trip.

I went to the first desk, *my application in hand,* and asked for Mr. Brown.

We need a fourth member of our bridge club, *Mary Ellen having moved to another town.*

CAUTION: *Never* punctuate an absolute phrase as a sentence.

Wrong: We need a fourth member of our bridge club. Mary Ellen having moved to another town.

18p. Use commas to enclose words in apposition.

My father, a physician, has just retired from active work.

This is Mr. Brown, our newly elected president.

My task, to compose a short story, seemed hopeless.

NOTE: 1. Omit the commas when the appositive is restrictive, or part of a proper name, or very closely associated with the preceding word.

> The river Mississippi is beloved of song writers.
> Richard the Lion-Hearted was an English king.
> My brother James is a senior in high school.

2. Omit the commas, usually, when the appositive is a noun clause.

> The fact that I was ill caused my absence.

3. Frequently, words in apposition are introduced by *namely, for example, for instance,* or *such as.* These words and phrases are enclosed by commas (NOTE: *such as* is *not* followed by a comma) as parenthetical expressions. If they and the apposition are fairly strong (that is, long and emphatic), dashes should enclose them. (See Section 21e, 1.)

> Two of the candidates, *namely,* John Smith and William Brown, are my friends.
> Any difficult subject, *for example,* chemistry, needs careful study.
> Some of our cities, *such as* New York, Chicago, and San Francisco, are thriving centers of commerce.
> The various seasonal sports—*for example,* football in the fall, basketball in the winter, and baseball in the summer—attract thousands of spectators.

18q. Use commas to enclose nouns or pronouns or a noun phrase in direct address (vocatives).

> *Mr. Brown,* will you speak next?
> I am proud, *Father,* of what you have accomplished.
> We are assembled, *ladies and gentlemen,* to discuss an important problem.
> Will you please, *sir,* speak more distinctly?
> Never doubt, *little boy,* that you will be rewarded.

18r. Use commas to enclose places and dates explaining preceding places and dates.

John left on June 20, *1949,* to go to Cincinnati, *Ohio,* for an interview.

Later he told us to send his mail to him at 147 Prospect Avenue, *Cincinnati 21, Ohio,* his new address.

NOTE: 1. The year and the state are completely enclosed by commas—the second comma must be used.

2. No comma is used before the postal-delivery zone number: Chicago 16; Philadelphia 27.

18s. Use commas to enclose initials or titles following a person's name.

Abbett, H. M., Abner, T. W., and Adams, R. B., head the list of names.

James Norman, M.D., and Frank Hale, D.D., are the featured speakers on the program.

The son of William McAdams, Sr., is listed as William McAdams, Jr., on our records.

18t. Do not use unnecessary commas.

Comma usage varies with different writers, but the fact that a reputable writer may vary occasionally from conventional practice does not establish a new principle. When practice varies so widely that no principle of punctuation can be stated, remember that every comma used must be needed for sense construction, clearness, or effectiveness. Modern punctuation usage omits more commas than formerly; therefore, be able to account for each comma you use. Above all, do not needlessly separate closely related sentence elements.

1. Do not separate a subject from its predicate or a verb from its object or its complement. (Remember that noun phrases and clauses act as the subjects, objects, and complements of verbs and should not be separated by commas.)

Wrong: What you say, is true.

To do satisfactory work, is my aim.

The man seated at the desk, is the secretary.

We asked, for a rereading of the motion.

The reason is, that I have been ill.

The letter informed me, that I should report for an interview.

2. Do not use a comma before the indirect part of a quotation.

Wrong: John told me definitely, that he would come.
The speaker asserted, that he stood squarely for progress.

3. Do not use a comma indiscriminately to replace a word omitted. The word *that* in indirect discourse and the relative pronouns *(who, whom, which, that)* are frequently omitted in informal writing.

Wrong: John replied, he would return next week. (Comma incorrectly substituted for *that*.)
The man, I met was a friend of a friend of mine. (Comma incorrectly substituted for *whom*.)
The last house, we lived in was just the right size for our family. (Comma incorrectly substituted for *which*.)

4. Do not use a comma to separate two words or two phrases joined by a pure coördinating conjunction.

Wrong: He has dignity, and integrity.
The leader has strength of body, and firmness of purpose.

5. Do not use a comma indiscriminately after a pure or simple conjunction. But the use of other elements may justify a comma after the conjunction.

Wrong: But, I shall never make that mistake again.
We are leaving early, and, I shall expect to receive your check before I go.
Right: But, as a lesson learned from experience, I shall never make that mistake again.
We are leaving early, and, to save trouble all around, I shall expect to receive your check before I go.

6. Do not use a comma before the first or after the last member of a series.

> Wrong: Avoid a mixture of, red, yellow, green, blue, and brown paints.
>
> We went swimming in a cool, clear, smooth-flowing, river.

18u. Avoid the comma splice: Do not use a comma to separate independent clauses not joined by one of the pure or simple conjunctions, and, but, for, or, nor, neither, yet.

A common and serious error (also named "comma blunder" and "comma fault") is the splicing of two separate, complete statements by a comma. This practice is confusing to the reader, who expects a sharper break between such clauses. Although an occasional example may be found in print, this error is usually avoided by reputable writers. (See also Section **62.**)

> Wrong: There was no reason for my going, I was not invited.
>
> Classes will begin on the twentieth of September, freshmen should be on the campus for orientation the preceding week.
>
> I spent money faster than I anticipated, therefore I had to drop out of school at the end of the first semester.
>
> I was able to borrow money to complete my first year, otherwise I should have had to leave at the end of the first semester.

To correct the "comma splice" error:

1. Use a period between the statements (partly objectionable because of resulting short and choppy sentences):

> There was no reason for my going. I was not invited.

2. Insert a pure conjunction between the statements:

> Classes will begin on the twentieth of September, and freshmen should be on the campus for orientation the preceding week.

3. Use a semicolon between the statements (preferable when a conjunctive adverb is used; see Section **19b**):

> I spent money faster than I anticipated; therefore I had to drop out of school at the end of the first semester.

4. Subordinate one of the statements (usually the most effective method):

> If I had not been able to borrow money to complete my first year, I should have had to leave at the end of the first semester. There was no reason for my going, since I was not invited.

EXERCISES

A. Supply commas where they are needed. Give the rule covering the use of each comma. (Refer to Section **18a-s**, if necessary.)

1. I am going home, but you may stay as long as you please. *separate independent clauses*
2. I think you are wrong, of course, but you have a right to stay. *parenthetical words*
3. The tree, which I saw for the first time, was a maple. *enclose nonrestrictive clause*
4. If John is certain, you may go. *separation from introductory adverbial clause introductory to independent clause*
5. Paris, France, is a lovely place not only because of its physical beauty, but because of its stimulating intellectual atmosphere.
6. The movement, as it sweeps along, becomes faster and faster. *enclose nonrestric. clauses*
7. It is food they want, not money. *separate contrasted coordinate elements*
8. Henry, the captain of the team, got a position in Gary, Indiana. *non restrictive*
9. Mr. Jones, please explain this problem to me. *direct address*
10. He wore a long, black, thick coat. *adjectives modify the same noun*

B. Directions given in Exercise A.

1. Your ideas are sound, nevertheless. *parenthetical word.*
2. President Wilson took office on March 4, 1913. *dates*
3. Having finished the course, John left the university for his home in Oakland, California. *absolute phrase*
4. "That is quite correct," said the girl. *comma after quotation*
5. The hall, a long, dark, narrow one, seemed foreboding. *series of adj.*
6. The captain of the team, a boy named Chester, was born in August, 1935. *nonrestrictive clause*
7. If you make money, you are judged a success, and strange as it seems, if you don't, you are counted a failure.

8. James Miley, LL.D, is a prominent lawyer; his address is 25 Valley Street, New Brunswick.

9. He discussed the economy of scarcity, the economy of plenty, the Republican platform; however, his words were meaningless to me, a mere child.

10. Boat travel fast and inexpensive has its delights, but Alice and John prefer the automobile, the airplane, and even the train as means of traveling.

C. Underline all the nonrestrictive clauses in the following sentences and supply the necessary commas.

1. Our team, which has lost four first-string men through injuries, can hardly expect to win.

2. A team, which has lost four first-string men through injuries, can hardly expect to win.

3. Freshmen, who on the whole are a carefree lot, generally forget their good intentions in a few weeks.

4. My old old Ford, which was the only car available at that moment, had two flat tires.

5. The car with two flat tires was the only one available at that moment.

6. Jim looked neat enough except for his rather seedy tie, which his roommate had lent him for the evening.

7. Some kinds of animals, such as raccoons, are commonly, wash their food.

8. Basketball players who are over six feet tall have a real advantage over their shorter teammates.

9. My story about the shipwreck of the *Mary Ann*, which took place off Hatteras on the Fourth of July, is exciting enough for a book.

10. We all thought that he had assigned Chapter XXI, which is the most difficult one in the book.

D. Select a page from any of your textbooks, or from a magazine, and encircle each comma. Try to account for the use of each comma by applying some part of Section 18. (Perhaps some of the commas are unnecessary or are incorrectly placed.)

E. Correct the "comma splices" in the following sentences by using as many methods, from 18u, as seem effective.

1. Mary is never on time, nevertheless, we'll have to wait for her.

2. I have not been in Philadelphia since 1949, that was the last time I saw a big-league baseball game.
3. You need not call me this evening, I shall not be at home.
4. I'll gladly lend you five dollars, in fact, I'll lend you ten.
5. There was some confusion about the nomination of officers, otherwise, the meeting was very well planned.
6. Mammoth Cave is on your way to St. Louis, you really should stop and see this natural wonder.
7. Father believed that every boy should earn his own spending money, consequently, I have had summer jobs since I was fourteen years old.
8. Dues are fifty cents a month, a fine of twenty-five cents, furthermore, is levied for each absence.
9. Please telegraph us your decision, our offer will remain open only three more days.
10. Susan is the most popular girl in her class, unfortunately, she is not the most studious.

THE SEMICOLON

19. The semicolon, as a mark of separation only, is a "stronger" mark of punctuation than the comma; it signifies a greater break or a longer pause between sentence elements. It is not, however, so forceful as the terminal marks of punctuation. The semicolon has definitely established uses which are not difficult to master. Remember: the semicolon is used only between elements of equal rank; it is entirely a mark of *coördination*.

19a. Use the semicolon to separate independent clauses not joined by a pure or simple conjunction: and, but, for, or, nor, neither, yet. (See Section 18d.)

I am certain you will like it; it will suit you perfectly.

Please close the window; the room is too cold.

My companion and I walked down the street; he saw only shop windows; I saw only people's faces.

19b. Use the semicolon to separate coördinate clauses joined by a conjunctive adverb (besides, however, nevertheless, therefore, thus, so, consequently, hence, in addition, likewise,

furthermore, <u>still</u>, <u>also</u>, <u>then</u>, <u>moreover</u>, <u>indeed</u>, <u>otherwise</u>, <u>meanwhile</u>, etc.)

We have been acquainted with the Smiths for many years; *still* we feel that we do not know them intimately.

There are many sharp curves in this road; *however,* a careful driver will have no difficulty.

Mr. Brown is a busy man; *nevertheless,* he seems busier than he really is.

NOTE: 1. The semicolon is used before the conjunctive adverb only when the conjunctive adverb comes *between* the two clauses. If the conjunctive adverb is shifted to a position within the second clause, the semicolon separates the two clauses (see **19a**), and the adverb, depending upon its parenthetic strength, is, or is not, enclosed by commas.

We have been acquainted with the Smiths for many years; we *still* feel that we do not know them intimately.

There are many sharp curves in this road; a careful driver, *however,* will have no difficulty.

Mr. Brown is a busy man; he seems busier, *nevertheless,* than he really is.

2. When the conjunctive adverb comes between the clauses, should there be a comma after it? There is no unvarying principle. A safe guide: decide upon the weakness or strength of the word in relation to the second clause. If it is weak, omit the comma; if it is strong, use a comma; if it is mildly strong, use or omit, depending upon your desire to indicate a pause. Another guide: commas follow longer conjunctive adverbs (*nevertheless, in fact,* etc.), rarely follow short ones (*thus, hence,* etc.).

The problem puzzled John for hours; *then* the solution flashed into his mind.

I do not favor spending the money; *nevertheless,* I shall not vote against the proposal.

Our climate is subject to sudden weather changes; *therefore,* you should bring a variety of clothing.

The Semicolon

CAUTION: Distinguish between a conjunctive adverb and a simple conjunction. A conjunctive adverb has an adverbial function which no simple conjunction possesses. Furthermore, it is used only between coördinate independent clauses, whereas a simple conjunction may join words, phrases, dependent clauses, or independent clauses.

Distinguish also between conjunctive adverbs and subordinating conjunctions, especially *because, whereas, although, inasmuch as.* These latter are not preceded by a semicolon unless they introduce the second of two independent clauses without a pure coördinating conjunction. (See 19a.)

I shall attend the lecture this evening, *although I can ill afford the time.*

I shall attend the lecture this evening; *although I can ill afford the time,* I believe that I shall learn something of profit.

19c. Use the semicolon to separate independent clauses joined by a pure conjunction if the clauses are long or contain internal punctuation. (See Section 18d, 5.)

He saw that the gasoline tank was full, each spark plug was clean, the carburetor adjusted; and then he felt that he was ready to start.

A distant relative on my mother's side, Harrison West, who had occasionally visited us, died last summer; and I was disappointed, although I had no right to be, that he had not left me a share of his fortune.

Success in college, so some maintain, requires intelligence, industry, and honesty; but others, fewer in number, assert that only personality is important.

NOTE: 1. Use semicolons to separate phrases of great length, as well as dependent clauses, and series of words in which clearness may not otherwise be attained.

The nominations for class president include the following: Adams, J. B., of New Richmond, member of Skull and Bones; Davis, H. M., of Bellville, formerly secretary of the Camera

Club; and Wilson, M. L., of Newtown, captain of the football team.

2. Do not overuse the semicolon. The longer a sentence becomes, and the more involved its punctuation, the less likely it is to be clear.

19d. Do not use the semicolon to set off a phrase or a dependent clause.

> Wrong: The excitement of the election being over; we settled down to our studies once again.
>
> Inasmuch as Joe has a fiery temper; we have to be careful what we say to him.
>
> The next meeting of the club will be postponed two weeks; because most of the membership will be on an inspection trip to Detroit.

THE COLON

20. The colon (:) is usually a mark of introduction, sometimes a mark of separation. It was once used as a form of semicolon, but the two now have distinctly different uses. The semicolon is a mark for *separating* coördinate sentence elements; the colon is primarily a mark for *introducing* lists, series, and quotations.

20a. Use the colon to introduce a word, phrase, or, occasionally, dependent clause when emphasis is desired. (See Section 18a.)

My aim in this course is easily stated: a high grade.

There is only one other possibility: to travel by air.

This is our next problem: where do we go from here?

I am positive there is one appeal which you cannot overlook: money.

These two things he loved: an honest man and a beautiful woman.

20b. Use the colon after an introductory statement which reveals that something is to follow: an enumeration, tabulation, or list.

You will need the following equipment for the trip: a change of clothes, a few toilet articles, and a supply of money.

There were three reasons for his success: integrity, industry, and a good personality.

Everything will be arranged: the paper provided, the pencils sharpened, the chairs placed.

NOTE: Do not overwork this introductory function of the colon. There must be a break between the introduction and what follows (frequently, *the following* or *as follows* is used). Colons do not separate verbs from complements or objects or prepositions from their objects. Nor is the expression *such as* followed by a colon.

Wrong: I am fond of: books, newspapers, and magazines.

I like to read: novels, detective stories, and biographies.

The three Ohio cities John visited were: Toledo, Cleveland, and Dayton.

In our community there are a number of popular sports, such as: basketball, tennis, and bowling.

20c. Use a colon to introduce a clause that summarizes or gives an example of a preceding clause.

The purpose of reading is not alone recreation: it is also information.

Many a man succeeds through sheer attention to industry: Benjamin Franklin was such a man.

NOTE: Do not overuse the colon for this purpose. Skillfully and infrequently used, it is effective. But the conventional mark between such clauses is the semicolon. (See Section 19a.)

20d. Use the colon to separate the introductory words from a quotation which follows, if the quotation is formal, long, or paragraphed separately. (See Section 18b.)

Robert E. Lee is reputed to have said: "Duty is the sublimest word in the English language."

The actor then stated: "I would rather be able adequately to play the part of Hamlet than to perform a miraculous operation, deliver a great lecture, or build a magnificent sky-scraper."

Then he arose, wiped his spectacles, adjusted his collar, and said: "It seems inevitable that we should have met together to discuss this problem."

The most important comment was made by William Brown, who spoke as follows: ". . . ." (one or more paragraphs of the speech)

20e. Use the colon after the formal salutation of a letter.

Dear Sir:
Dear Mr. Brown:
Gentlemen:
My dear Mr. Smith:

NOTE: The usual practice is to place a colon after the salutation of a formal or business letter and either a colon or a comma after the salutation of an informal, friendly letter. In this use, the comma suggests less formality, more friendliness than the colon.

20f. The colon also has the following uses: to separate hour and minute figures in writing time, the act from the scene of a play, the title of a book from the subtitle.

By my watch it is exactly 10:25 A.M.
The passage quoted occurs in Shakespeare's *Macbeth,* III:2.
Lew Wallace is the author of *Ben Hur: A Tale of the Christ.*

EXERCISES (Sections 19, 20)

A. Punctuate the following sentences, explaining the use of each semicolon and colon. If necessary, refer frequently to Sections **19** and **20.**

1. You should be able to write well you are able and willing to work.
2. He is lonely there without company besides, the trip would be good for you.
3. The wall paper was expensive it had an unusual design and was of good quality.
4. Above everything else he hated one thing hypocrisy.
5. He could barely read the sign "Danger, Explosives."

6. The players came from all over the world :Germany, Italy, Japan, Russia, China, and Canada.
7. The man advanced menacingly:"I don't wish to hurt you, but you must leave at once."
8. On this side of the street are trim hedges and neat lawns; on that side are tall weeds, ash cans, and gnarled trees.
9. He had little money therefore, he had to walk the whole way.
10. The lecturer said we must do three things: balance the budget, go back on the gold standard, and raise tariffs; however, he would not guarantee an immediate return of prosperity.

   B. Directions given in Exercise A.

1. He said the reference was to John 3:16 nevertheless, I was certain that it was to Luke 9:10.
2. This is his program for healthful living: drink plenty of milk; eat good-sized quantities of fresh, green vegetables; take exercise every day, preferably in the open air; sleep at last eight hours every night
3. A football team can be little better than its signal caller; that is to say, its success depends upon the plays it uses.
4. There are three things that I wish to do before I die: go to Europe, bathe in the warm, inviting waters of Waikiki Beach; see the Taj Mahal.
5. Do not despair of learning to punctuate correctly; keep on trying and you will learn eventually.
6. Stuart Chase once wrote: "For the milk of human kindness the most obvious substitute is soft soap."
7. He has a very sore leg; consequently, he cannot make the trip.
8. The professor told us this: to study at least three hours every day, to get enough sleep at night, to write to our mothers at least once a week, and to keep from worrying about the success of the football team, and spend more time in thinking about our classroom work.
9. The letter began: "Dear President Smith: I intended to answer your last letter more promptly than this; however, I have been so occupied that I have not had time to give my answer the thought it deserved."
10. Education is considered very desirable; therefore, every student should try to get at least a little while he is in college.

   C. Supply colons or semicolons where they are needed in the following sentences:

163

1. Not every trout fisherman has the time to tie his own flies, besides, the materials are very expensive.
2. Ken had seen that everything was in readiness, the gas, oil, and tires checked, the trunk packed, the lunch prepared.
3. Most books, particularly cheap ones, are slapped together so hastily that they have little durability, but with proper care, such as a true lover of books would bestow, they can be made to last through college, if not longer.
4. "There is no time for parley," he said, "there is no time for deliberation and soft words."
5. The notice had an ominous ring to it, "All lights must be extinguished at 10:15 sharp."
6. You should give that chair at least two coats of flat paint, then, in addition, you should put on one coat of varnish.
7. It has been our experience that success in college depends to a great extent on one trait, the ability to concentrate.
8. There is nothing very original about the street names in our town, Main Street, Broad Street, Bank Street, and so on.
9. After our first date she slammed the door in my face, hence I have never tried to see her again.
10. The group were as silent as stones. Hank slowly rose to his feet and faced us grimly, "All right, you cowards, I'll go."

THE DASH

21. The dash (—) serves the purpose of introduction, termination, separation, or (with another dash) enclosure.

The dash is a mark of punctuation most characteristically used to denote a sudden break or shift in thought. As George Summey, Jr., points out, it has been described as "the interruption, the mark of abruptness, the sob, the stammer, and the mark of ignorance." The last name probably refers to the fact that although the dash is useful, too frequent use of it reveals ignorance of the correct use of other marks of punctuation and makes for a choppy, incoherent style. A dash is approximately equivalent to a comma (both may be used in pairs or alone, and between expressions of coördinate or unequal rank). Logically, some other mark can usually be substituted for the dash, but its occasional use provides emphasis or surprise.

The Dash

21a. Use the dash to introduce a word, a phrase, or, occasionally, a clause when emphasis is desired. (See Sections 18a, 20a.)

My aim in this course is easily stated—a high grade.

There is only one other possibility—to travel by air.

Our next problem is—where do we go from here?

There is only one thing he needs for his complete success and happiness—love.

21b. Use the dash to indicate an interruption, an unfinished statement, or an unfinished word (usually in dialogue).

George began, "May I ask—"

"You may not," snapped the judge.

"I hardly know how to express—" and then the speaker blushed, and sat down.

"I can't spell the word 'erysipe—' "

NOTE: Omit the period when the statement terminates with a dash. Otherwise, never use the dash as a substitute for the period.

21c. Use the dash to indicate a break or shift in thought.

Here is a fuller explanation—but perhaps you are not interested.

He is the most despicable—but I should not say any more.

Do we—can we—propose such action to the trustees?

When John Smith comes in—oh, here you are now, John.

21d. Use a dash to separate a final clause summarizing a series of ideas that precede it.

The usual summarizing words are *these, those, such*.

Mathematics, chemistry, English—these give me more trouble than any other subjects.

The meek, the kind, the gentle, the pure in heart—such are of the Kingdom of Heaven.

Food to eat, a place to sleep, a pleasant occupation, a congenial companion—what more can anyone ask from life?

165

21e. Use dashes to enclose sharply distinguished parenthetical matter, in order to secure emphasis or suspense.

We are in favor—completely in favor, we repeat—of the proposal.

I was surprised—astonished, I should say—to hear of your splendid record.

My advice—if you will pardon my impertinence—is to apologize to your friend.

He was aware—he must have known—that his proposed solution was impossible.

My father is not afraid—he is a surgeon, you know—of performing the most delicate operation.

NOTE: 1. Long appositional phrases are likely to be enclosed by dashes (see Section 18p).

Three candidates for public office—Wilson of New York, Matthews of Illinois, and Adams of Colorado—are in favor of larger old-age pensions.

2. When the parenthetical material set off by dashes requires an exclamation point or question mark, such punctuation should precede the second dash:

If I should miss the train—heaven forbid!—please telephone me.

21f. Use the dash to indicate the omission of words or letters (other than contractions), or to connect combinations of letters and figures.

General B— was an excellent soldier.

The First World War, 1914—1918, was fought to end all wars.

John Kline is a pilot on the Chicago—New York run.

Monday—Friday classes will have one meeting more next week than Tuesday—Thursday classes.

Please study pages 3—14 for tomorrow's assignment.

21g. Use the dash sparingly.

Overuse of the dash is inadvisable. The dash is legitimately used in the instances cited in this section, but other marks of punctuation have their functions, too. Frequent use of the dash detracts from its special quality and effectiveness.

EXERCISES

A. Place dashes where they belong in the following sentences:

1. Col. John H. from Kansas, you know fought in France, 1916–1918.
2. When I looked up my heart misses a beat even now at the very memory I saw a huge beast before me!
3. You are too how shall I say? too matter of fact to do such a hot-headed thing.
4. From 1942 to 1945 perhaps it was 1941 to 1945 the man made a canvass of the city of T.
5. As I was walking along Waverly Place but before that I should mention the sight I saw on Twenty-first Street.
6. He was a large man who wore a straw hat and a topcoat a very odd sight, I assure you.
7. John was the laziest person at but I should not prejudice you in advance.
8. "Oh, Mary, do you could you will you give me a chance to try again?"
9. The food was excellent, but the boarders .
10. I am reasonably certain no, I am positive that you will like this if you will only give it a fair trial.

B. Encircle all the semicolons, colons, and dashes on one page of a textbook or a magazine. Account for the use of each.

THE HYPHEN—SYLLABICATION

22. The hyphen (-) is a mark of separation used only between parts of a word. Paradoxically, its most frequent use is unification, bringing together two or more separate words into a *compound* word which serves the purpose of a single part of speech.

The hyphen, therefore, is more a mark of spelling than of punctuation, to indicate that two or more words or two or more parts of one word belong together. It is a mechanical device necessary for correct, clear writing.

Syllabication is the act or method of dividing words into syllables, i.e., combinations of letters pronounced as one sound. Examples: re·sist; ad·vo·cate; ir·re·sis·ti·ble.

22a. Use a hyphen to join the parts of a compound word.

The use of a hyphen in joining compound words varies greatly. Do not attempt to learn the numerous rules; consult a standard dictionary (see Section 99). Dictionaries differ among themselves, however. It is wise to follow exclusively the dictates of some one good dictionary. The general principle of word joining derives, of course, from usage. When two words are first used together, they are spelled separately; as they grow to be more of a unit in common thought and writing, they are hyphenated; finally, they are written together as one word. This evolution is seen in the following, the third word in each series now being the accepted form: base ball, base-ball, baseball; basket ball, basket-ball, basketball; rail road, rail-road, railroad.

Hyphens are generally used:

1. Between two or more words modifying a substantive and used as a single adjective. These combinations may consist of
   a. an adjective or noun united with a present or past participle: *sad-looking, able-bodied, absent-minded, soft-spoken, battle-scarred, bell-shaped, wind-blown.*
   b. two adjectives, or an adjective and a noun, or a noun and an adjective: *Latin-American, ocean-blue, midnight-black, ten-foot, six-room.*
   c. a prefix or combining form attached to a capitalized word: *un-American, trans-Andean.*
   d. an adverb and a present or past participle (unless the adverb ends in *-ly*): *fast-moving, above-mentioned, swiftly moving.*
2. Between words of a compound noun:
   a. three or more words: *mother-in-law, jack-of-all-trades.*
   b. an adverb or a preposition as the second element: *go-between, looker-on, leveling-off.*
   c. compounds when *fellow, father, mother, brother, sister, daughter,* or a similar word is the first element: *fellow-citizen, mother-tongue, brother-classmates, sister-nations.*
3. Between compound words when, usually, *self, ex, half,* or *quar-*

ter is the first element: *self-control, self-respect, ex-president, half-asleep, half-truth, quarter-share.*

4. Between a single capital letter joined to a noun or participle: *A-flat, F-sharp, S-curve, T-shaped, U-turn.*

5. Between elements of an improvised compound: *make-believe, know-it-all, never-say-die, never-to-be-forgotten.*

6. Between the parts of compound numerals (from twenty-one to ninety-nine): *forty-three, sixty-seven, eighty-two.*

7. Between the numerator and denominator of a fraction: *two-thirds, four-fifths, one-thousandth* (but omitted when the hyphen already appears in either numerator or denominator: *twenty-four thirty-fifths; three ten-thousandths*).

22b. Use a hyphen to indicate the division of a word broken at the end of a line.

The rambling old house, it is true, would have looked considerably better if it had been freshly painted.

NOTE: 1. Do not divide a word at the end of a line if you can avoid it.

2. Place the hyphen at the end of the first line, never at the beginning of the second.

3. Never divide a monosyllable. Such words as *curse, through, though, ground, death, grace, quick, asked,* and *breadth* cannot be divided. Write them in their entirety on the first line; if that is not possible, leave a blank space and carry the whole word over to the next line.

4. Divide words of more than one syllable between syllables. But avoid dividing one-letter syllables from the remainder of the word: a·bout; i·talics; man·y.

5. Consult your dictionary to determine the correct syllabication of words. It is easier to consult an authority than to learn the various rules for dividing words. These simple suggestions may be helpful, however:

Prefixes and suffixes may be written separately.

Compound words are divided between their main parts.

Two consonants are usually divided.

23 The Apostrophe

22c. Do not use a hyphen in place of a dash, or a dash in place of a hyphen.

NOTE: With a typewriter the dash is made by striking the hyphen key twice: --.

EXERCISES

A. With the aid of your dictionary, determine which of the following words are compounds and should be written with hyphens: *notebook, pitchdark, fatherinlaw, understand, bull'seye, laborsaving, airtight, bathroom, foregoing, selfstarter, hangeron, blowout, quietspoken, hardworking, thirtynine, offstage, crazyquilt.*

B. Syllabicate the following words: *symphony, mystical, intangible, revolt, delicious, cohesion, radiation, carefully, torpedo, chemical, methodology, peregrinate, heighten, aphorism, throughout, deduction, grounded.*

C. Indicate where hyphens should be inserted in the following sentences:

1. The Farm Bureau is one of America's famous coop organizations.
2. An Xray picture of this steel shows that it should be retreated.
3. John's motherinlaw does not belong to the stay at home group.
4. A tight fisted miser is not known for his warm bloodedness.
5. Since Henry was an air minded individual, his father gave him for his twentyfirst birthday a twin motored airplane.
6. A blue green sedan has been wrecked on the Baltimore Washington highway.
7. My brother in law's malaria is a flareback to his service in the tropics.
8. Through self interest alone Anglo American relations should become friendlier.
9. Next Friday the president elect will become the new president, and the present president will become an expresident.
10. Every month sees all but unbelievable improvements in the industrial and manufacturing processes of our nation.

THE APOSTROPHE: POSSESSIVES AND PLURALS

23. The apostrophe ('), as a mark of separation, is used to indicate the possessive case of nouns and of indefinite pronouns *(an-*

other, everybody, no one, etc.). It is also used to mark omissions in contracted words and numerals and to indicate the plurals of letters and numbers. The rules covering the use of the apostrophe with possessives and plurals are not difficult to learn. Its use is as much a matter of spelling as of punctuation.

23a. Use an apostrophe and s to form the possessive of a noun (singular or plural) not ending in -s.

Man's, men's, child's, children's, dog's, women's, day's, week's.

As a specialist in *children's* diseases, the doctor, as well as the *doctor's* car, is ready for duty at a *moment's* notice.

23b. Use an apostrophe alone to form the possessive of a plural noun ending in -s.

Boys', dogs', doctors', days', weeks'.

During my two *weeks'* vacation I was a salesman of *boys'* clothing.

23c. Use the apostrophe alone, or the apostrophe with s, to form the possessive of singular nouns ending in -s.

Keats' (or *Keats's,* but not Keat's) sonnets are among my favorites.

Robert *Burns'* (or *Burns's,* but not Burn's) cottage is a shrine in Scotland.

NOTE: 1. The principle in **23c** applies usually to proper names. Most common nouns ending their singular in -s are the names of non-human objects and form their possessive with an *of* phrase.

Late in autumn *the greenness of grass* (not the grass' greenness) is unusual.

2. If the addition of the apostrophe and *s* causes difficulty in pronouncing, add only the apostrophe.

Every student of Greek knows *Aristophanes'* comedies.
Let's sing "Auld Lang Syne" for old *acquaintance'* sake.

23d. In compound nouns add the apostrophe and s to the element nearest the object possessed.

John borrowed his *brother-in-law's* car.

171

I could not afford that *attorney-at-law's* fee.

Charge these goods to *John Brown, Jr.'s,* account.

I left the restaurant wearing *somebody else's* hat.

23e. Add the apostrophe and *s* to the last member of a group to indicate joint possession.

I always use *Mason and Brown's* sporting equipment.

Let's get a soda at *Johnson and Stover's* drug store.

NOTE: Indicate individual possession by using the possessive case of each element of the series.

I am interested in the *Army's* and *Navy's* recruiting campaigns.

Mary is a baby-sitter for *Mrs. Brown's* and *Mrs. Wilson's* children.

23f. Use an apostrophe to indicate that letters or figures have been omitted.

John graduated with the class of *'49.*

Come now; you *don't* have to say, *"What's o'clock?"* That's a stilted way of saying, *"What's* the time?"

NOTE: Contractions provide common examples of this principle: *isn't, aren't, wasn't, weren't, hasn't, won't, he's, it's, they're, that's.*

23g. Use an apostrophe and *s* to indicate the plurals of figures, letters, and words considered as words.

I have trouble making legible *8's.*

Uncrossed *t's* look like *l's;* undotted *i's* are read as *e's.*

Don't overuse *and's, but's,* and *for's* in your writing.

John spent the first half of the *1940's* in uniform.

23h. Do not use the apostrophe in forming the plural of nouns.

Wrong: The *Smith's* are playing bridge with us tonight.

Right: The *Smiths* are playing bridge with us tonight.

Wrong: There have been more *boys'* than *girls'* among our freshman *student's* the past few *year's.*

> Right: There have been more *boys* than *girls* among our freshman *students* the past few *years*.

23i. Do not use the apostrophe to form the possessive case of the personal and relative pronouns.

Wrong:	our's	Right:	ours
	ours'		ours
	your's		yours
	yours'		yours
	his'		his
	her's		hers
	hers'		hers
	it's		its
	their's		theirs
	theirs'		theirs
	who's		whose

NOTE: 1. *Never* use the apostrophe with the possessive *its*—one of the most common errors in student writing. *Its* is the possessive form of *it; it's* is the contraction for *it is.*

When a dog wags *its* tail, that's a sign *it's* happy.

2. The possessive case of only the indefinite pronouns is formed with the apostrophe and *s: one's, someone's, somebody's, everybody's, each's, another's, either's,* etc.

EXERCISES

A. Use apostrophes correctly in the following sentences:

1. I like Burns' poetry better than I do Browns.
2. The girls picture was painted in 45; yours was done in 42.
3. Its a good thing the bread hasnt lost all its freshness.
4. Two years work wasnt enough for him to get his masters degree.
5. He said to us, "Mind your ps and qs and dont leave after ten oclock."

B. Form the possessive of: *Jones, men, Lord and Taylor, the, young prince, Ulysses, Roosevelt the First, oxen, it, Max, geese, Sally, Lewis and Conger, prince, Des Moines, mice, Dickens.*

C. Use apostrophes correctly in the following sentences:

1. I have already read most of Wodehouses' books.
2. The second years' work was also interesting.
3. Others are supposed to judge a person's ability because one can hardly consider himself objectively.
4. Don't tell me that that is the young miss's hat?
5. For appearances' sake, the Representative from Californias' vote was not counted.
6. Doctors sleeping hours are less regular than a clerk's.
7. You mustn't speak loudly; Charleys' ill.
8. Pericles' leadership coincided with Athens' golden age.
9. I'm not at all sure; perhaps its Johns' coat.
10. That's somebody else's job, not yours.

D. Encircle all the apostrophes on a page of prose and give the reason for each.

PARENTHESES, BRACKETS, AND MISCELLANEOUS MARKS

24. Parentheses ( ), sometimes called "curves," and brackets [ ] are marks of enclosure. The former find occasional use, but the latter are infrequently used (in fact, they are not included on the keyboard of standard typewriters).

24a. Use parentheses to enclose parenthetical material which is remotely connected with the context.

> This punctuation (I am convinced it is important) should be carefully studied.
> If you find any holly berries (surely they must be numerous now), please bring me some.

NOTE: In such constructions the parenthetical material merely amplifies the thought. Thus many writers prefer dashes to parentheses (see Section 21e). The marks may frequently be used interchangeably, although parentheses are more commonly used when the parenthetical material takes the form of a complete sentence not quite so closely related to the main statement.

24b. Use parentheses to enclose amplifying references and directions.

Study carefully the assignment on credits. (See Chapter V.)
Gulliver among the Lilliputians (see Book I) had some exciting experiences.

Shakespeare was born on April 23 (?), 1564.

I am studying medicine for three reasons: (1) I like the subject; (2) my father and grandfather are doctors; and (3) our town needs additional doctors.

24c. Use parentheses to enclose figures repeated to insure accuracy.

He paid ten dollars ($10.00) for the shoes.

There were thirty (30) claims for damages.

NOTE: Students often have an idea that a number written out *must* be followed by numerals. This is a mistaken notion; outside of commercial writing, words alone are sufficient.

24d. Do not use parentheses to cancel parts of your writing. Erase or draw lines through the words you wish to delete.

24e. Use brackets to enclose a comment of the writer inserted or interpolated in a quoted passage.

"On the first float rode the Queen of the Tournament [Miss Emily Miller] and her attendants."

"In April of that year [1942] Johnson took out his first patent."

"Milton portrays Satan as a fallen angle [*sic*] of tremendous size."

NOTE: Do not confuse brackets and parentheses. Brackets are used to set off inserted matter as extraneous or merely incidental to the context, especially editorial interpolations and comments not by the author of the text. Such interpolations may be corrections, comments, or explanations. Brackets are used to set apart the writer's addition to *quoted* material; parentheses are used to enclose the original author's *own words*.

EXERCISE

Place parentheses and brackets in the following sentences:

1. It was in December I think it was December that Mrs. Glass fell ill.
2. The measurements of the lot ninety by sixty feet were considered small.
3. The mean old ogre he is all of that made the child cry bitterly.
4. "The magazine was first published in the nineteenth century [1878] by Lee and Jones now known as Jones and Bushwick."
5. The letter ended: "Therefore, please let us have your check for two hundred dollars $200.00 in full payment for the article a rug your wife bought from us last January."
6. This article by James Jones you remember him? has been widely quoted.
7. The letter read: "John the boy I met at the dance has been asking about you every day since you left."
8. *Plain Sense* was published in the nineteenth century (1836) by an English firm.
9. Totalitarianism see Chapter 10 was eagerly discussed.
10. This book the one I referred to earlier is an excellent example of sixteenth-century thought.

MISCELLANEOUS MARKS

24f. Use a <u>caret</u> (∧) to insert an omitted expression or letter.

Place the caret below the line at the place of omission and write the inserted expression or letter directly above or in the margin.

24g. Use <u>ellipsis periods</u> (three) to indicate an intentional omission from a sentence or quotation.

This device is especially helpful when only part of a sentence or line of poetry is quoted. Thus:

". . . nothing walks with aimless feet."

—TENNYSON

"Your eyes smile peace . . ."

—ROSSETTI

NOTE: 1. A question mark or exclamation point may follow ellipsis periods.

2. Do not use ellipsis periods as a substitute for the dash. See Section 21f.

3. Do not use ellipsis periods purely as a stylistic device. Students

occasionally use them to indicate that much more could be said. Generally, they have nothing in mind.

4. Asterisks (* * *), three in number, serve the same purpose as ellipsis periods but are not frequently used to indicate omissions within a sentence. They are more likely to indicate omissions of paragraphs or long passages.

24h. Use a dieresis (¨) to show that the second of two vowels is pronounced in the following syllable.

With such words as *zoölogy, coöperation,* and *aërate,* there is a growing tendency not to use this sign. It is useful, however, in words like *reënforce* and *naïve,* in order to prevent momentary confusion or mispronunciation. A hyphen may also be used to indicate this separation of vowels in a word like *re-enlist.*

24i. Use an accent mark, usually with words of foreign origin, where the spelling requires it.

Acute accent (´): *passé*
Grave (`): *à la mode*
Circumflex (^): *hôtel de ville*
Cedilla (¸): *façade*

Let your dictionary be your guide.

QUOTATION MARKS

25a. Use quotation marks to enclose every direct quotation.

John asked, "What time shall I come?"
"Dinner will be served at seven," replied Mary.

NOTE: 1. Each part of an interrupted direct quotation begins and ends with quotation marks.

"Father," I said, "I need ten dollars."
"Bring your golf clubs," said Henry, "and we'll try to get in a round."

2. The *he said* or *said he* part, or its equivalent, inserted within a quotation is preceded by a comma (unless a question mark or

177

25 b-e

exclamation point is required). It is followed by a comma, unless a stronger mark (period or semicolon) is demanded by the grammatical elements. The test: What mark would be used if the *he said* were omitted? Use that mark after the inserted part indicating the speaker.

Joe Smith is a friend of mine, but I haven't seen him for five years.

"Joe Smith is a friend of mine," I said, "but I haven't seen him for five years."

I bought my hat at Johnson's Stores. It was on sale.

"I bought my hat at Johnson's Stores," Henry told us. "It was on sale."

There is no vacancy at present; however, we will keep your name on file.

"There is no vacancy at present," the employment director said; "however, we will keep your name on file."

25b. If a direct quotation extends for several paragraphs, use quotation marks at the beginning of each paragraph but at the end of only the last paragraph.

25c. In dialogue, use a separate paragraph for every change of speaker.

"Name, please?" asked the girl at the desk.

"John Brown," answered John.

"Did you have an appointment?" continued the girl, picking up a notebook.

"I certainly did," said John. "I've had it for weeks."

"Sit down, then. The doctor will see you in a few minutes."

25d. Use quotation marks to enclose technical terms in non-technical writing.

This is a heavily "watered" issue of stock.

The pilot made a "three-point" landing.

25e. In formal writing use quotation marks to enclose words which suggest a different level of usage.

If a word is appropriate, no quotation marks should be used as a form of apology. If it is not appropriate, the expression can usually be altered. In some instances, however, you may wish to shift to a different level of usage in order to communicate meaning exactly or emphatically:

> The prevailing opinion is that President Black informed Dean White that the recommendation of the faculty was "cock-eyed."
>
> The symphony was conducted by a "stuffed shirt."

CAUTION: Do not rely upon this use of quotation marks as an excuse for inexact choice of words. Find the word that means exactly what you wish to say. (See Section **89**.) Also do not sprinkle your writing with quotation marks; enclose only those expressions that would puzzle or mislead your reader.

25f. Use quotation marks to enclose chapter headings, titles of articles, titles of short stories, and the like, when used in a body of prose.

When both chapter heading and book are mentioned, or title and magazine, the latter should be indicated by italics (see Section **26a**).

> For such information consult the chapter, "Private Preparatory Schools," in the *American Educational Directory.*
>
> John B. Martin's article, "There Goes Upper Michigan," in a recent issue of *Harper's Magazine,* deals with the passing of an era in the realm of vacation lands.

If there is no chance of confusion, quotation marks may be used instead of italics to indicate the names of ships, trains, airplanes, and the like. (The use of italics is preferred; see Section **26a**.)

> "The City of Los Angeles" leaves the Union Station at nine o'clock.
>
> We have booked passage to England on the "Queen Mary."

25g. Use single quotation marks to enclose a quotation within a quotation.

> "Tell me," Father asked Mother after the wedding, "whether the bride said, 'I promise to obey.'"

The teacher said, "When you say, 'I'll turn in my theme to-morrow,' I expect it to be turned in tomorrow, not next week."

25h. Place quotation marks correctly with reference to other marks.

1. The comma and the period come *inside* the quotation marks. This principle applies even when only the last word before the comma or the period is enclosed.

> "I need your help now," she said. "I need it more than ever."
> Some praised the performance as "excellent," and others thought it was only "fair."

2. Every question mark, exclamation point, and dash comes *outside* the quotation marks unless it is part of the quotation.

> Did she say, "I have enough money"?
> She asked, "Have I enough money?"
> "Have I enough money?" she asked.
> What is meant by "dog eat dog"?
> That is demonstrably a "pip"!
> "It's a 'pip'!" he stated firmly.

3. Semicolon and colon come *outside* the quotation marks.

> Read E. B. White's "Walden"; it is, I think, his best essay.
> Look up the following in "A Glossary of Famous People": Theodore Roosevelt, Woodrow Wilson, Charles E. Hughes.

CAUTION: 1. Quotation marks *always go in pairs*. Be careful to indicate both the beginning and the end of a quotation.

> Wrong: "I like football better than baseball, he said. And I like tennis better than any other sport."
>
> Right: "I like football better than baseball," he said. "And I like tennis better than any other sport."

2. Do not put quotation marks around an indirect quotation.

> Wrong: The conductor asked "how many had their return tickets."
>
> Right: The conductor asked how many had their return tickets.

The conductor asked, "How many of you have your return tickets?"

3. In some books, magazines, and newspapers either no quotation marks at all or single quotes are printed where, according to rule, double ones would be used. Neither of these practices is any criterion because, in this country at least, they are usually experiments in typography or a kind of affectation.

4. Do not use quotation marks to indicate humor. Humor should be evident to the reader without the artificial indication given by quotation marks.

5. Unless the title of your theme is itself a quotation, do not enclose it in quotation marks.

ITALICS

26. Indicate words that you wish to italicize (i.e., in print, *slanting* letters) by underlining them once (whether you typewrite or write in longhand). Quotation marks may also be used to set off words that would be italicized in print, but since these marks have various other uses (see Section 25), the system of underlining is preferable.

26a. Use italics (underlining) to indicate titles of magazines, newspapers, books, long poems, plays, and the names of ships, trains, and airplanes.

I came from California to New York on the streamlined trains, the *City of Denver* and the *City of Philadelphia,* and sailed for England on the *Queen Mary.* From the ship's library I borrowed a copy of *Newsweek,* the New York *Times,* and Thomas Hardy's novel, *The Return of the Native.* As I was reading, I saw *Lucky Lady III* fly overhead on the first leg of her world flight.

NOTE: 1. When both the title of an article (or story) and the magazine in which it appears are written, in order to distinguish them use quotation marks to enclose the former and italicize the latter; apply the same principle to the chapter title of a book and the book.

Be sure to read Wilburn Cartright's article, "The Motorist Girds for Peace," in *Harper's Magazine*.

Your parents will enjoy reading Chapter 17, "Old-Age Pensions," in Allen Brown's *The Quest for Security*.

2. Do not italicize the name of the city in the title of a newspaper: the Philadelphia *World-Bugle*.

3. Do not omit an article which forms part of the title: *The Merchant of Venice; A Fable for Critics*.

4. Do not add an article to a title if none appears in the original work: Shakespeare's *Two Gentlemen of Verona*.

26b. Use italics (underlining) to indicate foreign words or phrases.

There is a *je ne sais quoi* quality about it.

This is an interesting proposal, but *cui bono?*

A vicious book of that kind has no *raison d'être*.

NOTE: 1. Because newspapers do not employ italics to indicate such expressions, this use of italics has lessened somewhat. Such words, however, should be italicized or set off by quotation marks. In formal theme writing, underline all such words and phrases.

2. Standard dictionaries use some consistent method to distinguish foreign words or words still felt to be foreign. In *The American College Dictionary,* every foreign word and phrase is followed by a label indicating the language. Other dictionaries use a symbol (*; for.; ||). You can thus determine whether a given word or expression should be underlined. Some dictionaries also contain a separate list of "Foreign Words and Phrases."

26c. Use italics (underlining) to refer to a word, letter, or number spoken of as such.

Every student should be able to use *its* and *it's* correctly.

Your undotted *i*'s look exactly like *e*'s.

You have written *6* every time that you meant to write *9.*

26d. Use italics (underlining) to emphasize a word, a phrase, or a statement.

Always sign your name to a letter.

> Never, *under any conditions,* keep poisonous substances in your medicine cabinet.

NOTE: Use italics for emphasis sparingly; never use more than one underlining for this purpose.

EXERCISES (Sections 25, 26)

A. Use italics and quotation marks correctly in the following sentences. Change the paragraphing, where necessary.

1. After you leave college, he said to me, you will find that work means work; just being a wise guy won't get you anywhere.
2. Mason Pryor, the columnist on the Richmond Clarion, says that Escape isn't as good a picture as it's cracked up to be.
3. Please substitute 3's for 4's in this addition, he told me. I answered, But will that be cricket? Never mind, do as you're told, he ordered.
4. Did you say one cent or one sou?
5. He read The Eve of St. Agnes and said he'd never come across a better poem.
6. Henry is really an enfant terrible; he says Zeitgeist is the cause of his actions.
7. The subtitle of William Makepeace Thackeray's novel, Vanity Fair, is A Novel Without a Hero.
8. The river tug John Henry Mason was rammed by the Cunard liner, the Queen Elizabeth.
9. Railroads are using novel expressions; for example, the City of San Francisco sails from Union Station in Chicago every evening at five o'clock.
10. Some students always misspell their and there, and here and hear. Do you?

B. Use quotation marks and italics correctly in the following. If necessary, change the paragraphing.

My father got the palsy, he said, and wasn't able to work on the Olympian any longer. My mother went out to work as a seamstress but I was a Dummkopf and stayed at home reading old copies of the Saturday Evening Post. But surely you didn't twiddle your thumbs all day, every day, I asked. You bet, he answered vehemently. We found a pied-à-terre on the Rue Mors and I didn't do much. I had a sort of Weltschmerz, I suppose; once in a while I made a few francs selling the Paris

Le Matin and got an occasional pourboire for holding someone's horse. But that's a poor way to live, I answered. Chacun à son goût, he replied. I didn't ask for what I got. I never wanted to come to France in the first place.

CAPITALS

27. Problems in capitalization are so numerous that rules or principles cannot be given to apply to every possible example. The stylebooks of various publishing firms usually contain from twenty to forty pages dealing with capitals. For the ordinary writer a few underlying principles may be helpful.

27a. Capitalize each important word in the title of a theme, article, book, play, poem, magazine, newspaper, musical composition, song, etc.

Autumn Chores on the Farm
The Manufacture of
  Ammonia
The Value of the Liberal Arts
Steinbeck's *The Grapes of
Wrath*

*A Midsummer's Night's
Dream*
Gray's *Elegy Written in a
Country Churchyard*
The Saturday Evening Post
The Moonlight Sonata

If you were to write an essay on "The Value of the Liberal Arts" for *The Journal of Engineering Education,* you might well include a critical discussion of Sheridan's *The School for Scandal* and Rossini's *The Barber of Seville.*

NOTE: Capitalize the first and last words of such titles, but within the titles do not capitalize articles, prepositions, and conjunctions, unless they consist of five or more letters: *Caught Between Storms; A Journey Through Darkest Africa; The Stars Pass By.*

27b. Capitalize the first word of every sentence and the first word of every direct quotation.

The first part of this rule is illustrated on every page.
Can you attend the meeting tonight?
John said, "Don't miss seeing that movie."

27c. Capitalize the first word of every line of poetry.

Her favorite simile occurs in the second stanza of Words-
worth's "She Dwelt Among the Untrodden Ways":
<blockquote>
A violet by a mossy stone
Half hidden from the eye!
—Fair as a star, when only one
Is shining in the sky.
</blockquote>

NOTE: Some modern poetry is written without capital letters.

27d. Capitalize proper nouns.

These include:

1. Names of people and titles used in place of specific persons:
   William Shakespeare, Theodore Roosevelt, the President, the
   Senator, the Treasurer, the General, Mr. Chairman, Father,
   Mother.

2. Names of countries, states, regions, localities, other geographic
   areas, and the like: United States, England, Pennsylvania, the
   Far East, the Dust Bowl, the Midwest, the Solid South, the
   Rocky Mountains, the Sahara Desert, the Mississippi River,
   Lake Michigan.

3. Names of streets: Michigan Boulevard, Fifth Avenue, Ross
   Street, Ravinia Road.

4. Names of the Deity and personal pronouns referring to Him:
   God, Heavenly Father, Son of God, Jesus Christ, Savior, His,
   Him, Thy, Thine.

5. Names for the Bible and other sacred writings: Bible, the
   Scriptures, Book of Genesis, Revelations, Koran.

6. Names of religions and religious groups: Protestantism, Ca-
   tholicism, Presbyterian, Jesuit, Unitarian.

7. Names of the days and the months (but *not* the seasons) Monday, Tuesday, etc.; January, February, etc.; summer, winter,
   autumn, fall, spring.

8. Names of schools, colleges, universities: Hill School, Morton
   Grade School, Horace Mann High School, Kentucky Military
   Institute, Wabash College, Cornell University.

9. Names of historic events, eras, and holidays: Revolutionary

185

War, Christian Era, Middle Ages, Renaissance, the Fourth of July, Labor Day, Thanksgiving.

10. Names of races, organizations, and members of each: Indian, Negro, Malay, League of Women Voters, American Academy of Science, National League, New York Giants, Big Ten Conference, an Elk, a Shriner, a Socialist.

11. Vivid personifications: Fate, Star of Fortune, Destiny, the power of Nature, the paths of Glory, the chronicles of Time.

12. Trade names: Studebaker Commander, Fordor sedan, Bon Ami, Ry-Krisp, Wheaties.

13. All names similar or comparable to the foregoing.

27e. Capitalize a common noun or adjective when it is a part of or helps to make a proper name.

Missouri River, Rocky Mountains, Wall Street, Fifth Avenue, Blackstone Theater, Washington High School, Swarthmore College, New York University, Roosevelt Dam, Yosemite National Park, Lake Erie, U.S. Highway 40, Route 33.

NOTE: Common nouns and adjectives used alone are not capitalized: river, mountain, street, avenue, theater, high school, college, university, dam, park, lake, etc.

He is not a professor.
This is Professor Smith.

My father is a dean in a college.
My father is Dean Williams of Seneca University.

These students attend the local high school.
John is a graduate of Rocktown High School.

The street in front of our house needs paving.
There are vacant houses on Forest Avenue.

I have explored many of the rivers in our country.
The Holland Tunnel runs under the Hudson River.

The Great Smoky Mountains are well worth a visit.

27f. Capitalize words derived from proper nouns.

Shakespearian, American, Episcopalian, Biblical, Scriptural, Italian.

NOTE: 1. The word *English* is always capitalized in reference to language and literature.

2. Some proper nouns and derivatives of proper nouns (the number is approaching two hundred) have been used so frequently that they are now considered common and are not capitalized. When in doubt, consult your dictionary. A fair sampling of such a list includes:

anglicize	macadam roads
bessemer steel	mentor
brazil nut	oxford shoes
brussels sprouts	pasteurize
castile soap	plaster of paris
chinaware	platonic friend
derby hat	quisling
english (spin imparted to ball)	quixotic
	scotch plaid
french dressing	turkish towel
german silver	venetian blind
india ink and rubber	vienna bread
italicize	watt (electric unit)

3. Does anyone need to be reminded that the first personal pronoun "I" is *always* capitalized?

27g. Avoid unnecessary and careless use of capitals.

1. Do not carelessly write small (lower-case) letters so large that they resemble capitals (upper-case letters).

2. Do not capitalize names of points of the compass unless they refer to a specific section.

Correct: My home is in the East.

John lives west of the Allegheny Mountains.

I should like to live in the southern part of California.

Walk two blocks west; then turn north.

3. Do not capitalize nouns of kinship unless they are used as a substitute for the proper name; when preceded by a possessive, they are common nouns.

Correct: My father is a dean.
At Seneca College, Father (i.e., Mr. Smith) is Dean of Men.
My sister thinks I am quiet, but Grandma and Mother say I talk too much.

4. Do not capitalize a noun or adjective if the reference is to any one of a class of persons or things rather than a specific person or thing. For example, do not capitalize names of classes or college class members as members (unless you have a specific class in mind): "This autumn I shall be a sophomore although I have enough course credits to be a member of the Junior class."

Do not capitalize names of college subjects unless they are proper names (but titles of specific courses are capitalized): "Next year I shall have courses in history, Spanish, and journalism, and although I do not like science courses, I shall be required to take Mathematics 2 and Biology 12."

EXERCISES

A. Encircle all the capitals on a page of prose in a textbook or magazine. Explain the reason for each capital.

B. Supply all necessary capitals in the following sentences:

1. You studied french, english, physics, and history your first year at college?
2. George Herbert wrote a poem, the elixir, whose first lines are
   "teach me, my god and king,
   in all things Thee to see . . ."
3. My sister said brother was going on saturday to see walter hampden play in rostand's cyrano de bergerac at the majestic theater.
4. The author of Temple Bells is writing about the eastern section of persia but he has never been out of the south of france.
5. The rape of the lock is a poem by alexander pope.
6. He walked south as far as the corner of exeter avenue and sixty-eighth street.

7. He was ex-president of some South American country and always insisted upon being called the Honorable Mr. Zalik.
8. Labor Day comes in September but father insists that every day is labor day for him.
9. He said that he had never learned the difference between Socialism and Communism but that he did believe in a democratic form of government.
10. The Catawba and Reedy rivers, which meet in the eastern section of the state, are not large, but they join to form a river which furnishes the power for the Genesee Cotton Mill of Dothan, Massachusetts.

ABBREVIATIONS

28a. Do not use abbreviations in formal writing or in idiomatic informal writing.

A good general practice to follow is this: In all writing intended for the information and convenience of a reader, avoid all abbreviations that would be puzzling or offensive to the eye; write out words and expressions in full, unless condensation seems necessary or the spelled-out words are unconventional and ultrafastidious.

Incorrect: A new sec. is to be elected to replace the sec.-treas. who has resigned.

Many a chem. prof. grades too severely; many a lit. prof. grades too easily.

Meet me in the Penn. Station Wed. p.m.

Chicago, Ill., lies n.e. of the Miss. R.

NOTE: 1. Themes and other college written work are (or should be) formal writing or good idiomatic informal writing. Usually, use abbreviations only in footnotes and bibliographies of term and research papers. Specifically, *avoid* in continuous formal prose abbreviations for:

a. Names of states, rivers, mountains, etc.: Ala., Pa., Ill. R., Appalach. Mtns.
b. Parts of geographic names: Ft. Wayne (for Fort Wayne), N. Dakota (for North Dakota), Pt. Arthur (for Port Arthur). (*Saint* is abbreviated before a place name: St. Louis, St. Bonaventure.)

28b   Abbreviations

c. Christian names: Jos. (for Joseph), Benj. (for Benjamin), Thos. (for Thomas).

d. Names of months and days: Jan., Feb., Sun., Mon.

e. Most titles: Prof., Gen., Lieut., Pres.

f. Names of school and college subjects: chem., math., ed., P.E.

g. Words denoting length, time, weight, or capacity: in., ft., yd., sec., min., hr., mo., yr., oz., lb., pt., qt., gal., pk., bu., bbl.

h. Miscellaneous words like st. for street, ave. for avenue, blvd. for boulevard, dr. for drive, pl. for place, r. for river, mt. for mountain; a.m. and p.m. (as substitutes for *morning* and *afternoon:* "this a.m. and p.m."); & for *and;* etc. for "and the like."

2. Certain very common abbreviations are permissible and should be used instead of the full word. These are usually conventional titles invariably used before names of people and the letters after the names indicating educational degrees:

Mr. William Brown; Mrs. John Smith; Messrs. William Brown and John Smith; Dr. Albert Jones; Hon. James E. Mason; Rev. Gordon Graham (but note: *The Honorable* James E. Mason, *The Reverend* Gordon Graham).

William Brown, A.B., A.M.; John Smith, Ph.D., LL.D.; Rev. Gordon Graham, D.D.

Harry Jones, M.D., and his brother, Henry Jones, D.D.S., share an office.

William Brown, Sr., and William Brown, Jr., were elected delegates.

Other necessary abbreviations are *a.m.* and *p.m.* with numbers (8:12 a.m., 2:10 p.m.); A.D.; B.C.; F. (for Fahrenheit); C. (for Centigrade).

28b. Do not use contractions in formal writing.

A contraction is a form of abbreviation: a word written with an apostrophe to indicate the omission of a letter. Usually considered as colloquial expressions (proper in speech but questionable in writing), such contractions as *won't, don't, can't, shouldn't, wasn't,*

190

and the like, seem out of place in formal writing. See Sections
84, 93.

NOTE: In reporting dialogue or conversation, a writer uses contractions correctly to convey the exact words of the speaker. Do
not avoid the use of contractions and other colloquialisms to the
extent of making your reports of conversation seem artificial and
forced.

28c. Use a period after every abbreviation.

NOTE: There are only a few exceptions to this rule. *No abbreviat-
ing period* is used after:

1. Contractions such as *don't, won't, isn't, haven't,* etc.
2. The ordinal numbers when written *1st, 2nd, 35th,* etc.
3. Nicknames such as *Bill, Joe, Al,* etc.
4. A few specialized abbreviations: percent, MS or MSS, TV,
   I O U, S O S, M (for thousand), etc.
5. Letters of radio stations: WENR, WABC, WBBM, WILL,
   KDKA, etc.
6. Certain government divisions and agencies, unions, associations:
   AAA, AEF, AF of L, AP, FBI, INS, TVA, UN, UNESCO,
   WAC, YMCA, YWCA, etc.

EXERCISE

Correct all errors in the use of abbreviations in the following
sentences:

1. The sts. run E and W in N Y C, & the aves. run N & S.
2. The king of G B from 1457 to 1509 was Henry VII; he was followed by Henry VIII.
3. The Pres. didn't make any speeches in Jan or Feb because he was
   taking a vacation in Fla those two months.
4. Tom said that thirty-two percent of the boys in school tried out for
   the swimming team.
5. Last mo I went to see the dr four times.
6. The agent asked to see the Mrs. of the house.
7. He said that he would arrive at eight ante meridian, D V.
8. "I regret that I shan't be able to accept your kind invit. of the
   fourteenth inst."

9. Ga. lies just across the Savannah R. from S C.

10. The rev. of the church also serves as a prof at the Univ across town.

NUMBERS

29a. Use words to represent numerals when no more than two words are required.

Nine; forty-seven; seven hundred; twelve thousand; five million.

A committee of seven members has been appointed.

Approximately ninety thousand spectators saw the Army-Navy football game.

29b. Use figures for numerals when more than two words are required.

$8.15   357   3,475   1,657,812

My check for $13.25 is enclosed.

Exactly 212 applications have been received.

29c. Do not use words in dates, street and telephone numbers, highway numbers, chapters of a book, or groups of numbers in the same passage.

My parents were married on June 28, 1928.

I live at 1607 Ravinia Avenue; my telephone number is Prospect 1874.

Take U.S. Highway 40 to Columbus and turn north on Route 33.

Read Chapters 5, 6, and 12 for the next assignment.

Trains for Chicago leave on Track 6.

For my bookshelves I need boards 6 feet long, 8 inches wide, and 1 inch thick.

29d. Do not begin a sentence with a numeral.

Wrong: 30 students are enrolled in Journalism 2.

Right: Thirty students are enrolled in Journalism 2.

29e. Write out fractions standing alone.

A margin of at least a half-inch should be left at the bottom.

These boards should be three-quarters of an inch thick.

General Exercises

Some business letters begin two and one-half inches from the top of the page.

CAUTION: **1.** Do not repeat a number in parentheses except where great accuracy is desired (see Section **24c**).

2. Use commas to set off figures in groups of three (except in dates and street and telephone numbers: 1,112; 365,107; 2,678,654; 2733 Broadway; June 1, 1939; Prospect 6187. (See Section **18l**.)

3. Do not use *st, nd, rd, th* with the day of the month when the year is mentioned: October 15, 1949.

EXERCISE

Correct all errors in the use of numbers in the following sentences:

1. He says that the last time he saw the witness was on Feb. 4th, 1949.
2. His telephone number is Hemlock 4,315.
3. 11 players constitute a football team.
4. There are only 500 women in the school, but there are at least one thousand five hundred men.
5. The Blacks have moved to a new home at 8,634 Avondale Street.
6. On March sixteenth his telephone number was changed to Oregon four six nine six two.
7. 2100 hundred men were at work on the project when the last check was made on April 2nd, 1949.
8. 4 boys and three girls failed the test, although they had studied diligently for ⅓ of the term.
9. Traffic over the bridge was very heavy: between four and four-thirty, 90 cars were counted, and between 4:30 and 5:00, 300 cars passed the tollhouse.
10. On March first, 1950, he received a check for $50, but he has received only twenty-two dollars and fifty cents since that time.

GENERAL EXERCISES: PUNCTUATION AND MECHANICS

A. The following sentences illustrate various errors discussed in Sections **16–29**. Punctuate the selections correctly, and give the number of the section or subsection which covers each mistake in punctuation or mechanics.

1. First because talking about the fair is hot news as it is during this very week.
2. But our troubles were only beginning once on the other side the going became worse.
3. He is just a healthy strong young animal ready for any fun but he can be serious and studious when necessary.
4. It was 18 years ago, that I was brought forth into the world.
5. Bernard Shaws play heartbreak house contains this passage no I dread being drunk more than anything else in the world.
6. I have read paul de kruifs accounts of great medical men.
7. the word literature has conjured up visions of reading matter extremely dull but highly educational.
8. So early the next morning i started for school. As mother thought.
9. The reason is quite obvious we had very little grammar and no more literature.
10. His name is theodore his friends call him teddy and children call him uncle teddy bear which makes him furious.

B. Directions given in Exercise A.

1. The former I liked because of its connection with history which is digestible to me at all times
2. He asked are you going but before I had time to reply he left as if he were angry.
3. When I feel like reading something in a lighter vein I turn to the witty and mirth-provoking thorne smith skin and bones the first of smiths books which i read still seems to me to be the funniest he has written, I suppose eventually all his books will begin to pall and I shall have to look elsewhere for humor.
4. Second because I myself feel more at ease recounting a past experience, than writing a personal sketch.
5. The teacher wouldn't let the child come into the room, she was required to wait outside the door.
6. The more i think about the subject however the more i wonder if anyone can ever learn all there is to know about the english language it is difficult to learn even enough to speak write and think coherently.
7. I answered twenty five percent. of the questions but there were twelve (12), which I couldn't answer at all.
8. Help help he cried but he was only trying to attract attention and the policeman paid no attention.

9. Mary thought she was naive because she still liked to read silly little books such as the little colonel at boardingschool but john told her that she was better off as she was that sophistication was not so hot after all.

10. Jones where Smith had had had had had had had had had had had the examiners approval.

C. Supply all necessary punctuation and mechanics in the following passage.

we found the baby sparrow hawk on june third 1949 he was one of 3 balls of white down lying in a hole in a gnarled old apple tree really he looked more like a baby chicken than a hawk except for his hooked beak and blue gray claws all the girls who saw him gurgled oh o o isn't he cute but they were not so sure of his cuteness when hed flop over on his back spread his claws and open wide his wicked looking mouth

the 2nd stage of his life I shall skip over the rest of his babyhood began when horace as we called him was from 20 to 25 days old his wings then were well developed but his tail amusingly enough was still too short to look good the white down had disappeared entirely except on his flat topped head where it still projected fuzzily when we fed him his one meal a day he ate only the best hamburger he would flap his wings and scream in a very loud mouthed fashion it was a minor hazard to feed him he would snatch the morsel avidly snapping at it with complete disregard for our fingertips I am sure however that he meant no harm for he seemed very very fond of us

the reactions of my family were threefold mother and dad were tolerant and amused jane thought him a nasty vicious monster or so she pretended mary our cook and I were devoted admirers coming down in the morning I would find mary likely as not sneaking some food to him oh glory be she would exclaim guiltily she knew it was against the rules I was just givin the poor darlin a wee morsel really mr edwin just a wee morsel of course I couldn't be angry with mary accordingly I would agree that it had been just a wee morsel

by mid july horace was flying well and I would not have sold him for $1,000,000 he lived in the trees around our house two thirty one 8th st coming like an aerial dog when I whistled for him unlike a dog however hed answer kill ee kill ee killee ee how that call made the sparrows disappear the thrill of seeing him swoop at me from one hundred feet up in the blue is one I never shall forget with the speed of an arrow he would drop straight at me coming and coming and coming and coming until it took a firm resolution to keep from dodging but he always stopped in time thank goodness

D. The following is part of a student's theme. Supply the deleted punctuation and mechanics (see Sections 16–29).

my first acquaintance with patrick ginsberg sherman began when i visited maurice in paterson new jersey maurice drove up to the bus terminal and as i seated myself in his auto patrick jumped upon my lap from the rear seat and looked me in the face as if to say my name is patrick what is yours i immediately thought of alexander popes epigram

> i am his highness dog at kew
> pray tell me sir whose dog are you

i put my hand forward saying hello pat he gave me his paw and we immediately became friends

patrick is white with a big brown spot on his head and another on his rump where his short stubby tail meets his body i thought he was a mongrel crossed between a poodle and a scotch terrier but on closer observation i found him to be a thoroughbred wirehaired fox terrier minus his whiskers and three fourths of his tail

when we arrived at maurices home patrick immediately rushed out of the car as i opened the door and bounding up the stairs butted the partly open door with his head he pranced into the house and was waiting for us with a ball in his mouth when we entered grabbing the ball i tried to take it away from him but he held on grimly it seemed to me his jaws held like a vise i pulled on the ball lifting patrick off the ground and swung him around in circles but he clung on firmly mirabile dictu finally i managed to get it from him and as i held the ball above his head he jumped for it a number of times then tiring he sat up and begged for it i threw the ball it was very small and of rubber into the air and he caught it before it fell this stunt we repeated several times

suddenly patrick ginsberg started to squeal his hind legs had become cramped and the muscles in them stood out like bumps on a potato or so they seemed to me in my fright i kneaded the muscles carefully and soon he was once more scampering around barking as if to say come on play with me

maurice then told me of a time not long before when a friend had come to visit him and as a form of greeting had slapped him on the back patrick seeing this had caught the stranger stranger to him by the

196

leg and before he could be called no pulled off he had torn a hole in the leg of the friends trousers

i stayed at maurices home for several hours when i started to leave i gave pat my hand saying as i did so goodbye he barked gave me his paw and walked sedately with me to the door the little rubber ball still in his mouth

perhaps youd like to meet him if so ill take you with me to 136 bevark drive paterson and introduce you to patrick ginsberg sherman the little fox terrier if youll play ball with him youll be great friends you know as well as i do that one could hardly have a firmer better friend than an intelligent loyal terrier who doesnt care whether you are good looking or wealthy he will ask for little and give a lot ive had many quarrels with maurice but patrick always acts as a friendly go between you really do want to meet my little friend dont you i want you to know all my friends and patrick ginsberg sherman is e pluribus unum

GLOSSARY OF APPLIED PUNCTUATION

30. In applying to your writing the generalized punctuation principles reviewed in the preceding pages, answer the following questions:

1. Exactly what is here that requires punctuation?
2. What purpose do I want my punctuation to serve?
3. What punctuation mark or marks will best accomplish that purpose?

When you are sure of the answer to the first question—"Exactly what is here that requires punctuation?"—use the following as a guide in answering the second and third questions. (Figures in parentheses refer to sections providing detailed discussion and illustration.)

1. **Abbreviations.** Use a period after a standard abbreviation. (16d)
2. **Absolute phrase** (nominative absolute). Use commas. (18o)
3. **Act—scene.** Separate by a colon. (20f)
4. **Adjectives.** Two or more adjectives modifying, coördinately, the same noun, separate by commas. See also **Series,** below. (18i)
5. **Adjective clauses.** See **Clauses, dependent,** below.
6. **Adverbial clauses.** See **Clauses, dependent,** below.

7. **Although.** Never preceded by a semicolon, unless other conditions warrant. See **Conjunctions, subordinating,** below.

8. **Apposition.** Use commas. For long or emphatic appositional phrases, use dashes. (18p, 21e)

9. **Because.** Never preceded by a semicolon, unless other conditions warrant. See **Conjunctions, subordinating,** below.

10. **Break or shift in thought.** Use a dash. (21b)

11. **Cancellation.** Do not use parenthesis marks to cancel. Erase or draw a line through the material. (24d)

12. **Chapter headings.** In a body of prose, enclose in quotation marks. As the heading of a chapter, use no punctuation. (25f)

13. **Clauses.**
 Independent clauses. (1) Joined by pure coördinating conjunction, use a comma. If the clauses are long with complicated internal punctuation, use a semicolon. (18d, 19c) (2) Not joined by any conjunction, use a semicolon. (19a) (3) Joined by a conjunctive adverb, use a semicolon. (19b) (4) Used parenthetically, enclose in dashes or parentheses. (21e, 24a)
 Dependent clause. (1) Adverbial clause preceding independent clause, use a comma. (18f) (2) Adverbial clause following independent clause: if restrictive, use no punctuation; otherwise, use commas if adverbial clause is nonrestrictive or fairly long. (18f) (3) Adjective clause: if nonrestrictive, use commas; if restrictive, omit punctuation. (18m) (4) Noun clauses: used as subject or object or complement, no punctuation. (18t) (5) Dependent contrasting clauses, use a comma. (18e)

14. **Complex sentence.** See **Clauses, dependent,** above.

15. **Compound predicate.** With two members only, usually no commas; with three or more, commas. See **Series,** below.

16. **Compound sentence.** See **Clauses, independent,** above.

17. **Compound words.** Separate the parts by a hyphen or hyphens. (22a)

18. **Conjunctions, coördinating.** (1) Pure conjunctions joining independent clauses, use a comma before, but not after. (18d) (2) Pure conjunctions joining two words or two phrases, no punctuation; joining three or more, commas. (18h) (3) Conjunctive adverb (see **Conjunctive adverb,** below). (4) Correlative conjunctions: apply same principle as for pure conjunctions. (18h)

19. **Conjunctions, subordinating.** Never place a comma or a semicolon

after, unless for other reasons; place a comma before if the clause is adverbial, is nonrestrictive, and follows the independent clause. (18f, 18t, 19b)

20. **Conjunctive adverb.** Use a semicolon before when placed between two independent clauses. Use a comma or no mark after, depending upon parenthetic strength. (19b)
21. **Contractions.** Use an apostrophe. (23f)
22. **Contrasted coördinate elements.** Use a comma. (18j)
23. **Coördinate adjectives.** See **Adjectives,** above.
24. **Correlative conjunctions.** See **Conjunctions, coördinating,** above.
25. **Dates and places.** Enclose in commas when they explain preceding dates and places. (18r)
26. **Decimal.** Use a period preceding. (16e)
27. **Declarative sentence.** See **Sentence,** below.
28. **Dependent clause.** See **Clauses,** above.
29. **Dialogue.** Use quotation marks and commas (18b, 25a, b, c)
30. **Diction.** Provincialisms, slang expressions, misnomers, and unusual technical terms, use quotation marks. (25e)
31. **Direct address (Vocative).** Use commas. (18q)
32. **Dollars and cents.** Use a period between. (16e)
33. **Doubt or uncertainty.** Use a question mark in parentheses. (17d)
34. **Emphasis.** Italicize. (26d) Also see **Surprise,** below.
35. **Exclamatory sentence.** See **Sentence,** below.
36. **Figures.** To insure accuracy, repeat and enclose in parentheses. (24c)
37. **For.** As a pure conjunction, use a comma preceding. As a preposition, use no punctuation. (18d)
38. **For example, for instance, namely, etc.** Used parenthetically, enclose in commas, unless they are followed by an independent clause; then use a colon or semicolon before, a comma after. (18n, 18p)
39. **Fractions.** Use a hyphen between the numerator and the denominator. (22a)
40. **Hour—minute.** Separate by a colon. (20f)
41. **Imperative sentence.** See **Sentence,** below.
42. **Independent clauses.** See **Clauses,** above.
43. **Indirect question.** Use a period, *not* a question mark. (16c, 17b)
44. **Indirect quotation.** Use neither commas nor quotation marks. (18t, 25a)

45. **Inserted material.** Indicate by a caret ($\wedge$). (24f)
46. **Interjections.** Mild, use a comma; strong or fairly strong, use an exclamation point! (17a, 18n)
47. **Interpolated material.** Use brackets. (24e)
48. **Interrogative sentence.** See **Sentence,** below.
49. **Interruption in dialogue.** Use a dash. (21b)
50. **Introduction.** Before a word, phrase, or clause being introduced, use a comma, colon, or dash. (18a, 20a, b, 21a)
51. **Irony.** Occasionally, indicate by an exclamation point within parentheses. (17a)
52. **Misreading.** Between words and elements that may be misread, use a comma, or recast. (18k)
53. **Namely.** See **For example,** above.
54. **Names of ships, trains, airplanes.** Use quotation marks or italics. (25f, 26a)
55. **Nominative absolute.** See **Absolute phrase,** above.
56. **Nonrestrictive clause.** See **Clauses, dependent,** above.
57. **Nonrestrictive phrase.** See **Phrases,** below.
58. **Noun clause.** See **Clauses, dependent,** above.
59. **Numerals.** Use a hyphen between the parts (from twenty-one to ninety-nine). (22a)
60. **Object.** Use no comma between a verb and its object or a preposition and its object (except for additional reasons). (18t)
61. **Oh.** As a mild interjection, use a comma following; as a strong interjection, use an exclamation point. Before a vocative, O (spelled thus) is followed by no punctuation. (17a, 18n)
62. **Omission of letters.** In a word, use a dash. In a contraction, use an apostrophe. (21f, 23f)
63. **Omission of words.** Use ellipsis periods or asterisks. (24g)
64. **Parenthetic words, phrases, clauses.** Weak, no punctuation; fairly to moderately strong, use commas; strong, use dashes or parentheses. (18n, 21e, 24a)
65. **Phrases.** (1) An introductory phrase containing a verb form, use a comma; not containing a verb form, use no punctuation, unless fairly long and then use a comma. (18g) (2) Nonrestrictive phrases, use commas; restrictive phrases, use no punctuation. (18m)
66. **Places.** See **Dates and places,** above.
67. **Plurals.** Formed by adding *-s, -es,* or change in form. *Never* use

an apostrophe, except to form the plurals of words as words, of letters, and of figures. (23g)

68. **Possessive case.** Use the apostrophe in forming the possessive case of nouns and indefinite pronouns. Do *not* use the apostrophe in forming the possessive case of other classes of pronouns. (23a-e, 23i)

69. **Predicate.** See Compound predicate, above.

70. **Preposition and object.** Use no comma or colon between. (18t)

71. **Provincialisms.** See Diction, above.

72. **Pure conjunctions.** See Conjunctions, above.

73. **Queries, series of.** Use question marks. (17c)

74. **Question.** After a direct question, use a question mark; after an indirect question, use a period. (17b, 16c)

75. **Quotation.** (1) Enclose a direct quotation in quotation marks; use no quotation marks with an indirect quotation. (25a) (2) A short direct quotation is set off by a comma; an indirect quotation is not set off by a comma. (18b) (3) A long formal quotation is introduced by a colon. (20d)

76. **Quotation extending over one paragraph.** Use quotation marks at the beginning of each paragraph, but at the end of only the last paragraph. (25b)

77. **Quotation marks with other marks of punctuation.** See Section 25h.

78. **Quotation within a quotation.** Use single quotation marks. (25g)

79. **References and directions.** When these amplify, enclose in parentheses. (24b)

80. **Restrictive clause.** See Clauses, dependent, above.

81. **Restrictive phrase.** See Phrases, above.

82. **Salutation.** In a business letter, use a colon after; in a friendly letter, use a comma or a colon. (18c, 20e)

83. **Sentence.** (1) After a declarative sentence, use a period. (16a) (2) After a mildly imperative sentence, use a period; if vigorous, use an exclamation point. (16b, 17a) (3) After an interrogative sentence, use a question mark. (17b) (4) After an exclamatory sentence, use an exclamation point. (17a)

84. **Series.** Three or more words or phrases or clauses, separate by commas, including one before but not *after* the conjunction. (18h). When the conjunction joins each two members of the series, use no punctuation. (18h) But see Clauses, above.

85. **Slang.** See **Diction,** above.
86. **Subheads.** Use no period following. (16g)
87. **Subject—predicate.** Use no comma to separate. (18t)
88. **Subordinating conjunctions.** See **Conjunctions, subordinating,** above.
89. **Such as.** Use a comma or no punctuation preceding; use no punctuation following. (18p)
90. **Summarizing final clause.** Use a dash preceding. (21d)
91. **Surprise, emphasis, strong emotion.** Use an exclamation point. (17a)
92. **Suspended elements.** Use commas, usually. (18n)
93. **Technical words.** See **Diction,** above.
94. **Title—subtitle.** Separate by a colon. (20f)
95. **Titles.** (1) Titles of books, magazines, newspapers, use italics or, less preferably, quotation marks. (25f, 26a) (2) Titles at the beginning of a theme or paper or chapter, use neither quotation marks around nor a period following. (25f, 16g)
96. **Transposed elements.** Use commas, usually. (18n)
97. **Unfinished statement or word.** Use a dash. (21b)
98. **Verb—object and verb—complement.** Use no comma or colon to separate. (18t, 20b)
99. **Vocative.** See **Direct address,** above.
100. **Word division.** Use a hyphen at the end of the line, between syllables, when the word is continued on the next line. Never use a hyphen at the beginning of a line. (22b)

The Whole Theme

Writing is not an exact science. When it is well done, it becomes an art; even when done poorly or only adequately, it reflects personal characteristics and is subject to numerous variations. But mere knowledge of words and their ways is worthless unless it can be applied. The word, the sentence, and the paragraph are only the means to an end, the bricks which make up a house. They must be correct, clear, and effective in order for the theme itself to contain these desirable qualities. Yet you can never be said to write well until you can achieve a completed whole, an entire composition.

To learn to write correctly, clearly, and effectively, you may require a semester of theme writing, or a year or two, or eternity, but everyone can improve his ability to write if he will conscientiously try. You can eliminate certain types of errors in your writing and you can become aware of other types of errors to be on guard against, by doing carefully the exercises at the ends of the various sections which follow. Such exercises are no substitute for writing. There is infinite truth in the familiar sentence: *The only way to learn to write is to write.* Other sections of this book deal with the word, the sentence, and the paragraph. This section deals with the whole theme or composition and with specific approaches to writing such longer units. But before examining them, ask yourself these questions about any composition you write:

1. Does my theme have a *central purpose?* (Have I carefully analyzed the subject?)
2. Does my theme have *ample substance?*
3. Is this substance *arranged* logically and effectively?
4. Is my theme *unified?*

5. Is my theme *clear?* (Will it mean to any reasonably intelligent reader exactly what it means to me?)

6. Is the substance presented so interestingly and emphatically that it will make a *definite appeal* to the reader?

7. Is my theme *correct* in all mechanical and grammatical details?

If you can truthfully and correctly answer "yes" to these seven questions, your task is completed. If you cannot, you need the guidance and criticism that your instructor will give. None of these requirements is beyond the ability of the ordinary student. That is, none is too difficult for the ordinary student who will work intelligently and industriously.

MANUSCRIPT FORM

31. There is no substitute for ample substance or content, well expressed, but you should not overlook the importance of neatness and legibility in the themes which you submit. Many a good composition has received a poorer grade or made a poorer impression than its actual content deserved because it was so improperly prepared and so untidily written that the reader lost patience in trying to decipher it. Conversely, many a thin theme or composition has received a comparatively high grade because of its extreme neatness and legibility. The conscientious writer will give to his ideas the outward form which will best insure their ready communication to the reader.

31a. Conform to specific standards in preparing manuscript.

If in your English composition or other classes there are particularized directions for the preparation of manuscript, follow those directions unvaryingly. Otherwise, use the following as a guide:

1. *Paper.* Use only standard-sized stationery, $8\frac{1}{2}$ by 11 inches in size. Ruled paper is convenient for longhand, but most standard paper is unruled. Use paper of good quality, clean white bond, which will take ink without blurring. Write on only one side of each sheet.

2. *Title.* Write the title on the first line, or about two inches from the top of the page. Center the title. Capitalize the first word and all other important words in the title (see Section **27a**). Use no period after the title (a question mark or exclamation point may be needed).

3. *Beginning.* Begin the theme about one inch below the title. If the paper is ruled, write on every line; if unruled, leave about one-half inch between lines.

4. *Margins.* Leave a margin of about one inch on the left side of each page. Standard theme paper has a margin of one inch ruled off; leave a similar blank space on paper not having this vertical line. Leave a margin of about a half-inch at the right. Make the margins even and fairly uniform down the page.

5. *Indentations.* Indent the first line of every paragraph about one inch. Use indentations of equal length for all paragraphs in the same paper. Make no exception if you have occasion to use *numbered* paragraphs.

Pay attention to the ending of the paragraphs. Leave part of a line blank *only* at the end of a paragraph. You thus indicate to the reader that a new paragraph will begin on the next line; he should not find that line beginning flush with the left-hand margin.

Indicate a paragraph division not shown by indentation by placing the sign ¶ before the word beginning the paragraph. Cancel a paragraph division by writing "No ¶" in the margin. But, in general, avoid the use of the marks ¶ and "No ¶." Preferably, you should recopy the entire page, correcting the indentation.

6. *Insertions.* Use a caret (∧) when inserting an omitted expression (see Section **24f**).

7. *Cancellations.* Draw a straight line through material that you wish to cancel. Do not use parentheses or brackets to cancel words. These marks have their own particular uses (see Section **24**) and should never be used to indicate deletion.

8. *Order.* Number and arrange the pages of your composition in correct order. Use Arabic numerals in the upper right-hand corner of each page. Arrange the pages in proper order: 1, 2, 3, etc. No reader likes to open a manuscript and find page 2 or page 3 before him.

9. *Endorsement.* With the pages in proper order, page 1 on top, fold the theme lengthwise through the middle. On the right-hand side of the back of the last page write your name, your course, your instructor's name, the date, and the number of the paper.

NOTE: For other "basic mechanics" in the preparation of manuscript, see "The Hyphen—Syllabication" (Section 22), "Capitals" (Section 27), "Abbreviations" (Section 28), "Italics" (Section 26), and "Numbers" (Section 29).

31b. Make your handwriting legible.

Illegible writing taxes the patience of a reader and causes him to give so much attention to the words themselves that his thought is turned away from the important ideas which should engage his interest.

1. *Do not crowd your writing.* Do not run words together; do not run consecutive lines too closely together; do not crowd the writing at the bottom of the page.

2. *Do not leave gaps in your writing.* The consecutive letters in a word should be joined. Do not leave a line partly blank, for no good reason, at the bottom of a page.

3. *Form your letters carefully and correctly.* Dot every small-letter *i* and *j*. (Use dots, not circles.) Cross every *t*. Make small letters *m* and *n* and *u* distinct, and small letters *a* and *o*. Do not carelessly write small letters as capitals, or capitals as small letters (see Section 27g).

4. *Write with a good pen, use clear ink* (preferably black or blue-black), and *write legibly.* Avoid the reader's possible comment on your theme: "This *looks* like a very interesting theme, but I can't *read* it!"

31c. If possible, type your themes and other written work.

Typescript is more legible than handwriting; also, it is easier for you, the writer, to detect errors in type than in handwriting. Observe the following conventions in typing:

1. Indent paragraph beginnings either five or ten spaces.

2. Leave margins at both the left and right: an inch or an inch and a half at the left, about an inch at the right.

3. Leave a blank space of at least an inch at the bottom of each page.

4. Double-space all lines (never single-space, except in business letters).

5. After terminating marks of punctuation (period, question mark, exclamation point), use the space bar twice or thrice; after internal punctuation marks, use it once.

The endorsement on a typewritten manuscript is usually placed in the upper left-hand corner of the first page. (If the manuscript is being submitted for printing, this endorsement contains, on three lines, the writer's name, his street address, and his city and state. For such submission, a manuscript is folded once through the middle, horizontally, or, if it is not bulky, like a business letter for a long-sized envelope.)

31d. Avoid numerous and unsightly erasures and corrections.

1. *Recopying.* Everyone is likely to make errors in writing. These mistakes must be corrected, but it is far better to recopy an entire page than to leave it filled with blots, blurs, and canceled and inserted words. If only one or two corrections must be made on a page, follow the directions given above (**31a**): "Indentations," "Insertions," "Cancellations."

2. *Proofreading.* Every manuscript should be reread slowly and carefully for errors of all kinds, and especially for careless errors. ("Oh, I knew better than that" is, afterward, slim excuse for the writer.) Though typescript makes detection of errors easier, typed papers often contain more errors than papers written in longhand because of the insidious way in which letters seem to change places and because of careless proofreading.

3. *Final Draft.* Always reread the final draft of a manuscript before passing it on to a reader.

THEME TOPICS

32. Every writer has had the discouraging experience of writing something with great care, something which pleased him and seemed to be correct and clear, only to find that others did not enjoy reading it, that it did not "get across." There is truth in the statement that "everything has interest for somebody," but it is equally true that some objects are inherently more interesting than others and can be presented more effectively.

Students manage to turn in themes of a sort when definite topics are assigned by their instructors, but they are often puzzled when required to write compositions on topics of their own choosing. After some thought, they select topics which frequently are neither original nor easily capable of effective treatment. But there are four simple tests which will enable you to choose subjects that you can handle effectively (Section 32a, b, c, d).

32a. Choose a topic of interest to yourself.

It is difficult to write effectively unless you are actually interested in the material. Vagueness, aimlessness, dullness, and sketchiness are sure evidence of uninterested writing; force and vigor are usually present when you are "wrapped up in your subject" and "let yourself go." You may not be interested in labor unions, for example, but if you have a friend who has lost his job because of joining or not joining a union, you are likely to write with genuine interest. You necessarily will write several themes on topics in which you are not really interested; but when you are choosing an effective topic, select one which has definite appeal for yourself in general, or in some particular aspect.

32b. Choose a topic of interest to your readers.

Except on rare occasions, like keeping a diary or writing notes, all writing is done primarily for a reader or a group of readers, with the purpose of giving either information or entertainment, or both. Far more important than yourself as writer are your readers. These may be your classmates, your friends, your relatives, readers of campus publications, or your instructor. Your paper may be specifically required as a class exercise, but you can indicate for what type of reader you intend it. Your instructor then becomes a kind of editor, a "reader over your shoulder," who visualizes himself as one of your designated readers and who judges whether your writing is appropriate.

A writer is a salesman: he has to "sell" his ideas to his readers. He will quite profitably spend considerable time in analyzing the likes and dislikes of his readers, their backgrounds, their general range of information on the chosen subject. He will plan ways to

overcome their "sales resistance" by interesting them in his material, or presenting in new or different ways material in which they
are already interested.

It can be dogmatically stated that the following subjects and
phases of these subjects have a genuine appeal for most people:

1. *Timely topics:* either new ideas or late facts, or the development
   of some old idea by emphasis upon its contact with recent developments.
2. *People:* unique, prominent, familiar, or unforgettable (even personal reminiscences and reactions).
3. *Places:* historical, unusual, scenic, even uncommon features of
   common places.
4. *Important matters:* those which involve the life and property of
   others, and which have a relation to the reader's own welfare.
5. *Conflict:* contests between people, between man and nature, and
   internal conflicts (within the person).
6. *Amusements and hobbies.*
7. *Occupations.*

NOTE: You may be aided in choosing topics by keeping in mind
the general purposes of the four kinds of writing: to tell a story
(narrative); to give a picture in words (description); to explain
(exposition); and to convince (argumentation).

32c. Choose a topic about which you know something.

Material from personal experience and observation can not only
be effectively incorporated in themes; an entire composition may
be suggested by, and written from, such material. If you write
about something you actually know, something you have thought
or seen or heard, you have a more than even chance of presenting
your material effectively.

Just as one cannot expect to handle a tool or machine efficiently
and expertly without some previous experience, some first-hand
acquaintance, so one cannot expect to write effectively without
some experience and first-hand acquaintance with the topic of the
composition. John R. Tunis' books and articles on sport are based
on many years of direct observation and study; Kenneth Roberts'
stories of Arundel—*The Lively Lady, Arundel, Captain Caution,*
etc.—come out of Roberts' personal familiarity with the Kenne-

bunk, Maine, area, his considerable study and research, and careful observation of people. Herman Melville shipped as a sailor before the mast in 1839. Two years later he sailed around Cape Horn in the whaler *Acushnet* and the following year lived briefly with cannibals in the South Seas. These experiences—and his keen observation of men and the sea—he utilized in *Typee, Redburn,* his great novel *Moby Dick,* and other writings.

Every good writer goes to his own experience—to those things he knows or has thought or seen or heard.

32d. Choose a topic which you can treat adequately.

You should have in mind, in choosing a topic, approximately the number of words that you plan to write. A short paper requires a limited subject; a longer paper naturally permits a broader subject, a more extended treatment, a wider point of view, the inclusion of more details.

The very word *theme* implies a single, well-defined *phase* of a subject. It is impossible to write an effective 500-word theme on a subject which requires 5,000 words. If you choose a broad subject and fail to limit it, you are likely to become discouraged and to write sketchily and illogically. You may select a topic which is interesting to both yourself and your reader, and about which you know something; yet it may not be a good one simply because you cannot treat it adequately in the prescribed number of words. *College Fraternities, Professional Football, Chicago,* and *Aviation* are examples of such topics. They cannot be treated in a short paper; and even if the paper is to be long, they will require more extended research than you can or will make. A small composition on a large subject is necessarily a fragmentary, disconnected, ineffective treatment.

General topics or broad subjects must therefore be narrowed. *The Duties of a Fraternity Pledge, How Professional Football Players Are Recruited,* and *When in Chicago, See the Planetarium* are examples of such limitation. *Aviation* is a hopelessly broad subject; limited to *Aviation in America,* it is still too large, even for a book; *The Career of Wilbur Wright* might be developed in a very long paper; *Wilbur Wright's First Flight* would be more suitable for ordinary-length theme treatment.

32e. Be prepared to write on assigned topics.

Many of the composition subjects in your college classes will be assigned. They may need some adaptation or limitation; they may need none.

Writing on such assigned subjects is excellent experience and also practical training for post-college work, since much routine writing (and speaking) is done on assignment. Answers to letters, research reports in business and industry, newspaper reporting, feature articles, and many of the nonfiction articles in general and trade magazines (as well as formal lectures and informal talks) are examples of assigned materials.

EXERCISES

NOTE: In addition to the theme subjects below, some 150 theme topics are suggested in the Exercise at the end of Section 46, page 262.

A. For each of the seven classes of subjects on page 209, make a list of five to ten limited topics, each suitable for a 350-word to 500-word theme.

B. Using the following as general subjects, for each write three to five limited topics which you think will interest specific readers whom you designate: Animals, Athletics, Atoms, Bravery, Business, Campus Activities, Childhood, Contests, Education, Flying, Food, Friends, Good Manners, Health, Heroes, Holidays, Illness, Medicine, Memories, Money, Music, Nature, Night, One Week, Personal Experience, Recreation, Relatives, Soil Conservation, Sorrow, Success, Superstition, Tall Stories, Travel, Vacations, Weather.

C. Prepare a list of ten limited theme topics designed to be developed by telling a story (narrative). Prepare a list of ten designed to be developed by giving a picture in words (description); ten to be developed by explaining (exposition); ten to be developed by convincing (argument).

D. Make a list of five incidents in your life which you think might be interesting to your readers, your instructor and the members of your class.

E. List five subjects about which you think you know details not known to your classmates.

F. Make a list of conventional theme topics which you think are trite and uninteresting. (*My Summer in Camp, A Fishing Trip, A Dream I Had,* etc.)

G. Apply the four tests for topics to the following suggestions for themes and indicate what readers you have in mind:

1. An interview with a well-known campus personality.
2. An account of a visit to a law court during a criminal trial.
3. The history, including a description, of one of the buildings of the college.
4. A description and character sketch of one of the best-known employees of the college.
5. A description of the college cafeteria during the luncheon hour.
6. Description of college "types": the athlete, the aesthete, the iconoclast, the bluffer.
7. A description of, and commentary upon, a popular radio program.
8. A criticism of a motion picture currently being shown.
9. An account of the conversation among a group of friends after a college dance.
10. A commentary upon the "easiest" and the "most difficult" courses and professors in the college.
11. My Favorite Magazine, and Why.
12. Why I Am a Liberal (a Reactionary, a Radical).
13. My Pet Aversion (radio crooners, tabloid newspapers, practical jokes, eight-o'clock classes, tourist camps, etc.).
14. An account of how you budget your time for a day, a week, a month of college life.
15. What I want to be, and to be doing, ten years from now.
16. What I expect to be, and to be doing, ten years from now.
17. The greatest personal disaster I can imagine.
18. A list of five books (with reasons for their choice) which I should like to take with me if I were to be marooned on a desert island for the remainder of my life.
19. The qualities I want my wife (husband) to have.
20. The Ideal English Composition Course.

THE TITLE

33. Just as a topic sentence is frequently helpful in keeping you on the track within the paragraph, a well-chosen title may help you stick to your subject throughout a theme.

The Title

But the title has another important function. A well-chosen title is a most effective means of gaining the attention of the reader. Who has not been led to read a certain book, magazine article, or story because of its attractive title? Motion picture producers frequently have paid thousands of dollars merely for the use of an effective title. Give your theme a good title, not a mere tag, and you have already taken an important step in making the whole composition more effective.

33a. Do not confuse title and subject.

The term *subject* is broader and more inclusive than the word *title.* If the instructor asks for a composition on "My Reading Habits," he has assigned a *subject,* not a *title,* and you should sharpen this subject to a more specific and more interesting title. Conversely, if the actual title is assigned, you must discover precisely what subject it covers. Do not assume that the title of a specific paper should be the same as a general subject which has been assigned. The best titles indicate not a general subject but the actual *theme* of the composition.

33b. Make the title suggest or indicate the material contained in the theme.

It is impossible, of course, for a title to mention everything which the theme contains. But a title should not be misleading; it should give at least a hint of the contents of the theme. Do not announce a title and then develop ideas which have no relation whatever to it. Motion pictures and novels are often misleadingly titled in an effort to attract attention, but you can usually phrase an effective title without any such subterfuge.

33c. Use effective phrasing in the title.

As has been pointed out, a good title is effective in interesting the reader. Occasionally, writers neglect to employ this "aid to interest."

1. *Do not use long titles. Browsing Among Magazines* is certainly more effective than *How to While Away an Afternoon Among the Magazines in the Periodical Room of the Belvedere Library.*

2. *Do not use vague and commonplace titles.* Titles like *College Football Is Overemphasized, A Camping Trip, Contemporary Etiquette,* and *The Importance of Using Short Words* can be re-

phrased for greater concreteness and uniqueness: *Dollar Marks on the Gridiron, Alone in a Civilized Wilderness, Best Foot Forward,* and *Little Words, But Mighty.*

To be effective, a title must usually be short, and fresh, and definite. Note these titles:

1. *Socrates Crosses the Delaware.* (An article about the "great books" program at St. John's College, Maryland.)
2. *Rich Land, Poor Land.* (A study of America's natural resources.)
3. *The Great Sports Myth.* (A criticism of the American system of sports.)
4. *That Burrowing Bean.* (An article about peanuts.)
5. *Only Yesterday.* (An informal history of the 1920's.)
6. "*I Love Him!*" (A profile of a popular religious leader.)

33d. Place and punctuate the title correctly on the page.

Center the title on the page, on the first line or two inches from the top of the page. Leave a space between the title and the first line of the theme. (See Section 31a.)

Capitalize important words (see Section 27a), but do not italicize the title or enclose it in quotation marks (unless it is itself a quotation) except when you quote it in the theme.

Do not place a period after the title; a question mark or exclamation point may be used, if needed.

33e. Do not vaguely refer to the title in the first sentence of the theme.

The title is independent of the composition. Avoid using *this, that, such* among the opening words of your writing. In a theme entitled *My Mexican Journey,* do not begin, "This trip was the most . . . ." The first sentence should be complete in itself, self-explanatory: "My trip to Mexico was the most . . . ."

EXERCISES

A. Buy, or consult in your library, current copies of three or four magazines like *The Saturday Evening Post, Collier's, The American Magazine, The Atlantic Monthly, Harper's Magazine.* Look at the titles of the articles; then skim through the content of these articles and decide whether the titles are commonplace, intriguing, novel (or too novel), appropriate. For those titles that you think skillfully chosen, put in parentheses the general subject of the articles.

B. Follow the procedure listed in Exercise A but apply it to the short stories in the same magazines.

C. Comment on the titles of the selections in your book of readings. Do for eight or ten of these selections what is asked under Exercise A, above.

D. Make the following titles more interesting and effective:

1. A Day in New York City.
2. A Canoeing Trip.
3. Why I Came to College.
4. My Religion.
5. Radio Programs I Dislike.
6. A Theme About Myself.
7. Autumn Activities on the Farm.
8. My Budget.
9. A Rainy Day.
10. Blind Dates.

ANALYSIS OF SUBJECT

34. The first step in writing a theme, after you have chosen (or been assigned) a subject and have limited it, should be a careful analysis of the subject. There must be an *objective* for the theme other than the completion of a required assignment, for there can be no such thing as good *purposeless* writing. You should attempt to understand what the subject involves by asking yourself (and answering satisfactorily) the following questions:

1. What special characteristics distinguish my subject?
2. What do I know about this subject?
3. What am I trying to do with it?
4. For what readers am I developing it?
5. How can I best convey my meaning and purpose to my readers?

34a. Make your analysis on the basis of the number of words you are to write.

Themes vary in length. Some may be as brief as 250 words, others may be 500 words or 1,000 words, and long research or term papers may run up to 5,000 to 8,000 words. (Similarly, in the presentation of a speech you may be asked to speak for two minutes, or five minutes, or ten or fifteen or twenty.)

Your choice of a single well-defined phase of the subject to be treated as well as your choice of details to be included and your plan of organization to be followed will all be affected by the important limitation of length.

34b. Determine your analysis according to your prospective reader.

Every theme—in fact, nearly every piece of writing—is a project for communicating to someone a series of thoughts and emotions. That "someone" may be a specially chosen individual (like the recipient of a letter) or one of a group. The group should not be too large: "the American public," "women," "college students," "high school graduates," and the like, include people of such varied interests and backgrounds that a composition aimed at them can at best be diffuse and general. On the other hand, writing aimed at a specific group is likely to be clear, concise, and effective. Often, your English teacher is simply the "reader over your shoulder" who tries to judge how appropriately and effectively you have written for the reader or readers you have designated.

For example, a theme on the subject, *My Background in English,* may be written for your present English teacher to indicate the strong and weak points of your training. It may be written for your high school principal, suggesting changes in the course for those students who go to college. It may be written to your former high school English teachers and may give a critical evaluation of their courses in the light of your present course.

34c. Determine the central purpose of the theme.

Before you begin to write, analyze the subject you plan to treat in order to find out how you may develop it most effectively. Put into words, which may or may not be included in the theme later, your central purpose or controlling idea. Find the *theme* within the theme. Writing is either a search for the means to accomplish a central aim or, as it all too frequently turns out to be, a

formal setting down of words according to mechanical requirements.

On the general subject, *A Camping Trip,* you might clarify your
purpose by writing for your own guidance: "My purpose is to
indicate, from my own experience, the kinds of recreational activities that boys between twelve and fifteen enjoy. My reader is a
recreational director who is beginning his first summer of service.
My paper is to be 1,000 words long."

Even when you have sharply limited your subject to fit the
number of allotted words and when you have chosen a specific
reader or readers, you must do still more in your analysis. You
must choose some method of development and treatment which
will most clearly accomplish your purpose, since not all subjects
can be developed in the same way.

In determining the central purpose of your composition and the
treatment and development, include in your analysis the following
three steps:

1. List fifteen or twenty details that you might possibly use. In
a theme on *When in Chicago, Visit the Planetarium,* your list
might include:

    a. What a planetarium is.

    b. History of the Planetarium.

    c. Location.

    d. Cost.

    e. Description of building (exterior).

    f. Description of building (interior).

    g. Special exhibits.

    h. Special lectures.

    i. Maintenance of Planetarium.

    j. Personnel.

    k. Comparison of Chicago's Planetarium and New York's.

    l. Value of planetariums.

    m. Mechanics of the projecting machine.

    n. Famous astronomers who have lectured there.

    o. Best days to go ("free" days or "fee" days).

    p. Necessity of making two or three visits.

Naturally you would not include all these details in your theme, nor in this order. But such a listing gives you an "overview" and can suggest direction and what details to include or exclude. Your central purpose might be limited to giving directions for reaching the Planetarium and to calling attention to special exhibits and lectures.

2. Choose a consistent method of development. You may wish primarily to use narrative (anecdote, history, biography, etc.); to describe (details of persons or places); to explain (give directions, define, classify, tell how a mechanism works or a process develops, etc.); or to argue (give reasons for and against, give advantages and disadvantages, show the need for or value of, etc.). Or one type of development may be aided by another: by the use of specific narrative incidents in an expository paper, or by a number of descriptive details, or by comparisons and contrasts. (See Section 46.)

3. Maintain a consistent tone (prevailing character or style). One adjective, which you should keep constantly in mind as you write, should describe your purpose and treatment: *serious, critical, humorous, ironical, satirical, dignified, flippant, facetious, formal, informal, persuasive, light, genial, gentle, conversational, breezy, witty, whimsical, contentious, savage, vitriolic,* or the like.

Notice the differences in tone in the following. Both are definitions (a form of exposition or explaining), both are on abstract and important subjects. Woodrow Wilson used a *serious* or *dignified* approach in defining liberty:

What is liberty?

I have long had an image in my mind of what constitutes liberty. Suppose that I were building a great piece of powerful machinery, and suppose that I should so awkwardly and unskillfully assemble the parts of it that every time one part tried to move it would be interfered with by the others, and the whole thing would buckle up and be checked. Liberty for the several parts would consist in the best possible assembling and adjustment of them all, would it not? If you want the great piston of the engine to run with absolute freedom, give it absolutely perfect alignment and adjustment with the other parts of the engine, so that it is free, not because it is let alone or isolated, but because it

218

has been associated most skillfully and carefully with the other parts of the great structure.

What is liberty? You say of the locomotive that it runs free. What do you mean? You mean that its parts are so assembled and adjusted that friction is reduced to a minimum, and that it has perfect adjustment. We say of a boat skimming the water with light foot, "How free she runs," when we mean, how perfectly she is adjusted to the force of the wind, how perfectly she obeys the great breath out of the heavens that fills her sails. Throw her head up into the wind and see how she will halt and stagger, how every sheet will shiver and her whole frame be shaken, how instantly she is "in irons," in the expressive phrase of the sea. She is free only when you have let her fall off again and have recovered once more her nice adjustment to the forces she must obey and cannot defy.

Human freedom consists in perfect adjustments of human interests and human activities and human energies.[1]

E. B. White uses a narrative, *humorous* approach in defining democracy:

We received a letter from the Writers' War Board the other day asking for a statement on "The Meaning of Democracy." It presumably is our duty to comply with such a request, and it is certainly our pleasure.

Surely the Board knows what democracy is. It is the line that forms on the right. It is the don't in don't shove. It is the hole in the stuffed shirt through which the sawdust slowly trickles; it is the dent in the high hat. Democracy is the recurrent suspicion that more than half of the people are right more than half of the time. It is the feeling of privacy in the voting booths, the feeling of communion in the libraries, the feeling of vitality everywhere. Democracy is a letter to the editor. Democracy is the score at the beginning of the ninth. It is an idea which hasn't been disproved yet, a song the words of which have not gone bad. It's the mustard on the hot dog and the cream in the rationed coffee. Democracy is a request from a War Board, in the middle of the morning in the middle of a war, wanting to know what democracy is.[2]

EXERCISES

A. Make a list of five theme subjects suitable for treatment in 250 to 500 words; five for treatment in 1,000 to 1,500 words; and five for treatment in 4,000 to 6,000 words.

[1] From *The New Freedom*. Copyrighted by Doubleday and Company.
[2] From *The New Yorker*, and included in *The Wild Flag*, Houghton Mifflin Company. Copyright, 1943, by E. B. White.

B. Choose one subject from each of the three length groups in Exercise A and write a sentence or two for each, stating your central purpose (see Section 34c).

C. For one subject chosen in Exercise B, list fifteen or twenty details that you might use in developing the theme.

D. For each of the subjects chosen in Exercise B, indicate your probable method of development (see 2, on p. 218).

E. Choose five of the "tones" given on page 218, and list for each three theme subjects which might be developed illustrating the particular tone chosen.

F. Restrict the following broad subjects to some phase which can be treated within the limits of a theme-length paper:

1. Communism in America.
2. The Cosmetics Industry.
3. How People Lived in the Gay Nineties.
4. My College Career.
5. Games of Chance.
6. The Art of Ballyhoo.
7. Social Security.
8. Americanizing the Displaced Person.
9. Radio Advertising.
10. The Motion Picture Industry.

G. Using one of the topics mentioned in Exercise F, discuss various methods of development to suit different purposes and different kinds of readers.

H. Make a list of subjects which are likely to be uninteresting to your fellow students. Mention methods of approach which might make these topics interesting.

SUBSTANCE

35. After you have chosen a subject or had it assigned to you, have limited it sufficiently, and have analyzed it for length, reader, and methods of treatment, you are faced with the problem of securing ample substance for its development. You must have something to say, perhaps more than you really need or can use, before you can write effectively. Lack of purpose, vagueness, and lack of interest inevitably result from lack of ample substance and full detail. Unless you have a special knowledge of your subject, you will find that securing ample substance requires considerable time and effort. The successful theme writer will exert genuine effort in collecting material for his theme *before* he begins actually to write.

35a. Gather substance from your own thought and experience.

Many students feel that their own ideas and experiences are not significant or interesting. Others have a false modesty, and so refuse to consider subjects in terms of their own experience. Actually, personal experience has a freshness and interest for the writer which are likely to be most effectively conveyed to the reader. One does not necessarily have an inflated ego when he uses experiences of his own as illustrative material. Significant and interesting material can and should be drawn from the writer's own *observation, curiosity, imagination,* and *reflection.*

Indeed, it is impossible for one to write wholly objectively; the writer necessarily puts something of himself into everything he writes. The more of himself he puts into his writing—that is, his own ideas, reactions, and observations—the more likely he is to write with full, interesting, concrete detail. There is no better source of substance than one's own self.

35b. Gather substance from the thought and experience of others.

Although a writer necessarily gathers substance from himself, he should not neglect the material he may derive from others, unless he is an acknowledged authority on the particular subject being treated.

The easiest and perhaps most pleasant way of getting material for themes from other people is *discussion.* This may take the form of an *interview* in which the ideas of the interviewed person may constitute almost the whole of the theme. Or it may be merely a *conversation* with a member of your family, an acquaintance, or an instructor, in which there is an interchange of ideas, a give-and-take which results in clarified and expanded thought. Classroom discussions are often an excellent source of material for compositions.

Another important way of getting substance from people is reading. Magazines, newspapers, and books are almost inexhaustible sources of material which may be utilized. Half-formed ideas of your own may be intensified and expanded by reading. Entirely new phases of thought may be suggested, which, when put through the hopper of your mind, may legitimately be used as your own. (For aids in using the library, see Section 48.) A fruitful source of material—a combination of conversation and reading—is discussing with your classmates and instructor the ideas (and their significance) in book-of-readings assignments.

For special information a letter of inquiry to a company or to a recognized authority may provide valuable substance (a method especially useful for a longer, research paper). Likewise, you may obtain material for themes from radio and television programs, motion pictures, and plays. Although these are usually listened to or seen, not read, they do constitute the experiences and thoughts of other people and as such are fruitful sources of substance.

In drawing upon the experiences and impressions of others, be careful to make them your own. That is, you should assimilate the ideas and then express them in your own words, unless you quote directly and mention sources. When you make use of an idea new to you, acknowledge your indebtedness courteously and fully. Sometimes a phrase is sufficient: "As Thomas Carlyle points out in *The French Revolution, . . .*" or "These novelists, Joseph Warren Beach says in *American Fiction, 1920–1940,* were profoundly affected by the social conditions. . . ." Sometimes—in a research paper, for example—fuller acknowledgment is necessary; for the proper method and forms of documentation in research papers, see Section 50e. The charge of plagiarism must be avoided; taking the ideas and words of another and passing them off as your own is plagiarism.

EXERCISES

A. For each of the following groups make a list of five limited subjects which can be developed using your own thought and experience:

1. Past and Present Physical Activities.
2. Past and Present Social Activities.
3. My Environment (home, community, college).

4. Recreation and Avocation.
5. Education.
6. Vocational Experiences (full-time; part-time).
7. Financial Responsibilities.
8. Religion.
9. Politics.
10. Philosophy of Life.

B. Mention some personal experience (or incident which you have witnessed) that could be used in developing a theme based on one of the following topics:

Social Fraternities Should (Should Not) Be Abolished.
Few Athletes Are Good Students.
Buying Second-Hand Books.
The Care and Feeding of Bookshelves.
The Value of a Time Budget.

C. Name a book, magazine article, motion picture, or play from which ideas might be drawn for a theme dealing with:

Underprivileged Children.
Social Injustice.
Man's Greed.
The Horror of Dictatorships.
Safe Automobile Driving.

D. What is the most successful theme you have written? How much of its material was based upon personal thought and experience? How much was derived from other people?

OUTLINES AND OUTLINING

36. After you have analyzed your subject, gathered ample substance, and, perhaps, selected a title, you must consider the problem of *arranging* the material which you have chosen. *Order* is of even more importance in the whole theme than it is in the paragraph.

The most frequently used method of ordering the parts of a theme is an outline. An outline is a sort of blueprint for the "builder" of the theme, or a recipe which contains the names of ingredients and directions for using them.

Many students object to preparing and using outlines. They

assert, with some vehemence, that the preparation of formal outlines requires too much time, proportionately, and that their use
acts as a sort of brake, or clamp, upon the free flow of ideas. But
outlines need not be elaborate; they are only a guide to the writer,
to be consulted occasionally as he writes; moreover, if you revise
carefully, you may need to consult your outline only *after* you have
written the first draft of your theme.

Many instructors require outlines for themes which are to be
submitted to them because they know that (1) nearly everyone
thinks illogically and haphazardly when several different ideas are
being considered; (2) a theme must be clearly ordered and proportioned to be effective; and (3) an outline aids the reader as well
as the writer in grasping immediately the plan of organization.
Certainly no one will deny that a writer must know where he is
going, whether his outline be actually written or only in his mind.
No one can write an orderly composition without using some kind
of outline, formal or informal, actual or implied.

There are three types of outlines:

1. The *topic outline,* which consists of words and phrases—an
   outline primarily of meaning only to the writer.
2. The *sentence outline,* which is made up of complete sentences—
   an outline which is clear to both writer and reader.
3. The *paragraph outline,* which consists of groups of sentences—
   perhaps, but not necessarily, the topic sentences—indicating the
   contents of whole paragraphs. Such an outline is of value when
   the theme is to consist of only three, four, or five paragraphs;
   summarizing sentences can be numbered with Arabic numerals
   and used as paragraph topics. It is valuable also as the first
   step in outlining someone else's work, like a magazine article
   or an essay; from these sentences a topic or sentence outline
   can be built, showing major and minor divisions.

These three types of outlines are illustrated in Section **36a,** below.

36a. Make outlines mechanically correct.

The conventional outline is based, first of all, on division of
material into major parts. Your analysis of your subject shows
what the major divisions of your topic are and in what order you
can best discuss them. You then make the divisions the founda-

tion of your outline (generally by using Roman numerals, I, II, III, etc.) and examine these main points to determine what subtopics you need to include to make your discussion complete. For such subtopics, use capital letters (A, B, C, etc.). Frequently you need to subdivide subtopics further, for greater clarity. Indicate such further division by Arabic numbers (1, 2, 3, etc.). But do not divide too minutely; avoid cluttering an outline with excessive detail; keep the number of main headings to a minimum. Use indentation as a further aid to clarity: all I, II, III divisions begin at the left; all A, B, C subdivisions are indented an equal distance, and under these all 1, 2, 3 subdivisions are also indented equally.

Study the following models for use of symbols, indentation, and content:

Topic Outline:

MY COLLEGE

I. Its location.
II. Its past.
    A. Founding.
    B. Progress.
        1. First fifty years (to 1900).
        2. 1900–'50.
III. Its condition today.
    A. Buildings.
    B. Faculty.
    C. Students.
        1. Three hundred men.
        2. Four hundred women.

Sentence Outline:

MY COLLEGE

I. Mission College is well located.
    A. It is near a large city.
    B. It possesses a large, beautiful campus.
II. Mission College has had an interesting history.
    A. It was founded by Quakers in 1850.
    B. The student body was small at first.
        1. In the first graduating class there were only ten students.
        2. For thirty years, the student body averaged only fifty students.
    C. In 1900, the college entered an era of expansion.

Paragraph Outline:

ON GETTING TO THE PLANETARIUM

1. The easiest way to reach the Planetarium is to drive, either in your own car or by taxi.

2. Buses also run to the Planetarium every thirty minutes.

3. Streetcars are a possibility, but you will have a fifteen-minute walk from the car line to the Planetarium.

The paragraph outline, as indicated above, is most helpful in setting down summary sentences to represent the thought of successive paragraphs in a selection being studied. Here, for example, is a paragraph outline of the thirty-two paragraphs of James Harvey Robinson's well-known essay, "On Various Kinds of Thinking":

1. The quality and quantity of the stream of thought are varied, interesting, and deserving of attention.

2. We are constantly engaged in reverie which is concentrated upon the ego.

3. Reverie, which was neglected by earlier philosophers, is significant, but it does not increase knowledge.

4. Making practical decisions, distinguishable from reverie, may or may not increase knowledge.

5. Rationalizing is a third kind of thinking in which the ego comes to the defense of *our* ideas.

6. Rationalizing causes us carelessly to accept ideas.

7. There is a distinct and important difference between "good" reasons and "real" reasons for our opinions and actions.

8. "Real" reasons are unknown, are products of association and suggestion, not honest decision.

9. "Real" reasons lack "primary certitude" and are not personal.

10. "Good" reasons are personal but do not promote enlightenment.

11. Rationalizing is a form of self-justification and self-exculpation.

12. Rationalizing is essentially personal.

13. The import of rationalizing is exemplified.

14. Examples are given of the fact that all mankind thinks in the ways thus far described: reverie, making practical decisions, rationalizing.

15. We must revise our thinking concerning social and economic questions.

16. The age of an idea is no warranty of its truth.

17. Creative thinking is described and its characteristics are listed.

18. Creative thinking, the most significant kind of thought, has changed the world and our concept of it.
19. The ego is not concerned in creative thinking.
20. Curiosity is the first step in creative thinking, but curiosity may be personal.
21. Impersonal (idle) curiosity is the real starting point of creative thinking.
22. Curiosity sometimes leads to examination and research and, in turn, to real knowledge.
23. Galileo is cited as a person with curiosity.
24. His reverie changed to curiosity and subsequently resulted in scientific hypothesis.
25. Galileo examined and tested the observations resulting from his curiosity; his successors did likewise.
26. The example of Faraday and his curiosity is cited.
27. Creative thinking does not apply only to the natural sciences.
28. Without creative thinking on various levels of activity, no advance of mankind is possible.
29. We use and abuse creative thinking, but all too often we fail to recognize, appreciate, or apply it.
30. The four kinds of thinking mingle in practice, but reverie and rationalizing naturally predominate.
31. We are not reasonably entitled to opinions on many subjects concerning which we hold and express definite ideas.
32. Our opinions are frequently not the result of self-interest, but they are "pure prejudices," a form of mass or herd tradition for which we are not responsible.

36b. Make outlines logically correct.

You must construct your outline logically if the theme you write from it is to be coherent and clear. Therefore you must examine your outline critically and revise it carefully. You must analyze it even as you have analyzed the subject. Delete repetitions, reorganize for most effective organization, correct violations of unity, remove illogical relationships, add specific details where necessary. A rough sketch is not a blueprint; a few words and phrases jotted down at random are not an outline.

To attain these aims in outlining, follow these suggestions:

1. Make headings (main divisions or subdivisions) of the same rank parallel in form.

227

Wrong: A. Buildings.
       B. The faculty contains forty men.

2. Do not make subordinate any matter that is coördinate, and do not make coördinate any matter that is logically subordinate.

Wrong: B. Progress.
       1. First fifty years (to 1900).
         a. 1900 to 1930.
       • b. 1930 to 1950.
Wrong: B. Progress.
       1. First fifty years (to 1900).
       2. 1900 to 1930.
       C. 1930 to 1950.

3. If a single minor topic must be mentioned, express it in, or as part of, its major heading, or add another coördinate minor topic. Remember that outlining is division, that subdivision means division into at least two parts.

Wrong: A. Founding.
       1. By Quakers in 1850.
       B. Progress.

4. Avoid meaningless headings such as *Introduction, Body, Conclusion, Reasons, Causes,* etc., unless they are accompanied by explanatory material or subheads. An outline must be actually revealing. Although intended primarily for the writer's own use, it should furnish a reader a general idea of the organization and content of a paper.

NOTE: Do not slavishly follow a prepared outline. If you do, you are merely putting a little flesh on a skeleton whose bones will stick out. Follow a definite plan of some sort, yes. But following that form too closely will result in stiffness and artificiality, qualities which detract from effective writing fully as much as does lack of order or proportion. As you write, you may find certain changes in plan effective and necessary.

36c. Use an outline to give your theme proportion.

A good outline will enable you to achieve proper order, and it can assist you in achieving correct proportion (see Section 37). Place in parenthesis marks after each part of your outline the number of words you plan to write on that division or subdivision. The sum of the subdivision words should equal the major division; the sum of the major divisions should equal the number of total required words. This allocation is only tentative; you may find expansion or contraction necessary.

EXERCISES

A. Point out all errors in the following outline:

ARE COLLEGE BOYS STUDENTS?

I. Definition of word, *student*.
   a. Reference to several dictionaries.
II. Many boys come to college to engage in athletics.
   A. Some come to enjoy the social life.
   B. Others to keep from working.
III. A minority come to get a real education.
   1. Preparation for various professions.
      a. Medicine, dentistry.
         1. Law, teaching.
IV. Summary and Conclusion.

B. Make a correct *topic* outline of the material in Exercise A.

C. Make a correct *sentence* outline of the material in Exercise A.

D. Make correct topic outlines for the three themes indicated by the subjects you chose in Exercise B (p. 220).

E. Make a correct sentence outline for five themes that you could write on the topics chosen in Exercise A (p. 219).

F. Make a paragraph outline of one of the essays in your book of readings.

G. Change the paragraph outline (Exercise F) into a topic outline.

PROPORTION

37. Proportion in paragraphs is discussed in Section 57. Also, much of the above discussion on outlines deals with proportion in themes. But the element of proportion is so important that it merits additional treatment as it applies specifically to whole compositions.

37a. Develop divisions of a theme in proportion to their importance.

Proportion requires that the development given each division of a theme (paragraph or group of paragraphs) be in accord with the relative importance of the division. Note the word *relative;* importance is not absolute. In determining which parts of a theme should be developed at length and which less fully, you must be guided by the *purpose* of the theme and the *readers* for whom it is written. Ordinarily, do not give disproportionate space to less closely related or incidental sections of your theme; ordinarily, also, give greater space to sections which may be difficult to understand otherwise, or which are to be emphasized.

For example, if your purpose in writing on *Radio Advertising* is to show that such advertising is blatantly overdone, your theme will be badly proportioned if you devote more than half the space to a discussion of the origin and growth of radio broadcasting and only a small part of the composition to the central theme.

Similarly, if you are writing a composition on *Fraternity Dances* for your classmates, you can correctly give less space to many important details well known to them than if you are writing on the same subject for a group of foreign students. Or if you are writing a composition on *Color in Motion Pictures,* you can assume that certain elementary, important details about photoplays in general are known to anyone who can read, and thus give the greatest space to a discussion of *color* as used in motion pictures.

37b. Achieve proportion by proper use of your outline.

A good outline not only indicates proper order but also assists in achieving proportion (see Section **36c**). Careful thought and planning in both outline and theme are necessary. If you do not *plan* your themes and if you do not follow some guide to proportion, you may write a narrative of ten pages, of which nine deal with relatively unimportant details and only one with the important conflict of the story. Or in an expository theme, you may write four hundred words of introductory material and then suddenly realize that you have only one hundred left. Into these few words you will attempt to compress the important ideas which, perhaps, should have had the 400-word space.

The principle of proportion is simply that of rendering "unto Caesar the things which are Caesar's." Give any part of a theme the space and attention which are commensurate with its importance in relation to the reader and the subject itself.

EXERCISES

A. Study the amount of space given each division of one of your recent themes. Can you justify the proportion from the standpoint of both subject and reader?

B. Prepare a topic outline of one of the essays in your book of readings (or in a current magazine). Write down after each of your main divisions and subdivisions the number of words used by the author. Study this outline with the essay or article from the point of view of proper or inadequate proportion.

C. Look up in a good dictionary these words: *perspective, distortion, proportion.* Illustrate them by reference to motion pictures, paintings, statuary, and architecture which you have seen.

BEGINNING THE THEME

38. After you have gathered material and correctly outlined and proportioned this substance, you are faced with the problem of *beginning* the composition.

A theme, like any written paper, does have a beginning, a middle, and an end. Do not make the mistake of thinking that the body of a theme is the only important element and that beginnings and endings are merely tacked on as appendages. Prefixes and suffixes are very real parts of words; likewise, the introduction and conclusion are of genuine importance to the whole theme, because they are analogous to first and last impressions. Introductions and conclusions of short themes should be direct, clear, and effective. They should be neither abrupt nor diffuse. In a short theme, every sentence should count. In a longer one, introductory and concluding paragraphs must be concise and emphatic; if such material is not carefully composed, the whole theme is likely to lack proportion.

38a. Avoid unnecessary formal introductions.

Do not write an introduction unless your theme requires one. Avoid writing a formal beginning for every theme, because, usually, only long papers require extended definition of terms, or a history of the subject, or a long statement of its significance. Be careful not to make a formal series of general statements or to give needless explanations and details. Of course, you must not bewilder your reader by beginning so abruptly that he is unable to understand what follows. If antecedent details are needed, you must give them.

38b. Begin themes directly and clearly.

To begin at the beginning, directly and clearly, is not easy. Many writers ramble for some time before they warm to their subject and really come to grips with it. They seem to be building a platform from which to "take off." But if you will think through what you have to say, you can make the important opening position really count by attacking the heart of the subject, and thus avoid false starts and loose generalities.

Four direct and clear beginnings are illustrated in the following, on *The Evils of Radio Advertising*:

1. Repetition of the title in the opening sentence.

   The evils of radio advertising project like pinnacles above the lesser evils of other forms of advertising.

2. Rephrasing or paraphrasing the title in the opening sentence.

   Of all forms of advertising, radio broadcasting is the most blatant and least effective.

3. A setting or framework within which the subject will develop.

   Everyone is familiar with radio broadcasting, but not everyone realizes that radio programs are used, not only to give information and entertainment, but also to enrich those who prepare, present, and pay for them.

4. A summary or outline paragraph enumerating the main divisions to be discussed.

Radio advertising at the present time is guilty of four deadly sins: the sin of exaggeration, the sin of false taste, the sin of usurpation, and the sin of greed.

Such direct beginnings—a kind of topic sentence for the whole composition—immediately inform the reader of the subject to be discussed; each such beginning gives the central thought or *theme* of the theme.

38c. Begin themes effectively.

A good beginning gains the reader's attention and so interests him that he wishes to continue reading. A direct beginning is usually emphatic, but there are several other specific ways—alone or in combination—in which effectiveness may be gained.

1. *An Illustrative Incident.* Since people are interested in narrative, a well-chosen anecdote will gain the reader's interest and simultaneously illustrate the theme itself. Many good writers begin articles in this way. A single issue of a magazine such as *Harper's, The New Yorker,* or *The Atlantic Monthly* will contain several articles which have narrative leads.

In Tolstoy's novel *The Cossacks,* there is a scene where a man swimming is shot dead and drifts to the shore, while his slayer swims over the flooded river to get him and crouches down exhausted at his side. There the two lie, looking almost the same. But one is full of a turmoil of desires and aspirations, mingled feelings of pride and misery; and the other is dead. And the only sign of difference is a light steam rising from the body of the living man.

So small a sign, and yet all the difference that can be!

—GILBERT MURRAY

2. *A Combination of Narrative and Descriptive Details.* An article on skiing begins as follows:

Late last autumn, when the first snow flurries dusted across the northern half of the United States, an estimated three million pairs of knees began to twitch. This mass flexing was the first symptom of a seasonal phenomenon that has progressed in twenty years from the status of a foreign foolishness to that of a national mania. Although still in early stages of development, this phenomenon has reversed migratory instincts, cut scars in the faces of ancient mountains, created an economic revolution in rural areas, upped the income of the medical profession, and released several million inmates of modern society into flights of ecstatic freedom.

—ERIC SWENSON

3. *A Significant or Startling or Paradoxical Statement.* But such statements should not be used only to gain attention and interest; they should have some connection with what is to follow.

The Black Death, six hundred years ago, was beyond comparison the greatest catastrophe mankind has endured.

—EDWIN MULLER

Some wise man once wrote that each victorious war costs us a few more of our liberties.

—HANSON W. BALDWIN

4. *A polite command or a direct personal appeal.*

Any afternoon at six, walk down the Boulevard de la Gare, the principal avenue of Casablanca, and stop at the Café le Roi de la Bière.

—EDWARD TOLEDANO

Doctors and teachers are not the only people who should take refresher courses. All of us would be the better for an occasional refresher course in the essence of right living.

—NINA WILCOX PUTNAM

5. *A Direct Question.*

Is American Big Business getting too big to be good for business or for America?

—JOSEPH C. O'MAHONEY

You have been asleep for hours. You open your eyes in the darkness and listen. You hear a footfall on the staircase. What would you do?

—FULTON OURSLER

6. *The Report of a Conversation, or Quoted Material of Some Kind.* An apt, familiar quotation, or an exclamation is often an effective beginning.

"Oh, the immovably shining, smiling man!"

234

Thus William Bolitho described Woodrow Wilson as he appeared to Europe in 1919.

"The perfect model of the Christian cad."

Thus H. L. Mencken described Woodrow Wilson as he appeared to a considerable number of Americans in 1920.

—Gerald W. Johnson

7. References to People, Contemporary or Historical, Prominent or Not.

In a dim hut in the wild Arctic Circle region of Sweden, an area of impenetrable forests and howling storms, a doctor knelt by a stricken patient to wrestle with death.

—Ralph Wallace

The largest private builder of houses in the Eastern United States is the firm of Levitt & Sons, of Manhasset, Long Island, whose president —William J. Levitt—is to the housing industry somewhat as Robert R. Young first was to railroads.

—Eric Larrabee

8. Timely News Events or Seasonal Occurrences.

One warm day last May there were many vacant desks in Chicago public schools and the truant squad swung into action. Some officers headed for beaches and amusement parks, but Mrs. Mary Lusson, famous for her annual bag of hooky players, stalked her prey in a huge building on the shore of Lake Michigan. Here she nabbed sixty happy vagrants. These children, believe it or not, were caught visiting a museum.

—Harland Manchester

Last September at Forest Hills I sat in the fierce sun and watched one of the greatest tennis players of the past decade nearly fly apart.

—Mr. Harper

ENDING THE THEME

39. Like the beginning, the ending is an important position. It is the last thing that the reader sees; it should be emphatic and effective; it should make a final impression upon the reader.

39 a-c

39a. Avoid unnecessary formal or rambling conclusions.

The most important thing to remember in ending themes is this: When you have said all you intended to say, stop. Do not write a conclusion simply for the sake of the conclusion. A short composition usually requires no formal conclusion; a summarizing sentence will suffice. A rambling and wordy ending will destroy the effect of what has been said. Except in argumentative writing, there can be little excuse for the "thus we see's" and "in conclusion, let me state's."

39b. Avoid abrupt and incomplete endings.

Do not make the ending abrupt; that is, you should leave an impression of completeness, of having rounded out a discussion and reached a goal. Also, do not close with a statement that concerns only some detail; you should bring the reader back to some phase of the main thought of your theme.

39c. End themes effectively.

Although short compositions do not usually require formal conclusions, they should end effectively. This means that they should not end too abruptly, and that the ending, because of its very position, should contain a thought of such importance that it is a real contribution to the theme. There are several specific methods by which endings may be made effective.

1. The closing statement may deal with the main thought of the composition, may restate the title or central idea. In well-planned themes, afterthoughts are never so important as main thoughts.

. . . Only the free can be educated, but only the truly educated will find the spiritual spark of genius and morality necessary to remain free. [Title of article: "Only the Educated Shall Be Free."]

—SIDNEY J. FRENCH

Since skiing is one of the worst spectator sports in the world, owing to the weather, the region, and the terrain it requires, it must be tried to be believed. It cannot be explained satisfactorily to anyone who never has stood on a mountain top commanding a view of a few hundred miles of winter, felt the wind whip through his clothes, quaked at the thought of the plunge ahead, and then shackled himself to a pair of hickory boards and let fly downhill.

—ERIC SWENSON

2. The closing sentences may summarize or clinch the *theme* of the composition.

. . . If there were no other reasons in the world for hating women, that one would be enough. In fact, you can leave all the others out.

—JAMES THURBER

America depends for its growth upon bold young men willing to take a chance in pioneering new fields of service. And it bountifully rewards the skillful pioneer, whatever his origin.

—CHARLES C. SPAULDING

There is strength in moderation, strength above all in the basic American concept that military power is and must remain subordinate to civilian authority.

—HANSON W. BALDWIN

3. The closing sentences may show that the subject has some new or practical application, or some significant meaning.

. . . We shall find in all these people qualities and accomplishments from which we may learn and refresh ourselves, and by which we may enrich our inheritance and our posterity. Some day, let us hope, it will be permitted us to love our country without betraying mankind.

—WILL DURANT

Nevertheless, through the new accomplishments of natural science, the opportunity to diminish and possibly end the food crisis will exist. If no progress is made toward resolving the crisis, it will not be for want of technical means.

—LEONARD ENGEL

4. The closing sentences may link the subject with some matter of current interest, or may suggest a course of action.

The American Dream is a lovely thing, but to keep it alive, to keep it from turning into a Nightmare, every once in a while we've got to wake up.

—LOUIS ADAMIC

237

It is up to pedestrians to save their own lives, not only by being more careful but by vehemently demanding that officials give them at least an even break in the battle of motorist vs. pedestrian.

—DAVID G. WITTELS

The age of television is already here. The moment has arrived to decide how this medium can best be utilized for the benefit of the public. Tomorrow will be too late.

—BERNARD B. SMITH

EXERCISES

A. Choose six articles from your anthology and study their beginnings: What methods do they use to begin directly and clearly (Section 38b)? What methods, or combination of methods, do they use to gain effectiveness (Section 38c)?

B. Study the beginnings of all the articles in one issue of a standard magazine like *The Atlantic Monthly, Harper's Magazine, The Saturday Evening Post, Collier's, Time, Newsweek.* Apply to these beginnings the directions given in Exercise A.

C. Of the articles that you choose in Exercise A, examine the endings: What methods of effective ending are used (Section 39c)?

D. What methods of effective ending are used in the articles that you consulted for Exercise B?

E. Analyze the beginning and ending of two of your recent themes. If necessary, rewrite the introductions and conclusions, making them more direct, clearer, and more effective.

UNITY

40. Unity in the paragraph and the sentence is discussed in Sections **55** and **65**. But unity in the whole theme is also important, for every sentence and paragraph in a composition may be unified in itself, and yet the theme as a whole may lack unity.

The word *theme,* as applied to compositions, means a single *phase* of one subject. A theme should clearly and fully develop this one phase, but it should avoid being "more than complete." In other words, it should not contain irrelevant material or "pad-

238

ding"; it should stick to the oneness of its central idea, its controlling purpose.

40a. Discuss in your theme only one phase of a subject.

Proper limiting of the subject and proper analysis of the subject (see Sections 32d and 34) should show you exactly what you plan to discuss and what you plan to exclude. A writer is not likely to violate unity so grossly as to discuss basketball in a composition whose theme is the horrors of war. The danger is that he may thoughtlessly slip from one division of his subject into another division which is related but which has no immediate bearing upon the central theme. There is nothing more confusing or irritating to a reader than the insertion of irrelevant detail whose connection with the main theme is not obvious.

An irrelevant introduction and a conclusion that is merely tacked on violate the principle of unity. A story which has nothing to do with the subject but is told merely for its own sake violates unity. When a student has a paucity of ideas and a great need for words, he is likely to resort to "padding"; that is, he may fill a paragraph or two with words that deal with a phase of the subject other than the particular one being treated. An illustration: A student, writing on the subject, *The Ingenuity of Robinson Crusoe on the Desert Island,* began his theme: "Before beginning a discussion of Robinson Crusoe's ingenuity on the deserted island, I think it well to give the main facts of Daniel Defoe's life"; over half the paper was devoted to Defoe's biography.

40b. Build your theme around only one central purpose.

Every composition should have only one main idea or *theme;* it must stick to this one phase of the subject and must utilize it to achieve only one central purpose. For example, let us assume that the title of a theme is *My High School.* The particular phase of the subject is the *instruction* in the school; the purpose of the theme is to prove that the school which you attended furnished you with instruction which enables you to do your college work successfully. If in this composition you enter upon a discussion of the school building itself, attempting to point out that it is badly in need of

239

repair, you will have shifted the purpose, the central idea, of the theme.

To achieve unity, you must set your sights for some definite target and aim straight at the mark. You must decide exactly what you wish to do—inform, amuse, interest, arouse to action—*before* you begin to write. After you have determined your purpose, be careful to attempt nothing except reaching this predetermined goal.

40c. Give your theme unity of tone.

If you plan to write narration, do not overburden your writing with description. If you plan to explain, do not become involved in detailed arguments over applications. If you plan to argue, do not introduce anecdotes which have little bearing on the evidence.

Also, do not unnecessarily mix tragedy and comedy, pathos and satire, humor and stateliness, reverence and irreverence, dignity and absurdity, or any two similar extremes. For example: A paper on Abraham Lincoln's assassination should not introduce the humorous anecdotes of which Lincoln was fond; a paper on the pleasures of eating should not conclude with serious moralizing about the dangers of overindulgence; a paper on international relations on the campus should not include humorous or satirical stories about any particular race or nation.

EXERCISES

A. Try to find places in a recent theme where you have dealt with more than one phase of a subject, or where you have not confined yourself to one central purpose.

B. Show how a theme may lack unity even if all its component sentences and paragraphs are themselves unified.

C. Discuss violations of unity in the following plan for a theme:

MY ROOMMATE'S FATHER

I. My roommate's father is an excellent dentist.
II. He studied hard while he was in college and dental school and took many scholastic honors.
III. His mother died during his last year at dental school.
IV. My roommate is not a hard student; he is more interested in dancing and playing football.

V. After he was graduated, my roommate's father studied abroad for several years.
VI. He now has a large and lucrative practice in Mobile.
VII. His health is poor, and he has engaged an assistant.
VIII. My roommate has many excellent characteristics.

COHERENCE

41. Coherence means "holding together." It is an essential quality of the good theme because, without coherence, there can be no clear communication of thought from writer to reader. A composition is coherent when its parts have been so carefully woven together that the reader is never confused about the relationships of ideas.

An outline (see Section 36) is helpful in achieving coherence because it aids in arranging ideas in proper order. But a definite plan alone will not insure coherence; you must be certain that you have left no gaps in thought, and you must make sure not only that you *have* order in the theme but that you *reveal* this order to the reader.

41a. Do not leave any gaps in thought.

In writing a composition you must remember that your reader is not likely to be so quick as you are in seeing the relationships of ideas. The association of two ideas may seem logical to you but very illogical to him, because you have omitted to put down the thought which bridged the two ideas. For example, a student may be writing a theme on *The Pleasures of Walking,* in which he jumps from a paragraph on walking in city streets to one which deals with a description of the Black Hills. The relation is not obvious to the reader, but it would be if the writer had linked the thoughts in some such manner as this: "Walking the streets of a city is pleasant, but another equally pleasurable form of walking is mountain climbing. One summer I took several enjoyable hikes among the Black Hills of South Dakota. . . ."

41b. Attain coherence in a theme by the use of transitional devices.

If the parts of a composition have orderly arrangement and if no gaps in thought occur, coherence is usually attained. Occasionally, however, the progress of thought must be actually *marked,* so that the reader will immediately know when one point has been finished and another is taken up.

The use of transitional devices accomplishes this purpose and shows consideration for the reader:

1. Transitional words and phrases, such as *moreover, however, consequently, in addition, in the second place,* etc. (For a longer list of transitional words and phrases, see p. 376.)

2. Transitional sentences. Such sentences come usually at the beginning or the end of paragraphs, that is, between integral parts of the theme. Example: "The greatness of a college depends not only upon its buildings and equipment; it depends also upon its faculty and students."

3. Transitional paragraphs, each usually consisting of one or two sentences which look back to the preceding paragraph and point forward to the paragraph which is to come.

The thoughtful writer remembers that he is attempting to *transfer* ideas to readers, and in this effort he will ask, "Will my readers understand this? What will insure their seeing exactly what I have in mind? Shall I summarize here? Shall I warn my readers that I am taking up a slightly different idea here?"

In a coherent theme each paragraph must seem to grow out of the preceding one, and each group of paragraphs dealing with one division of the theme must be clearly connected with other paragraph groups (just as within each paragraph each sentence is logically and coherently related to the sentences that precede and follow). Finally, the reader must be able to see clearly that the whole theme has made orderly progress from beginning to end, without gaps in thought, without obscurity, without fruitless backward movement.

CLARITY

42. Correctness, clarity, and effectiveness are essentials of all good writing. In some respects, clarity is the most important of the three. An idea may be incorrectly and ineffectively expressed, and yet, if it is understood by others, communication, the purpose of all writing, has been achieved. But it is certainly possible for a theme to be substantially correct in the details of writing and not be clear to the reader. It is theoretically impossible for writing to be effective without being clear; but who has not read and reread material which was obviously correct and seemingly emphatic enough, without being able to understand its central meaning?

Thus, because clarity is an essential, a prime essential, nearly every section of this book deals with it. But three special suggestions for attaining clarity deserve particular attention.

42a. Define all terms which are not completely clear.

It is perhaps too much to say that you should consider your readers to be entirely ignorant. But remember that certain terms may be known to you and yet be foreign to your reader. All thinking begins with terms (concepts, ideas, names), and the reader cannot understand your thought unless he understands the terms used.

If it is necessary to use technical words—that is, terms peculiar to and generally understood only by members of a certain sect, class, or occupation—define them clearly. Not every reader will understand such terms as *cassock, quinazoline, gravamen, counterpoint, idiopathy,* and *syncope.* If you use them, you should clearly define them. Naturally, you should consider the reader or class of readers for whom you are writing; for example, if you are writing a paper for presentation to a group of musicians, you need not explain the word *counterpoint.*

42b. Give every statement the quality of reasonableness.

Reasoning is based upon facts and inferences, that is, conclusions drawn from facts. Avoid making questionable statements unless you are prepared to prove them, and do so. Make your meaning clear to the reader by offering evidence based upon facts. If you make a statement which is false in analogy, or is based upon a faulty premise, or is a mere generalization, the reader will become confused. Sound thinking is essential to clarity. (See pages 12–18.)

Note the illogicalness in these statements taken from actual themes:

1. He knows all there is to know about the game of football.

2. Any student who will not engage in some form of extracurricular activity should be expelled from college.
3. All fast drivers are reckless.
4. Because football is the most dangerous of all sports, my mother refused to allow me to play it.
5. Gambling quickly becomes a habit, and everyone should avoid it because habits are bad.
6. The actions of King Charles prove that monarchy is the best form of government for that country.
7. My ancestors came over in the *Mayflower;* therefore I am naturally opposed to intolerance.

42c. Check your theme and your outline for orderly arrangement.

There is no easier way to confuse your reader than to develop your theme in a series of illogical steps or in a puzzling order. Test each part of your outline; test each paragraph; and test each sentence within each paragraph. Does each element lead logically and clearly to the element that follows? Are there any gaps? Have you omitted necessary transitions which will indicate orderly development?

EXERCISES

A. Make a list of some technical, or cant, terms which you know and which you think your classmates may not understand.

B. List the cant terms well known in your college.

C. Clarify the possible meanings of the sentences quoted in **42b.**

D. Define the following terms: *evidence, authority, inference, deduction, induction, analogy, premise, syllogism.*

E. "It is never safe to reason by analogy." Comment on this statement.

POINT OF VIEW

43. The point of view of a writer is the position that he takes relative to the object under observation or the subject under consideration. Lack of clarity in the theme may result from an inconsistency in the physical point of view from which something is seen or in the mental point of view from which the specific details of a subject are considered. In order to test the consistency of your point of view, ask yourself of a given theme: Have I shifted my point of view? If so, did I have a purpose in making the shift? Are the shift and the reason for making it fully clear to my readers?

43a. Do not carelessly shift the physical point of view.

Before you begin your composition, you usually have to choose some point in *space* (inside or outside a building, an elevation, a point of the compass, etc.) or *time* (hour, season, weather, year), from which the subject is to be considered. The selection of a definite point of view is particularly important in descriptive and narrative writing. After you have chosen your position and time, do not needlessly shift them; and, when a shift is necessary, make such shift clear to your reader by using adequate transitional phrases.

For example, if you are describing a building, do not shift carelessly and without warning from the back to the front of it, or from the inside to the outside, or from one floor to another. The reader will be confused if he thinks that you are looking at the outside of the house and suddenly you begin to describe a picture in one of the bedrooms or the furnace in the basement.

A confusion in time is just as mystifying to the reader. Do not carelessly jump from one year to another, or make him think that it is night and suddenly inform him that it is the afternoon of the next day. If the time is midwinter, do not suddenly interject details about June beetles or growing cotton.

43b. Do not carelessly shift the mental point of view.

Point of view implies *mood* or *tone* as well as place and time. Select the style or tone which you think most suitable for the particular phase of the subject being developed and do not shift from it unless you have good reason to do so. Avoid shifting from a formal to a colloquial style, or from a serious to a humorous style. If your mood is gay and light, avoid a careless and sudden shift to a sad and heavy mood (see Section **34c, 3**). If you are discussing intercollegiate athletic competition, you may properly present arguments for and against it, but you must make perfectly clear when you shift from one side to the other. Similarly, if you are arguing that intramural sports are preferable to intercollegiate athletics, do not present arguments in favor of the latter unless you use them to further your central point. And do not subtly shift to a different phase of the subject, such as women's part in intramural sports, without indicating the shift. Never cause confusion in the mind of the reader about your mental point of view.

43c. Do not carelessly shift the personal point of view.

In discussing any subject, you may use one of four points of view: the first person (*I, my, me, we, our, us*), the second person (*you, your*), the third person (*he, his, him, she, her, they, their, them, one, a person,* etc.), or the impersonal (omitting all personal pronouns or using the passive voice). Do not carelessly or needlessly shift the point of view in any discussion from the "I" to the "we" or "you" or "one" point of view, or from any one of these to another. When a shift is necessary or effective, as it sometimes is, give your reader warning of what you are doing.

This principle is especially valuable in writing narrative, which may be told from one of three points of view: (1) from that of a major character, perhaps the author himself; (2) from the point of view of a minor character in the story; (3) from an omniscient angle, in which the author knows all that his characters think, feel, and do. Each of these has its special effectiveness. The thing to remember is that the teller of a story must choose a single narrative point of view and stick to it. It is confusing to the reader to be changed from the point of view of one character to that of another, unless the shift is made clear to him immediately.

EXERCISES

A. Determine the *physical* point of view (in *space*) of the author of some piece of description which you have read. Does this point of view shift? If so, explain.

B. Determine the *physical* point of view (in *time*) of the author of some narrative that you have read. Does this point of view shift? If so, explain.

C. Determine the *mental* points of view expressed in one or more of several essays which you have studied recently.

246

D. Determine the *personal* point of view in several essays and short stories that you have read recently.

E. Determine the *narrative* points of view of several short stories or narrative sketches in your book of readings.

EFFECTIVENESS

44. If a composition is correctly, clearly, and fully expressed and coherently arranged, it will usually be decisive and striking. Ample substance expressed with correctness and clearness is not always effective, however; you must never forget that in order to communicate ideas you must *interest* your readers. Many students, with the aid of textbooks and instructors, learn to write correctly and clearly; comparatively few achieve the ability to express their ideas in such a manner as to gain and hold the attention of their readers.

The title of an opera by Verdi, *Aïda,* contains the letters of a mnemonic device which you should remember: A—Attention; I—Interest; D—Desire; A—Action. That is, a theme should first command the attention of the reader, then attract his interest so that he will actually wish to read it and perhaps be led to agree or disagree with what is said, or wish to do what the theme suggests, or fall in with whatever your purpose is.

Such effectiveness in writing is dependent upon correctness and clarity, but their presence does not insure effectiveness; this can be achieved, however, by the proper position and proportion of ideas, and by statements which are expressed definitely and with animation.

44a. Achieve effectiveness by conveying an actual sense of fact.

Many papers which are reasonably correct and clear are not genuinely effective because of abstractness, indefiniteness. Good writing is definite, concrete; it contains specific details which arouse interest. In other words, it either contains facts or conveys a sense of fact. A composition on taxation will hardly be effective so long as you abstractly discuss the theory of taxation; but when you make a statement such as this you make your work come alive: "Whether or not you own real property, you pay taxes.

According to a recent estimate, the citizens of our town paid an average tax of $350.00 this past year."

Specific answers to the questions Who? What? Where? When? Why? How? always achieve effectiveness. They furnish realistic touches, clear imagery, which the reader has a right to expect. Note the difference in effectiveness between these two excerpts taken from student themes:

1. My roommate was selfish. He cared nothing for me or anyone else and was completely absorbed in looking out for his own interests.
2. John was selfish. He borrowed my neckties and razor-blades, sometimes without asking permission, but he hated for me to borrow even a sheet of paper from him. When he had to get up for an early class, he walked around noisily, and made no effort to keep from waking me. But he grumbled for ten minutes one morning when I accidentally dropped my history book and waked him.

These suggestions can help you convey an actual sense of fact:
1. Enumerate specific details.
2. Narrate specific and dramatic incidents.
3. Use specific people as examples, whenever possible.
4. Use comparison and contrast.
5. Show definite relationships of causes and effects.

44b. Achieve effectiveness by making your compositions alive.

Writing which is studded with facts may be very dull and lifeless. History books are commonly considered dull, for example, but they are certainly not thin in facts. Neither are stock market statistics, or insurance reports, or legal briefs. But none of these are interesting, effective, *alive*. They have little dramatic effect, human interest, movement, humor, satire, or any of the other qualities which make writing more than merely readable. Not every writer can be humorous or satirical or urbane, but everyone can make occasional use of dialogue, or of a series of questions or exclamations, and everyone can get *movement* of some kind into his narrative and descriptive writing. Study the following:

1. She was not certain that she should have stopped payment on the check. She thought she might be sued for nonpayment.

Should she have stopped the check? What could Mr. Jones do to her? What would he do? Oh, if only she could get her father's advice!

2. The house had been freshly painted, and shone in the afternoon sun.

"I see you have had your house painted, Mr. Dodge."

"Yes, Lem and I decided a fresh coat of green and white would help, so we bought paint and brushes, and did the job ourselves."

"Did you, indeed? Well, the house certainly does look lovely in the afternoon sun."

44c. Achieve effectiveness by the use of parallel structure.

Parallel structure is a valuable aid in gaining effectiveness because of the obvious similarity it gives to related ideas. (See Section 74.)

44d. Achieve effectiveness by the skillful repetition of words and structure.

Note the effectiveness achieved by such repetition in the following:

Verse is patterned language. That is, verse is composition in which words are arranged according to a pattern, a form which is metrical, rhythmical. Verse may be mere doggerel, such as
"Here lies the body of Samuel Blank;
He dropped a match in a gasoline tank."
These lines are verse because they consist of words arranged according to a pattern.

Poetry is patterned language, plus. That is, poetry is composition arranged in a pattern. But poetry is more than verse. It signifies high thought, imagination, or emotion.
"Heard melodies are sweet, but those unheard
Are sweeter; therefore, ye soft pipes, play on."
These lines are poetry because they are patterned language which contains genuine thought and imagination. All poetry is verse, but not all verse can be called poetry.

But avoid a long series of paragraphs which are similar in structure. Variety in paragraph structure is fully as desirable as variety in sentence structure. Just as a reader will tire of pages with no paragraph breaks at all, he will lose interest in a group of paragraphs which are monotonously similar in construction.

44e. Achieve effectiveness by avoiding frequent use of the passive voice.

Make your themes *move* or create an impression of movement, with the subjects of your sentences acting and not being passive or acted upon (see Section 11). To say "A trip was made" when you mean "I made a trip" is to commit a fault in structure which is simple and easy to correct. Students overuse the passive voice and the verbs *to be, to make, to have, to do,* and *to cause.* Use verbs in the active voice whenever you want to express or imply action, mental or physical, unless the point of the sentence is to represent the subject as being acted upon. And avoid shifting from active to passive, since so doing confounds sense and tends to confuse your reader (see Section 75b).

44f. Achieve effectiveness by avoiding trite expressions.

Aim at explaining, describing, or narrating from a *fresh* point of view: use vivid, concrete words which suggest feeling, which appeal to the reader's sense of shape, color, sound, touch, taste, smell (see Section 92).

EXERCISES

A. In terms of an actual sense of fact and aliveness, discuss the effectiveness of an article selected from your book of readings.

B. What are the psychological bases for the effectiveness of dialogue, of movement or impression of movement, of narrative detail, in themes?

C. Does the discussion in this section help to account for the difference in people's interest in the news columns of a daily paper as contrasted with their interest in editorials?

D. Analyze one issue of *Time* ("the weekly newsmagazine") in order to determine the reasons for its effective style.

REVISION

45. "There is no such thing as good writing; there is only good *rewriting.*" Many students are likely to object to such a statement; they will recall a time when they really "got going" and turned out a first and only draft which was superior to anything they had laboriously revised, or they will recall having heard that Scott or O. Henry or this or that writer never rewrote. But the statement on rewriting is basically sound.

Frequently a student will say: "I wrote this theme in an hour and got a C grade on it; my last week's theme took me three hours, and yet was marked D." Such an instance is offered as proof that revision does not pay, is not worth the effort it requires. But, nine times out of ten, the writer of a good "hour" theme has composed his theme before actually writing it. He has thought it through many times; he has, as Charles A. Brooks puts it, composed "on the hoof." He has collected something to say, perhaps unconsciously, and has secured some real interest in saying that something. His "quickly written" theme is thus not quickly written at all.

No one, not even an accomplished professional writer, can plan, write, and proofread a theme all at one time. Perhaps the best plan to follow is this: First, gather material for your theme, and then plan and arrange it. Next, without paying special attention to grammatical, rhetorical, or mechanical details, write the theme with all the vigor and interest you can. After that, and preferably some time later, revise the theme carefully. "Easy writing makes hard reading; hard writing makes easy reading."

45a. Proofread your theme for accuracy.

Anyone who will use a reference handbook (making the most of its index) and a dictionary should be able to write at least *correctly*. But in the haste of composing a first draft, you may frequently make careless slips not due to ignorance or neglect to check matters about which you are not sure. After you have written your first draft, reread it and entirely rewrite it, eliminating all possible errors.

1. Go through the theme once for the sole purpose of making sure that all the words are *spelled correctly* (see Section 81).

2. Read the theme through again to insure *grammatical correctness.*

3. Read the theme through again to insure *correct punctuation.* Pay especial attention to commas (see Section 18).

4. Read the theme again to insure *effective diction.*

5. Proofread the final draft, looking for errors carelessly made in recopying and for errors in mechanical form (see Section 31).

Helpful hints for the first and final drafts of any written papers are given on pages 19–28, "Your First Themes."

45b. Proofread your theme to secure better sentences.

Read the preliminary draft to improve the sentences in phrasing and structure. Make sure that all the sentences are unified and complete (Sections **61, 65**); that the ideas are properly coördinated or subordinated (Sections **76, 77**); that there are no "period fault," "comma fault," or "fused" sentences; that the sentences are clearly and effectively phrased; and that the sentences are varied in structure (Section **80**).

45c. Proofread your themes for unity, coherence, emphasis.

Read the theme once more in order to make sure that it is unified, coherent, and effective as a whole. Delete the extraneous material; rephrase all vague or rambling thought; substitute specific details for vague generalities.

CAUTION: Allow as much time as possible to elapse between writing the theme and revising it. If there is sufficient time between the two steps (the actual composition and the suggested rereadings), you will see errors which are not apparent to you when you have just completed writing it. You can approach your theme more objectively; errors not seen before will be prominent. Every writer has noted that he can detect errors in another's work more easily than he can in his own. If you will allow your work to "jell," you can see it almost as objectively as you can the compositions of someone else.

45d. Revise your graded and returned theme according to a specific plan.

As in many other activities, one does not improve merely by having his attention called to his errors. He must correct those errors under supervision. So, too, with theme writing.

When your theme is graded and returned to you, observe carefully the errors that are marked and profit by the comments that your instructor has written.

If there are errors in organization or in various types of sentence structure, you may be asked to rewrite and resubmit the theme. If there are errors in spelling, grammar, punctuation, or diction, you may be asked to make out a correction sheet. Your instructor will indicate by some method, such as underlining the symbols, which errors are to be corrected, and he may further indicate by some mechanical device such as brackets [....] or ∠....∖ or double parallel lines ‖....‖ how much material is to be included on the correction sheet. These correction sheets can be a valuable guide in future writing. (For fuller discussion of correction sheets—their importance, use, and form—see pp. 21–22.)

EXERCISES

A. Find out what you can about the amount of revision done by Robert Louis Stevenson, Benvenuto Cellini (see the *Autobiography*), John Galsworthy, or any modern essayist or short-story writer.

B. Make an honest analysis of the time spent on various of your themes. Estimate the amount of time spent on "thinking before writing," the actual time spent in writing and in revising.

C. "Technical errors hinder communication in writing as much as stammering does in conversation." Discuss the meaning and application of this statement.

D. Below are given two short themes. Proofread them carefully, marking all the errors that you see. Give each theme a grade, assuming that the writers have had ten weeks of college English instruction. Write for each theme a paragraph of comment that should aid the writers in future themes.

"APPLE POLISHERS"

Many people have a poor idea of the "apple polisher." When this is done by an expert it is a fine art, it takes long years of practice. The expert will always stand out from the crowd because of the ease with which he goes about his work. This man is by far the most disliked man in the party. It is easy to see why when we

analysis him. He always tries to get something
for nothing, and many times, at the next mans
expence. He is a far cry from the type of man
you and me would like to know and work with.
But after all aren't we all just a little in-
clined towared this means at some time or another? I think we are. A kind word or a forced
smile may sometimes made a great difference.
But so far as abdicating this as a general
practice, that's out. I have seen quite a few
"apple polishers" in the last four years. In
that time I have come to believe that it is no-
always his falt. As you know there are many
people who will call a man an "apple polisher"
for no reasion at all. In my opionion these
people are more at falt than the man himself.

THE PAISANOS' CODE OF CONDUCT

In 1935 John Steinbeck wrote the book
Tortilla Flat. In this book he wrote of the
characteristics, the standard of living, and
inhabitants of Tortilla Flat. Tortilla Flat
lays in the upward hill district from the
heart of Monterey, California. The paisano is
the main inhabitant in this sector of the city.
He is a mixture of Spanish, Indian, Mexican,
and Caucasian bloods. He speaks broken English
and when questioned about his race claims pure
Spanish blood. The paisano has black course
hair, black beddy eyes, dark complexsion and
usally not very tall.

The paisanos song is wine, women, and song.
He is a lazy character, who never worries about
the happenings surrounding him. Danny, Pilon,
and Pablo lived off the "fat of the land" and
each other. The paisano spends much time in
jail, not that he does any serious crime but
for his moral and scruple way of living. In
their own crude way the paisanos are always
trying to do something nice for each other. The
paisano doesn't realize he is committing a
crime or cares less when he takes the pleasure
of another man's goods or steal his wine. The
paisano doesn't have an education and any home

254

life, this resulting in his worthless way of living.
The paisanos have lived in a very low standard for many years and probably will never change. Their entire life is based on wine, and cheap women. If they have these two things they are happy.

THE BASIC FORMS OF WRITING

46. All writing can be classified according to one of four forms or types: narration, description, exposition, and argument. *Narration* (or *narrative*) tells a story; *description* gives a picture in words; *exposition* explains; *argument* seeks to convince. No one form exists alone, pure and unmixed; for example, descriptive details may be used in narrative or in exposition; narration helps to clarify in exposition or argument; and argument may be used in exposition. Predominating tone and purpose and characteristics determine the classification of any piece of writing.

Cutting across boundaries and classifiable according to content are such varieties of writing as the précis (see pp. 266–269), the paraphrase (see pp. 269–272), the research paper (see pp. 287–306), and letters (see pp. 475–502).

46a. Use narration to tell a story, true or imagined.

Narration, in telling a story, answers the questions: "What happened? How? When? Why? Where? With or by whom?" It varies in length from extremely long to extremely short: novels, novelettes, dramas, biographies and autobiographies, histories, news stories, short stories, incidents, and anecdotes. Longer types of narrative are beyond the scope of freshman writing, as are some of the shorter ones; one-act plays, news writing, and short stories require specialized study.

The plan or order in simple narrative is chronological; that is, you relate the various events as they occurred in time. The point of view may be first person, third person, multiple, or omniscient (see p. 244); be sure to keep to a consistent point of view.

Shorter or shortened forms of narrative (and narrative-exposition) that you may choose or be assigned are the anecdote, incident, autobiography, interview, and profile.

1. The *anecdote* is a narrative bit told or written to illustrate some specific point. Its chief characteristic is that it presents individuals in an action which illustrates some definite idea, illuminates some aspect of personality or character. Dialogue, setting, and characters are subordinate to the main point. The anecdote rarely stands alone but is a powerful method of making understandable a possibly difficult idea.

2. An *incident is* a short narrative told for its own sake. It deals with a single, simple situation. Its primary emphasis is upon the character of the narrator or some person involved in the action, or upon the action itself. (For examples, see the department, "Life in These United States," in *The Reader's Digest*.) The incident involves characters, setting, action, and dialogue, but it is simple in structure, brief, and without undue emphasis upon dramatic conflict.

3. In *autobiography*, you give a rounded and understandable picture of yourself (just as in biography you give such a picture of another person). In analyzing your subject *(you)* and gathering material, give consideration to the following: a brief account of your heredity and environment; a series of descriptions of people, places, and events (including education) which have genuinely influenced you; your social beliefs; your religious beliefs; your political beliefs; your moral beliefs; your interests and hobbies; your ambitions; your personal characteristics (qualities of character); your ideas of happiness. An autobiographical theme composed in whole or in part of a smoothly articulated discussion of these and similar important matters should be genuinely significant and revelatory to both writer and reader.

4. The *interview* is a narrative account of some person's opinions, beliefs, and attitudes told through dialogue and direct quotation. The person need not be "an important personage"; almost anyone who has an interesting occupation or hobby is a good subject. Before the interview, find out as much as you can about the person. Plan in advance the questions you are going to ask and

the topics which you would like to have discussed (modify these as necessary during the interview). Be inconspicuous in the use of a notebook or in taking notes; try to rely upon your memory in the subject's presence. Avoid an exclusive use of a "question and answer" style in writing up the report of the interview. Try to give something of the background of the person. Build your interview around some high point or central thesis of the conversation. Finally, be careful to insure the mechanical accuracy of your interview, such as the use of punctuation marks and the paragraphing of conversation.

5. The *profile* combines biographical material with character interpretation. The profile differs from biographical writing in that it contains more anecdotes, human-interest stories, and humorous or ironic comment. As its name indicates, it is not a full-length portrait; it merely seizes upon highlights and bears somewhat the relation to a full-length biography that a short story does to a novel. Anyone, regardless of who he is, is a potential subject for a profile.

Include in your profile much more than merely "who's who" detail, which ordinarily constitutes a minor part of the whole. Be thorough in getting information, not only from the subject himself but from his friends and acquaintances, the members of his family, his roommate, his enemies, his teachers or students. Do not make your profile didactic: you are not writing a sermon, a moral lecture, or a piece of propaganda. Build the major portion of the profile around some dominant characteristic of the subject. Use incidents, anecdotes, description of appearance and actions, direct quotations, and account for his attitudes toward various topics.

Follow some clear plan of organization. A good and typical profile may be written as follows: First, describe your subject's physical appearance and follow up with a few "flashes" of him or her in action—teaching a class, serving a customer, treating a patient, etc. After that, give a rapid story of the subject's life, stressing those details of heredity and environment which have an important bearing. Then come back to him as of the present, showing why he is important, interesting, amusing, or is bitter, frustrated, or happy, or what not. Here you will develop his guiding "philosophy of life," his primary motives, his aims and hopes, the worth of his actual achievements. Such an outline is merely a suggestion; rearrangement of the items is permissible.

46b. Use description to give a picture or an impression.

Description is that kind of writing which tells how something looks, tastes, smells, sounds, feels, or acts. It deals with objects, people, places, scenes, animals, moods, or impressions. It may supplement narrative, exposition, or even argumentative writing. The primary purposes of description are to portray a sense impression and to indicate a mood.

1. Maintain a consistent point of view to make description clear and effective. *Physical* point of view (see Section **43**) deals with considerations of time and place; *mental* point of view with mood and tone. Do not shift your point of view without good reason; when you do shift, warn your reader by means of transitions.

2. Use the "space order," ordinarily, in writing description. Space order means choosing some point in space or geography as an anchor from which your description moves: from north to south or east to west, from left to right or right to left; from near to remote or remote to near; or, in personal description, from head to foot. Sometimes you can develop description by beginning with prominent characteristics and moving to the less prominent.

3. For effective description, use words that appeal to one of the senses or that portray a mood: shape, size, color (*rectangular, bulbous, bluish*); sound words (*tinkling, harsh, melodious*); smell words (*pungent, acrid, rose-scented*); taste (*sweet, sour, tangy, bitter*); touch words (*hard, hot, soft, cold, caressing, velvety*); mood words (*sad, brooding, mournful, melancholy*). A piece of descriptive writing should have a single effect, provide a unified dominant impression.

4. A common form of descriptive writing is the *sketch*, a study of character or setting or mood. It contains little action or plot but places emphasis on descriptive details. Unlike the anecdote, it is not concerned with making a point or illustrating a thesis; unlike the incident, it puts emphasis upon characterization to the virtual exclusion of action.

46c. Use exposition to explain or clarify or interpret.

Exposition includes the greatest part of what we write and read: textbooks; long and short magazine articles; newspaper editorials; and criticisms of books, motion pictures, radio and television programs, and musical compositions. All of these except the first you may be called upon to write.

1. Follow a logical plan or order in writing exposition. Choose one of the following:

a. *Known to Unknown.* Begin with what your reader knows and proceed to the unknown material about which you are to give information.

b. *Simple to Complex.* Begin with easily understood matters; proceed logically to the more difficult.

c. *Classification.* Divide your subject into its various parts according to a consistent, logical plan and discuss each part in order.

d. *Time.* Develop your subject according to the way its phases develop in time, as, for example, giving instructions on how to paint furniture.

e. *Space.* Follow the order that the parts of your subject occupy in space, such as a discussion of regional characteristics or of particular attitudes or habits in various countries.

f. *Deductive.* Begin with a general statement or truth and show how it applies to specific or particular instances or examples.

g. *Inductive.* Discuss particular instances or examples from which you draw a general conclusion or make a generalized statement.

h. *Analogy and Contrast.* Explain your subject, or some part of it, by using analogy, which shows a similarity to some familiar object, or by using contrast, which emphasizes differences.

2. Choose the form of exposition which will most appropriately and effectively develop your subject.

a. *Expanded Definition.* Other than giving a simpler synonym to define a term, most definition assigns a term to a general class (*genus*) and then shows how it differs from other members of this class (*differentia*). In all such definitions, use simple words; exclude everything from the definition that does not belong in it;

include everything that does belong; and avoid using the term being defined or any derivative of it. Expanded definition proceeds by giving further details or examples; by using comparison or contrast; by showing cause or effect; or by dividing the term into its component parts. (Apply to writing definition some of the varied methods of paragraph development discussed in Section 54a.)

b. *Narrative Exposition.* So called because it explains by telling a story and usually follows a time order, narrative exposition is commonly used in the explanation of a process. Subjects using the words "how," "the method," "the principle," and the like, are developed by narrative exposition—for example, *How Petroleum Is Refined* and *Methods of Obtaining Penicillin from Mold.*

c. *Giving Directions.* An important subdivision of narrative exposition is giving directions. Subjects may be impersonal, *How to Ride a Bicycle,* or personal, *How I Learned to Ride a Bicycle.* In either, directions should be so clear that your reader will have no trouble in following them.

d. *Descriptive Exposition.* So called because it explains by describing and ordinarily using space order, descriptive exposition is commonly used in the explanation of mechanical objects like a spark plug, the telephone receiver, a fishing reel. Frequently, descriptive exposition and narrative exposition are used together; excellent examples appear in any issue of a semitechnical or popular scientific magazine.

e. *Criticism.* Whether of a book, magazine article, movie, radio or television program, or musical composition, a criticism is an estimation of worth or value. Ordinarily, as critic, you will answer four questions: What was the author's purpose? What methods did he use in accomplishing his purpose (scope, characters, setting, kind of plot, dialogue, point of view, style, etc.)? Was the purpose successfully accomplished? Was it worth accomplishing?

The following suggestions for writing a critical review may be helpful: Always give some indication of the contents. Select a controlling idea and mold your review around it. Make some use of quotations from the work. Be specific; avoid vague terms. Do not hesitate to inject yourself and your ideas into the review. Avoid contradictions and afterthoughts which destroy the unity of purpose and tone of your review.

f. *Informal and Formal Essays.* The informal or personal essay is usually a friendly and conversational explanation of the writer's attitudes or opinions or moods toward some specific subject, using some dominant tone like whimsy, satire, irony, lightness, wittiness, humor. The formal essay or article is a dignified and usually impersonal treatment of some serious subject; it may be descriptive or argumentative, but it is usually expository. Examples of both informal and formal essays can be found in contemporary magazines: the former is fairly infrequent in this decade; the latter is a preponderant or integral part of the contents of almost all modern magazines. Formal essays are specialized types of exposition. However, by following the directions already given for the writing of themes (choosing and limiting and analyzing subjects, Sections 32, 34; getting material, Section 35, and organizing, Section 36), and by adapting the directions for writing the research paper (see Section 50), you should approach successful writing of the formal essay or article. Bear in mind only that the formal essay is now usually written in an appropriately popular style and, although based on fact, is not accompanied by the paraphernalia of documentation (footnotes and bibliography).

46d. Use argument to persuade or convince.

Formal argument is a complicated subject, using four specialized steps: establishing the proposition, analyzing the proposition, formulating the argument, and preparing the brief (a special form of outline).

Less formal argument—usually used in themes, magazine articles, and occasional newspaper editorials—is built around subjects containing the words "advantages," "disadvantages," "value," or "why": *The Advantages of Belonging to a Social Fraternity, The Value of Intramural Athletics, Why Mission College Should Abolish Final Examinations.*

The order or plan to follow in informal argument is classification: a listing of the reasons for or against, sometimes in the order of climax (progressing to the most important), sometimes more or less arbitrarily. Under each reason, discuss the facts or materials (known as evidence) which support and establish that particular phase of the argument. Guard against any weaknesses or errors that would destroy the effectiveness of the chain of reasoning or logical thinking (see pp. 12–18).

Make all argumentative substance lead to an inevitable conclusion. But sometimes you may give both sides and leave the reader to make his own decision about the conclusion: *The Advantages and Disadvantages of Final Examinations.*

EXERCISES

In writing on any of the following subjects, remember that you should have in mind, and indicate, a specific reader or limited group of readers (see Section **34b,** pp. 216–217).

A. Examine three selections in your book of readings; determine how many of the four basic forms of writing (narration, description, exposition, argument) are contained in each selection.

B. From the vantage point of a window overlooking a busy street, observe details which are primarily expository, descriptive, argumentative, and narrative. For each type of writing, compile a list of ten subjects based on your observation.

C. Write an anecdote to "prove" or "disprove" any one of the following statements.

1. Women are more emotional than men.
2. Men are better automobile drivers than women.
3. Young people are no ruder than their elders.
4. Chivalry among modern youth is nonexistent.
5. Few people have the courage of their convictions.
6. Informal education is more valuable than formal education.
7. Most important people have inferiority complexes.
8. The honor system on our campus is successful.
9. Athletes receive special consideration from their instructors.
10. Our campus does not know the meaning of "campus politics."

D. List five incidents in which you have recently been involved and which you think would be of general interest.

E. Read the department, "Life in These United States," in several issues of *The Reader's Digest.* From your own experience write several similar incidents (limit, 300 words).

F. Write a brief autobiographical theme (about 500 words), introducing yourself to your instructor.

G. If you do not write a fairly complete autobiography, you may be assigned (or wish to write) sections or divisions of your autobiography: Ancestry; Early Childhood; Environment; Early Education; College; Summer Activities; People, Places, and Events That Have Had Influence; Friends; Religion; Politics; Travel; Ambitions; Interests and Hobbies; Personal Characteristics; Ideals.

H. Choose someone on or near the campus who has a responsible position or who is known for some achievement or activity. Plan, carry out, and write an interview with this person. Suggestions: A Dean; A Head of a Department; An Interesting Teacher; The College Business Manager; A Student Pastor; The Manager or Owner of a Cafeteria; A Bookstore Owner or Manager; The Librarian; The President of Some Class or Organization; The Manager of a Student Activity; A Campus Band Leader; A Campus Policeman; A Janitor; A Night Watchman; A Bus or Taxicab Driver, etc.

I. Write a *profile* of one of the people mentioned in Exercise H or in Exercise M.

J. Copy from a guidebook a formal description of some place which you have visited. Then write a brief description in which you try to convey to the reader some idea of the *impression* which the place made upon you. Make liberal use of your five senses.

K. Make each of the following specific; then write a brief, literal description of any two: A Soda Fountain; A Chemistry Laboratory; A Student Room; A Dentist's Office; A Bus Station; The College Cafeteria; A Professor's Office; A Chain Grocery Store; A Skyscraper; A Filling Station; Back Stage at a Theater; A Projection Booth; A Student's Notebook; An Airport; A Stadium; A Golf Course; A City Park; A Bridge; A Modernized Farm; A Mountain.

L. Assume that a friend of yours in a distant city has agreed to meet at the station someone he or she has never seen. Write for that friend an adequate description of a relative, your roommate, a classmate, or a close friend.

46 Exercises

M. Make individual and write a character sketch of one of the following: A College Dean; A Typical Clubwoman; A Member of My Family; My Best Friend; The Cashier at a Motion Picture Theater; A Camp Counselor; A Fraternity Brother; A Coed; An Actress as She Appears in the Part of a Specific Character; Our Family Physician; A Good Teacher; My High School Principal; A Campus Leader; An Unforgettable Character; Man (or Woman) of the Year.

N. Write an informal (expanded) definition (300 to 500 words long) of one or more of the following: Dictatorship; A Roommate; An English Composition Class; A Theme; Hydroponics; A State Fair; Sorority Tea; Fraternity Rush; A Good Sport; The Ideal Wife (or Husband); Television; Student Government; 4-H Club; Campus Politics; Code of Honor; Rewriting; S O S; Cutthroat Competition; Scholars and Students; any limited term in sport (Lateral Pass; Offside; Strike; Net Ball; Three-Bagger; Technical Foul; Knockout; Hole in One; etc.).

O. Write a narrative exposition explaining one of the following processes:

1. How an Automatic Washing Machine Works (or any similar mechanism).
2. The Manufacture of Paper (or any similar process that you know about or have observed in a factory).
3. Producing an Amateur Play.
4. Dressing for a Formal Dance.
5. The Principle of Jet Propulsion.
6. Mimeographing.
7. Cooking with a Pressure Cooker.
8. Fluorescent Lighting.
9. The Method of Electing Class Officers.
10. Air Conditioning.

P. Write a "giving directions" theme on one of the following:

1. How to Make a Tossed Salad (or some other appetizing food).
2. How to Lead a Boy Scout (Girl Scout) Troop.
3. How to Change an Automobile Tire.
4. How to Study Successfully.
5. How to Make an Eight-O'clock Class.

264

6. How to Prepare for an Examination.
7. Rules for Driving in City Traffic.
8. A Guide to (or Through) a Building, Factory, Park, Campus, Historical Site, etc. (make definite).
9. Directions for Getting to (name some place).
10. How to Make a Strike in Bowling (or any other limited action in a sport).
11. How I Learned to Swim (or some other physical activity).
12. How I Budget My Time.
13. How I Earn My Spending Money.
14. How I Taught My Dog Tricks.
15. How I Developed My Hobby of —.

Q. Write a theme for a named person on a subject beginning: "So You Want to Learn to . . . ."

R. Write a descriptive exposition on one of the following: Automatic Washer, Deep-Freeze Unit, Electric Fan, Camera, Opaque Projector, Movie Film, Ball Point Pen, Desk Calendar, Microscope, Lawn Mower, Can Opener, Storm Windows, Drawing Board, Model Airplane, Electric Shaver, etc.

S. Choose from each of the following groups one that you liked (or like) best and one that you liked (or like) least. Write a criticism of each: book (fiction), book (nonfiction), magazine, newspaper, movie, radio program, television program, musical composition, dramatic production, short story.

T. Write a theme for a named person on one of the following subjects. Begin each theme title with the words "This is a . . . ."

Town You Should Visit; Program You Should Hear; Meal You Would Enjoy; Girl (Boy) Whom You Should Know; Professor Whom You Should Have; Activity You Should Enter; Book You Should Read; Profession You Should Enter; Hobby You Should Have; Movie You Should Not Miss.

U. Make a list of twelve theme subjects to be developed as argument. Distribute your subjects equally among the following:

1. The Advantages of —.
2. The Disadvantages of —.
3. The Value of —.
4. Why I Am in Favor of —.
5. Why I Am Opposed to —.

6. Why — Should — (Example: Why Mission College Should Adopt the Honor System).

THE PRÉCIS AND THE PARAPHRASE

47. "You went to the movies last night, didn't you? What was the picture about?" "What did you do in the city this afternoon?" "Write a brief statement concerning the essential ideas in Thackeray's essay on Addison." All such questions, asked in conversation and on examinations, require summarizing answers—an indispensable form of communication in modern college life. Many times each day we are called upon to give, in written or oral form, condensed versions of events, ideas, or impressions.

In fact, the method of summary is generally prevalent. Such a popular magazine as *The Reader's Digest* is largely composed of summaries of more detailed articles in other periodicals, and the editorial technique involved has been employed by dozens of imitative "digest" magazines. Certain periodicals publish digests of even entire books. Radio news commentators furnish what are essentially summaries of the latest news developments. ("For further details, see your daily newspaper.") Magazines such as *Time* and *Newsweek* contain short articles which are, in one sense, condensations of events. Business and industrial executives frequently have occasion to ask their employees to submit brief reports concerning developments in their departments or trends in business or research, or to write brief introductory summaries of longer reports. The illustrations need not be continued; all of us could mention other examples of the use of summaries.

A summary, as a condensed version of a longer passage or a more extended account, has several forms: the *abstract,* the *digest,* the *synopsis,* the *résumé,* the *epitome,* the *précis.* Of these forms of summary, the most widely used is the précis.

THE PRÉCIS

A précis (form both singular and plural, pronounced *pray-see'*) is a brief summary of the essential thought of a longer composition. It attempts to provide a miniature of the original selection,

on a 3000 comp. a 750 précis

reproducing the same proportions on smaller scale, the same ideas, and the same mood and tone, so far as possible. The maker of a précis cannot interpret or comment; his sole function is to give a reduced photograph of the original author's exact and essential meaning. Nor can he omit important details.

Instructors frequently require précis in both oral and written form because they realize how effective the summarized method is in developing students' capacities for *careful reading* and *constructive thinking*. English teachers often assign as a theme topic the making of a précis of some selected passage, because they realize the importance of teaching *exact writing*. The composition of a good précis is difficult, therefore, because careful reading, constructive thinking, and exact writing require time and effort. In making a précis, follow these suggestions:

47a. Select carefully the material to be condensed.

Some selections can be reduced satisfactorily, but others are so tightly knit that condensation is virtually impossible. You can make précis of novels, short stories, speeches, or poems, but do not select material the style of which is especially compact and epigrammatic. Avoid material which has already been summarized, edited, or abridged; "continual distillation" cannot accurately indicate the essential thought of the original composition.

47b. Read the selection carefully.

The major purpose of a précis is to present faithfully, as briefly and clearly as possible, the important ideas of the selection being "cut down." In order to grasp the central ideas, you must read carefully, analytically, and reflectively. Look up the meanings of all words and phrases about which you are in doubt. Do not skim, but look for important or key expressions. Before starting to write, you must, to use Sir Francis Bacon's phrase, "chew and digest" the selection, not merely "taste" it or "swallow" it whole in a single gulp. You must see how the material has been organized, what devices the writer has used, what kinds of illustrations support the main thought. You must be sure to distinguish fact and opinion, and you will want to question critically the writer's statements. These suggestions are, of course, those which you would ordinarily follow every time that you attempt to read and to think as intelligently as you can.

47c. Use your own words.

Quoting sentences—perhaps topic sentences—from each paragraph results in a sentence outline, not a précis. You must use your own words for the most part, although a little quotation is permissible. Ordinarily, the phrasing of the original will not be suitable for your purposes. Once you have mastered the thought of the selection, your problem is one of original composition. You are guided and aided by the order and wording of the material, but the précis itself represents your own analysis and statement of the main thought.

47d. Do not use too many words.

The précis should usually be about one-third to one-fourth as long as the original. Nothing of real importance can be omitted, but you must remember that the central aim of a précis is condensation. The length of a condensation cannot arbitrarily be determined, but it is safe to say that most prose can be reduced by two-thirds to three-fourths. Some verse is so compact that it can hardly be condensed at all; other verse can be shortened far more than most good prose.

47e. Do not alter the plan of the original.

Follow the logical order of the original so that the condensation will be accurate. Thoughts and facts should not be rearranged; if they are, the essence of the original may be distorted. Give attention to proportion. Try to preserve as much as possible of the mood and tone of the original.

47f. Write the précis in good English.

The condensation should not be a jumble of disconnected words and faulty sentences. It should be a model of exact and emphatic diction and clear, effective sentence construction, because it must be intelligible to a reader who has not seen the original. Transition from sentence to sentence must be smooth and unobtrusive, emphasizing the unity of the summarization. The précis is not often likely to be so well written as the original, but it should read smoothly and possess compositional merit of its own.

The following example of a précis was written by a student:

268

ORIGINAL

For a hundred years and more the monarchy in France had been absolute and popular. It was beginning now to lose both power and prestige. A sinister symptom of what was to follow appeared when the higher ranks of society began to lose their respect for the sovereign. It started when Louis XV selected as his principal mistress a member of the middle class, it continued when he chose her successor from the streets. When the feud between Madame Du Barry and the Duke de Choiseul ended in the dismissal of the Minister, the road to Chanteloup, his country house, was crowded with carriages, while familiar faces were absent from the court at Versailles. For the first time in French history the followers of fashion flocked to do honor to a fallen favorite. People wondered at the time, but hardly understood the profound significance of the event. The king was no longer the leader of society. Kings and presidents, prime ministers and dictators, provide at all times a target for the criticism of philosophers, satirists, and reformers. Such criticism they can usually afford to neglect, but when the time-servers, the sycophants, and the courtiers begin to disregard them, then should the strongest of them tremble on their thrones. (208 words.)

—DUFF COOPER, Talleyrand

PRÉCIS

For more than a hundred years the monarchy in France had been absolute and popular. But Louis XV lost the respect of the upper ranks of society by choosing his mistresses from lower classes. When the feud of the Duke de Choiseul with Madame Du Barry resulted in the Minister's dismissal, the court turned its attention to him, away from the king. The king, no longer the leader of society, could well tremble for his throne. (76 words.)

THE PARAPHRASE

Not a form of summary but another type of "report on reading" widely required in college work is the paraphrase. A paraphrase is unlike a précis in that the latter is a digest of the essential meaning of an original passage, whereas a paraphrase is a full-length statement of that meaning. It is a free rendering of the sense of a passage, fully and proportionately, but in different words.

The paraphrase is most frequently used to make clear any wording which is vague, obscure, or difficult, a process usually consisting of both simplification and modernization. Each of you has read a particularly difficult poem or an especially abstruse discussion in philosophy which you could not make sense of until you put it into your own words. After you did so, its meaning was clear, and you felt that you had actually translated the passage into your own thought processes. Much of the discussion in English and social science classrooms begins with a paraphrasing of the ideas expressed in assignments from textbooks. In other words, every student has almost daily need for reshaping source material to suit his own discussional purposes.

In making a paraphrase, follow these suggestions:

47g. Study the original passage.

"Study" here means that you should read the original passage as often as necessary in order to understand its full and exact meaning. It is impossible properly to paraphrase a passage until you have mastered its essential content, until you are familiar with its purposes, organization, and method of getting at the central idea. Just as in making a précis, you must read as well and think as consistently as you can. Some phrases and sentences you will probably have to reread several times, carefully and reflectively, before their meaning will "come alive" for you. If the passage contains obscure words and allusions about which you are in doubt, consult a dictionary or other reference book to determine their meanings.

47h. Use your own words.

Try to find understandable equivalents for words and phrases which are obscure, but do not strain for synonyms. Repeat words whose meaning is unmistakably clear; restrict your changes to passages which actually require simplification or modernization. Do not fail to make necessary changes just because it is difficult to do so.

47i. Leave out nothing of importance.

A paraphrase is a restatement and, as such, should contain the thought of the original in its entirety. Omitting significant detail is a violation of the original and results in distortion.

47j. Add nothing which is not in the original.

A paraphrase is not designed to be a *full* interpretation; it should not contain the paraphraser's own comments. Interpretation and explanation should be confined to making clear what the original author had in mind and should not convey the paraphraser's additional ideas. Whether you like or dislike what the writer has said, whether you agree or disagree with him, whether you think his logic is sound or faulty—these considerations do not enter into the making of the paraphrase. To make a paraphrase does not mean that you cease to think; it means that your thinking produces fulllength statement of another's meaning.

47k. Retain the form and tone of the original.

As closely as clarity will permit, follow the form and tone of the material being paraphrased. If obscurity cannot otherwise be overcome, recast the passage, but be careful not to distort or to parody. Obviously, a paraphraser can hardly hope to achieve the same mood and tonal quality as the author of, say, a great poem, but he should try to preserve as much of these existing qualities as possible.

47l. Use good English.

Any paraphrase of a good poem or prose passage is worth far less than the original, but the better the paraphrase, the less the difference between it and the original. In addition to careful reading and constructive thinking, the making of a good paraphrase, just as of an effective précis, requires exact writing. Correct, clear diction and sentence structure are indispensable to the successful paraphrase.

The following is a paraphrase made by a student. Criticize it in terms of the suggestions given above.

ON FIRST LOOKING INTO CHAPMAN'S HOMER
>Much have I travell'd in the realms of gold,
>And many goodly states and kingdoms seen;
>Round many western islands have I been
>Which bards in fealty to Apollo hold.
>Oft of one wide expanse had I been told
>That deep-brow'd Homer ruled as his demesne:
>Yet did I never breathe its pure serene
>Till I heard Chapman speak out loud and bold:
>Then felt I like some watcher of the skies
>When a new planet swims into his ken;
>Or like stout Cortez, when with eagle eyes

> He stared at the Pacific—and all his men
> Look'd at each other with a wild surmise—
> Silent, upon a peak in Darien.
>
> —John Keats

PARAPHRASE

I have read widely in the great classics of literature and have noted many examples of great poetry. I had often been told of the work of Homer and the poetry which he had created, but I never really understood or appreciated its great beauty and power until I read Chapman's translation. Then I felt as awed as some astronomer who unexpectedly discovers a new planet, or as surprised and speechless as Cortez (Balboa) and his followers when they saw the Pacific Ocean for the first time, from Panama.

EXERCISES

A. Look up in your dictionary these words: *précis, abstract, summary, epitome, outline, compendium, synopsis, abridgment, digest, résumé.*

B. Write several précis of materials from your book of readings. Include one narrative and one expository selection.

C. Select several articles in a current *Reader's Digest.* In your library obtain the magazines referred to. Compare the shortened versions with the original versions.

D. Choose an article in a current magazine and condense it as *The Reader's Digest* would.

E. Write a précis of these three paragraphs from a speech by Franklin D. Roosevelt:

Experts in vital statistics now calculate that we shall have reached a point of stationary population within approximately the next twenty-five years.

For two centuries the dramatic aspect of national growth was territorial expansion—successive waves from the Atlantic to the Allegheny Mountains, to the Mississippi Valley, to the prairies, to the Rocky Mountains, to the Pacific Coast. The addition of improved lands has come to a stop; in fact, in many parts we have overdone it and must restore some of them to more natural conditions.

With these have appeared other evidences of maturity. For a period following the establishment of the Union, about 85 per cent of our people lived on farms; today nearly 75 per cent live in cities and villages. During our earlier years, the proportion of young people in the population increased much more rapidly than the proportion of old people. Today, for various reasons, the proportion of old is increasing more rapidly than the proportion of young people.

F. Write a précis of the following selection from James Harvey Robinson's "On Various Kinds of Thinking":

A third kind of thinking is stimulated when anyone questions our belief and opinions. We sometimes find ourselves changing our minds without any resistance or heavy emotion, but if we are told that we are wrong we resent the imputation and harden our hearts. We are incredibly heedless in the formation of our beliefs, but find ourselves filled with an illicit passion for them when anyone proposes to rob us of their companionship. It is obviously not the ideas themselves that are dear to us, but our self-esteem, which is threatened. We are by nature stubbornly pledged to defend our own from attack, whether it be our person, our family, our property, or our opinion. A United States Senator once remarked to a friend of mine that God Almighty could not make him change his mind on our Latin-America policy. We may surrender, but rarely confess ourselves vanquished. In the intellectual world at least peace is without victory.

Few of us take the pains to study the origin of our cherished convictions; indeed, we have a natural repugnance to so doing. We like to continue to believe what we have been accustomed to accept as true, and the resentment aroused when doubt is cast upon any of our assumptions leads us to seek every manner of excuse for clinging to them. The result is that most of our so-called reasoning consists in finding arguments for going on believing as we already do.[3]

G. Write a précis of this passage from Louis R. Reid's "American Movies Today":

Unchallenged is Hollywood's technical supremacy. In such details as photography, sound recording, set and costume designing, the California producers lead the world. Their artistic progress is still hampered by the seemingly inescapable necessity of making their dominant appeal to childish intelligence. Of secondary importance is that production

[3] From *The Mind in the Making*, by James Harvey Robinson. Copyright, 1921, by Harper & Brothers.

based upon a maturity of story and treatment. Upon those occasions when progressive and imaginative directors break away from trite and childish formulae to make pictures of mature intelligence, the result, in many instances, has been astonishingly profitable. Such films have been received with rejoicing among that portion of the public to whom movie-going means something more than a time-passing habit or an escape from realities.

So responsive are the West coast artisans to this acclaim that they have fallen into the grievous error of copying their newly-found formulae to tiresome lengths. Thus has come a succession of films, built upon the themes which had proved refreshingly adult. So impressed is Hollywood by what seems sure-fire that variety and change of pace, the mainstays of all genuinely successful amusement, are neglected.[4]

H. Look up in your dictionary the meaning of *paraphrase, translation, parody, version, interpretation.*

I. As your instructor suggests, write either a paraphrase or a précis of each of the following poems. All of them have been selected because they particularly lend themselves to both of these methods of study.

From SONNETS
XXIX

When, in disgrace with Fortune and men's eyes,
I all alone beweep my outcast state,
And trouble deaf heaven with my bootless cries,
And look upon myself and curse my fate,
Wishing me like to one more rich in hope,
Featured like him, like him with friends possessed,
Desiring this man's art, and that man's scope,
With what I most enjoy contented least;
Yet in these thoughts myself almost despising,
Haply I think on thee; and then my state,
Like to the lark at break of day arising
From sullen earth, sings hymns at heaven's gate;
  For thy sweet love remembered such wealth brings
  That then I scorn to change my state with kings.

—WILLIAM SHAKESPEARE

[4] From *America Now*, edited by Harold E. Stearns.

Sonnet I *from* DIVINA COMMEDIA

Oft have I seen at some cathedral door
A laborer, pausing in the dust and heat,
Lay down his burden, and with reverent feet
Enter, and cross himself, and on the floor
Kneel to repeat his paternoster o'er;
Far off the noises of the world retreat;
The loud vociferations of the street
Become an undistinguishable roar.
So, as I enter here from day to day,
And leave my burden at this minster gate,
Kneeling in prayer, and not ashamed to pray,
The tumult of the time disconsolate
To inarticulate murmurs dies away,
While the eternal ages watch and wait.

   —Henry Wadsworth Longfellow

DOVER BEACH

The sea is calm to-night,
The tide is full, the moon lies fair
Upon the Straits;—on the French coast, the light
Gleams, and is gone; the cliffs of England stand,
Glimmering and vast, out in the tranquil bay.
Come to the window, sweet is the night air!
Only, from the long line of spray
Where the sea meets the moon-blanch'd sand,
Listen! you hear the grating roar
Of pebbles which the waves suck back, and fling,
At their return, up the high strand,
Begin, and cease, and then again begin,
With tremulous cadence slow, and bring
The eternal note of sadness in.

 Sophocles long ago
Heard it on the Aegean, and it brought
Into his mind the turbid ebb and flow
Of human misery; we
Find also in the sound a thought,
Hearing it by this distant northern sea.

The sea of faith
Was once, too, at the full, and round earth's shore
Lay like the folds of a bright girdle furl'd;
But now I only hear
Its melancholy, long, withdrawing roar,
Retreating to the breath
Of the night-wind down the vast edges drear
And naked shingles of the world.

  Ah, love, let us be true
To one another! for the world, which seems
To lie before us like a land of dreams,
So various, so beautiful, so new,
Hath really neither joy, nor love, nor light,
Nor certitude, nor peace, nor help for pain;
And we are here as on a darkling plain
Swept with confused alarms of struggle and flight,
Where ignorant armies clash by night.
                                                —MATTHEW ARNOLD

USING THE LIBRARY

48. A library is virtually a laboratory where deposits of the written word and the graphic portrayal of thought preserved in manuscripts, print, and picture are available to the reader, the investigator, and the creative worker. A knowledge of what these resources are and an understanding of how they are organized are prerequisites for your effective use of this library-laboratory.

Libraries differ greatly in actual content and physical arrangement, but the basic principles which determine the organization of library resources have been sufficiently standardized to enable the student familiar with them to proceed with an investigation in any library. Whether familiar or not with library organization, you are urged to examine *Guide to the Use of Libraries* (by Margaret Hutchins, et al.) or *A Handbook of Library Usage* (by Merrill T. Eaton and C. M. Louttit).

There are three important kinds of material which a student has at his disposal in every library: reference works, periodicals, and the general collection of books.

48a. Become familiar with the reference works in your library.

In doing research, unless you know in advance what books and magazine articles are best suited to your needs, you should start with a study of condensed, authoritative articles in reference books. Any book may be used for reference purposes, but reference books "are usually comprehensive in scope, condensed in treatment, and arranged on some special plan to facilitate the ready and accurate finding of information."[5] Such works are usually segregated as a special collection on shelves open to the student in the main reading room or in a nearby reference room.

The following list contains the titles of works which are likely to be most valuable to the undergraduate student. The page references in parentheses are to I. G. Mudge's *Guide to Reference Books*.[6]

1. BOOKS OF GENERAL INFORMATION.

   A. General Encyclopedias.
      Columbia Encyclopedia. (p. 42)
      Encyclopædia Britannica. (p. 43)
      Encyclopedia Americana. (p. 41)
      New International Encyclopaedia. (p. 41)
   B. General Dictionaries.
      Funk and Wagnalls New Standard Dictionary of the English Language. (p. 53)
      Murray's *New English Dictionary on Historical Principles.* (Often referred to as the Oxford Dictionary.) (p. 54)
      Webster's New International Dictionary of the English Language. (p. 53)
   C. Special Dictionaries and Wordbooks.
      Crabb's English Synonyms. (p. 58)
      Fowler's *Dictionary of Modern English Usage.* (p. 56)
      Mencken, Henry Louis, *The American Language* and Supplements I, II. (Supplement to Mudge, 1944–1946, p. 14)
      Roget's *Thesaurus of English Words and Phrases.* (p. 58)

---

[5] I. G. Mudge, *Guide to Reference Books* (6th ed.; Chicago: American Library Association, 1936), p. 2.

[6] *Ibid.* The student is urged to consult these references. The *Guide* furnishes full bibliographic details and helpful critical discussions. There are supplements for 1936 to date.

Webster's Dictionary of Synonyms. (Supplement to Mudge, 1941–1943, p. 16)

D. Yearbooks.

American Year Book. (p. 121)
Americana Annual. (p. 42)
Annual Register (British). (p. 343)
New International Year Book. (p. 43)
Statesman's Yearbook. (p. 122)
Statistical Abstract. (p. 123)
The World Almanac. (p. 121)

(Outstanding events, changes, and progress in the fields of industry, government, literature, and education should be sought in the yearbooks for the period. The *Statesman's Yearbook,* for example, gives data regarding the government, area, population, education, religion, and industries of every nation and state in the world, including the United States.)

2. BOOKS OF SPECIAL SUBJECT INFORMATION.

A. Some Basic Reference Works in Various Fields.

Cambridge Ancient History. (p. 340)
Cambridge Medieval History. (p. 341)
Cambridge Modern History. (p. 341)
Catholic Encyclopedia. (p. 108)
Dictionary of American History. (Supplement to Mudge, 1938–1940, p. 72)
Encyclopaedia of the Social Sciences. (p. 113)
Grove's Dictionary of Music and Musicians. (p. 224)
Jewish Encyclopedia. (p. 111)
O'Rourke, Charles E., *General Engineering Handbook.* (Supplement to Mudge, 1938–1940, p. 40)
Van Nostrand's Scientific Encyclopedia. (Supplement to Mudge, 1944–1946, p. 34)

(Subject encyclopedias are usually broader in scope than their titles indicate. They are especially useful for supplying a brief history of a special subject, together with a selected bibliography for further study.)

B. Biography.

Authors Today and Yesterday. (p. 301)
Current Biography. (Supplement to Mudge, 1938–1940, p. 57)
Dictionary of American Biography. (p. 284) *D A B*

Reader's Guide
Poole's Index

Dictionary of National Biography. (English) (p. 286) *DNB*
Living Authors. (p. 301)
Who's Who. (Principally British) (p. 287)
Who's Who in America. (p. 285)

C. Literature—Special Indexes.

A.L.A. Index . . . to General Literature. (p. 27)
Essay and General Literature Index. (p. 27)
Firkins' *Index to Short Stories.* (With Supplement) (p. 241)
Firkins' *Index of Plays, 1800–1926.* (With Supplement) (p. 240)
Granger's *Index to Poetry and Recitations.* (p. 242)

D. Literature—General Reference Books, Quotation Books, and Guides.

Baker's *Guide to the Best Fiction.* (p. 241)
Baker's *Guide to Historical Fiction.* (p. 241)
Bartlett's *Familiar Quotations.* (p. 234)
Book Review Digest. (p. 13)
Cambridge History of American Literature. (p. 243)
Cambridge History of English Literature. (p. 243)
Masterpieces of World Literature in Digest Form, ed. by Frank N. Magill, 1952. (Not listed in Mudge.)
Oxford Companion to American Literature. (Supplement to Mudge, 1941–1943, p. 50)
Oxford Companion to Classical Literature. (Supplement to Mudge, 1945–1947, p. 39)
Oxford Companion to English Literature. (p. 244)
Sonnenschein's *Best Books.* (p. 414)
Stevenson's *Home Book of Quotations.* (p. 234)
U. S. Catalog, with *Cumulative Book Index.* (p. 382)

Of the *general* encyclopedias, the *Britannica* is the most scholarly, the *Americana* the most recent, the *New International* the most useful at time of publication but somewhat outdated for subjects of current interest. (Annual supplements to each of these encyclopedias may be used to bring material up to date.) Among the *special subject* reference books, the *Encyclopaedia of the Social Sciences* (E.S.S.), the *Dictionary of National Biography* (D.N.B.), and the *Dictionary of American Biography* (D.A.B.) are indispensable.

In general, students should prefer the special encyclopedias for

279

subjects within their scope. *Encyclopaedia of the Social Sciences* (E.S.S.), for example, is usually superior to the general encyclopedias for treatment of political, social, and economic subjects and for all topics relating to human welfare and relationships. The "best" encyclopedia to use for a given topic often depends upon the phase of a subject being investigated. For example, *advertising* is touched upon in the general encyclopedias, but *Advertising as a Business* is more satisfactorily treated in E.S.S.

The American Yearbook is often used in supplementing E.S.S. (and other reference books) and is quite satisfactory for the general type of topic discussed in the *Americana* and the *New International*.

48b. Become familiar with indexes to periodicals.

If you are doing research on a subject of contemporary interest or recent occurrence, you will need to consult magazine files. Libraries usually display current issues of the best general magazines and some of special interest, but older issues are bound in book form and can be obtained most easily after you have consulted the reference books which contain catalogues of the magazines' contents. The most helpful of these indexes are:

1. *Reader's Guide to Periodical Literature.*
   (This catalogue indexes many important magazine articles from 1900 to date, usually under headings of author and subject.) Cf. Mudge, *op. cit.*, p. 7.
2. *Poole's Index to Periodical Literature.*
   (This is an index of articles, by subject only, from 1802–1906.) Cf. Mudge, *op. cit.*, p. 6.
3. *International Index to Periodicals,* 1907–
   Cf. Mudge, *op. cit.*, p. 8.
4. *Public Affairs Information Service.*
   Cf. Mudge, *op. cit.*, p. 16.
5. *The New York Times Index,* 1913–
   (This is a guide to events of national importance by reference to date, page, and column.) Cf. Mudge, *op. cit.*, p. 25.
6. *Agricultural Index,* 1916–
   (This is a cumulative subject index of a selected list of agricultural bulletins and periodicals.) Cf. Mudge, *op. cit.*, p. 11.
7. *Engineering Index,* 1884–

(Since 1928 this index has been an author-subject index of periodicals in all engineering fields.) Cf. Mudge, *op. cit.,* pp. 16–17.

8. *Industrial Arts Index,* 1913–

(This is a subject index of a selected list of engineering, trade, and business periodicals, books, and pamphlets.) Cf. Mudge, *op. cit.,* p. 17.

9. *Facts on File,* 1940–

(This is both an index and a digest of world events.) Cf. Supplement to Mudge, 1941–1943, p. 63.

10. *Art Index,* 1929–

(This is a cumulative author and subject index to magazines dealing with the fine arts.) Cf. Mudge, *op. cit.,* p. 12.

11. *Education Index,* 1929–

(This is a cumulative author and subject index to magazines in the entire field of education.) Cf. Mudge, *op. cit.,* p. 13.

12. *Index to Legal Periodicals,* 1908–

Cf. Mudge, *op. cit.,* p. 14.

48c. Become familiar with the general collection of books in your library.

The most important part of a library is the main collection of books. In order to obtain them for your own use, you need to consult the card catalogue. This catalogue is the index of the whole library. It consists of 3 x 5 inch cards which are filed alphabetically in a series of cabinets. Book information may be found in the card catalogue in three ways: (1) by author, (2) by title, and (3) by subject. Each book in the library is represented in the catalogue by several cards.

The three catalogue cards on p. 283 are subject, title, and author cards for the same book. In all libraries, every nonfiction book is represented by at least three cards, usually identical except that the subject headings are typed, in either black capitals or red type, at the top of the card. The subject headings (i.e., entries for the subjects with which the book deals) follow the Arabic numerals near the bottom of the card. A separate card is filed in the card catalogue for each such entry. Title cards, joint author cards, etc., are typed in black.

If you know the author or the title of a book you want, you can most easily get the needed information about the book from the author or title card. But if you know neither author nor title, turn to the cards that list books dealing with the subject upon which you are working and make your choices from the collection there.

In addition to revealing the resources of the library, the card catalogue gives the call number by means of which each book is located on the shelves. Some libraries are so arranged that all or part of the books are placed on open shelves easily accessible to the students. In other libraries the main collection is shelved on enclosed stacks. To obtain a book in this case, you must fill out a "call slip" furnished by the library and present it at the Circulation or Loan Desk.

The student who has access to the book collection will soon discover that the books are arranged according to a definite system, the notational expression of which is the first part of the call number. The two classification systems most commonly used in this country are the Dewey Decimal Classification and the Library of Congress Classification. Books classified by either system are arranged according to the subjects they treat.

Students who are baffled and bewildered by myriad trays of cards filed in the card catalogue see neither rhyme nor reason in the filing system. Some libraries follow a strictly alphabetical order, but the majority observes the rules outlined below.

All libraries file by entry, i.e., according to what appears first on the card, whether author, subject, or title. Articles appearing as the first word of a title are ignored; most libraries file letter-by-letter to the end of the word. This means that the title card, *The American way,* is filed in front of the subject card, AMERICANISMS, just as all cards beginning "New York" are filed in front of cards with "Newark" as the entry word. Libraries which file in strictly alphabetical order, of course, place *-isms* before *way* and *-ark* before *York.* Incidentally, encyclopedias, as well as library catalogues, differ in this fundamental rule.

Books *about* an author (considered subject entries and typed in red or in black capitals) are filed before or after all books *by* that author.

Author cards having the same surname as the entry word are

filed according to the given name; always make a note of the first
name, or at least the initials, of an author and of the *exact* title of
the book you want.

Abbreviations and numerals are filed just as they would be if
the word they represent were spelled out.

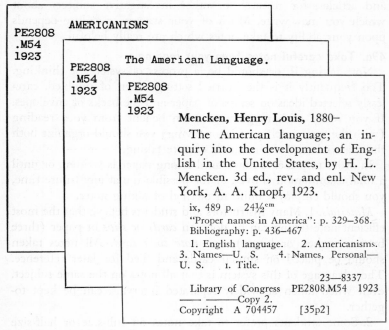

When the entry word is the same, all authors by that name
precede all subjects, and all subjects precede all titles. For example,
Washington, George (books by), WASHINGTON, GEORGE
(books about), *Washington merry-go-round* (title) are entered in
that order.

The regulations which any one library establishes for its users
appear in various forms. Before beginning research on any subject
or for any paper or article, you should find out whether your
particular library has a guide or handbook which explains or
interprets its organization.

49 a

TAKING NOTES

49. As a college student you will spend much time taking notes in your room, in the library, and in the classroom. Both now and later you will be faced with the problem of taking notes, on books and articles, for research or other investigative subjects about which you may write. Much of your success or failure depends upon your ability to take notes which are really helpful.

49a. Take careful notes from your reading.

Note taking is, or should be, a process of systematic thinking. Too frequently it is the hurried setting down of jumbled, carelessly selected ideas on scraps of paper and the backs of envelopes. If you really wish to get maximum benefit from your reading (with the most intelligent labor saving) you should organize both the materials and the methods of note taking.

In order to preserve notes until a long paper is written, or until a final examination is over, or for possible use at any future time, you should employ a uniform method of taking notes.

Materials. 1. Many instructors and students believe that the most efficient note taking can be done on *cards or slips* of paper (three by five inches, or larger), *one note to a card*. All notes taken should be placed on similar cards and filed for later reference. The advantage of this system is that all notes on the same subject, even when taken at widely separated intervals, can be kept together.

2. Some students prefer to take notes on full-size or half-size sheets of paper, or *loose-leaf notebook* paper. (Bound notebooks are usually unsatisfactory.) If you use such materials, remember to keep notes on a particular book or article together and organize your notes on the various phases of the subject as you proceed.

Methods. More important than the materials used for recording notes are the methods employed. In order to save time and trouble later and to prevent assembling a hodgepodge of quotations and undigested raw material, follow this technique, however tedious and cumbersome it may seem:

1. Before you begin to take notes on a book, study its Preface and Table of Contents. From these you will find out the scope

284

and purpose of the book. If you are going to read only one chapter from a book, or a magazine article, skim through it first, and then begin to read carefully and take notes. If the book has an index, you may save time by examining it for your particular subject or for related materials.

2. Record accurately and fully the details about the source of information. Your notes must be clear and full, or you will have to make trip after trip to the library to supply missing information. Get all the information you need and *get it the first time.* Notes must be *clear,* so that you can read and understand them later; *full,* so that you can supply adequate information about sources in both footnotes and bibliography; *exact,* so that you can quote or paraphrase accurately; *organized,* so that you can make ready use of what you have assembled.

3. Condense your notes. They should be as full as needed but not so lengthy that main ideas are obscured in a mass of detail. Make frequent use of topic sentences (see Section 53), summaries, and synopses.

4. Rearrange and regroup your notes as your work proceeds. Keep your notes on a single subject together; do not let notes become mixed with others even on the same general subject. This segregation is especially important whenever numerous books or articles are consulted. (If you are writing a research paper, you will of course be analyzing your subject, and you will be making— through your analysis and through the arrangement and grouping of your notes—a preliminary outline of your paper. In this way, you will be able to keep on the main track of the investigation and not be totally surprised at the end of your note taking by the manner in which your investigation has run away with you. And you will be more thoroughly prepared for the next major step in the preparation of your paper.)

5. Be careful to distinguish fact and opinion in your reading and in the notes themselves. In weighing opinions, consider the facts upon which the opinions are based, the point of view of the author, and the date of publication of the material.

The specimen cards on page 287 illustrate use of the methods suggested.

Not all cards will note material directly quoted. Some will digest or summarize in your own words the ideas of the source; such a summarization is called a précis (see pp. 266–269). Some will give in your words a full-length statement of the meaning of the source material; such a statement is a paraphrase (see pp. 269–272). But all cards should be so complete that you need not return to the source to discover how much of the material is direct quotation, how much paraphrase, or what the bibliographical facts are.

49b. Take usable notes on lectures.

Lecture notes have various uses, two of which are as a possible source for themes and as material for basic research. In reading, you have all the time you need, but in listening to and taking notes on lectures, you have to think and write rapidly. In taking notes while reading, you have ample time to reflect and to condense and organize your notes. Lecture notes have to be taken as you listen and must be reviewed later. Thus, taking lecture notes is more difficult than making notes on reading.

The majority of students take lecture notes in bound or loose-leaf notebooks. If you are farsighted—as in taking notes on reading —you will use cards or slips. Whatever the mechanical method, keep together all the notes taken in a single course. Record the date and the subject of each lecture. Utilize the following aids:

1. "Stop, look, and listen" before you write. Do not copy the introductory words dealing with a subject, unless they are really important; wait until the point can be summarized.

2. Do not try to take down everything the lecturer says. The best lecture notes are always condensed; they contain in summary and outline form the gist of what was said.

3. Abbreviate in order to save time. Make up a list of abbreviations, such as $\bar{c}$ for "with"; $\therefore$ for "therefore"; $=$ for "equal"; & for "and"; tr. for "translation," etc.

4. Try to keep your mind on the lecture. Psychologists state that full attention cannot be maintained for more than a short time, but you can learn so to concentrate on what is being said that your "attention lapses" will be less frequent and shorter in duration.

5. Read over your notes on a lecture as soon as possible after

---

(*Lincoln*)

Democracy, definition of
" As I would not be a _slave_ so I would not be a _master_.
This expresses my idea of democracy. Whatever differs from this,
to the extent of the difference, is no democracy."

The Writings of Abraham Lincoln, edited by A. B. Lapsley, New
York, Putnam, 1906, vol. 7, p. 389.
    Quotation dated "[August 1?], 1858." Footnote to the quo-
tation: "From the original manuscript in the possession of
James B. Bradwell, Esq., Chicago, Illinois."

(*Becker*)

Democracy, definition of
    That form of government "in which the citizens, or a sufficient
number of them to represent . . . the common will, freely act from
time to time, and according to established forms, to appoint or recall
the magistrates and to enact or revoke the laws by which the community is governed."

      Carl L. Becker, Modern Democracy,
        New Haven, Yale University Press, 1941, p. 7.

---

they are taken. If they are blurred, jumbled, or difficult to read,
copy them over neatly; if your abbreviations may later lose meaning for you, write them out at once.

THE RESEARCH PAPER

50. The research paper (also called an *investigative theme* or a
term report or *term paper*) is a long theme—usually from two to
six thousand words—assigned in most college courses which require outside reading. Such a paper is designed to be more than a
mere report; its purpose is to make a careful investigation of some

subject and to present and interpret the source material in the light of the researcher's findings. It should not be merely a reading report based on several books or articles read more or less haphazardly; it should be a study, carefully controlled, which sets out with a definite purpose and accomplishes its end. The best research papers are usually extensions of phases of work actually mentioned in connection with courses for which they are prepared.

The preparation and writing of a successful research paper depend upon four major steps: (1) choosing and analyzing the subject; (2) making a thorough investigation of the subject; (3) preparing an outline; and (4) writing and revising.

50a. Choose and analyze your subject carefully.

The choice of a good subject will save you much time later. Keep these points in mind:

1. If possible, choose a subject in which you are already interested or one in which you think that you can become interested. Furthermore, do not select so abstruse or technical a subject that your readers cannot be interested.

2. Do not select too large or too small a subject. Some subjects can be treated adequately in one thousand words; an attempt to develop such subjects in five-thousand word papers results in padding, repetition, dullness. On the other hand, do not choose a subject which cannot be handled in the assigned space.

3. Choose a topic upon which enough has been written for you to obtain adequate information. Always keep in mind the resources of the library in which you will do your investigating; for example, avoid a subject which will depend heavily upon back copies of magazines which your particular library does not have. Remember that your paper should be based upon material from *several* sources: reference books, periodicals, books, perhaps newspapers and personal interviews.

4. Select a central purpose, or thesis, or controlling idea. Any logical assembling of material presupposes the support of some proposition, and all the facts you gather should lead in the direction of and help you to state your conclusions, the really important part of any research paper. You may have to change your thesis when acquired facts prove your purpose and plan untenable, for

you should never start out with a rigid, preconceived idea that you want to establish in spite of all contrary facts and evidence. A research paper, like any theme, must develop one phase of a subject, fairly and convincingly, in order to achieve one central purpose.

5. Select, but modify if necessary, the basic type of writing for your research paper. Your report may be *descriptive exposition:* for example it may describe and explain the processes involved in making rayon. It may be *narrative:* a setting forth of exactly what took place at the time of the sinking of the *Lusitania.* Or it may be *analytical;* for example, a comparison of socialism and communism would require analytical treatment of the likenesses and differences of the two systems. But whether the plan of the report is logical or chronological, the research paper must have a clear, unmistakable *purpose.*

50b. Make a thorough investigation of the subject.

The conscientious researcher ferrets out all the information he can about a given subject. A student, pressed for time, is not likely to ascertain *all* the facts, but at least he should make as thorough search as possible for pertinent detail. You must utilize the information to be found in reference books, periodicals, the general collection of books in your library, and newspapers. It is an illusion that writing a term paper and using an encyclopedia are one and the same thing. A term paper has no real value unless it does more than merely dip into a subject.

In order to make a thorough investigation of the subject:

1. Learn how to use, efficiently, the resources of your library: reference works, periodical indexes, the card catalogue and general collection of books (see Section 48a, b, c). From these resources—notably the first three—prepare a preliminary bibliography on three-by-five-inch cards, that is, a list of books and magazine or newspaper articles that are *likely* to contribute material.

2. Take careful notes from your reading (see Section 49a).

50c. Prepare an adequate outline of your paper.

Not until you have read and taken notes on available material will you be in a position to outline your research paper completely

289

and accurately. When you have worked long enough to reach definite conclusions and to see the framework of the whole structure, you can then rearrange your notes in final form, under the appropriate headings, and from them prepare a topic or sentence outline. (See Section 36.)

In making an outline for your paper, bear in mind that the object of your investigation is to find out the facts, arrange and interpret them, and present conclusions based upon them. The writer of a research paper is not necessarily a propagandist—rather is he a discoverer of fact—but he must assimilate and absorb what seems to him the truth so that he can present it to a reader who will see what definite purpose he had in mind.

50d. Write your research paper correctly, clearly, and forcefully.

After you have investigated the field thoroughly and have organized your notes and prepared an outline, you are ready to write the paper. If you have taken careful notes and arranged them properly, your work is much more than half done. But be careful to give the results of your study correct, clear, and forceful expression. To this end, you should write the body of your paper as clearly and forcefully as you can; you must take great care with footnotes and bibliography; and you must revise your paper to insure correctness and accuracy.

There is no reason why a term report should be dull and lifeless. If you have chosen an attractive subject and investigated it thoroughly, you should have little difficulty in making your paper "come alive." No penalty is attached to an occasional bit of humor in a research paper; the vitality which can be achieved by vigorous diction and neatly turned phrases will add effectiveness to the thoroughness and accuracy which the paper must have. Careful investigation and vigorous writing are not incompatible. A jumbled series of quotations and paraphrases is not a term paper. A good research report is smoothly articulated and written; the reader can grasp the thesis in pleasant, easy reading.

In addition to being correct, clear, and forceful, every investigative theme worthy of the name must be carefully documented. The suggestions which follow should enable you to provide your paper with adequate and accurately listed footnotes and bibliography, *provided your notes on reading were carefully taken.*

50e. Use footnotes to document your research paper adequately and properly.

The purpose of a footnote is to mention the authority for some fact stated or to develop some point referred to in the body of the paper.

Generally known facts or quotations do not require substantiation in footnotes, but charges of plagiarism must be avoided. Unless the idea and the phrasing are completely your own, you should refer the reader to some source for your statement. In order to be entirely honest, you will acknowledge every source of indebtedness, even when no direct quotation is used.

Frequently the writer wishes to develop, interpret, or refute some idea but does not wish an extended comment to clutter up the body of his paper. He uses a footnote.

It is impossible to state how many footnotes should appear in a research paper. One investigation may call for twice as many as another. Some pages of your paper may require a half dozen or more footnotes, others may need none or only one or two. Your guiding principle should be to acknowledge credit where it is due and to supply discussion footnotes where they are needed for understanding.

1. Adopt a standard form of footnote, and be consistent in its use.

Methods of footnoting are numerous, but whatever system you employ should be consistent throughout your paper and immediately clear to any intelligent reader. Standard usage favors this form: (1) author's Christian name or initials followed by surname; (2) title of book or periodical (in italics); (3) place of publication; (4) name of publisher; (5) date of publication; (6) volume and page reference.

In listing information about periodical material, place the title of the article or story after the author's name and before the name of the periodical. The title is put in quotation marks, the name of the magazine is italicized (underlined). The volume number, in

Roman numerals, is placed immediately after the name of the periodical. By putting the volume number in Roman numerals and the page numbers in Arabic, you avoid the necessity for volume and page abbreviations. Study the correct forms for listing the following kinds of information:

BOOKS

A. Book by one author:

[1] John R. Tunis, *This Writing Game* (New York: A. S. Barnes & Company, 1941), p. 26.

[2] Henry Louis Mencken, *The American Language* (4th ed.; New York: Alfred A. Knopf, Inc., 1936), p. 168.

B. Book by two or more authors:

[1] John Tasker Howard and Arthur Mendel, *Our American Composers* (New York: Thomas Y. Crowell Company, 1941), p. 82.

C. Book of two or more volumes:

[1] Douglas S. Freeman, *George Washington* (New York: Charles Scribner's Sons, 1948), II, 142.

D. Book cited under editor:

[1] Richard Aldington, ed., *Great French Romances* (New York: Duell, Sloan, and Pearce, 1946), p. 17.

[2] *Letters from W. H. Hudson,* ed. by Edward Garnett (New York: E. P. Dutton & Co., 1923), p. 62.

E. A translation:

[1] Homer, *The Odyssey,* tr. by George Herbert Palmer (Boston: Houghton Mifflin Company, 1891), p. 46.

ARTICLES (ESSAYS, STORIES)

A. From a magazine:

[1] Walter D. Edmonds, "Arrival of the Lily Dean," *The Saturday Evening Post,* CCX (May 7, 1938), 5.

[2] "Personality Tests," *Life,* XXI (October 7, 1946), 55.

B. From a collection:

[1] Katherine Mansfield, "Bliss," *A Study of the Short Story,* ed. by

Henry S. Canby and Alfred Dashiell (New York: Henry Holt and Company, Inc., 1935), p. 303.

NOTE: Your instructor may prefer a shorter form or one in which the information is arranged differently. For example, he may permit or require you to omit the author's first name, the place of publication, or the name of the publisher. But the examples above are models and, if other instruction is not given, should be followed. After the form has been determined upon, be consistent in its use.

2. Use the following standard footnote abbreviations.

ibid.: The same. If a footnote refers to the same source as the one referred to in the footnote *immediately* preceding, the abbreviation *ibid.* (from the Latin *ibidem* meaning "in the same place") may be used. If the volume, page, title, and author are the same, use *ibid.* alone. If the volume and page differ, use, for example, *Ibid.*, III, 206. *Ibid.* usually comes at the beginning of a footnote and is capitalized for that reason only.

op. cit.: The work cited. After the first full reference to a given work, provided no other work by the same author is mentioned in the paper, succeeding references may be indicated by the author's surname, followed by *op. cit.* (from Latin *opere citato* meaning "in the work cited") and the volume and page. Examples:

Jones, *op. cit.*, IV, 19.
Hasty, *op. cit.*, p. 94.

passim: To be employed when no specific page reference can be given. It means "everywhere," "throughout."

loc. cit.: The place cited. If the reference is to the exact passage covered by an earlier reference not immediately preceding, use *loc. cit.* (from the Latin *loco citato* meaning "in the place cited").

p.: (plural, pp.) page   v.: verse
l.: (plural, ll.) line   ante: before
vol.: volume   art.: article
chap.: (plural, chaps.) chapter   sec.: (plural, secs.) section
ff.: following   n.: (plural, nn.) note

The abbreviations *ibid.*, *op. cit.*, and *loc. cit.*, as well as *passim*, are always italicized (underlined).

Many writers now use the short title convention for footnote references other than the first. The following examples illustrate this form:

First entry:
  [1] Sir Arthur Quiller-Couch, *On the Art of Writing* (New York: Putnam, 1930), 84.

Subsequent entry for the same book:
  [2] Quiller-Couch, *Art of Writing*, p. 92.

First entry:
  [1] Clifton Fadiman, "Herman Melville," *The Atlantic Monthly*, CLXXII (October, 1943), 88.

Subsequent entry for the same article:
  [2] Fadiman, "Melville," p. 90.

3. Place the footnote numeral properly.

A footnote is indicated by an Arabic numeral placed above and to the right of the word to be commented upon. If the reference is to a quotation, place the numeral at the end of the passage. Before the actual footnote at the bottom of the page repeat the number used in the text. Do not use asterisks or other symbols in place of Arabic numerals.

Footnotes may be numbered consecutively throughout the manuscript or separately for each page. Most instructors prefer the former method.

Footnotes may be put at the bottom of pages, between lines in the manuscript proper, or all together at the end of the paper. Most instructors greatly prefer the first of these methods. If the footnotes are placed at the bottom of the page, they should not be crowded. Always leave a clearly defined space between the text and the footnotes.

50f. Use a bibliography to document your research paper properly and adequately.

A bibliography is a list of books or magazine or newspaper articles relating to a given subject and placed at the end of the manuscript. It is usually a *classified* list containing the names of all the works actually quoted from or used generally in the body of the paper. Thus a bibliography may contain more references than the sum of all the footnote references. Every formally prepared research paper should contain a bibliography.

Arrange bibliographical items correctly and consistently. Usage in the arrangement of bibliographies varies. However, keep these standard rules in mind:

Arrange the items alphabetically by the surnames of the authors. If the author's name is not given or is unknown, list the item alphabetically according to the first word (except *the* or *a*) in the title. List titles by the same author chronologically according to dates of publication. When more than one work by the same author is cited, use a 3-em dash (approximately one-half inch) in place of the author's name after its first appearance.

If the items are numerous, you may classify them in groups— books, magazine articles, and newspaper accounts. Such classification is indicated below, although the items there are not so numerous as to require separate listings.

A sentence or phrase following each item in the list is frequently helpful. Such statements should indicate the scope or content of the book or article; they comprise what is known as a *descriptive bibliography*.

Place the bibliography at the end of the paper and begin it on a separate page, not on the last page of the text.

The following is a short specimen bibliography:

BIBLIOGRAPHY

A. Books

> Allen, Hervey. *Israfel, the Life and Times of Edgar Allan Poe*. New York: Farrar & Rinehart, Inc., 1934.
>
> Boyd, Ernest Augustus. *Literary Blasphemies*. New York: Harper & Brothers, 1927, pp. 163–185.
>
> Campbell, Killis. *The Mind of Poe and Other Studies*. Cambridge, Mass.: Harvard University Press, 1933.
>
> *Encyclopædia Britannica, The* (14th Edition, 1929), XVIII, 104–105.
>
> Krutch, Joseph Wood. *Edgar Allan Poe: a Study in Genius*. New York: Alfred A. Knopf, Inc., 1926.
>
> Woodberry, George Edward. *Life of Edgar Allan Poe, Personal and*

Literary, with His Chief Correspondence with Men of Letters.
Boston: Houghton Mifflin Company, 1909, 2 vols.

B. Magazine Articles

Cooke, A. L. "Edgar Allan Poe—Critic," *Cornhill Magazine,* LXXII (November, 1934), 588–597.

Huxley, Aldous Leonard. "Vulgarity in Literature," *Saturday Review of Literature,* VII (September 27, 1930), 158–159.

Macpherson, Harriet Dorothea. "Dumas and Poe Again," *Saturday Review of Literature,* VI (February 22, 1930), 760.

Wilson, James Southall. "Devil Was in It," *American Mercury,* XXIV (October, 1931), 215–220.

50g. Revise your research paper rigorously.

After you have written the report with all the vigor and interest which you can muster, and after you have correctly indicated the footnotes and bibliography, you should allow the paper to "jell." That is, if time permits, put the report aside and forget about it for some time, several days if possible. After this "cooling" process, you will be able to come back to it with more objectivity than was possible just after you finished it. The errors which everyone makes will be more apparent to you, and you can at this time give the theme its final polishing. Give your research paper the rereadings suggested on pages 251–252, and to them add another for the sole purpose of making certain that the footnotes are accurately and uniformly listed and that the bibliography is correctly and consistently arranged.

The following research paper (reprinted by permission of the President and Fellows of Harvard College) illustrates proper methods of documentation.

THE LESS TRAVELED ROAD
by Caroline Ford

"There are two ways of coming close to poetry," says Robert Frost. "One is by writing it, and the other is by reading it."[1] After a glance at this remark, the critic probably turns the page, considering it too obvious to

[1] Robert Frost, "Education by Poetry, a Meditative Monologue," <u>Amherst Alumni Council News,</u> IV (March, 1931, Supplement), 13.

ponder over. But a little thought would convince him that the statement is not just another platitude. Although more people aspire to
be good readers than good writers of poetry,
few of these carry away from their reading anything more than personal impressions. But the
reader's personal reaction is not enough; he
will come closer to the real meaning if he
strives to understand the author's feelings
when the poem was written.

Little has been known of Frost's opinions
about poetry beyond those suggestions gleaned
from the poetry itself. For he has rarely expressed his opinions in prose and hence it is·
not surprising that readers have interpreted
his aims freely. Some learned critics differ on
the question of whether the provinciality of
Frost's subject-matter implies a limitation of
its significance; others argue that he does, or
does not, write about the world of men.[2]

It is a difficult task to follow a man's mind
through the process of creation without an
initial understanding of the man himself. Fortunately Frost draws such a vivid portrait of
himself in "New Hampshire" that the reader is
furnished with just the background he needs.
Here the poet proclaims himself a lover of New
Hampshire and of nature, a "sensibilitist and
environmentalist." As a devotee of the genuine
and as an optimist, he knows he is not a mere
juggler of words, a poseur, or a salesman of
ideas. Although he does not describe himself as
such, the poem shows him also to be a humorist.
He is, in fact, a perfect embodiment of his
poetry and has seen to it that no one shall de-
prive him of the conditions that make this
possible.

Since poetry has always been a natural medium
of expression for Frost, he has little difficulty in describing the manner in which he com-

[2]F. E. Carpenter, Review of Frost's Collected
Poems, New England Quarterly, V (January,
1932), 159; Robert Hillyer, "Robert Frost
'Lacks Power,' " ibid., V (April, 1932), 404.

poses. A reporter once heard him remark: "An
idea flashes into my mind anywhere. . . . If
I'm where I can sit right down and work it out
I do. If I'm not I tuck it away and keep my
mind averted from it."[3] This analysis brings to
mind the familiar polished phrases of Wordsworth: "Poetry is the spontaneous overflow of
powerful feelings; it takes its origin from
emotion recollected in tranquility; . . . the
tranquility gradually disappears, and an emotion kindred to that which was before the
subject of contemplation is gradually pro-
duced. . . ."[4] Clearly both poets react in much
the same way to the initial emotion and the
period of incubation that follows it. Frost,
like Wordsworth, describes the recollection of
the emotion and the new form which makes it
worthy of being written down.

That this process is not confined to these
two poets is now a matter of common knowledge.
Mr. Lowes demonstrated this fact in his analysis of Coleridge's mental processes during
creation. "In genius of the highest order,"
says Mr. Lowes, "that sudden, incalculable, and
puissant energy which pours up from the hidden
depths (of the mind) is controlled by a will
which serves a vision--the vision which sees in
chaos the potentiality of form."[5] Mr. Lowes's
"vision," Wordsworth's "emotion," and Frost's
"idea" are all expressions of the same primary
urge to creation. Mr. Lowes describes the
period of suspension of thought as "the hidden
depths of the mind"; Wordsworth implies it when
he says that the new emotion is "recollected";

---

[3] "I Will Teach Only When I Have Something to
Tell," Boston Globe, CVI (November 23, 1924,
Supplement), 3:1-5.
[4] William Wordsworth, Lyrical Ballads (1798),
preface, ed. by Harold Littledale (London:
H. Frowde, 1911), p. 246.
[5] John L. Lowes, The Road to Xanadu (Boston:
Houghton Mifflin, 1930), p. 432.

Frost plainly states that he keeps his mind
averted from his first idea.

Fortunately Frost has also described the new
emotion recollected in tranquility. His expression for Mr. Lowes's controlling will is
"believing the thing into existence," a belief
which makes you find yourself "saying as you go
more than you even hoped you were going to be
able to say, and coming with surprise to an end
that you foreknew only with some sort of
emotion."[6] This is identical with Wordsworth's
"spontaneous overflow of powerful feelings"
which has resulted in something much greater
than even the poet could anticipate. Frost
calls his definition of poetry "Words that have
become deeds." "In making a poem," he continues, "you have no right to think of anything
but the subject-matter. After making it, no
right to boast of anything but the form."[7] This
seems to imply that the poet cannot keep his
original control over the subject of his poem,
for his ideas have obtained a character of
their own during the process of being moulded
into shape. The sudden inversion of position
from riding an idea to being ridden by it is a
natural occurrence in a work of art in which a
philosophy of life is expressed. Philosophy
takes time and thought to develop and thrives
most favorably in the process of thinking, suspension of thought, and rethinking, which produces the greatest poetry. Speaking as a man
who has undergone each process with great care,
Frost has a right to his scorn for poets of
"fluid inspiration" who fake the process of
thinking by substituting a window display of
lacquered ideas.

In Frost's opinion, sincerity and individuality, which form the backbone of deep thinking,
are also characteristic of a great writer. His
requirements for such a writer, along with his

[6]Frost, "Education by Poetry," p. 15.
[7]Gorham Munson, Robert Frost (New York:
Doran, 1927), p. 97.

description of poetic method, bear a striking
similarity to those of Wordsworth, whose model
poet possesses "a greater readiness and power
in expressing what he thinks and feels"[8] than
other men. To Frost what a man thinks and
feels, which he calls his "prejudice," demands
serious cultivation:

> All that makes a writer is the ability to
> write strongly and directly from some un-
> accountable and almost invincible personal
> prejudice. . . . But most people end as
> they begin by acting out the prejudices of
> other people.[9]

The word "prejudice" as used here is typical of
Frost in its pungency and exaggeration. It
seems to me inevitable that poetry should express stronger bias than prose, since it deliberately emphasizes the striking aspects of a
given thought. One realizes that the unbiased
point of view makes tepid poetry, that it requires dogma to write anything that can burn.
Frost's particular bias is fortunate in that
both urban and rural readers respond to his
moods. Poets like Sandburg only supplement him
in stories concerning the misery of city life.
Speaking from the prejudice that man's greatest
opportunity for spiritual growth is in close
association with nature, Frost appears to have
had no contact with the newsboys and elevated
railways of urban life. Yet the prejudice he
has developed in favor of country life has
gained power through his spasmodic contacts
with the city. Not wishing to meddle with
struggles of civilization, he is yet aware of
their inevitability, as he says in "The Flood":

Blood has been harder to dam back than water.
Just when we think we have it impounded safe
Behind new barrier walls (and let it chafe!)
It breaks away in some new kind of slaughter.

One can understand how a natural lover of the
country would be even more overcome by its

[8] Wordsworth, op. cit., p. 246.
[9] From a letter to Frederick Skinner.

quiet power, knowing as he does that it cannot
be a permanent possession.

To write from a prejudice requires the most
careful analysis of one's self and one's beliefs. Frost's remarks to a friend indicate
that he has fulfilled the requirements. "I
don't want you to be a writer of exercises," he
says. "You know best whether you are haunted
with any impatience about what other people see
or don't see. That will be you if you are a
you."[10] Frost realizes that a sincere critical
view of humanity does not appear at the mere
press of a button. He knows that potential
writers are walled in by the prejudices of the
people with whom they live and by those of the
authors whom they admire. In an introduction to
the poetry of some Dartmouth undergraduates, he
says that a poet "has to begin as a cloud of
all the other poets he ever read. That can't be
helped."[11] He then demonstrates, by an elaborate metaphor, his belief that it is possible
to cease from reflecting the opinions of other
people and to coin the imprint of your own.
Frost is competent to stress the importance of
individuality because he has taken personally
each step that he describes. As a college
undergraduate he followed the accepted tradition of coming close to the world's great
thinkers. The fact that he left college without
a degree and took up residence in the country
indicates a sudden development of his individuality. He soon found out that his major
interest was New England and that he was able
to reproduce the impression it made on him.

Frost's subject is a region inhabited by many
unhappy individuals. His New England, the scene
of a diminishing farm population, is one where
fear and poverty form the axis of many lives.
Sympathy for the Yankee temperament, whether in
repressed farmers or suspected witches, makes
him capable of acute psychological interpreta-

[10] Ibid.

[11] Robert Frost, Introduction to Dartmouth
Verse (Portland, Maine: Mosher, 1925), p. vii.

tions of its moods. This insight is sharpened
by the similarity of his own philosophy of life
to that of country people. Yet his ability to
speak for them hinges also on his knowledge of
the relation of their lives to the alternative
city existence. For their sake it is fortunate
that Frost can be their spokesman from his
superior vantage point. The attainment of this
insight is a result of the fundamental process
which he follows in the creation of poetry.
Although he preferred the simple life from
early youth, it was through his subsequent experience of life in cities, when his country
sympathy was in limbo, that his feeling became
coherent. On his return to the country, he
found that the emotions he had always felt had
become well organized and could take shape as
poetry.

Many people shiver as they read about Frost's
New England characters, just as he shivered on
first meeting them as a ten-year-old alien from
California. "They seemed narrow to me," he
tells us:

   I could not get used to them. Then, when
   I was about 18 or 19, there came to me the
   pride of discernment and I found some good
   in them. I went on finding good in them,
   and after that it was hard for me to find
   any bad in them.[12]

The failure of some critics to see the greatness in these characters that Frost eventually
saw can usually be attributed, I believe, to
their unfamiliarity with the type of person
described. This would be likely to cause a lack
of sympathy with the problems of his characters.

Of these critics Amy Lowell seems to me the
most dangerous because she professes to criticize Frost's characters from a New England
standpoint. Yet her critical notes emerge
through a haze of cigar smoke and Beacon Hill
individuality. She finds his people untrue to
type in that they do not have "that pungency of

   [12] Boston _Globe_, November 23, 1924, p. 3.

thought or expression which is so ingrained in the New England temper. . . . Characters and situations impress (Frost), speech does not. It is probably for this reason that he uses no dialect in his poems."[13] Frost refutes this charge against his interest in speech, for he says distinctly: "What I am after is tones of voice."[14] In short, he is tremendously interested in speech and strives to mould the cadences of his verse along the rise and fall of conversation. It was Ezra Pound who first detected the power and accuracy of these conversations, which apparently escaped his fellow poet. I think the test of their truth lies in Pound's instinctive dislike of these "real people." "I don't want much to meet them, but I know that they exist,"[15] he says. It will be remembered that this is the precise reaction Frost felt on first acquaintance with them. If his poems can recreate that sensation, they must have the breath of life.

What Frost has succeeded in doing is to describe something "common in experience uncommon in writing,"[16] in accordance with his own definition of ideal subject-matter. In describing it he is following a great literary tradition, for this combination has appealed to all the great poets. Mr. Lowes analyzes it as something that "arises as a rule from things familiar enough to give the pleasure of recognition, yet not so trite as to rob us of the other pleasure of surprise."[17] There is familiarity in the themes of love, work, and man's relation to nature, which have always formed experience.

[13] Amy Lowell, Tendencies in Modern American Poetry (New York: The Macmillan Company, 1917), p. 125.
[14] Munson, op. cit., p. 90.
[15] Ezra Pound, "Modern Georgics," Poetry, V (December, 1914), 129.
[16] Munson, op. cit., p. 90.
[17] John L. Lowes, Convention and Revolt in Poetry (Boston: Houghton Mifflin, 1930), p. 97.

The novelty of Frost's warped individuals in
situations typical of New England gives the
touch of surprise necessary for great poetry.
Although the reader is steeped in the tradi-
tions of parental sorrow over the death of
children like Little Eva's in Uncle Tom's
Cabin, the living description of a particular
situation of this kind in the "Home Burial"
rings true because it portrays in a fresh manner an event common to everyone's experience.
In this poem a farmer's wife could not bear the
seeming callousness of her husband's attitude
after he had buried their child:

> You could sit there with the stains on your
>   shoes
> Of the fresh earth from your own baby's
>   grave
> And talk about your everyday concerns. . .

Frost's ability to handle this emotion is made
possible by his knowledge of women's reactions
to common things in such a crisis. The mud on
the husband's shoes, which in the woman's mind
has suddenly become symbolic of the child,
makes her feel he is callous, because mud was
formerly a symbol of matter-of-factness to her.
Her violent reaction to the new symbolism carries over to the reader, who then sees new
meaning in an old experience.

In contrast to the theory of many critics,
Frost has been deliberately provincial in subject-matter in the belief that in order to
cross any barriers of sectional differences,
each section must first be understood for what
it is.[18] With his comprehension of New England
peculiarities, which is necessarily keener than
ours because of his daily contact with them, he
is actually describing representative humanity
for those who recognize the common element in
different types of provincialism. The census-
taker in commenting on New England combines the
gloom of all humanity with its inherent desire
for happiness.

[18] Frost, "Education by Poetry," p. 15.

It was a local fact that rural population was
diminishing in New England, but the sadness of
the census-taker holds one's interest as a
trait common to most people on viewing deserted
settlements. Like him we "want life to go on
living." Frost sees that the instinct in both
cases is really one of self-protection. The
fear of failure, haunting even the most successful men, may be aggravated by contact with
the failure of others.

On the other hand, it is not easy to make a
man sad if he approaches life in a sufficiently
cheerful mood. Even deserted settlements are
sometimes objects of humor for Frost, as in his
satire on a deserted Mormon settlement, entitled "A Fountain, a Bottle, a Donkey's Ears
and Some Books." This time the theme is treated
in a far lighter vein than that of the "Census-
Taker." Frost's range also includes such subjects as decaying marriage laws and concern for
death, a quarrel about a cow, farmers covering
each other with hay for vengeance, and family
reunions. In the last case the question under
discussion is:

> What will we come to
> With all this pride of ancestry, we Yankees?

By probing one of New England's most characteristic attributes, her family pride, Frost
forces one indirectly to consider the nature of
family loyalty in general and its relation to
one's own family.

BIBLIOGRAPHY[7]

A. Books
    Boynton, Percy. Some Contemporary Amer-
       cans. Chicago: University of Chicago
       Press, 1924, pp. 33-50.
    Cox, Sidney. Robert Frost. New York: Henry
       Holt and Company, Inc., 1929.

[7] This bibliography would of course be begun on a separate page in the theme
itself.

Frost, Robert. Introduction to Dartmouth
Verse. Portland, Maine: Mosher, 1925.
———, Collected Poems. New York: Henry Holt
and Company, Inc., 1939.
Lowell, Amy. Tendencies in Modern American
Poetry. New York: The Macmillan Company,
1917.
Lowes, John L. Convention and Revolt in
Poetry. Boston: Houghton Mifflin, 1930.
———, The Road to Xanadu. Boston: Houghton
Mifflin, 1930.
Munson, Gorham. Robert Frost. New York:
Doran, 1927.
Wordsworth, William. Lyrical Ballads, 1798,
ed. Harold Littledale. London: H. Frowde,
1911, preface.

B. Periodicals and Newspapers

Carpenter, F. E. Review of Frost's Col-
lected Poems, The New England Quarterly,
V (January, 1932), 159-160.
Frost, Robert. "Education by Poetry, a
Meditative Monologue," Amherst Alumni
Council News, IV (March, 1931, Supple-
ment), 13-15.
Hillyer, Robert. "Robert Frost 'Lacks
Power,' " The New England Quarterly, V
(April, 1932), 402-404.
"I Will Teach Only When I Have Something to
Tell," Boston Globe, VI (November 23,
1924, Supplement), 3:1-5.
Pound, Ezra. "Modern Georgics," Poetry, V
(December, 1914), 127-130.

The Paragraph

Writing is a process of building. Just as letters of the alphabet are combined into words, and words are linked to form phrases, clauses, and sentences, so sentences are combined to form paragraphs. Good themes or compositions are the result of good paragraphs.

Good paragraphs are difficult to compose, but anyone can create them who has ideas to rub together and who will write and rewrite thoughtfully. We must train our minds to deal fully and logically with ideas, to develop concepts and relate them to each other. We may speak in sentences, but we should and must think and write in larger units. For example, you may decide to write a character sketch of your friend George. After selecting the subject, you ask yourself, "What can I say about him?" Your answer, often arrived at after considerable mental anguish, might consist of a series of statements, each of which indicates one phase of the subject. You phrase these thoughts:

1. He is tall, handsome, athletic.
2. He has always been interested in how things work and is now studying mechanical engineering at college.
3. He is generous and fun-loving but lacks will power.
4. The outstanding influence upon his life has been his mother, who has always pampered him and restrained his normal development.
5. He is completely sincere in his belief that success can be measured only in terms of money and consequently he cares little for so-called culture.

The five sentences about George will mean little to the reader until they are expanded into paragraphs. Their shaping and expansion require thought, more thought than is ordinarily used in conversation. Good paragraphs, which are fundamental to all good writing, are predicated upon clear thinking. These five ideas indicate different and interesting characteristics and will, perhaps, serve as the nucleus of an effective description. Your writing problem is to arrange and develop these statements and combine them into a whole. Your "developed" statements will be the paragraphs of your theme. Your theme will be as effective, and only as effective, as the individual paragraphs. It is as simple, and as difficult, as that.

To achieve good paragraphs, therefore, you should understand the meaning, the purposes, and the characteristics of paragraphs and paragraphing.

DEFINITION AND CHARACTERISTICS

51a. Understand clearly the meaning and purpose of paragraphing.

A paragraph is a group, or bundle, of sentences developing either one single topic or a specific part of a larger topic. The purpose of the paragraph is to aid in communicating ideas by setting off the single topic which is developed or by providing clear distinctions between the separate parts of a longer composition.

Good paragraphing is essential for clarity and effectiveness. Properly separated groups of sentences enable the writer to plot his course and see the progress he is making. They serve the reader by making the structure and development of the ideas easily apparent. Paragraphing involves some of the principles of punctuation in that it separates certain ideas from others because of their structural relationships; it thus furnishes the reader signposts or road markers to guide him along the paths of thought which the writer is developing. A series of carefully constructed paragraphs aids clarity just as does a series of correctly punctuated sentences: by developing ideas so that the reader, following the signs laid out for him, can obtain, quickly and clearly, a grasp of the parts and of the whole which they constitute.

Likewise, paragraphs have an effectiveness which derives from the fact that readers easily tire unless a page of writing is broken up into smaller units. The sign of the paragraph, *indentation,* is a helpful lure to the reader; he feels that he has completed a unified section of writing and can go on to another unit. Many books, magazine articles, and even short stories are divided into chapters or sections, not so much to keep closely related ideas or parts of the action together (unity) as to furnish the reader a "breathing space."

51b. Make your paragraphs correct, clear, and effective.

A well-constructed paragraph, like good diction or a good sentence, should be *correct, clear,* and *effective*—characteristics dependent upon careful thinking. Such a statement may seem vague, but it has specific meaning if you thoroughly understand the elements which give paragraphs correctness, clearness, and effectiveness. For convenience and ready reference, eight desirable paragraph characteristics are listed below; each one will be fully discussed in following sections. Each necessitates using your mind. If your paragraphs possess these eight qualities, they evidence careful thinking and resultant correctness, clarity, and forcefulness. If they do not, they show that you have been guilty of careless, insufficient thought, or ignorance, or both.

1. A good paragraph is *mechanically* correct. It is properly indented; it contains the words which belong with it, not with the preceding paragraph; in dialogue, it correctly represents every change of speaker.

2. A good paragraph contains a *topic statement,* expressed or implied.

3. A good paragraph contains a *body of thought,* not a mere fragment. The well-developed paragraph is never sketchy or incomplete.

4. A good paragraph must be *unified.* Oneness of purpose is desirable; extraneous detail must be eliminated.

5. A good paragraph contains full, unified material arranged in proper *order.* The sentences in it are so worded and arranged that they have a maximum appeal to the reader. Good arrangement of ideas implies logical thinking.

6. A good paragraph is well *proportioned.* If the thought of the paragraph is important, the paragraph should be so fully and com-

309

pletely developed that the reader can readily understand the significance of that thought. If the paragraph discusses an idea, or a group of related ideas, of comparatively less importance, the proportion of the paragraphs should reveal the difference in weight.

7. A good paragraph has suitable *length*. This statement implies what is said above under proportion; it also means that a series of short, choppy paragraphs, or a group of very long ones, should usually be avoided.

8. A good paragraph contains *transitional aids*. The thoughts within paragraphs should make orderly, clear progress, and there should be clear passage from one paragraph to another.

MECHANICS

52. *Mechanical correctness* in the handling of paragraphs is simple to attain. The rules pertaining to indentation, the paragraphing of dialogue, etc., are few and easily learned. But they must be mastered. The absence of errors is a mechanical and negative aspect of style, but it is an element without which style loses much of its effectiveness.

52a. Indent the first line of every paragraph.

Every paragraph should be indented one-half inch or more. The break of distinct paragraph indentation is a real aid to both writer and reader in recognizing the divisions of thought within the whole theme. Further, paragraph indentation aids in reading; the break serves as a signal that a clear distinction between separate parts of the whole composition is about to be made. In typing, common practice is to indent five spaces.

Use indentations of equal length for all the paragraphs in the same theme. Make no exception for *numbered* paragraphs.

Avoid in general the use of the marks "¶" and "no ¶," meaning, respectively, "a new paragraph intended" and "not a new paragraph." If possible, you should recopy the entire page, correcting the indentation.

52b. Do not leave part of a line blank within a paragraph.

A part of a line should not be left blank unless a new paragraph begins on the next line. Blanks in lines which are not last lines of paragraphs mislead your reader, who expects such a break to finish the discussion of one phase of the subject. Furthermore, such blanks in lines not only cause a jagged appearance but also make less efficient the mechanical process of reading—the eye, in sweeping over the line, has to make several extra movements in order to adjust itself and to transfer meaning to the brain. Margins at the left of the page should, of course, always be uniform for the same reasons.

52c. Paragraph separately each speech in writing dialogue or quoting conversation.

Dialogue and quoted conversation require separate paragraphs for each speech. Notice the mechanical forms in the following excerpts from Mary Porter Russell's short story, "Arrival." Three particulars may be observed: correct paragraphing of conversation, correct paragraphing of explanatory material, and correct form for introductory and explanatory words within paragraphs which contain dialogue.

"Are we *here?*" she called to the driver, and something inside her seemed trying to burst.

"You bet," he answered. "See that building? That's the church. And d' yer see that one? That's the school."

Such funny little houses they were. Not at all like a church and a school.

"And here's the post office," said the driver, drawing up before a building that was really a grocery store.

Mother hadn't said anything for a long time, but she had reached over for Joan's hand, and was squeezing it very hard. "I see Father," she cried out all at once, in a choky sort of voice.

"Yeah, that's him," said the driver.[1]

THE TOPIC SENTENCE OR STATEMENT

53. A topic sentence or statement gives the gist of the paragraph; it contains the heart of the idea which is to be, or has been, developed. It does not mention everything that the paragraph

[1] From *Story*.

contains, nor does it summarize the full contents of the paragraph. It merely indicates the unity of the paragraph by pointing out the topic, the central thought with which the group of sentences is concerned.

53a. Use a topic sentence or topic statement to aid in gaining paragraph unity.

A topic sentence or statement is a guide to both writer and reader. It may be, perhaps should be, a simple sentence. A well-planned outline, in which you have already decided the divisions to be expanded into paragraphs, will readily provide topic sentences; a sentence outline will present topic sentences ready-made. (The paragraph outline, usually made of others' writing, consists of authors' topic sentences.)

Frequently the topic sentence, although so called, is only part of a sentence: perhaps the main clause of a complex sentence or one of the clauses in a compound sentence. The topic statement may be a phrase within a sentence, or even a single word. But whatever its grammatical form, it is always the *topic* or *subject* of the paragraph, and it is the guide by which you keep on the subject and avoid introducing irrelevant material.

Not every well-constructed paragraph contains an expressed topic sentence or statement, but every good paragraph is so well knit that it at least *implies* one. The reader, reflecting, can sum up the central thought of the paragraph in his own "topic sentence."

53b. Vary the position of topic sentences within paragraphs.

In some paragraphs, where clarity otherwise may be difficult to attain, the first sentence should be the topic sentence. But series of paragraphs beginning with topic sentences become monotonous. Used in different positions within the paragraphs, topic sentences contribute to effectiveness. Attain variety in paragraph structure by placing the topic sentence at different positions, or occasionally letting it be implied, or by expressing it in different forms. Its form, for example, may be interrogative as well as declarative, and it may generalize as well as summarize. Also, topic sentences may appear in the middle or at the end of the

312

paragraphs, as well as at their more usual position, the beginning. Study the following four examples. Note the unifying, clarifying effect of the topic sentences; note also their position and function.

1. The topic sentence is the first sentence; it affirms what is to follow.

Fireworks indicate happiness and rejoicing. On every Fourth of July, millions of firecrackers are exploded in a sort of national rejoicing over our independence. They are not fired in memory of the war which achieved our independence so much as in explosive utterance of our happiness in being free.

2. The topic sentence is the last sentence; it sums up what has been said.

She takes a walk every day. Walking makes her feel better, she says, because it strengthens her muscles and gives her a good appetite. Walking also relaxes her mind, because it is rhythmical, and noiseless, and requires no conscious thought. Walking is, for her, excellent physical and mental relaxation and exercise.

3. The topic sentence is the first sentence, an interrogative sentence; the answer to the question constitutes the remainder of the paragraph.

In the face of this one may ask: Why does the great and universal fame of classical authors continue? The answer is that the fame of classical authors is entirely independent of the majority. Do you suppose that if the fame of Shakespeare depended on the man in the street it would survive a fortnight? The fame of classical authors is originally made, and it is maintained, by a passionate few. Even when a first-class author has enjoyed immense success during his lifetime, the majority have never appreciated him so sincerely as they have appreciated second-rate men. He has always been reënforced by the ardor of the passionate few. And in the case of an author who has emerged into glory after his death, the happy sequel has been due solely to the obstinate perseverance of the few. They could not leave him alone; they would not. They kept on savoring him, and talking about him, and buying him, and they generally behaved with such eager zeal, and they were so authoritative and sure of themselves, that at last the majority grew accustomed to the sound of his name and placidly agreed to the proposition that he was a genius; the majority really did not care very much either way. (From Arnold Bennett's "Why a Classic Is a Classic.")[2]

4. The topic sentence is the fourth sentence; the sentences before and after it illustrate and expand the idea expressed.

Suppose, however, that we had called that same animal a "mongrel." The matter is more complicated. We have used a word which objectively means the same as "dog of mixed breed," but which also arouses in our hearers an emotional attitude of disapproval toward that particular dog. A word, therefore, cannot only indicate an object, but can also suggest an emotional attitude toward it. Such suggestion of an emotional attitude does go beyond exact and scientific discussion because our approvals and disapprovals are individual—they belong to ourselves and not to the objects we approve or disapprove of. An animal which to the mind of its master is a faithful and noble dog of mixed ancestry may be a "mongrel" to his neighbor whose chickens are chased by it. (From Robert Thouless' "Emotional Meanings.")[3]

These illustrations indicate the variety of ways in which a topic sentence may be used. But the important thing to remember is this: One criterion of the good paragraph is that it must be so unified that its gist, or pith, *can* be stated in a topic sentence, even though this sentence is not expressed. Only thus can you be certain that you have kept to the subject; only thus can the reader follow clearly the development of your idea. But keep in mind that a topic sentence contains merely the main point, or points, of a paragraph, not every idea mentioned.

EXERCISES

A. Underline the topic sentences or topic statements of a number of paragraphs in one of your textbooks; in an article in a current magazine; in an article in your book of readings.

B. From your reading, select a well-constructed paragraph which has no topic sentence or topic statement. Give the implied topic.

[2] From *Literary Taste: How to Form It,* by Arnold Bennett.
[3] From *How to Think Straight,* by Robert H. Thouless, copyright, 1939, by Simon and Schuster, Inc.

C. Write a paragraph based on this topic sentence: Every student should take part in some college activity.

D. Use this topic sentence (Exercise C) in various forms and at different positions within other paragraphs.

E. By means of topic sentences make an outline of some essay in your anthology.

F. List five or more topic sentences to be used in developing each of the following theme subjects:

1. Why I Am Attending — College.
2. The Problem of Cheating.
3. The Best Way to Sell Used Textbooks.
4. The Quaintest Character in My Town.
5. How to Improve in Writing.

SUBSTANCE

54. After you have determined the thought to be expressed in the paragraph and put it in a topic sentence, expressed or implied, you then encounter the problem of developing the thought. Many students have no difficulty in expressing a main idea or a group of ideas, but all writers are vexed with the ever-present problems of expanding, shaping, and explaining thoughts so that they will be clear and effective.

Topic sentences are but the trunk of a tree; they must be developed in such a way that the reader will see a tree with branches and leaves. Readers will not fully understand a series of topic sentences because only the skeleton, the bare outline, of the thought is presented. Completely developed paragraphs contain an abundance of vital, pertinent detail. Everyone who has read the closely woven essays of Emerson or Bacon has sighed, "Each sentence is a paragraph, or a whole paper, in embryo. If only the author had expanded the main ideas, I could understand so much better."

Themes frequently contain flabby, ineffective paragraphs not so much because the central ideas of the paragraphs are weak as because their substance is thin, vapid, and meaningless. In other words, getting something to say requires genuine mental activity.

"He is generous and fun-loving but lacks will power." Such a topic sentence is easily thought and easily written. But to develop the idea contained in that sentence is another matter. Neither hazy generalizations nor mere repetition of the central thought builds good paragraphs. After you have phrased the topic sentence, you must draw upon your own experience and the experience of others as revealed in newspapers, magazines, books, and conversation. You must make use of your own observation, curiosity, imagination, and reflection. Full paragraph development requires time and careful thought. An effective, clear theme is the sum total of a series of paragraphs rounded with ample substance. If you know something about the subject upon which you are writing and have some real interest in expressing your ideas, you can always avoid weak, incomplete paragraphs by making enough mental effort, and taking enough time, to fulfill the statement of a topic sentence. The five topic sentences listed (p. 307) for a theme about George may be quite satisfactory; the effectiveness of the theme will depend upon how those bare ideas are developed.

54a. Be consistent in developing the idea contained in the topic sentence.

Your topic sentence, if well chosen and phrased, will often indicate the most desirable method for amplifying it into a paragraph. Sometimes it will suggest several methods from which you should choose the one that will most clearly and effectively accomplish your purpose. The choice of any one method does not preclude occasional use within the paragraph of other methods.

Several different methods of developing topic sentences, involving the use of different kinds of material, may be employed alone or in combination. The most frequently used are explication, illustration, comparison or contrast, division, proof, and definition.

1. Development by *explication* means explaining the various aspects of the idea contained in the topic sentence. A series of specific details or concrete particulars, arranged in a logical order, are the supporting materials used. The method of explication is similar to the method of definition.

Expository details:

We all appear to ourselves to be thinking all the time during our waking hours, and most of us are aware that we go on thinking while we are asleep, even more foolishly than when awake. When uninterrupted by some practical issue we are engaged in what is now known as a *reverie*. This is our spontaneous and favorite kind of thinking. We allow our ideas to take their own course and this course is determined by our hopes and fears, our spontaneous desires, their fulfillment or frustration; by our likes and dislikes, our loves and hates and resentments. There is nothing else anything like so interesting to ourselves as ourselves. All thought that is not more or less laboriously controlled and directed will inevitably circle about the beloved Ego. It is amusing and pathetic to observe this tendency in ourselves and in others. We learn politely and generously to overlook this truth, but if we dare to think of it, it blazes forth like the noontide sun.[4]

Narrative details:

The bare, indisputable facts in the life of Mary Todd Lincoln are few and simple. She was born of a good Kentucky family, in 1818, ten years after her husband. In 1839 she came to live with her sister, Mrs. Edwards, in Springfield. After a stormy courtship Lincoln married her in 1842. Her life then led her through Illinois law and politics to the White House, and the war, and the culminations of triumphant peace. All the triumph and hope were blasted by the assassination of her husband, and her remaining years, in spite of a brief sojourn in Europe, were darkened by sorrow and misfortune till a temperament, always impulsive and intense, was unbalanced to a point of oddity approaching and at times reaching actual derangement. She died in 1882.[5]

2. Development by *illustration* uses a series of sentences which, in relation to the topic sentence, furnish an *example* or *specific instances*. Because an example familiar to the reader carries its own explanation, there is no surer way of anticipating the reader's question about your topic sentence, "What does it mean?" *Instances* and *examples* serve to answer this question, to drive home to the reader the idea expressed.

The following paragraph from Robert Louis Stevenson's essay, "El Dorado," is developed by *specific instances*:

[4] From *The Mind in the Making*, by James Harvey Robinson. Copyright, 1921, by Harper & Brothers.

[5] From *Wives*, by Gamaliel Bradford.

One who goes touring on foot with a single volume in his knapsack reads with circumspection, pausing often to reflect, and often laying the book down to contemplate the landscape or the prints in the inn parlour; for he fears to come to the end of his entertainment, and be left companionless on the last stages of his journey. A young fellow recently finished the works of Thomas Carlyle, winding up, if we remember aright, with the ten notebooks upon Frederick the Great. "What!" cried the young fellow, in consternation, "is there no more Carlyle? Am I left to the daily papers!" A more celebrated instance is that of Alexander, who wept bitterly because he had no more worlds to subdue. And when Gibbon had finished the *Decline and Fall,* he had only a few moments of joy; and it was with a "sober melancholy" that he parted from his labours.

In the following, an *example* develops the paragraph:

My college roommate, a blessed boy full of good humor and serious purpose, was as incapable of acquiring the daily theme eye as a cat of obeying the eighth commandment. His idea of a daily theme was a task, not a pleasure. If there was no chance to write a political editorial, he supplied an anecdote of his summer vacation. Once he described a cliff he had seen in Newfoundland, and, determined to be pictorial, he added "tumbling waterfalls" and "sighing pines." Unfortunately, the instructor who read it had also been in Newfoundland, and he pointed out that his investigations of the cliff in question had failed to disclose either "tumbling waterfalls" or "sighing pines." My roommate treated the matter as a joke; he could not see that he had been guilty of any fault. And yet he is a much more moral man than I, with a far more troublesome conscience. Truth to his principles he would die for. But truth to the picture his mind retained and his hand tried to portray in the medium of literature, to him so trivial and unimportant, he could not grasp. What did it matter? So it would never occur to him to record in his themes the fleeting impressions of his daily life, to sit up half the night trying to pack into the clumsy frame of words the recollection of a strangely innocent face seen suddenly in the flash of an opened door down a dark, evil alley where the gusts of winter swirled. He went to bed and never knew a headache or jumpy nerve. Yet I could not help thinking then that there was something in life he was missing besides the ultimate mark in our composition course. And I cannot help thinking that there is something in life he misses still.[6]

—WALTER PRICHARD EATON

[6] From *The Atlantic Monthly.*

3. A topic may be made clear and effective by the use of *comparison* or *contrast*. The former shows the likeness between the topic and some concept or object familiar to the reader; the latter shows differences. Not infrequently both comparison and contrast are used within the same paragraph.

By *comparison:*

Compare the lot of the youngsters who compete for top honors in tennis with those who do the same thing in music. If you fail to make the big time in tennis, the really big time that pays off handsomely, you can always give up the game and become a "once fine amateur" and a credit to the sport. In music, if you practice eight hours a day for eight years and still don't make the grade, you are a music teacher or a second string fiddler, and you are tagged as a professional who wasn't good enough to get big billing. There are surely many concert musicians who would be glad to "turn pro" if that opportunity meant anything but a chance to play third bassoon in the overture to "Allegro."[7]

By *contrast:*

There is a real difference between the so-called "social sciences" and the "natural and physical sciences" that has an important bearing here. It is not that there is anything "unnatural" about the social sciences. Man is a part of nature, and the study of human society is just as truly "natural science" in the real sense of the term as any other study. The difference arises from the peculiar factors and particular functions pertaining to the co-operative way of life. Whereas the scientific use of things may be achieved through the efforts of a very small minority of the citizens, provided with adequate facilities for research, the scientific organization of society in a democracy can be achieved only when the majority of its citizens have the scientific attitude toward social problems and act in accordance with that attitude of mind. In other words, only a few physicists, chemists, and technologists are required for the mastery of our physical environment, but for victory in the struggle with ourselves every man must be his own sociologist.[8]

4. Developing a topic by *division* means that the writer calls attention to two or more parts of the topic and discusses each one briefly. The following paragraph is developed by this method:

[7] From "After Hours," *Harper's Magazine,* January, 1948, p. 93.
[8] From Kirtley F. Mather, "The Future of Man," *The Scientific Monthly.*

The mind has to do two essential things if it is to keep its vigor: It has to take in new experience, and it has to transform this experience into fresh thought, emotions, intentions, plans, and activities. When the mind stops taking in, it merely lives along on its past. When it fails to turn its experiences smoothly and effectively into new ways of thinking and doing and acting, it suffers a kind of mental poisoning, much as the body suffers poisoning when intake of food remains undigested. It is under such conditions that the mind becomes suspicious, fearful, opinionated, stubborn, cranky, bitter.[9]

To the fatalism of the Orient and the other-worldliness of the Christian Middle Ages must be added a second idea opposed to the concept of progress—that is, utopianism. This idea takes two forms. In the minds of some thinkers it is related to the past; there has been a golden age, in the "good old days of the fathers" or in some remote period of the early evolution of mankind. In seeking to escape the evils of the present, we must return to the perfection of long ago when people lived in peace, happiness, innocence, and plenty. But, in other minds, utopianism is related to the future: by doing this or that we can establish a static order of bliss—a fixed scheme of things so nearly perfect that they will never have to be changed. A variant on these aspects of dreaming may be called the utopianism of whitewash: the present order is so nearly perfect that it is almost profane to inquire into its evils or to propose modifications, for the possibility of doing harm is always greater than the chances of doing good. Historians, with all their searching, have not been able to find the golden age in the past, and skeptics doubt the perfection of the present. Still the illusion of utopianism shadows all human thought about public and private affairs, challenging the idea of progress.[10]

5. The method of *proof* means that support or evidence is given in the paragraph to establish the truth of the topic statement. Sometimes such evidence is in the form of relevant details; sometimes the paragraph shows the *cause,* sometimes the *effect* of the statement in the topic sentence to be proved.

Proof by *details:*

Even before the eighteenth amendment, books about the United States Constitution were apt to be pretty dry. They usually tell what the

[9] From *Let Me Think,* by H. A. Overstreet; The Macmillan Company, publishers.
[10] From *A Century of Progress,* by Charles A. Beard.

Supreme Court says in a lot of cases and try to show how what it says in one case will jibe all right with what it says in the other cases. After the writers tell what happens in each case, then they try to forget it and to put all the cases together and make up a set of rules to show what the Supreme Court has been up to and what it is going to do next. This is a very hard thing to do, and it is very hard to read after it has been done. You have to think very hard all the time, and even then you get all mixed up. This kind of book makes you tired because you have to try so hard to think, and so you usually stop trying to read it.[11]

Proof by *giving causes* or *reasons:*

The real attraction of skiing is probably the fact that it is a magnificent form of escape. For those great numbers of Americans who are too deeply mired in the complexities of present-day society to attempt permanent simplification of their lives, skiing offers a brief, uninhibited respite. The sensation of complete freedom, both physical and mental, that overcomes a skier while flying down a mountainside can be almost miraculous. For a short space of time his life is his private property, dependent on no time schedules, restricted not one whit by his own intellectual limitations or by those of others. His whole being is absorbed in what he is doing and in where he is doing it, and both considerations are physical. In the concentration essential to the moment, the past of desk calendars, time clocks, phone calls, social forms, train schedules, personal relationships, self-examinations, and world idiocies is blotted out; and the only perceivable future is involved with the pine tree that marks the turn ahead. The sensation of grace and speed, independent of devices, that a skier feels while competing with nature and with himself may be elusive, and it may end abruptly with a crash into the underbrush, but once felt it gains a grip which again and again brings him out of his cave and up to the timberline in winter.[12]

Proof by *effect:*

To most participating nations, a modern war brings complex economic results. Science and industry are occasionally advanced by researches derived from the stimulus and energy of war. Life and property are destroyed; vast sums are consumed in armament; impossible debts

[11] From Thomas Reed Powell, "Constitutional Metaphors," *The New Republic.*
[12] From Eric Swenson, "Let Fly Downhill," *Harper's Magazine,* January, 1948, p. 27.

accumulate. Repudiation in some form becomes inevitable; currencies are depreciated or annulled, inflation relieves debtor governments and individuals, savings and investments are wiped out, and men patiently begin to save and lend again. Overexpansion in war is followed by a major depression in peace. International trade is disrupted by intensified nationalism, exalted tariffs, and the desire to develop at home all industries requisite in war. The vanquished are enslaved—physically, as in antiquity, financially and by due process of law today. The victorious masses gain little except in self-conceit; the ruling minority among the victors may gain much in conquered lands, markets, spheres of influence, supplies, and taxable population.[13]

Occasionally the topic is developed by *refutation* or *negative proof:* giving evidence to show that the statement in the topic sentence is not true. The following paragraph uses this method:

The only plausible alternative to the conclusion that earth and sun will continue the even tenor of their ways for an inconceivably long period of time is that the sun will some day imitate the supernovae occasionally detected among the stars and terminate the existence of the entire solar system by a gigantic explosion. Precisely one such supernova has been observed within the galaxy of the Milky Way and several such in all the other galaxies of stars during the past few decades. The astronomers could therefore calculate for us the chances on a statistical basis that any individual star—the sun, for example—would suffer such a fate within any given period of time. The result would be a figure so infinitesimal as to set at rest the mind of even the most jittery of questioners. Pending the discovery of the kind of premonitory symptoms displayed by stars about to blow themselves to atoms, the best that can be done is to rest content in history. Since the earliest records of living creatures were left as fossils, if not indeed since the earliest sedimentary rocks were formed, the sun has faithfully maintained its energy output within a fairly narrow range and has given no evidence of any fluctuations that might suggest any significant change in its behavior.[14]

6. Development of a topic by *definition* involves the use of substance which answers the implied question of the reader, "What do you mean by this?" To be clear and effective, the paragraph developed by this method also uses some of the foregoing methods:

[13] From Will Durant, "Why Men Fight," *The Saturday Evening Post.*
[14] From Kirtley F. Mather, "The Future of Man," *The Scientific Monthly.*

details and particulars, cause and effect, illustration. A straightforward definition is the following:

Science is a method of knowledge that arose and first proved its usefulness within the realms of mechanics, physics, and chemistry. In essence it is remarkably simple. The first step is to discover the pertinent facts. Next, you make a guess as to the law which accounts for these facts. And finally, you test the correctness of this guess by experiment. If your experiments do not verify the first guess, you admit that you were wrong, and make another guess. And so on, until you have found a piece of demonstrable knowledge, or demonstrated that the truth with regard to that particular matter is so far unknown.[15]

In his essay, "Why a Classic Is a Classic," Arnold Bennett writes the following paragraph, which, descriptive of the term used, is actually a definition:

A classic is a work which gives pleasure to the minority which is intensely and permanently interested in literature. It lives on because the minority, eager to renew the sensation of pleasure, is eternally curious and is therefore engaged in an eternal process of rediscovery. A classic does not survive for any ethical reason. It does not survive because it conforms to certain canons, or because neglect would kill it. It survives because it is a source of pleasure, and because the passionate few can no more neglect it than a bee can neglect a flower. The passionate few do not read "the right things" because they are right. That is to put the cart before the horse. "The right things" are the right things solely because the passionate few *like* reading them. . . .[16]

54b. When necessary, combine various methods of developing the topic sentence.

You can write clear and effective paragraphs by developing them according to any *one* of the methods described above (whichever is most appropriate for the purpose). On the other hand, as some of the methods and quoted illustrations show, you may need to use several; in fact, a few of the methods involve the use of others. It is impossible to be rigidly logical, impossible always to eliminate the overlapping of some of the methods.

[15] From Hugh Stevenson Tigner, "The Pretensions of Science," *The Christian Century*.
[16] From *Literary Taste: How to Form It*, by Arnold Bennett.

In the following paragraph from Aldous Huxley's "Comfort" are elements of explication, illustration, comparison, contrast, and even repetition:

Another essential component of modern comfort—the adequate heating of houses—was made impossible, at least for the great ones of the earth, by the political structure of ancient societies. Plebeians were more fortunate in this respect than nobles. Living in small houses, they were able to keep warm. But the nobleman, the prince, the king, and the cardinal inhabited palaces of a grandeur corresponding with their social position. In order to prove that they were greater than other men, they had to live in surroundings considerably more than life-size. They received their guests in vast halls like roller-skating rinks; they marched in solemn processions along galleries as long and as draughty as Alpine tunnels, up and down triumphal staircases that looked like the cataracts of the Nile frozen into marble. Being what he was, a great man in those days had to spend a great deal of his time in performing solemn symbolical charades and pompous ballets—performances which required a lot of room to accommodate the numerous actors and spectators. This explains the enormous dimensions of royal and princely palaces, even of the houses of ordinary landed gentlemen. They owed it to their position to live, as though they were giants, in rooms a hundred feet long and thirty high. How splendid, how magnificent! But oh, how bleak! In our days the self-made great are not expected to keep up their positions in the splendid style of those who were great by divine right. Sacrificing grandiosity to comfort, they live in rooms small enough to be heated.[17]

Not infrequently a single topic is developed in a series of paragraphs. To establish a certain statement, a number of illustrations may be given, each in a separate paragraph. Similarly, a series of paragraphs may support the truth of a major division or topic; they may give the causes; they may give the effects. Such a paragraph series usually results from the desire of the writer to make his materials convenient to the reader (as opposed to one long, complicated paragraph) and to attain both clearness and effectiveness.

[17] From *Proper Studies,* by Aldous Huxley.

54 c-d

Knowing and using various methods of paragraph development is valuable, but after practice and experience you will find choice and use almost automatic. All methods of paragraph development have essentially the same purpose, and their different technical names are of little importance. The primary aim in writing paragraphs is to make the reader see exactly and fully the ideas contained in expressed or implied topic sentences. The only test of the substance of a paragraph is that of clear and effective communication.

54c. Avoid developing paragraphs with hazy generalizations.

Adequate substance consists of definite, concrete ideas, impressions, reflections, and observations. Generalizations are frequently trite, vague, and ineffective. Note the lack of worth-while substance in this student-written paragraph:

Cheating never pays. After all, "honesty is the best policy"; also when one gets something for nothing he does not appreciate it. I think that every student should be on his own, even if his "own" is not good enough for him to pass his course. One should be honest, no matter what the cost. The student who thinks cheating is a sin only when it is detected is fooling nobody but himself. Sooner or later, his sins will find him out, and he will have nobody but himself to blame.

The student rewrote this paragraph with greater effectiveness because he used a specific illustration:

Cheating never pays. A friend of mine, whom we shall call John, thought that it did. He once said to me: "Why should I study when it is so easy to get the desired results without work? The only sin in cheating is being caught." And so John was dishonest all through his four years at school. But when he took the college board examinations, he could not cheat because the proctors were efficient. He failed, and was bitterly disappointed, because he wanted very badly to enter — College. Now he believes, as I do, that cheating never pays.

54d. Avoid meaningless, ineffective repetition of the topic sentence.

Repeating the topic sentence in different words is a device auxiliary to other methods of paragraph development. Such repetition should add clearness and should expand and develop the idea by

54

Exercises

the introduction of specific details (note the use of repetition in the Arnold Bennett paragraph, p. 323, above). But repetition alone, no matter how varied the words, is rarely used as the sole or major method of developing a paragraph. Repetition which adds nothing new is merely an indication of little thought, or of thought going round in circles. Note the inadequacy of this pararaph:

People pay too much attention to their diet. They spend hours every day wondering if they should eat this or that. They are too concerned about their digestive processes. One would think their greatest concern was food and, indeed, it is. Diet is not nearly so important as these people think it is. It does not warrant so much concern.

EXERCISES

A. Write twelve topic sentences which you would like to develop into paragraphs. Compose these topic sentences so that you could develop two paragraphs according to each of the following methods: (a) explication, (b) illustration, (c) comparison or contrast, (d) division, (e) proof, and (f) definition.

B. Choose six of the topic sentences (Exercise A) and write six paragraphs, one illustrating each of the methods listed.

C. Develop each of the following topic sentences into a paragraph, each paragraph to illustrate a method of development listed in Exercise A:

1. Henry is a man of infinite tact.
2. Most lectures are forgotten in a day.
3. Is it true that girls are usually more conscientious students than boys?
4. Grandfather's generation lived a happier life than ours does.
5. A small college has (does not have) more to offer a student than a large university.
6. There are several aids to correct spelling.
7. The future of America depends upon the proper conservation of its oil.
8. The era of the small independent farmer is (is not) passing.
9. There is (is not) a vast difference between sports and athletics.
10. Television and radio are distinctly twentieth-century forms of entertainment.

326

D. From your reading, select several paragraphs which illustrate each of the methods of development discussed in Section 54.

E. Use at least three methods (and write three paragraphs, illustrating each) in developing each of the following topic sentences:

1. Hazing may be beneficial, but it is always cruel.
2. A sound use of connectives reveals more clearly than anything else a writer's mastery of his material.
3. Lucy was the stingiest girl whom I have ever known.
4. I believe that — is the most interesting magazine published in America today.
5. There are more disadvantages than advantages in living in a big city.
6. College football is no place for amateurs.
7. College athletics should not be carried on for profit.
8. We all talk about sex, but few of us know much about it.
9. A man's best friend is his —.
10. College is a poor place in which to get an education.

UNITY

55. As it is important that every sentence should be unified, should contain only facts and ideas that belong together and present a clear and consistent point of view, so is it important that the related sentences forming a paragraph should develop consistently a larger idea which presides over the whole group. If a paragraph contains substance, no matter how excellent, which is irrelevant to the central theme, it is not unified. A lack of unity causes a lack of effectiveness because the reader, prepared for a discussion of topic A, is confused by the introduction of detail about topic B; he shifts his attention from both A and B in an attempt to see how they are related.

55a. Omit any idea not related to the main thought of the paragraph.

Any idea which is not related to the main thought of the paragraph should be omitted, or placed in another paragraph where it does belong. Our minds do not always work logically; frequently, unrelated ideas occur together, and you should avoid automatically setting them down. The only test for unity is this: Does this statement refer to the thought contained in the expressed or implied topic sentence? If you introduce irrelevant details into your paragraphs, you will both confuse and irritate your reader. Let each paragraph develop and convey its own idea—and no other.

The following paragraphs do not possess unity:

She loved the wild flowers which grew near our home. Nearly every day she would wander into the fields and return with an armful of daisies or Queen Anne's lace which she would carefully arrange in bowls of water. *These bowls were of all kinds: pewter, silver, and copper. We had bought them at Woodward and Lothrop's, many years ago.* She would put the flowers in every room in the house and walk from room to room admiring their texture and color.

It was a lovely summer day. The green of the trees and grass was brilliant; the sun shone brightly from a blue sky which was filled with fleecy, white clouds. Hardly a sound could be heard save for the birds which were happily singing in the trees and the distant shouts of a group of tennis players. *Two of these players were students from a nearby college, where they were attending summer school.* Such days as this were rare, even in June.

55b. Include all material necessary for adequate development of the topic sentence.

Frequently you may be tempted to expand your paragraphs to greater length than you should by including too much material suggested by the method or methods of development that you are using. But include *only* enough material so that the discussion of your topic sentence will be complete. In choosing substance to achieve this purpose, however, you will need to check carefully to see that you have included *all* essential information, that you have left no unanswered questions to puzzle your reader.

In the following paragraph, one of the two ideas forming part of the topic statement—the man's education—has not been adequately discussed:

John Johnson was qualified for the position of City Sanitary Engineer by both education and experience. He had been assistant to the

City Sanitary Engineer of Indianapolis for five years; during one of those years, when his superior was ill, he had been in sole charge. He then became a consultant for the Indiana State Conservation Commission, which was making a survey of stream pollution. Two years of private practice in Louisville followed. When our city decided that it had grown large enough to need a sanitary engineer, our City Council looked over the field of applicants carefully, and felt fortunate in obtaining the services of John Johnson.

In revision, this writer has two choices. He can omit mention of "education" as part of the topic, or he can include adequate developing materials. A third possibility is, of course, a separate paragraph on education.

55c. Attain unity by consistently following specific methods of paragraph development.

Such methods of paragraph development have been discussed in the preceding section (Section 54). Skillful use of one method or of a combination of two or more methods can guide you in including or excluding material so as to produce a well-rounded, unified paragraph.

EXERCISES

Show why the following paragraphs do not possess unity.

A. The year Robert, my brother, first entered college, the war was just beginning to show its effects but not to any great extent. When he first started, he commuted for a while and had a locker at Craven Hall where he threw his coat and books along with perhaps three or four hundred other boys. He sometimes ate lunch there and once in a while at the Union, where the freshmen who lived on the campus ate. At that time there were no graduate students living on the campus.

B. Henry Adams embarked on an intellectual career. He toured all of Europe and gained the friendship of many great men of his time such as John Hay and St. Gaudens. All the time he was seeking reasons and rules for the actions of life. He was influenced by Darwin and Marx, but he was constantly being disappointed by seeing one of his theories disproved. Adams was sincere in all the inquiry he made into the meaning and culture of humanity. His philosophy is simple and understandable although it is often untrue. His dynamic theory of history and his belief regarding the dynamo are well known to all those who read the *Education of Henry Adams*. Without a doubt, Henry Adams was a great intellect, yet he did not continue in the lines of his forefathers. To be a statesman at the time of the capitalistic era was not typical of the Adams style.

C. Malta lies almost in the middle of the Mediterranean—55 miles from Sicily and about 150 miles from Africa. Its area is less than one hundred square miles. The island was originally all rock, no soil whatever. Legend has it that all the soil was shipped in from Sicily years ago. The highest point on the island is the small town of Rabat, 700 feet above sea level. Malta's strategic location made possible raids on Italian and German shipping to Africa, when Rommel was in Egypt and Tunisia.

D. During the greater part of the last century, Cuba was ruled by a captain-general, later called governor-general. The population of Cuba was divided into four classes: (1) the Spaniards, who occupied the offices and positions of power; (2) the Creoles, who were the planters, business men, and lawyers of the island; (3) the free mulattoes and Negroes, making up one-sixth of the population; and (4) the slaves, estimated at one-third the total population. The third class was excluded by law from holding any civil office; the fourth class were mere chattels. Although the native Cubans had little civil, political, or religious freedom, they were heavily taxed to maintain Spanish military forces on the island and a large number of Spanish officials.

ORDER

56. The first great problem in writing a paragraph is securing full, interesting, unified material. The second great problem is *arranging* the material. Even excellent substance will lose much of its effectiveness if it is incorrectly and illogically arranged.

56a. Arrange sentences in a paragraph in logical sequence.

Just as hasty and inaccurate thinking causes a lack of paragraph unity, so it may result in the sentences of a paragraph being arranged not in order, but in disorder. Because our minds do not always work logically, we tend to place ideas ahead of the place where they belong, or we temporarily forget them and insert them later in the paragraph. Anyone who has ever attempted to tell a long story, or who has heard one told, knows how difficult it is to arrange ideas in their proper order.

A paragraph may consist of five good sentences; a meal may consist of five excellent courses. Those five sentences should follow each other in an orderly sequence; those five courses should do likewise: the dessert is not served first and the soup last. Do not shuttle back and forth between the sentences. Keep related parts together; finish one phase of the thought before you begin another.

56b. Make the arrangement of sentences show progress or a forward movement.

The arrangement of sentences within a paragraph depends upon the substance itself; there is no standard rule. However, there is one essential of order: it requires progress, a forward movement of some sort. The thought must go from some place to some other place. This progress may be of several kinds: (1) *chronological* (time) order, which serves for much narrative writing, expository processes, and descriptions which progress as the writer changes his temporal point of view; (2) *point-of-view* order or *"space"* order, in which details are arranged from near to remote, or remote to near, from outside to inside, left to right, and conversely; (3) *logical* order, in which the writer makes a general statement and then supplies details (deductive method), or, vice versa (the inductive method), in which he states an effect and then gives the causes.

The following paragraph is developed in *logical* order:

From time immemorial work has been glorified. Song and story yield their homage to the solid merits of work, however romantically they may extol the delights of indolence, while essay and biography axiomatically acclaim work as the sure means to personal success and social esteem. The more prosaic and academic discussions of contemporary life, in their exaltation of work as the great social panacea, do but reëcho the words of Carlyle, who describes it as "the grand cure of all the maladies and miseries that ever beset mankind." The Rotarian mind makes work co-equal, if not identical, with service. Nowhere has this doctrine been better summed up than in the words of that past master of pious platitudes, Calvin Coolidge: "To provide for the economic well-being of our inhabitants, only three attributes, which are not beyond the reach of the average person are necessary—honesty, industry, and thrift." (Oh, if it were only so simple!)

—HENRY PRATT FAIRCHILD in *Harper's Magazine*

56c. Arrange sentences in a paragraph in effective order.

Order in the paragraph involves not only logic but effectiveness. There are two easily attainable methods of effectiveness within the paragraph.

1. *Beginning and ending as effective positions.* The effectiveness of any paragraph can be improved by a careful arrangement of thoughts. Ordinarily, the sentences developing the most important phase of the idea of the paragraph should be placed at the beginning or the end. It is not always advisable to place significant detail in these positions; consistently doing so will cause monotony of structure. The most trenchant statement of the paragraph, however, should usually not be embedded somewhere within the paragraph. First and last impressions of paragraphs, as of people, are genuinely important.

2. *Order of climax.* A second method of achieving effectiveness in the paragraph is to arrange the thoughts in climactic order; that is, each successive idea is followed by a more important one, the most important coming last. If the dramatic idea is saved for the end, the reader will eagerly read on, lured by the prospect of a climactic statement. Notice how Norman Thomas builds up to a trenchant statement in this paragraph from "Is Decline of the Profit Motive Desirable?":

Economic experts tell us that we in America have the capacity for a minimum income of $2,000 or $2,500 a year. Why, then, our bitter poverty? If the profit system isn't to blame, what is? You can't laugh off the desire of the masses for abundance. But you will never conquer the movement to abolish the profit system, unless temporarily by the despicable means of force, unless you can dispose of the Great Agitator, poverty in the midst of potential plenty.[18]

If you consistently fail to "keep something in reserve," if you always fully inform your reader in advance of what your statement

[18] From *The Rotarian*.

implies, you will lose the effectiveness which climactic arrangement affords.

EXERCISES

A. Rewrite the paragraph below, following a correct *point-of-view* order. Supply any transitional aids which will insure greater coherence.

Viewed from the outside, the house seemed large and rambling. It was enclosed by a picket fence which needed a coat of paint. The agent who was accompanying me said that the house had only nine rooms, but that they were large. The dining room was covered with wall paper which was faded and torn. The lawn needed mowing, and ugly weeds were growing in the cracks between the front steps. The bedrooms badly needed repairing. I reached the property early in the afternoon. After going over the house thoroughly, I decided not to lease it. The agent was from St. Louis; his name was Brown.

B. Write a paragraph which involves *chronological* order, from *earlier* to *later* time, or vice versa.

C. *He became desperately ill.* Consider this as a topic sentence which states an effect and write a paragraph in which the sentences are logically ordered as *causes* for his illness.

D. Rewrite the following poorly ordered paragraph:

1. He was a good athlete. 2. At first, his freshman coach thought that John would never make his letter. 3. At the end of his junior year, John almost made the trip abroad with the Olympic team. 4. His high school coach knew he had ability, and when John left for college, the coach wrote the athletic director not to overlook him. 5. John did not make the freshman team, but he worked diligently and showed great improvement. 6. Although he did not make the Olympic team, he went as a spectator. 7. This year he won a first place at the Western Conference Meet. 8. He sailed on the *Olympic*.

E. Rewrite a paragraph from a theme so as to place the most important idea at the beginning or the end.

F. From your book of readings select a paragraph which is effective because of its climactic arrangement.

G. Write a paragraph in which the details are arranged in the order of climax.

PROPORTION

57. Paragraphs should have not only adequate substance, unity, and correct order of sentences, but also right proportion. This term implies *symmetry;* a paragraph should be developed according to its relative idea value. If a paragraph contains discussion of a proportionately important idea, its length should be greater than that of a paragraph which develops a comparatively minor topic. Readers are likely to attribute importance to ideas on a basis of the length of the paragraphs in which they are discussed. Often such emphasis is undue; it causes distorted, out-of-proportion understanding.

57a. Make sure that paragraphs are correctly proportioned.

In writing a theme of five hundred words, a student may compose a long introductory paragraph, follow it with a transitional paragraph, and have left only one hundred words or so for the final paragraph which contains the actual *theme,* the central idea of the entire paper. Such a composition is badly proportioned. Do not expand ideas that are relatively subordinate or treat sketchily ideas which are of fundamental importance. Between these two extremes of overexpansion and underdevelopment there is a golden mean: paragraphs which adequately deal with their topics and which, added together, give a unified, well-proportioned discussion of the subject.

57b. Achieve proportion through careful overall planning.

Correct proportion necessitates careful planning. The writer who dwells at length upon some phase of the theme because he is interested in that phase or knows it thoroughly may not be taking into account its importance in relation to the reader. The thoughtless writer will consider only his own interest or knowledge; to achieve correct paragraph proportion, he must consider the relation of the paragraph to the whole subject, and also his reader's reaction. Study the following suggestions:

1. Consider the subject as a whole before writing an individual paragraph.

334

2. Think of the reader; determine the central purpose which each paragraph is to have in communicating ideas to him.

3. Do not hesitate to shorten paragraphs if they are out of proportion in relation to the subject and the reader, even though they contain favorite ideas and their revision will sacrifice precious words.

4. Do not hesitate to lengthen paragraphs if they contain ideas which need amplification, illustration, or repetition, so that their significance may really be felt by the reader.

EXERCISES

A. Study one of the essays in your book of readings. Comment upon the paragraph proportion. Are the paragraphs symmetrical?

B. Comment upon the apportioning of space (time) in some lecture or debate you have recently heard. Did some phases (paragraphs) seem *unduly* long, or sketchy?

C. Choose a few topics for 500-word themes, and estimate the proportionate importance of the several developing paragraphs.

D. Indicate the number of words proportionately correct for each paragraph of a 500-word theme based on the following plan:

LEARNING TO SWIM
1. Correct mental attitude for the beginner.
2. Correct body position.
3. How to handle the arms.
4. How to handle the feet.
5. Errors to be avoided.
6. Summary.

LENGTH

58. The principle governing proportion is that the length must be determined by the relative importance of the thought unit the paragraph embraces. But the problem of paragraph length not considered proportionately is also troublesome. No specific rule for paragraph length can be laid down, save the principle mentioned above, and the principle of appropriateness (see Section **60,** below). Two general recommendations may serve as guides.

58a. Avoid a series of short, choppy paragraphs.

Short, choppy paragraphs confuse the reader, who expects a central idea or topic to be clearly and effectively developed within a paragraph. Such a series, therefore, usually implies that you have not developed fully and coherently the central idea of such paragraphs, or that you have failed to see the relationship of ideas and have thus violated the principle of unity (Section 55). Note the choppy, confusing effect of the following paragraphs:

Each day he arises at an early hour and sets out for the city with his vegetables.

He arrives there before most people are awake and has his produce neatly arranged before the housewives start out to market. Because his vegetables are fresh, and attractively displayed, he usually has little difficulty in selling them.

By noon each day he has completed his sales and returns to his farm to work in the fields until sunset.

Short paragraphs may correctly be used to gain emphasis. For example, in description or narration, short paragraphs are often used to achieve a vigorous, emphatic style. Frequently they are necessary in dialogue to indicate change of speakers. But remember: very short paragraphs should not be written except for a definite stylistic effect. The short paragraphs in some newspapers and advertisements are used for effect, not thoughtlessly.

58b. Avoid a group of long, heavy paragraphs.

A series of long paragraphs is likely to strain your reader's attention. He may finish one, or even two, distended paragraphs, but he will lose interest, and his attention will shift, unless he is furnished with an occasional paragraph break which will afford him an opportunity to "catch his breath" and summarize the thought.

Another objection to very long paragraphs is that all too frequently they contain material which does not properly belong, thus violating the principle of unity. It is difficult to write a unified paragraph of over 250 words.

Often it is possible to break a long paragraph into two or more shorter ones without violation of unity, provided that transitional words or phrases are used to insure coherence.

NOTE: Do not awkwardly and artificially avoid either long or short paragraphs. Use them according to the proportionate value of the thought units they express. It is only a *series* of either that is usually ineffective. Many excellent writers now tend to write shorter paragraphs than formerly were used, but in scholarly or technical papers the paragraphs still run to considerable length. In popular magazines and the better newspapers of today, the average length is about one hundred words. The use of long or short paragraphs, or a compromise between the two, is often a matter of convention and appropriateness (Section **60**).

EXERCISES

A. Compare the average length of the paragraphs in an article in *The Atlantic Monthly* with the length of those in an article in *Collier's Magazine.*

B. Ascertain the average length of the paragraphs in a newspaper story and in a full-page advertisement printed in a popular magazine. What effects are achieved, in your opinion, by the brief paragraphs?

C. Count the number of words in several consecutive paragraphs of some essay in your anthology.

D. Compare the number of words in the opening three or four paragraphs of any two of the essays in your book of readings.

E. Place in larger units these choppy paragraphs:

Every year, except during years when civilian production is curtailed, thousands of people buy new radio sets for the first time. Other thousands replace their old sets with new ones.

Why?

All these people want entertainment. Buying a radio set is buying a seat for the big show.

Who gives the show?

The advertisers give the show. They want the attention of the public, and they are willing to pay heavily to get it.

But some advertisers seem to forget that the entertainment value of the programs they provide is, for the public, of paramount importance. The advertising message is accepted only if it is not too insistent and blatant.

If advertisers wish to be repaid for the show, if they wish to win good will, they must avoid antagonizing the public with too obvious intrusion of the advertising message into the entertainment of the program.

TRANSITION

59. When we say that paragraphs should be coherent, what we really mean is that they should be properly tied together. That is, each paragraph should contain sentences which are logically related, and separate paragraphs within the same theme should be unmistakably connected. Coherence depends upon clarity of thought, but the secret of coherence lies in the use of connectives, *transitional expressions*. Even though a paragraph contains ample substance, with its sentences logically and clearly arranged, it will not seem coherent if the sentences appear to the reader to be loosely joined. A series of paragraphs will be coherent to him only if the connections between them are unmistakably clear.

59a. Make transitions between paragraphs clear by using transitional words and phrases or by repetition.

Shifts in thought are always puzzling to a reader unless he is prepared in advance for them. Signs on highways, such as "Curve, 100 yards" and "Slow Down: End of Pavement," are similar in function to transitional aids. When a writer has finished one section of his discussion, he often finds it necessary to mention what has been said and to indicate what is to follow. Such reference and indication are of real help to the reader.

Important as transitions are, they should be brief and inconspicuous. Their function is to lead the reader smoothly and easily from one idea to the next. Transitions are a mechanical feature of style; they should not be labored, they should not protrude so much that they distract the reader's attention from *ideas*. The writer should lead the reader from one idea to the next with clarity and skill.

That clarity and skill can be gained by the use of transitional words and phrases. Such words and expressions as *for example,*

338

however, on the other hand, but, similarly, a second cause, another reason often furnish adequate transition. (A fuller list is given in Section 72a, p. 376.) Employed at the beginning of a paragraph, although not necessarily as the opening words, they serve to connect what is to follow with the thought in the preceding paragraph. An entire sentence may also be used transitionally. Likewise, coherence may be gained by the repetition of words at the close of one paragraph and the beginning of another. Note the following italicized expressions:

. . . This concludes the author's comments on taxation.
But taxation is not the only problem which he discusses . . .

Thus we may say that he is a splendid specimen, physically.
On the other hand, his mentality is of a low order . . .

. . . The valence of certain elements varies in different compounds.
But let us first discuss the valence of two common elements, oxygen and hydrogen . . .

59b. Make transitions between paragraphs clear by using transitional paragraphs.

Sometimes the shift in thought between two paragraphs, or two groups of paragraphs, is so marked that a word or phrase is not sufficient fully to indicate the transition. In such a situation a short transitional paragraph may be used to give a summary of what has been said and to suggest what is to follow. Note the following italicized paragraph:

There are three primary essentials to the good theme: correctness, clearness, and effectiveness. If a theme lacks any one of the elements, it is not a good theme; if it lacks more than one, or lacks any one to an unusual degree, it is a very poor theme.

These elements, then, are the sine qua non *of the good theme. It now remains for us to define each of these terms and apply them to such matters as diction, punctuation, and sentence structure.*

A good theme must be correct in its diction. Correct diction implies . . .

59c. Make transitions clear by leaving no gaps in thought.

Frequently paragraph connection is faulty because the writer fails to give all pertinent details of relation. For example, in a descriptive theme, one paragraph may end with a description of the exterior of a house, and the next begin with a discussion of the view from an upstairs room. Or one paragraph may discuss the value of good roads, and the next begin: "Good roads are a menace to life and property." The reader naturally asks why? A gap has been left in the thought and must be filled in with, perhaps, statement that good roads, because they are a temptation to speed and reckless driving, are also a menace.

Good writing is always characterized by skill in the revelation of thought relationships. Transitional aids are indispensable to the writer who wishes *fully* to *communicate* his thoughts, and the exact shadings of his thought, to the reader.

EXERCISES

A. Underline all the transitional words and phrases which occur in one of your recent themes. Compare them with the list given in Section **72a.**

B. Underline all the reference words and transitional expressions to be found on one page of a selection in your book of readings. Note especially the transitional devices which occur at the *beginnings* of paragraphs.

C. Expand into a short transitional paragraph some linking phrase or sentence which you have used in a recent theme.

D. From your book of readings select three paragraphs which seem to you particularly skillful in the use of connectives.

APPROPRIATENESS

Depending upon your purpose, you will choose certain kinds of paragraphs which will most appropriately and effectively accomplish that purpose. In addition to the "normal" paragraph or series of paragraphs which develop the various phases or divisions of a subject and are unified by being built around a specific topic (Sections **53–59**), other paragraphs, according to length or content, perform special and specific functions.

60. Use paragraphing that is appropriate.

1. In *writing dialogue* or *quoting conversations,* use short para-

graphs, and a separate paragraph for each speaker's words. (See Section **52c.**)

2. As *introductory paragraphs,* as *concluding paragraphs,* or as *transitional paragraphs* between longer divisions of a subject, use short paragraphs. (See Section **59b.**) The following is an introductory paragraph listing the topics to be expanded in the following paragraphs:

The causes of war are psychological, biological, economic, and political—that is, they lie in the impulses of men, the competition of groups, the material needs of societies, and fluctuations of national power.[19]

For the material introduced by the preceding paragraph, the following serves as a brief summary and conclusion:

These, then, are the causes of war. How natural it seems now, in the perspective of science and history; how ancient its sources and how inscrutable its destiny![20]

3. In *business letters,* use short paragraphs. Such paragraphs vary from two to six lines. Longer paragraphs are seldom used; they retard getting the message at a single glance, a major purpose of most business-letter paragraphs.

4. In developing briefly *a single topic* or *a simple subject,* write only one paragraph. Such a paragraph, in developing only a single topic, is of course independent; in a sense it is a miniature theme. Many newspaper editorial writers, columnists, and advertising writers make frequent use of independent paragraphs. At the beginning of the term especially, freshman English students are often required to write independent paragraphs. Later they are required to write on larger topics, and paragraphs become units of larger compositions. Here is an example of the independent paragraph developing a single topic:

We were encouraged at reading the prediction that this country would be out of gas in about ten years. There is probably nothing in the report. Still, it bucks a man up. We can now dismiss the revolting

[19] From Will Durant, "Why Men Fight," *The Saturday Evening Post.*
[20] *Ibid.*

picture of the world which has been painted for us—a world agitated by an unlimited supply of petrol and by the spirit of total motion. The automobile, the helicopter, the family plane, the stratoliner, and the folding house which flaps together and jumps around from place to place have been woven into a dream in Technicolor by the excitable prophets of industry. They push this dream down our throats at every turn of the page. Unless a man believes that the highest form of life is that which darts about, he can face the future only with an effort of will. As for us, we are an exponent of the sit-still, or stay-where-you-are, theory of life and have always had more respect for the horned toad than for the black ant. The bicycle is our idea of a decent acceleration of the normal body movements and the Model T Ford is the highest point to which we deem it advisable to develop the gas engine. We therefore hail with cries of unprincipled joy the news of the drying up of the wells. Ah, lovely wilderness, if only it were true![21]

5. For *summaries, conclusions, recommendations,* and certain kinds of *directions,* use a paragraph consisting of not too closely related sentences. The unifying topic of such paragraphs, usually implied, is one of the foregoing italicized words. The following is an example of a summary paragraph:

We have now examined the various classes of thinking which we can readily observe in ourselves and which we have plenty of reason to believe go on, and always have been going on, in our fellow-men. We can sometimes get quite pure and sparkling examples of all four kinds, but commonly they are so confused and intermingled in our reverie as not to be readily distinguishable. The reverie is a reflection of our longings, exultations, and complacencies, our fears, suspicions, and disappointments. We are chiefly engaged in struggling to maintain our self-respect and in asserting that supremacy which we all crave and which seems to us our natural prerogative. It is not strange, but rather quite inevitable, that our beliefs about what is true and false, good and bad, right and wrong, should be mixed up with the reverie and be influenced by the same considerations which determine its character and course. We resent criticisms of our views exactly as we do of anything else connected with ourselves. Our notions of life and its ideals seem to us to be *our own* and as such necessarily true and right, to be defended at all costs.[22]

[21] © The F-R Publishing Corporation, 1944.
[22] From *The Mind in the Making,* by James Harvey Robinson.

6. For *effectiveness* in writing summaries, conclusions, recommendations, and certain kinds of directions, occasionally use *paragraphs of isolated statements:* that is, paragraphs consisting of single sentences or parts of sentences. Such paragraphs are frequently numbered. For example:

As a result of this investigation, our conclusions are as follows:
1. Weather conditions that morning were not suitable for flying.
2. The engine of this plane had mechanical defects that should have been corrected before the take-off.
3. The pilot, and owner, of the plane was comparatively inexperienced in flying under unfavorable weather conditions.
4. The Brooktown Municipal Airport authorities, since their advice and commands were ignored, should be absolved of responsibility for the accident.

Not infrequently such paragraphs of isolated statements come within the body of an article. For example:

Part of the [water-famine] solution is to stop the reckless waste. The engineers of the Department of Water Supply estimated that it would be possible for the eight million New Yorkers to conserve 196.8 million gallons of water per day. They urge that citizens
1. Repair, or have the landlord repair, any leaking faucet or other wasting fixture.
2. Don't wash dishes under an open faucet.
3. Don't heat or cool the baby's bottle under a running faucet.
4. Keep a bottle of water in the refrigerator to get a cool drink quickly.
5. Don't overrinse in using washing machines.[23]

EXERCISES

A. From a magazine or your anthology, choose a short story and examine the paragraphing of dialogue. Note how much, if any, explanatory material is included in the paragraphs giving quoted speeches.

B. Write a short paper in order to illustrate paragraphing and

[23] Arthur H. Carhart, "Turn Off That Faucet!" in *The Atlantic Monthly,* February, 1950, p. 39.

the use of quotation marks (see Section **25**) on the subject, *A Dialogue Between — and —*.

C. In one article in a magazine or in your book of readings, mark all the short paragraphs (two to six lines). Determine what purpose they serve: introductory, concluding, transitional, etc.

D. Look through such magazines as *The New Yorker, The Nation, The New Republic,* or *The Reader's Digest* for one-paragraph articles or discussions. Estimate their length. Find the topic sentence or statement and discuss the method or methods of paragraph development used.

E. Comment on the length and purpose of the paragraphs in several business letters (written to you or to relatives and friends).

GENERAL EXERCISES

A. Study the following paragraphs. Pick out the topic sentence or topic statement of each (or phrase the topic if it is merely implied); identify the method of development (professional writers often use a *combination* of methods); notice the transitional words and phrases; discuss the specific devices employed to make each paragraph effective:

1. The migratory passage of birds, like the movements of the stars, can be a great consolation to men whose minds continually search for an established order and progression in the universe. The knowledge that, whatever we may make of ourselves in the moment of our existence, the stars will continue in their appointed courses, the seasons will move in their confirmed order, the birds will pursue their destined biannual migrations, carries with it a sense of ultimate security which the works of man alone fail to convey. It seems to give us the intimation of a will that directs us. It belies our orphaned state in the universe. Order, harmony, regularity, these elements implicit in the recurrent flight of birds, are beyond the touch of the good and evil that men do in the numbered hours of their survival. Knowledge of the integrated pattern of the universe in which the birds share, of the final cosmic autocracy whose imposed limits no organism may transcend, secures us from the nightmare of anarchy.[24]

—Louis F. Halle, Jr.

[24] From *Birds Against Men*, by Louis F. Halle, Jr.

General Exercises

2. The proper use of social insurance is akin to that of drugs. In carefully measured doses it will keep the economy healthy. Used recklessly, it will destroy the body politic. What we can afford in the future for the welfare of our people will depend upon an expanding productivity. All the more reason, therefore, to ensure that productivity not only for the protection of old age but also to give all our children an equal opportunity for self-development and for the creation of an emotional poise and security which economic security alone cannot provide.[25]

—AGNES E. MEYER

3. Life for most of these attractive, brown-skinned Micronesian peoples is simple and primitive. They have no literature. Few of them have any but the most elementary education. For centuries before the white man came they maintained a fairly happy existence, developing a culture admirably adapted to the conditions under which they lived. Theirs was a subsistence economy undisturbed by worries of buying and selling. Mother Nature is for the most part kindly in the South Seas. Coconuts, bananas, breadfruit, pandanus, taro, and fish are easily to be had; clothing presents no trouble—the less the better; and shelter is easily furnished by the leaves of pandanus or palm. Sustained work was quite unnecessary. A strongly developed communal family or clan system removed the fear of individual want or capacity, and promised care in time of sickness or old age.[26]

—FRANCIS B. SAYRE

4. That tenement had a certain quiet distinction; there was no sign upon its face that he made for any of the Royal Family—merely his own German name of Gessler Brothers; and in the window a few pairs of boots. I remember that it always troubled me to account for those unvarying boots in the window, for he made only what was ordered, reaching nothing down, and it seemed so inconceivable that what he made could ever have failed to fit. Had he bought them to put there? That, too, seemed inconceivable. He would never have tolerated in his house leather on which he had not worked himself. Besides, they were too beautiful—the pair of pumps, so inexpressibly slim, the patent leathers with cloth tops, making water come into one's mouth, the tall brown riding-boots with marvelous sooty glow, as if, though new, they had been worn a hundred years. Those pairs could only have been

[25] From *The Atlantic Monthly*, January, 1950, p. 64.
[26] *Ibid.*, p. 70.

made by one who saw before him the Soul of Boots—so truly were they prototypes, incarnating the very spirit of all footwear. These thoughts, of course, came to me later, though even when I was promoted to him, at the age of perhaps fourteen, some inkling haunted me of the dignity of himself and brother. For to make boots—such boots as he made —seemed to me then, and still seems to me, mysterious and wonderful.[27]

—JOHN GALSWORTHY

B. The following section lacks unity, order, and proper transitional aids. Make all necessary changes for correct paragraphing.

Several hundred years ago, it was customary for European towns to hold annual fairs in their market places. To these fairs came farmers who wished to sell their products and peddlers who wished to sell their wares. Only small businessmen went to customers' homes to make sales. Large business houses hire men and women to sell wares from door to door. One day a young man came to my home. When the lady of the house appeared, he began to talk rapidly. I answered the doorbell and let him into the house. "How do you do, Mrs. Johnson? Any of the articles I have may be bought for one dollar. Each is worth more. Which would you prefer?" And he kept on and on. Finally my mother had a chance to say, "I am very busy and, furthermore, do not wish to buy anything. Please go at once." But the sale was eventually made, and the canvasser left for the next house. This type of canvasser can never amount to much, for he relies more upon the appeal of sympathy than upon salesmanship. I was sitting in a friend's home one afternoon when one of these dynamic salesmen appeared. It was a very cold day, and I had gone to see my friend in preference to playing football. He carried a small vacuum cleaner in one hand and a valise in the other. He rang the doorbell and made himself at home. He demonstrated the machine, explaining its mechanism clearly. He was close to thirty years of age, and his hair was graying around the temples. Then he compared his prospect's machine with his new one, and made a trade-in offer. The gentleman's sales argument was perfect. He departed as soon as the sale was made. She accepted the offer and bought a new vacuum cleaner. He did not give the customer time to regret the purchase. Modern canvassers are indeed different from the peddlers who sold their wares in medieval times. Today in all parts

[27] From *The Inn of Tranquillity*, by John Galsworthy.

346

General Exercises

of the world, especially in thickly populated districts, these modern peddlers can be found.

C. The following paragraphs are choppy and ineffective. Revise them.

He is now a physician, but it took him many years to become one.

He was a poor boy and had to work his way through high school, college, and medical school.

He worked in a department store in St. Louis for four years while he was going to college.

He made good grades while he was in college and had no difficulty in gaining entrance to a medical school.

He made his tuition money at medical college by tutoring some high school students who lived near his room.

He is now a successful practitioner of medicine. He says that his own son wants to become a doctor and he is willing for him to do so, provided money is plentiful enough. His own experience was rather bitter, and he has no desire for his son to have to earn money while attending school.

D. Comment upon the lack of unity and the ineffectiveness of the following paragraph:

Henry Adams wrote as a person who knew the answers to nearly every question—as a man who had the final word. Since Mr. Adams had found no order or pattern in the universe, he claimed there was none. True, he was not satisfied with the conclusions he drew, but he felt that they were the only answers. I don't think Adams had any right to criticize life because he had never really lived. He tended to float through things and thus never got as much out of the world as most people do. I think everyone gets out of a thing what he puts into it. Adams had potentially great talents to give but he never gave them. Instead, he remained inactive, studying and drawing his almost useless conclusions. I am not condemning Adams for living the life of a student and a philosopher. Many philosophers have greatly helped the world. However, Adams drew conclusions based on what life had been to him and attempted to apply these conclusions to people in general. They were, however, invalid to ordinary people because Adams had disassociated himself too far from the life that the average person led.

The Sentence

"We think in terms of words, speak in terms of sentences, and write in terms of paragraphs." Such a statement is not wholly true, but it at least implies that by the use of concepts (words) we phrase sentences which we tie together into complete paragraphs. A sentence is the link between a thought and the full development of that thought, and, like all links, it is of great importance. Good sentences derive from good diction, good paragraphs from good sentences, and good themes from good paragraphs. The paragraph can be only so good as its component parts, its sentences, the units of expression.

Thus, if your sentences are awkward, or faulty, or vague, the primary purposes of your writing at all have been defeated. Obviously, then, you must know how to avoid writing cumbersome, faulty, or cloudy sentences; you must know how to give your sentences unity, completeness, clearness, and effectiveness. But one cannot shingle a house or paint the roof before he has laid the foundation or built the framework. Neither can one understand how to obtain such characteristics in sentence structure as those mentioned above before he has a solid foundation, a substantial framework. You must first know what a sentence *is;* you must understand grammatical structures and functions and upon that foundation and framework construct sentences that are direct and clear and complete.

A sentence is a group of words containing a complete, independent thought or a group of closely related thoughts. This definition, together with a full discussion of the forms and patterns of sentences, may be found on pages 51–55. A review of this material may be helpful before you study the following sections, which

The Sentence

deal specifically with errors frequently made in writing the sentence and suggest definite ways of avoiding them. As in any study, you should relate the rules, suggestions, comments, and exercises to your particular needs.

Actually, the problems of writing sentences may be classed under only three main heads: *correctness, clearness,* and *effectiveness.* Sections **61–80** deal with these three topics as follows:

Correctness

  Period fault—Section **61**
  Comma splice—Section **62**
  Fused sentences—Section **63**
  Dependent clauses misused—Section **64**

Clearness

  Sentence unity—Section **65**
  Incompleteness—Section **66**
  Word order—Section **67**
  Split constructions—Section **68**
  Dangling modifiers—Section **69**
  Reference of pronouns—Section **70**
  Mixed constructions—Section **71**
  Transition—Section **72**

Effectiveness

  Conciseness—Section **73**
  Parallelism—Section **74**
  Point of view—Section **75**
  Faulty coördination—Section **76**
  Faulty subordination—Section **77**
  Choppy sentences—Section **78**
  Position and arrangement—Section **79**
  Variety—Section **80**

Such a listing as this may help you to keep in mind the three main problems you are attacking. You should note, however, that these topics are not mutually exclusive. Effective sentences result from both correctness and clearness; sentence unity is probably as much a problem of correctness as of clarity and could have been placed under either heading. Or, for another illustration, inexact transition is both ineffective and incorrect. But keep your attention focused on sentence *correctness,* sentence *clearness,* and sentence *effectiveness.* Doing so will keep you from becoming mired in the many details of the twenty sections which follow.

PERIOD FAULT

61. Do not write a subordinate part of a sentence as if it were a complete predication.

The word *sentence* means "a stated opinion." Accordingly, any group of words may be called a sentence. But in grammar, a sentence is not a sentence unless it has a subject and predicate, implied or expressed, even though the predicate be merely a single verb, and unless this word group can stand alone, make sense in itself, be complete.

"Sentences" are occasionally incomplete because the writer is unable to distinguish between a complete predication and a group of words which is incapable of standing alone and "making sense." A phrase or a dependent clause cannot be written as a complete sentence; to write and punctuate one of them as such constitutes a *period fault.* Verbal and appositive phrases, and dependent clauses of all kinds must be included in the same sentence with the main clause. (See "Phrases" and "Clauses," pp. 47–51.)

> Wrong: I had no money for a trip to Europe. *When suddenly I was left a fortune.* (Dependent clause.)
> I studied hours every night. *Finally giving up all my efforts.* (Participial phrase.)
> The bank was destroyed by those who needed it most. *The small depositors.* (Appositive phrase.)

Such fragmentary sentences may be corrected by rewriting or by joining the dependent clause or phrase to a preceding or following whole sentence.

> Revised: I had no money for a trip to Europe. Suddenly I was left a fortune.

I studied hours every night but finally gave up all my efforts.

The bank was destroyed by those who needed it most, the small depositors.

NOTE: There are, however, two kinds of incomplete sentences which are permissible.

1. *Elliptical sentences,* although not grammatically complete, imply complete predications, and are correct, for ellipsis means that parts are omitted which are understood from what precedes or follows. The italicized expressions which follow are thus allowable violations of Rule 61.

"Did you buy it?"

"Yes."

"For how much?"

"Five dollars."

2. *Fragmentary sentences* are frequently used by skilled writers for stylistic purposes. For example: "He walked as though he were dreaming. Dreaming? Hardly. He was more detached than that. He was hypnotized! Far away. Lost in another world."

Students frequently complain that their instructors mark all fragmentary sentences as incorrect, even those deliberately written for stylistic effect. The truth is that most teachers wish their students to use fragments for rhetorical purposes only after they have demonstrated their knowledge of sentence completeness. After you have shown that you know what a sentence is, you may be allowed to experiment. (For further discussion of sentence fragments, examples, and methods of correction, see pp. 23–24.)

EXERCISES

A. Correct the period faults in the following sentences by expanding the fragments into complete sentences:

1. The grass needed moisture. No rain for four weeks.
2. He wrote all his themes very rapidly. An hour for each.
3. She discussed politics avidly. But unintelligently.
4. It has an excellent climate. At the same time offering many recreations.

5. There were only two people who did not listen. The poorest students.

    B. Correct the above sentences by attaching the fragments to the remainders of the sentences.

    C. Correct the following sentences by attaching the fragments or by expansion:

1. The trip is not long or tedious. Lasting only one hour and offering excellent scenery.
2. He had a small appetite. Eating only once a day.
3. The airship was put into its hangar. So that curious spectators could not damage it.
4. My brothers studied law. One at Columbia and one at Virginia.
5. He has been here many years. Coming from Illinois in 1935.
6. Mr. Gory submitted a bid for the property. The lowest we have seen. It was immediately accepted.
7. Tom could not understand why he was defeated. He had worked hard to win the election. Harder than anyone else in the race.
8. Some of Thackeray's characters are memorable. Indeed, unforgettable.
9. This sentence is not difficult to correct. Very easy indeed. At least that's my opinion.
10. She spoke haltingly. Brushing away the tears from her eyes.

COMMA SPLICE

62. Do not write two sentences with only a comma between them.
    Sentences must be complete (see Sections **61, 66**) and they must be unified (see Section **65**). Students frequently write two independent statements as one sentence, thus violating the principle of unity. A writer who does this reveals a deficiency of thought or the fact that he does not know where one sentence ends and another begins. A frequent occurrence of this "double sentence" error is the "comma splice" (also called "comma blunder" and "comma fault"). Remember that this error is using a comma between two sentences or between two independent clauses not joined by a simple coördinating conjunction. The comma splice may be corrected by substituting a period for the comma. If the two ideas are related, however, the blunder may be corrected by using a comma

and a simple conjunction (see Section **18d**); by using a semicolon (see Section **19a**); or by subordinating one of the two statements. (For further discussion of the comma splice, examples, and methods of correction, see p. 25.)

> Wrong: The trees are very tall, they were planted ten years ago.
>
> Right: The trees are very tall. They were planted ten years ago. (Period.)
>
> The trees are very tall, for they were planted ten years ago. (Comma and conjunction.)
>
> The trees are very tall; they were planted ten years ago. (Semicolon.)
>
> The trees are very tall because they were planted ten years ago. (Subordination.)

EXERCISE

Correct the following "double sentences" by the use of a period, by the substitution of a comma plus a conjunction, by the use of a semicolon, or by subordination. Be careful to separate completely ideas not at all related.

1. This lawyer is prominent in his own community, he is not known nationally.
2. He had a bad cold, this was due, he thought, to a sudden change in the weather.
3. The storm was furious, John said he had never seen one like it.
4. The population of the United States is growing, it may soon be 160,000,000.
5. The bell is ringing now, this means that you will be late.
6. The man hurried, it was cold and he wanted shelter.
7. The sophomore knows what he can do in life; the senior is uncertain about his future.
8. I answered the call, it sounded like Henry's voice.
9. We walked a mile farther to Madison, there a tramp asked us if he could join our party.
10. Baltusrol is a splendid golf course, and many experts say it is comparatively easy, I like to play tennis better than golf.

FUSED SENTENCES

63. Do not write two sentences with no punctuation whatever between them. Use a terminal mark (period, question mark, exclamation point).

A serious grammatical error and violation of the principle of unity is to write two grammatically complete sentences with no mark of punctuation between them. The "fused," or "blended," sentence error is an even more flagrant violation of correctness than the comma splice, for the writer of a comma splice shows that he senses the need for punctuation of some sort.

A sentence is a complete and independent predication and should always be followed by a full stop, that is, a terminal mark of punctuation.

> Wrong: The automobile ran smoothly the train was rough. The next day he departed for Atlanta this city is the capital of Georgia.

Judged by their grammatical form, each of these two "sentences" contains two independent statements. Each "sentence" may be written as two separate sentences or, if the writer feels that the statements are sufficiently related in thought, other punctuation may be used. The result might be a compound sentence with a semicolon separating the clauses and a terminal mark at the end:

> Revised: The automobile ran smoothly. The train was rough. The automobile ran smoothly; the train was rough.

The methods used to avoid the comma splice (p. 352) may be applied to some fused sentences. For example, you may subordinate one of the statements:

> The next day he departed for Atlanta, the capital of Georgia.

(For further discussion of fused sentences, examples, and methods of correction, see pp. 24, 25.)

EXERCISES

A. Use periods, question marks, or exclamation points (and capital letters; see Section 27) where they are needed:

354

1. He talked for two hours, when he finished I had no idea what he meant.
2. Are you going so soon I shall go with you as far as the corner.
3. Turn out the lights hurry they may see us.
4. I gave the watch to John, the gardener, he was pleased and thanked me heartily.
5. "Help Help" the man cried, I hurried to the edge of the river, but I could see that he was only playing.

B. Correct the following by using terminal marks of punctuation or by subordination:

1. They will surely be arrested, they are breaking the law.
2. He remained in Germany for two years, then he returned to enter college.
3. The storm was raging, I stayed at home instead of going.
4. He is an excellent performer, one of the best in the state, I think, do you think so, too?
5. He was garrulous I did not pay any attention to his harangue.

DEPENDENT CLAUSES MISUSED

64. If you recognize the clearness and emphasis which proper subordination contributes to your sentences, you will be likely to use a large number of dependent clauses. But proper subordination is difficult and requires careful thinking. Errors in subordination sometimes cause lack of clarity and sometimes result in ineffectiveness. Those which are primarily matters of correctness are mentioned in this section.

Dependent clauses have the functions of separate parts of speech (noun, adjective, adverb); to use one of them for another is considered by some grammarians as serious an error as to misuse the parts of speech.

64a. Do not use an adverbial clause as a noun clause.

Wrong: I heard *where the weather forecaster said cold weather was coming.*

The reason the automobile stopped was *because it had run out of gasoline.* (Substitute *that* for the sub-

355

ordinating conjunctions *where* and *because* in these sentences.)

Because he had no money was the reason John dropped out of school. (Substitute *The fact that* for *Because.*)

64b. Do not use an adverbial clause in place of a noun.

When and *where* are the chief offenders in this type of incorrect subordination.

> Wrong: Plagiarism is *where* you take the work of another and pass it off as your own.
> Anemia is *when* the blood has certain deficiencies.
> *When* you graduate from college is the time to take life seriously.
> (Substitute nouns with modifiers for the adverbial clauses.)

64c. Use a noun clause, not a sentence, as the subject or complement of is and was.

> Faulty: I had sprained my ankle was the reason I could not go to the dance.
> His only fault is he has a bad temper.
> Better: The reason I could not go to the dance was that I had sprained my ankle.
> His only fault is that he has a bad temper.

NOTE: A quoted sentence may be used as a noun clause.

> Correct: "Her little face is like a walnut shell" is a line from an English poem.

EXERCISES

A. Correct the following sentences:

1. I see in the paper where the weather has been unusually cold this winter.
2. The train left by daylight time is why I missed it.
3. A conflict is when people or things are opposed to each other.
4. He did not concentrate was why he failed the course.

5. The reason the mower did not cut the grass was because its blades were dull.
6. Perjury is where a man swears to tell the truth and then tells a lie.
7. Because I bought a new suit is why she thinks I have money.
8. His excuse is he did not hear the command.
9. His definition of freedom is when you can look any man squarely in the eye.
10. His home is where you can always have a good time.

B. Compose sentences correctly illustrating dependent clauses used as nouns, adjectives, and adverbs.

C. Rewrite the following sentences, correcting the misuse of dependent clauses:

1. My one great advantage is I was born on a farm.
2. A state of rebellion is when armed forces seize control of the government.
3. The reason the steeple toppled over was because termites ate it.
4. Her father pointed out where she had been making the same mistakes for years.
5. Just after the hero sings to the heroine is where we came in.
6. The thing that upset our chickens was a skunk came into the henhouse looking for eggs.
7. The seat of the chair has been stood on so often by you children is the cause for its giving away under Mrs. Smith.
8. After examining the stomachs of a thousand malarial mosquitoes, the biologist stated the danger was when their stomachs were full.
9. The greatest benefit I received from my training was it taught me how to take care of myself.
10. Only because they have formal clothes is why the dance is being held.

SENTENCE UNITY

65. Unity means *singleness of purpose*. Sentence unity does not mean that only one object or idea should be mentioned, or that the sentence must be short. A unified sentence may refer to several people, places, objects, or ideas, and may extend to considerable length. For example, this is a unified sentence: "Although the weather had turned warmer during the night, nevertheless Jim and

I decided to pack our provisions and sharpen our skates in the hope that our guide would decide the ice was still safe for skating." The sentence is long and refers to several things and people; but it is unified because it has a singleness, a oneness, of purpose. The ideas are closely related and form a unit of thought. But a sentence could be one-fourth as long as this and refer to only one person, and yet violate the principle of unity: "Joe was a good student, being the possessor of a new hat." The reader of this sentence very properly asks, "What have the two ideas in common?" The answer is, of course, "Nothing. The sentence is not unified."

(1) Introducing too many details and (2) combining unrelated ideas violate sentence unity, essential to clear writing.

65a. Avoid rambling sentences which introduce too many details.

Wrong: They offered to meet our party at Moose Junction, a little town in Minnesota which has only five hundred inhabitants, but which contains two general stores, three churches, and, since 1946, a drive-in restaurant and a golf course owned by a wealthy man named Parks.

Revised: They offered to meet our party at Moose Junction, a little town in Minnesota which has only five hundred inhabitants, two general stores and three churches. Since 1946 it has also had a drive-in restaurant and a golf course. The latter is owned by a wealthy man named Parks.

65b. Avoid placing incongruous ideas in the same sentence.

Wrong: The grass was cut short, and she had bought the seed from Mrs. Thomas.
The girl wore a white dress, and she had a good time at the dance.

NOTE: Sometimes unity can be attained by making one idea subordinate to the other in the sentence, but ideas so unrelated as those immediately above probably should be placed in separate sentences.

EXERCISES

A. Rewrite the following sentences, remembering that often unity can be attained by proper subordination as well as by complete separation:

1. Bill was, a good pole vaulter and he was a graduate of Erie High.
2. The noise in the hall gradually increased until the din was so terrific that only by shouting could we make ourselves heard, and, the seats were hard wooden benches. *It*
3. We feel that our fraternity is the best at State College, which was founded in 1899 by two brothers, George and Daniel Slate.
4. The *Saturday Evening Post* is my favorite among the weekly magazines, and it is, published in Philadelphia.
5. My last grade in History XV was a 93, and I decided to go to the movies instead of studying.
6. We drove steadily for five hours between Harrisburg and Washington, and the Lincoln Memorial looked very beautiful in the twilight.
7. Ping-pong is a game that requires tremendous concentration if it is to be played well, but Jack would beat me six games out of ten.
8. He is a much better dancer than his brother, who took lessons at a studio and works at a local store.
9. Theodore Roosevelt believed in living a strenuous life, and was fond of his family and home at Oyster Bay. *He*
10. We lived in a boarding house which was managed by an elderly woman whose father had been an army officer. *Her*

B. Correct any violations of unity which occur in the following sentences:

1. After he left college he got a job teaching school in Madison, where he met Joe, a man who was to be his fast friend for life.
2. The man at the station said that the train left at four and, since I was hungry, I bought a sandwich.
3. Oyster fishermen live along Chesapeake Bay, and the pearls found in oysters are sometimes valuable.
4. People in North Carolina like hot breads, and the largest city is Charlotte.
5. The father was a physician, having studied at Jefferson Medical College in Philadelphia, the third largest city in the United States.
6. He is a good student, his sister having lived in Paris for several years.

7. Woodrow Wilson was an eminent statesman, ~~and he~~ had a prominent chin.
8. He was a constant smoker and owned a large factory in Kenyon.
9. When he was at Camp Sapphire, the boys agreed to go on an overnight hike and, after getting permission from Mr. Brown, the headmaster, an alumnus of Coe College, they packed their knapsacks and started for Moon Mountain, a peak about four miles from the camp, which was in a valley.
10. Finally, I arrived at the Aquarium, the world's largest fish museum, and behind it were parked two great fireboats which were red, with shining brass fittings.

INCOMPLETENESS

66. A sentence not only must contain a single thought, or a group of closely related ideas, but it must also be *complete;* that is, it must be capable of standing alone and "making sense." Because of their inaccurate thinking, many writers do not express their ideas so completely that the latter will be fully understandable units of thought. The fault is that the writer knows, or thinks he knows, what he has in mind, but does not take the trouble fully to convey his idea. Likewise, some "sentences" are incomplete because the writer does not know the grammatical essentials of a sentence. (See Section **61.**) Sound thinking and a minimum understanding of the "grammar" of a sentence should enable you also to avoid two serious kinds of sentence incompleteness: (1) the omission of *words* necessary for clear, full expression and (2) the omission of essential *ideas.*

66a. Do not omit a necessary main verb or an auxiliary verb.

Informal usage sanctions the omission of words which must be expressed in formal writing and speaking. Even in formal writing, such a sentence as "He made such a speech as only a politician can [make]" is complete and correct without the bracketed *make.* The following sentences, however, involve more serious breaches of clarity:

Doubtful: The lawn is mowed and the hedges trimmed.
Improved: The lawn is mowed and the hedges *are* trimmed.

Doubtful: He always has and always will study hard.
Improved: He always has *studied* and always will study hard.

66b. Do not omit a necessary article, pronoun, or preposition.

The president and chief executive received my plea. (This sentence means that one man is both president and chief executive.)

Doubtful: He built an automobile which could go ninety miles an hour and pleased many people.

Improved: He built an automobile which could go ninety miles an hour and *which* pleased many people.

Doubtful: I have interest and regard for your work.
Improved: I have interest *in* and regard for your work.

66c. Do not omit words necessary in a comparison.

Do not omit the standard of comparison or one term of the comparison. Do not omit *as* or *than* in a double comparison; place the second element at the end.

Doubtful: He is so weak.
Improved: He is so weak that he cannot do any work.
He is very weak.

Doubtful: This is the best cake.
Improved: This is the best cake that I have ever eaten.

Doubtful: I study my lessons harder than Fred.
Improved: I study my lessons harder than Fred does.
I study my lessons harder than I study Fred.

Doubtful: He is as strong, if not stronger, than John.
Improved, but awkward: He is as strong *as,* if not stronger than, John.
Preferable: He is as strong as John, if not stronger.

66d. Do not fail to express every idea essential to the sense or proper structure of the sentence.

It is difficult to determine whether incompleteness in thought causes incompleteness in structure, or vice versa. But you should remember not to leave any sentence elements grammatically in-

66 e Incompleteness

complete by starting with one construction and shifting to another
(see Section **71**).

> Not clear: An automobile, unless you take good care of it,
> you will soon have to have it repaired.
> Improved: An automobile will soon have to be repaired un-
> less good care is taken of it.
> Not clear: With these eleven men functioning as a team is
> the reason for our successful season.
> Improved: With these eleven men functioning as a team, we
> had a successful season.
>
> or
>
> Because these eleven men functioned as a team
> we had a successful season.

66e. Avoid a telegraphic style in formal writing.

Writing can be understood even when important words are
omitted. Otherwise, many important telegrams would be misin-
terpreted. The following, however, is not good style in formal
writing: "Letter received. Leaving tomorrow noon. Reserve room
Carter Hotel. Regards."

EXERCISES

A. Correct the incompleteness of words or idea in the following
sentences:

1. This is the worst hotel.
2. A typewriter, unless you know how to use it, it can be a genuine
   nuisance.
3. Will accept offer. Am writing further details.
4. The town of Florence is as large, if not larger, than Sumter.
5. The house was painted and the blinds hung.
6. The first years were not so bad.
7. He was interested and excited about his trip.
8. The teacher's pronunciation is like any other educated person.
9. Paved streets are more comfortable and last longer.
10. Aviation is no longer considered a novelty, but one of our chief
    industries.

B. Directions given in Exercise A.

1. In our college there is a course for almost everyone except modern American poetry.
2. It is perfectly possible that a dog's brain contains images very similar to ours.
3. My sympathy goes out to a boy who is so stupid.
4. Our team always has and always will fight clean.
5. For ten cents the children bought a pedometer which was entirely inaccurate but pleased them greatly.
6. I can handle cars better than Dad.
7. Stony Brook is as deep, if not deeper, than Otter Creek.
8. Father took me to the Exchange where I met several of the "big shots," including the president and treasurer.
9. Naturally, my reaction was entirely different from my family.
10. As we were very timid in a gathering of such important people, forgot all about introducing ourselves.
11. His hair is combed neatly and his hands washed clean.
12. I am very enthusiastic and fond of his sketching.
13. Since I have just had the flu, is a good reason for not going out for football.
14. He was always saying he could walk faster than any of us.
15. Mr. Jones changed a great deal after his accident and helped his employees with all the generosity he would have his own children.

WORD ORDER

67. In highly inflected foreign languages, the relationships of words in a sentence are shown by their endings. English is not highly inflected, and lack of clearness will result if such functional words as prepositions and auxiliary verbs are not properly used. Even if they are, vagueness will occur in a sentence in which words are incorrectly placed. Try to keep related words together in order that the reader may see their connection, and place every modifier so that it is logically and naturally connected with the word it modifies.

67a. Avoid a "squinting modifier."

A modifier is said to be "squinting" when it may refer to either of two parts of a sentence.

The man who can do this *well* deserves your praise. (*Well* may modify either *can do* or *deserves*.)

One way to correct this ambiguity is to add *certainly* after *well*. Then, the adverb *well* will apply to *can do* and the second adverb, *certainly*, to *deserves*. Or the sentence may be recast.

The student who does his work faithfully *from the point of view of his teachers* is praiseworthy. (The italicized words may refer to either the preceding or the following part of the sentence.)

To remove ambiguity here, place the italicized phrase at the beginning or end of the sentence. Doing either will remove the ambiguity but will result in a construction which probably should be recast.

67b. Do not misplace such words as <u>only</u>, <u>not</u>, <u>even</u>, <u>hardly</u>, etc.

Modifiers should be so exactly placed in a sentence as to convey precisely the meaning intended. In such a sentence as "I *only* want ten dollars," *only* apparently modifies the verb *want*. Actually, it is intended to modify *ten dollars:* "I want *only* ten dollars." The former position of *only* is so normal in both speech and writing, however, as hardly to be misunderstood by anyone. But remember that the placing of *only* or of any other modifying expression can have a decided effect upon meaning:

He *hardly* has enough stamina for that. (*Hardly* here may be construed as modifying the verb *has;* actually it should modify the adjective *enough*.) To remove any possible doubt in the reader's mind, write: He has *hardly* enough stamina for that.

Vague: Any woman who sees this picture, *even the most unattractive,* will identify herself with the lovely heroine.

Improved: Any woman, *even the most unattractive,* who sees this picture will identify herself with the lovely heroine.

Split Constructions **68 a-b**

67c. Do not misplace clauses and phrases.

Vague: I picked up the gloves and put them on my hands, *which I had bought in San Francisco.*

Improved: I picked up the gloves *which I had bought in San Francisco* and put them on my hands.

Vague: In his remarks he discussed everyday matters and people whom you and I know *as simply as a child.*

Improved: In his remarks he discussed, *as simply as a child,* everyday matters and people whom you and I know.

SPLIT CONSTRUCTIONS

68. As is pointed out in Section **67,** English is not a highly inflected language. Because many of our words show little if any change, it is important to keep logically related elements together. Because of inaccurate thinking, writers sometimes unnecessarily split constructions. Emphasis is not reflected in such constructions nearly so often as are awkwardness and ambiguity.

68a. Do not aimlessly separate the parts of a verb phrase.

Awkward: This tree *has,* although you would not think so, *been* here for thirty years.

Improved: Although you would not think so, this tree *has been* here for thirty years.

Awkward: He *is,* despite many objections from his parents, *going* to sea.

Improved: He *is going* to sea, despite . . .

or

Despite many objections from his parents, he *is going* to sea.

68b. Place coördinate sentence elements together.

Poor: *Although he was a good tennis player,* he never was ranked among the first ten, *although he practiced daily.*

With fair weather we should have an enjoyable trip, *with good luck.*

Improved: *Although he was a good tennis player* and *although he practiced daily,* he never was ranked among the first ten.

With fair weather and *with good luck* we should have an enjoyable trip.

68c. Avoid unnecessary separation of subject and predicate, verb and object, verb and complement, preposition and object, and other closely related sentence elements.

On occasion, greater smoothness may be achieved by separation, as, for example, in the last sentence in Section **67c,** where verb and object are split. But separation of closely related elements should be made for deliberate stylistic effect, never aimlessly. Remember, too, that informal speech and writing permit more freedom in splitting constructions than does formal writing. In the latter, you have opportunity to revise your sentences so that they will be unmistakably clear.

Faulty: He threw, in one sweeping and uncontrolled motion, both books and newspaper on the floor. (Verb and object.)

Improved: In one sweeping and uncontrolled motion he threw both books and newspaper on the floor.

Faulty: He walked into, although he was terrified, the house. (Preposition and object.)

Improved: Although he was terrified, he walked . . .

68d. Avoid the split infinitive.

There is little reason for putting an adverb or phrase between an infinitive and its sign *to:* to + adverb + infinitive. Many good speakers and writers use and defend the split infinitive; consequently, it no longer is considered a heinous fault. However, clearness and naturalness should be the tests for its use.

Occasionally a "faulty" split infinitive and a split construction are not faulty, but desirable. In such a sentence as "He failed to *entirely* pay for it," *entirely* is correctly placed next to the verbal *pay,* which it modifies. To place it after *failed* or after *it* or after *pay* would result in a confusing or awkward construction. You should master the rule, however, before testing the exceptions. The following example illustrates questionable splitting:

> He ordered us *to as soon as possible leave.*
> Improved: He ordered us *to leave* as soon as possible.

DANGLING MODIFIERS

69. A modifier dangles when it cannot unmistakably be connected with the sentence element that it modifies. Verbal phrases and elliptical clauses (see pp. 350-351) are the chief sources of trouble; their correct position is dependent upon careful, logical thinking. Such phrases and clauses are properly used only when the substantives to which they refer are expressed in the sentences and when these phrases and clauses are placed so near the modified substantives that there can be no ambiguity (see Section **67c**).

69a. Avoid dangling verbal phrases.

Infinitives and participles, as well as gerunds used in a preposition-gerund phrase, are not inflected for number or person and hence must be connected logically and clearly with the words they modify. Sentences containing dangling verbal phrases may be corrected in one of three ways: (1) by expanding the verbal phrase into a dependent clause; (2) by supplying the substantive which the dangling construction modifies; (3) by placing the construction so near the substantive that there is no confusion.

> Wrong: To oil this machine, the wheels must be removed.
> In buying a ticket, the price should be considered.
> Being very expensive, I did not buy the ticket.
> Correct: When one oils this machine, he must remove the wheels. (The dangling infinitive phrase is expanded into a dependent clause.)
> In buying a ticket, one must consider the price. (The dangling preposition-gerund phrase is sup-

367

plied with the substantive *one*, which it modifies logically.)

The ticket being very expensive, I did not buy it. (The dangling participial phrase is placed next to the substantive, *ticket*, which it modifies.)

Participial phrases tacked on to the end of a statement with *thus, thereby,* and *therefore* are also dangling.

Questionable: He was ill for several weeks, thus causing him to fall behind in his work.

Improved: He was ill for several weeks and thus fell behind in his work.

or

His several weeks' illness caused him to fall behind in his work.

NOTE: When a verbal is used to specify a general action, it is not considered a dangling modifier: *"In diving,* the feet should be kept together."

Such words as *considering, concerning, according to, owing to,* etc., are used prepositionally, not as verbals. Thus: *"Considering* everything, the proposal was fair" is a correct sentence. But avoid such constructions as "Thinking it over, it seems reasonable."

69b. Avoid dangling elliptical phrases and clauses.

An elliptical expression is one from which something has been omitted. An elliptical clause, usually a dependent clause, is one from which the subject or verb, or both, have been left out. Sentences containing dangling elliptical clauses can be corrected by (1) supplying the omitted subject or verb or (2) changing the independent clause so that the subject is that which is understood in the dependent clause. Elliptical phrases can similarly be corrected.

Wrong: Never race the engine *before thoroughly warmed up. While entering the house,* the bell rang.

Correct: Never race the engine before it is thoroughly warmed up. (The dangling elliptical clause is corrected by supplying the necessary words, *it is.*)

While entering the house, he heard the bell ring.

(The dangling elliptical phrase is corrected by changing the main clause.)

REFERENCE OF PRONOUNS

70. The relation of a pronoun to its antecedent (the substantive to which it refers) must be clear and unmistakable. The reference word should generally be placed as close as possible to its antecedent in order that no intervening words may cause confusion. A *relative* pronoun must be in the same sentence as its antecedent, but a *personal* or *demonstrative* pronoun may be placed some distance away, even in another sentence if there are no intervening substantives to cause confusion. (See Section **7.**)

70a. Avoid double reference for a pronoun.

Double reference occurs when there are two possible antecedents for a pronoun. The antecedent of every pronoun must be clear and definite (see Section **7e**).

Ambiguous reference can be corrected by (1) repeating the antecedent; (2) using a synonym for the antecedent; (3) changing the construction of the sentence.

> Vague: The professor told George that *he* would vote in the next election.
>
> He took the books from the boxes and placed *them* on the floor.
>
> Better: The professor told George that he intended to vote in the next election. (The double reference is corrected by changing the construction of the verb phrase.)
>
> Clear, but awkward: The professor told George that he (the professor) would vote in the next election. (The double reference is corrected by repeating the antecedent.)
>
> Better: He took the books from the boxes and placed the volumes on the floor. (The faulty reference is corrected by using a synonym for the antecedent.)
>
> He removed the books and placed the boxes on the

floor. (The faulty reference is corrected by changing the construction of the sentence.)

70b. Avoid implied reference for a pronoun.

Implied reference occurs when the antecedent of a pronoun is not actually expressed and must be inferred from the context. One of the most common forms of implied reference is the use of the pronouns *this, which, that,* etc., to refer to an entire preceding statement rather than to some substantive in that statement.

Vague:	His brother is a dentist. *This* is the profession he intends to enter.
	I like to travel in Switzerland. *They* are always pleasant to visitors.
	I cannot answer your letter *which* makes me very sad.
Improved:	His brother is a dentist. Dentistry is the profession he intends to enter.
	I like to travel in Switzerland. The Swiss are always pleasant to visitors.
	I cannot answer your letter, a fact which makes me very sad.

NOTE: Faults in the reference of *this, which, that,* etc., may be corrected by (1) summing up the idea of the preceding statement in a noun which acts as the antecedent; (2) making the statements coördinate; (3) rephrasing the sentence.

70c. Avoid the indefinite use of it and they.

Wrong:	In this picture *it* showed that war is horrible.
	They have good roads in Delaware.
Improved:	This picture showed that war is horrible.
	Delaware has good roads.

70d. Avoid the indefinite use of you.

When using *you,* be sure that you mean the person or persons whom you are addressing. For example, the following is inappropriate in a paper designed for reading by an adult: "When *you* become a Boy Scout, *you* learn many useful things."

Exercises

67-70

EXERCISES (Sections 67-70)

The exercises which follow deal with errors commented upon in Sections 67-70. Refer frequently to these sections, as well as to Section 7, when you are doing the exercises.

A. Rearrange the words in the following sentences so as to make the meanings of the sentences clear. Point out and correct all faulty split constructions, dangling modifiers, and reference of pronouns.

1. Horticulture is interesting work, but she does not want to be one.
2. The boy who works hard in time feels repaid.
3. He does not know even whether he can.
4. She had, in many different ways, greatly improved.
5. The advertisement read: "For sale: a new house, by an elderly gentleman painted white who is forced to leave town for business reasons."
6. If my father gives his permission, we can go swimming this afternoon, if it does not rain.
7. He removed the chains from the wheels and stored them in the garage.
8. When baking biscuits, the oven should be very hot.
9. In this book it says that Holmes was a great jurist.
10. She was playing the piano, which pleased her mother very much.

B. Directions given in Exercise A.

1. I enjoyed reading Lewis' *Dodsworth* because he was a strong character.
2. They do not serve good food in this cafeteria.
3. She offered to give him old clothing for the work, but he refused it.
4. Being very tired, the bed was a welcome sight.
5. I have never, in all these years, known such a dry summer.
6. He did not like to fish when it was raining, because they would not bite well.
7. To in every way do the best you can was his advice.
8. She almost plays golf as well as he does.
9. The person who reads good books constantly betters himself.
10. They almost have enough money for a European trip.

C. Directions given in Exercise A.

1. While engaging him in conversation, he seemed very attentive.

371

2. In walking to town, Prospect Avenue must be followed.

3. I do not wish to positively and finally give an answer now.

4. She does not nearly have enough strength to do the work.

5. She read the magazine for two hours, which she had bought at the station.

6. The person who saves his allowance toward the end of the month has money.

7. They were, in the opinion of all their teachers, considered brilliant students.

8. When the sun sets, the air becomes cooler, when the evening breezes blow.

9. In repairing this damaged tank, a plug should be placed in the side.

10. They say that Denver is an attractive city, which makes me want to go there.

11. Seated on the step of any farmhouse, and staring up into the mountains, the charm of the sight is almost hypnotic.

12. Tall, with gawky legs, two pieces of invisible hair, and a peculiar penchant for falling over everything, the future held little promise of the great and noble deeds I was to accomplish.

13. Look at the type of people slums are breeding. They must be exterminated.

14. Lumbering drowsily out of bed, my eye caught the picture standing upon my dresser.

15. While very young her mother tells her that she always insisted on cream for her cocoa.

MIXED AND ILLOGICAL CONSTRUCTIONS

71.   Lack of clarity in sentences frequently results from ignorance of grammar or slovenly thinking, or both. Sections 67-70, for example, have shown how a knowledge of grammar and careful thinking can improve faulty or ambiguous word order. Another result of ignorance of grammar and of carelessness is mixed and illogical constructions. Such expressions have already been mentioned in Sections 64 and 66 and are further discussed in Sections 74, 76, and 77. They are sufficiently important and common to merit separate attention in this section.

You may expect your reader to give careful attention, but you cannot expect him to untangle involved and mixed constructions or to correct your mistakes in logic. He may make the necessary corrections as he reads, but his attention is unwillingly attracted to the errors and away from the important communication of ideas. Therefore, if you wish to present your thoughts clearly and effectively, avoid the following errors.

71a. Do not leave a grammatical construction unfinished.

The error of "unfinished grammatical construction" occurs when a writer or speaker forgets, or fails to notice, how he began a sentence and inadvertently shifts to another construction. Every statement must be related, both logically and grammatically, to the remainder of the sentence.

> Wrong: The fact that he had always been a good student, he did well at medical college. (The first part of the sentence is left unfinished; the noun *fact* requires a full construction.)
>
> Correct: The fact that he had always been a good student accounted for his doing well at medical college.

> Wrong: Anyone who can be really happy, most people would look upon him with envy.
>
> Correct: Anyone who can be really happy would be envied by most people.
>
> Most people would envy anyone who can be really happy.

71b. Avoid mixed, illogical syntax.

Unless we are careful, certain "blends" will creep into our thinking and writing. In a sentence such as "He had no automobile in which to ride in," we have faultily blended *in which to ride* and *to ride in*. In speaking, we might well say "Despite of what you think, I say you are wrong." Here we have blended *in spite of* and *despite*. Such syntactical constructions are as much a result of careless thinking as of grammatical ignorance. When we write "Irregardless of that, he decided to stay," we have illogically blended *regardless* and *irrespective*.

71c. Avoid illogical double negatives.

Perhaps the most common violation of logical syntax is the double negative. Informal speech abounds with such expressions as "can't hardly," "can't scarcely," "haven't scarcely," and the like. In strictly formal English, however, they should be avoided. Although double negatives have been allowable in the past, they are currently out of style and unacceptable. We are not likely to say or write "I didn't get no food" or "I didn't see nobody," but we should always be careful in using *not* with such "negative words" as *no, but, nor, only, hardly, scarcely,* and *except.*

Allowable and occasionally useful, however, are certain double negatives expressing a weak positive: *not* with a negative prefix or suffix of an adjective or adverb.

> A spare tire is a *not unnecessary* piece of equipment.
>
> This position calls for a *not irresponsible* person.
>
> Despite the punishment the boxer walked *not unsteadily* to his corner.

EXERCISES

A. Correct the mixed or illogical constructions in the following sentences:

1. He doesn't have no time in which to play checkers.
2. The motion picture shows how a man, who, having returned from the war, tries to make a living selling chickens.
3. The tree which stands so sturdily in the hurricane, it must have long, strong roots.
4. He hardly never goes to see a play.
5. He is not able to run nor even to walk.
6. He made a proposal, but to tell what it was they were unable to do it.
7. I do not question but that he will pay the money.
8. It was a small rock on which he stumbled on.
9. The player completely forgot the signals; he missed one earlier in the game made him forget all of them.
10. In all his attempts to make money caused him to go further into debt.

B. Rewrite the following sentences, correcting the mixed or illogical constructions:

1. In all his efforts to get up on his feet made his wound bleed more.
2. This is the identical pillar where the prisoner of Chillon was chained to.
3. The chairman stated that if we wanted Reilly for secretary let us get his name on the printed ballot.
4. With two beds, two dressers, two desks, and two chairs, is it any wonder that we have no space in which to exercise in?
5. Our dog has never learned that it can't eat but one mouthful at a time.
6. The cartoonists exaggerate all the president's idiosyncrasies, which, I know from personal acquaintance, some are deserving of it and some are not.
7. The tall buildings, with their hundreds of cell-like apartments, house people who after several years do not even know or recognize their neighbors, seems cold and unfriendly.
8. After being up for two whole nights, I was so tired when the initiation came I wasn't hardly able to keep my eyes open.
9. It was a good speech but, disregardless of that, I was not convinced.
10. The fact that you can't take but one girl to the dance, you should not invite two.

TRANSITION

72. Individual sentences may be correct, clear, and effective, and yet not be either clear or effective when they are put together in a paragraph. If the order of the sentences within the paragraph is fully logical, then any lack of clarity probably is due to faulty *transition*. Transition means "passage from one place, state, or act to another." There are three kinds of transition, as applied to writing: within the sentence, between sentences, and between paragraphs.

Our own processes of thought are so familiar to us that we are likely to forget that our readers do not understand quite so readily and fully as we do the exact relations of our ideas. The writer's thoughts not only must progress logically; they must be *marked* so plainly that the reader can readily grasp both them and their interrelations. Only thus can effective communication be achieved.

72 a-b

72a. Make transitions clear by frequent and correct use of transitional words and phrases.

Transitional devices are not needed within or between all sentences, but they are needed, for example, in this faulty series:

> Baseball is said to be the national game; I do not like it. If it is the national game, thousands must enjoy watching it, or playing it. I know people who do not ever attend a game; I know people who see as many as fifty games a year. I should not make a dogmatic statement about the appeal of the sport; I have never witnessed a game.

Note the greater clarity and smoothness caused by the italicized words:

> Baseball is said to be the national game; *however,* I do not like it. *Yet* if it is the national game, thousands must enjoy watching it, or playing it. *To be sure,* I know people who do not ever attend a game; *on the other hand,* I know people who see as many as fifty games a year. *Perhaps* I should not make a dogmatic statement about the appeal of the sport; *you see,* I have never witnessed a game.

The competent writer has a knowledge of *connectives* and their proper use. The following is a list of some of the more frequently used transitional words and phrases: *at that point, and, again, accordingly, as a result, as I said, afterward, but, for, for example, for instance, fortunately, furthermore, hence, here, however, in like manner, in short, likewise, meanwhile, moreover, now, of course, on the contrary, on the other hand, similarly, soon, temporarily, therefore, truly, thus, well, while.*

72b. Avoid inexact transition.

Use transitional devices frequently, but correctly.

> Inexact: He did not get the telegram in time *as* it was delivered late. (Substitute *because* or *since* for *as.*)
> I wanted to study architecture, *and* my father wanted me to become a lawyer. (Substitute *but* for *and.*)

I did not pay the bill *because* I have the money in my pocket. (Substitute *for* for *because*.)
I was so tired *until* I could not study. (Substitute *that* for *until*.)
George wished to go; *on the other hand,* his father also wanted him to go. (Substitute *and* or *fortunately* or *similarly* for *on the other hand*.)

EXERCISES

A. Supply correct transitional words and phrases where they are needed within and between the following sentences:

It seemed to be a cold day; the temperature was only 30°. I had risen early; my alarm clock went off too soon. John was still asleep. I shook and shook him; he did not move. I left him behind, hurried to George's house. He was asleep. He got up, dressed himself; we set out on our long-anticipated hike. Both George and I like to walk; we had a good time. The winter day was too short; we had to return in a few hours. John had stayed indoors all day.

B. Correct the inexact connectives in the following sentences:

1. He did not recite well as he had not studied his lesson.
2. I don't know if I can go.
3. They did not arrive by airplane because I was at the landing field.
4. She tiptoed to the window so she could hear what was being said.
5. When we left the house, yet they stayed.
6. He is a good musician, while his parents do not encourage him to practice.
7. I wanted him to feed the horses, and he wanted to shell the corn.
8. He would not take good care of himself, so he contracted pneumonia.
9. I returned to the station, as it was late.
10. We had hardly started than we had to repair a puncture.

C. Study the brief list of connectives given at the end of Section 72a. Determine how many of them you use in your own themes.

D. Mark all the transitional words and phrases occurring in some selection in your anthology. Try to read the sentences, omitting the transitional devices.

CONCISENESS

73. A sentence may be complete and unified and yet be ineffective because it is wordy. Clear, effective sentences demand accuracy of thought and conciseness of expression. This does not mean that you should use a telegraphic style (see Section **66e**). Nor does it mean that all sentences must be brief. A sentence of one hundred words may be concise, and one of twenty may be quite wordy. But sentences can hardly be effective when they contain superfluous words or ideas.

In making sentences concise you can eliminate unnecessary words, turn clauses into phrases, and use word-saving suffixes. For example, you would certainly not refer to "a great, big, enormous man." Probably only the last adjective would suffice. "Any student who is matriculated can become a member of the squad" may be shortened to "Any matriculated student can become a squad member." And a sentence such as "I was waiting for that telephone call until I became frantic" can be written: "I was waiting frantically for that telephone call." If such condensation violates meaning, it should not be employed. But you will effectively hold your readers only when your sentences are lean and vigorous.

Wordiness is also treated in Section **96,** but the following rules apply primarily to sentence construction.

73a. Avoid the useless repetition of an idea.

This fault is called *tautology*. Frequently, a writer who is not thinking carefully will repeat an idea, for no purpose, in different words. The result is a tautological construction.

> I was very anxious for him to succeed and eager that he do so.
> This absolutely new and novel innovation will please them; they will like it very much.

73b. Avoid piling up unnecessary details.

This fault is called *prolixity*. A prolix sentence may be unified (see Section **65**), but it is always ineffective because its details obscure or weaken the point of the main idea.

Last summer I won the local golf tournament with a set of clubs that I had purchased five years before from a friend who had bought a new set and who sold me his old clubs at a bargain price.

The town in which he formerly lived was small, it having a population of only one thousand, more than half of whom worked in the Smith and Brown Mattress Factory, Inc.

These two sentences are so verbose that whole ideas must be deleted. From the first, delete the last two-thirds of the sentence: "Last summer I won the local golf tournament with a second-hand set of clubs." The second sentence contains two distinct ideas which may be placed in separate sentences or which may be combined and shortened: "He formerly lived in a town of only one thousand, more than . . ."

EXERCISES

A. Condense the wording of the following. Make separate sentences, if necessary.

1. He drew a perfect circle on the piece of paper and, if I may be permitted to make such a statement, seemed more than well pleased with what he had done.
2. They were circular in form, big in size, and many in number; in all important essentials they were everything which we had been led to expect.
3. The grass had not come up to a good stand, and Mr. Jones thought that this was owing to the fact that the man from whom he had bought the seed was not an honest dealer and did not have the necessary requisite of integrity.
4. There were ten of us who went, on Hallowe'en evening, to pay a call upon Harold, our fellow-playmate, who had been sick and ailing for a long period of time.
5. I cannot attend to my reading and listen to your discourse at one and the same time.

B. Look up, in a good dictionary, the following words: *redundancy, tautology, circumlocution, verbosity, verbiage, periphrasis, prolixity, pleonasm, diffuseness, terseness, succinctness, curtness, brevity, sententiousness.*

C. Directions given in Exercise A.

1. It was a clear, sunny day without a rain cloud in the sky.
2. She was a great talker who spoke well and who often had a great deal to say on each and every possible occasion.
3. Anyone who knows anything about the young people of this day and age knows that the more tactfully and diplomatically they are handled the better their social behavior will be as far as the other sex is concerned.
4. That side of the structure receives the morning sun but during the time that the sun is in the west and afternoon shadows begin to fall, it is dreary and cheerless.
5. I waited for the signal which would indicate that the hunt had begun, but the dogs with their barking and the horses with their stamping drowned out all other sounds and noises.

PARALLELISM

74. Parallelism means "like construction for like ideas." You will convey your precise meaning to your readers, surely and effectively, if you construct your sentences so that the reader can immediately see what ideas are of equal importance. Parallel construction for like ideas is indispensable to clear, grammatically correct, effective sentences. Parallel movement, correctly handled, is one means of attaining an emphatic, vigorous style. In striving for matching word structure, however, do not make the errors discussed below.

74a. Sentence elements that are coördinate in rank should be parallel in structure.

An infinitive should be followed by an infinitive of similar form, a phrase by a phrase, a clause by a clause, etc.

> Wrong: He liked to run and playing tennis.
> Right: He liked to run and to play tennis.

> Wrong: He bought a radio with seven tubes and having a beautiful mahogany finish.
> Right: He bought a radio with seven tubes and [with] a beautiful mahogany finish.

Wrong: He wanted to make Phi Beta Kappa and that he
        might earn a varsity letter.

Right: He wanted to make Phi Beta Kappa and to earn a
        varsity letter.

NOTE: Absolute parallelism is not always required. But although
in the following the form is not parallel, the functions are:

He talked *slowly* and *with a stammer.*

I saw *John, Henry,* and *a man whom I have not met.*

74b. Avoid misleading parallelism.

Do not use the same structural form for sentence elements
which are not of equal value. Avoid a series of elements which
appear to modify the same element, but do not.

Wrong: For your sake for fifty dollars I will help you.

        It is important that each of you should bring his
        own ammunition, and that it should be good am-
        munition.

        They left immediately, and they had a good auto-
        mobile.

74c. Avoid ineffective partial parallelism.

In using the formula A, B, and C, make certain that the three
sentence elements are parallel in form. If they are not, a faulty
and unemphatic series will result.

Undesirable: The story is vivid, interesting, and has a simple
             plot.

Improved: The story is vivid, interesting, simple in plot.

                            or

        The story is simple, interesting, and vivid.

74d. Sentence elements following correlative conjunctions should be parallel in form.

Faulty: He is either indolent or he doesn't feel well.

Improved: He is either indolent or ill.

74e. Do not join a relative clause to its principal clause by **and**, **but,** or **or.**

And, but, or, and other coördinating conjunctions connect only elements which are equal in rank. The most frequent violation of this rule is the "and which" construction. Do not use *and which, but which, and who, but who* unless there is a preceding "which clause" or "who clause."

> Wrong: He showed much energy at first, *but which* soon vanished.
>
> He is a man of intelligence, *and who* is an industrious worker.
>
> This is a beautiful tennis court, *and which* you will enjoy playing on with your friends.

The simplest method of correcting these three sentences is to omit the conjunctions (but remember the punctuation of restrictive and nonrestrictive clauses!). Parallelism can also be attained by adding a "who clause" or "which clause": "He is a man who is intelligent and who is an industrious worker." Such revision, however correct, is usually wordy and ineffective, as it is here. The sentence should be rewritten: "He is intelligent and industrious."

EXERCISES

A. Change the incorrect or misleading parallelism in the following sentences:

1. He enjoyed playing billiards and to shoot pool.
2. She is a lovely girl and whom everyone likes.
3. I being tired, the weather hot, and no mail had come for weeks, it was difficult for me to feel cheerful.
4. Mr. Jones enjoys swimming, golf, and to play bridge.
5. George being interested in his stamp collection, and Helen played with the other girls, so I had no difficulty in reading.
6. Your job will be answering the mail, to collect bills, and run errands for me for twenty dollars a week.
7. Walking is less exercise than running, and to do nothing is better than either.
8. The article is concise, thoughtful, and appeals to thousands of people.
9. The story is a dramatic narrative, and which concerns the lives of fishermen.

10. The automobile was sent to the garage to be washed and have the tires inflated.

B. Rewrite the following sentences, making coördinate sentence elements parallel in form:

1. His power lay in his ability to spellbind his audience and thinking faster than his enemies.
2. The sergeant ordered us to dismount our guns, to assemble our equipment, and we were to be ready for general inspection.
3. After considering all the breeds, he bought a dog with short hair, a docile disposition, and having great intelligence.
4. He stated that he not only would write to the judge but also writing the jurors.
5. It is easy to fool Grace by pretending to be dumb and that you are not able to hear her.
6. None of the fans was expecting such a hard-fought game or that it would last so long.
7. The boat is relatively new, unusually clean, and proving to be absolutely seaworthy.
8. The pup wanted to be loved and having someone play with him.
9. Not only was Purdy shifty on his feet but that he was also clever at passing.
10. The detective believed either he was the thief or to act as an accomplice.

POINT OF VIEW

75. Point of view means the relative position from which something is seen or a subject is considered. Point of view requires *consistency,* so far as the sentence is concerned, although it has other uses when applied to the theme (see p. 244). *Consistency* in the sentence means that the parts must be in agreement and must so remain unless there is good reason for shifting.

75a. Avoid unnecessary shifts in tense.

Maintain one point of view in time unless there is excellent reason for changing. Do not change the tense from present to past or from past to present in narration.

Incorrect: George was walking slowly down the street when

suddenly an automobile turned the corner. It dashes
wildly down the avenue, careening and twisting
as if its driver is crazy. George jumped behind a
tree to protect himself. (Change *dashes* to *dashed,*
is to *were*.)

75b. Avoid aimlessly shifting the subject or voice in a sentence.

Faulty: The furnace burns little coal, and at the same time
Jim says it is easily cleaned. (Jim says the furnace . . .)
As you look across the street, tall trees can be seen.
(. . . street, you can . . .)

75c. Avoid unnecessary shifts in number.

Incorrect: A small child can be a great joy, but they require
much care. (Change *they* to *he* or *she; require* to
requires.)

75d. Avoid shifting the class or person of pronouns.

If one tries hard enough, you will inevitably succeed. (*One*
is an indefinite pronoun in the third person; *you* is a personal
pronoun, second person.)

EXERCISES

A. Correct the faulty or undesirable points of view in the following sentences. See Sections **6, 7,** and **10,** if necessary.

1. Jack likes apples, but oranges taste better to me.
2. You should study your lesson; they will be giving you an examination in them soon.
3. The club is opposed to changing their constitution.
4. Woodrow Wilson was born in Virginia, but Georgia and South
Carolina claim him as their own.
5. We took a long trip, and many things happened to us.
6. I do not see how anyone can fail to like *Arrowsmith;* they must
not have understood it.
7. I talked and talked until the bell rings and it was time for recess.
8. He was hit by a batted ball, but baseball still claims much of his
time.
9. If a student tries to engage in too many extracurricular activities,
his lessons will not be learned.

10. If you buy this coat, it will be most useful to you.

B. Rewrite the following sentences, correcting the faulty or undesirable points of view:

1. Be careful to remove all rubbish from the cellar, and one can reduce the fire risk greatly.
2. I followed the dog down into the ravine and can make out the opening of the old mine.
3. Jack and his father drove to Canada last summer, and many exciting adventures were experienced by them.
4. I insist that if a college man really works hard, they are bound to succeed.
5. The class made a tour of Radio City, where the air-conditioning apparatus particularly amazed us.
6. When the alarm bell clanged in the hall, Mary lost her head and screamed, "Fire!"
7. I walked all around the structure, but its much-touted charm was missed by me.
8. Every little girl loves a kitten, but they can be a real nuisance to the parents.
9. He joined the track squad last spring, but his lack of perseverance kept him off the team.
10. Our fraternity was asked by the dean to explain their attitude toward dancing.

FAULTY COÖRDINATION

76. In order to be correct and clear, sentences must be unified and complete. In order to be effective, they must be so constructed that the relative importance of their elements is fully apparent.

The immature writer will phrase his sentences as a child speaks. That is, he will construct a series of independent clauses loosely held together by coördinating conjunctions. A child very naturally might say: "We went to the circus, and we saw all the freaks, and we drank pink lemonade, and we had a grand time." You should avoid such "run-on" sentences, however; if you think carefully you can express your ideas in constructions which will show their varying importance. Subordinate minor ideas so that the important statement may be more emphatic.

Avoid excessive coördination, then, because it is childish and monotonous and reveals a lack of judgment. Avoid inaccurate and illogical coördination because it reveals that you have not really "thought through" the ideas you wish to express; it results in haziness and causes the reader to get incorrect impressions of the thoughts presented to him.

76a. Avoid stringy, "run-on" sentences.

Do not overwork the compound sentence; avoid the excessive use of coördinating conjunctions between independent clauses. Reduce predication; that is, change an independent into a dependent clause, a dependent clause into a phrase, a phrase into a single word.

> Immature: George bought a new automobile, and it had free-wheeling, and there was a radio.
>
> He took us for a short drive, and we stopped at a store, and we bought some candy.
>
> Improved: George bought a new automobile which had freewheeling and a radio.
>
> He took us for a short ride during which we stopped at a store and bought candy.

76b. Avoid "seesaw" sentences.

"Seesaw" sentences are compound sentences with the two independent clauses of approximately equal length. A succession of such sentences is monotonous and ineffective. Usually one of the clauses can be subordinated.

> Ineffective: I prepared carefully for the test, and I was sure I would pass. The questions were difficult, but I knew all the answers. I waited a few days, and then the papers were returned. My grade was high, and I was not disappointed.

76c. Avoid the overuse of so.

Even though *so* is correctly used as a conjunctive adverb with a semicolon preceding, its overuse is common and ineffective. In constructions like that below, it can often be replaced by *therefore, thus, accordingly,* and the like, or predication may be reduced.

> Ineffective: He had to study, so he did not go.
> A bridge was out on Highway 40, so we had to detour on Route 28.
> Improved: He had to study; therefore he did not go.
> Since a bridge was out on Highway 40, we had to detour on Route 28.

76d. Avoid inaccurate and false coördination.

Coördinate means "of equal rank." An independent clause cannot be joined to a dependent clause by a coördinating conjunction. Use the *correct* coördinating conjunction between independent clauses: do not use *and* if *but* is called for (see p. 110). But if two statements belong together, do not incorrectly place them in separate sentences.

> Inaccurate: He told me this and with his voice quivering.
> The nurse was a pleasant person and had had good training, but who was a failure. (See Section **74e.**)
> She wanted to go, and she did not have the proper clothes to wear.
> The automobile is a Chevrolet. It was made by General Motors.

FAULTY SUBORDINATION

77. Careful, thoughtful writing contains much subordination. The good writer recognizes that not all of his ideas deserve equal rank, and he judiciously places them in constructions which correspond to their importance. Thus he writes sentences which are unified and effective. His thoughts are more clearly communicated to his readers, for they can see what the relationship of the sentence elements actually is.

The diligent writer will avoid excessive and faulty coördination (see Section 76), but in so doing he is likely to make errors in subordination. Reducing predication requires thoughtful care; the writer must be certain that he knows exactly what he wishes to express in order not to obscure fine shades of meaning.

The errors mentioned below are quite common.

77a. Avoid the use of a subordinate form for a coördinate idea.

> Inaccurate: He was heavy and slow, *while* his sister was lithe and active.

To make this sentence more effective, delete the *while* or substitute a correct coördinating conjunction, *but.*

> *Born in Canada in 1890,* he became an American citizen in 1935.
>
> I called to her, *though she refused to answer.*
>
> More effective: He was born in Canada in 1890 and became . . .
>
> I called to her, but she refused to answer.

77b. Avoid putting the main idea of a sentence into a subordinate construction.

This is called "upside-down subordination." It shows that you have not evaluated the worth of your statements, and it frequently causes your reader to attach undue importance to a subordinate idea. It should be said, however, that it is sometimes difficult to determine which is the subordinate idea. Usually, the most dramatic incident and the effect, rather than the cause, are major ideas; preliminaries (place, time) and attendant circumstances are minor, that is, subordinate, ideas.

> Inaccurate: Our muscles were getting very tired, when we decided to hail a taxicab.
>
> I saw an automobile heading straight toward me, when I was unable to move, from fear. (In each of these sentences, transpose *when.*)

77c. Avoid excessive subordination.

Sentences which contain a series of overlapping subordinate clauses are not effective. In such a series, each clause depends upon the preceding. Sentence elements should be linked together, but they should not be built like an accordion.

> Ineffective: It was an inexpensive toy which had been made in Japan which has cheap labor.
>
> These are the children who feed to the squirrels the nuts which they buy on the corner that is near the park.

Each of these statements should be broken up into two sentences.

EXERCISES (Sections 76, 77)

A. The following sentences are badly coördinated or subordinated. Rewrite each sentence, making it more effective. Refer frequently, if necessary, to Sections 76 and 77.

1. I wanted to take her the flowers, but which my mother would not let me do.
2. He thought that he was going to get the job, when he fell ill.
3. He is the idol of all the people of this town of four hundred inhabitants.
4. Jane loves animals, and she has many of them for pets, and she takes excellent care of them.
5. This is the book which I spoke to you about which was written by John Galsworthy.
6. I thought that it would snow, although I did not put the car in the garage.
7. He inherited a fortune, and gave money to each of his relatives, and bought a new house.
8. He sawed the tree through, and it did not fall.
9. Born in 1860, he died in 1920.
10. The dog pointed the bird, as I dropped my gun.

B. Rewrite the following sentences, correcting the faulty coördination and subordination.

1. I was just drifting off into sleep when he rushed in yelling "Murder!"
2. This is the car which I bought for $25 from the man who has a gas station near Tilton where I went to school.

3. He can easily get a 90 on his last quiz, and he already has a general average of 89, giving him an A– in the course.
4. He made the football team although he was a splendid singer.
5. My favorite sport is tennis, while my brother's is lacrosse.
6. I put on my overshoes, and then I wrapped a muffler about my neck, and drew on a heavy coat, but I was still cold.
7. He had little resistance to disease, because he died in a week.
8. He looked at me queerly and with his eyes blinking.
9. The man was desperate, being out of work, and he had no money.
10. The musician arose from his seat, hurling his violin to one side.

CHOPPY SENTENCES

78. Do not chop up the thought of one unified sentence into a series of short, jerky sentences.

Unity, clearness, and effectiveness are all thwarted by a series of jerky, short sentences which logically belong in a single predication. Such a series is monotonous and does not permit variety of sentence structure (see Section **80**); it also gives undue emphasis to relatively unimportant ideas (see Sections **76, 77, 79**). The separate ideas should be properly coördinated and subordinated and placed together in a longer, unified sentence.

> Faulty: He picked up the pocketbook. He saw that it contained a large sum of money. He naturally wanted to keep it.
>
> Better: When he picked up the pocketbook, he saw that it contained a large sum of money which, naturally, he wanted to keep.
>
> Faulty: It was dark. She was afraid to enter the room. She called her brother. He did not hear her. This terrified her more than ever.
>
> Better: Because it was dark, she was afraid to enter the room. When she called her brother, he did not hear her, and consequently she was more terrified than ever.

EXERCISE

Combine the following groups of sentences into complex or compound sentences. Use more than one sentence if unity is violated. See Sections **65, 76, 77.**

1. I walked down the street. The snow was falling fast. I turned up my collar.
2. The baby reached for the rattle. He took it in his hands. He shook it. Then he dropped it.
3. He and Henry were good friends. They formerly lived together. Now they are enemies. Henry called him a liar and a thief.
4. He was preparing to study medicine. In college he enrolled for biology. He also took chemistry.
5. Tobacco is a plant. From its leaves are prepared cigars. Cigarettes are a popular form of tobacco. Some people like to chew tobacco.
6. The ice broke up in the spring. We boys used to "hop cakes." We would ride downstream on the cakes. We received dire threats and warnings from our parents.
7. Dawn had just begun to light up the east. Joe woke me by throwing stones against my window. We had agreed upon this signal. We thought it the one least likely to wake my parents.
8. People were standing outside the theater. They stood on the sidewalk. The group assumed the proportions of a mob as word got around that Violet Beauty was there. She is the film star in *Life and Death.* She was attending the benefit performance of *Romeo and Juliet.*
9. I went to the carnival in a voluminous costume. The carnival was right after Easter. I went as an Indian dancer. It took three yards of cloth to make the turban. The pantaloons had six yards of cloth in them, and my cape took eight yards.
10. The steam roller chugged down the street. Small boys tagged after it. The driver appeared not to notice the urchins. He was conscious of them, though. He enjoyed their unabashed admiration.

POSITION AND ARRANGEMENT

79. Effectiveness in sentence structure implies that the words are so chosen and arranged that they have maximum impressiveness. Students frequently attain correctness and clarity in their sentences, but only the more diligent or more gifted write sentences which really "get across" decisively and emphatically. Effective diction may be studied in Section **92;** effective word arrangement has been mentioned in Sections **67–69** and **72–74.** Especially important phases of sentence effectiveness are discussed separately in Sections **78, 80.**

Not all the words or ideas in a sentence are of equal importance; consequently, you must attempt to place the elements of your thought so that relatively unimportant items will remain in the background and important ones will achieve prominence. You can attain such effectiveness only by proper coördination and subordination (see Sections **76, 77**). As an effective writer, you will also repeat important ideas, for emphasis, and will consciously avoid weak and inconclusive constructions.

79a. Do not begin or end a sentence with weak and relatively unimportant words or ideas.

The most conspicuous parts of a sentence are the beginning and end. Sentences should usually be built with the most important idea at the beginning or end, the places of stress, the places where the attention of the reader is most keen. You should remember, however, that transitional words and phrases, although seemingly colorless, are really important and frequently deserve beginning positions (see Section **72**).

Prepositions and parenthetical expressions are usually not "pivotal," or important, words. Thus they should be placed within the sentence, although artificiality and awkwardness must be avoided in so placing them.

> Ineffective: He had no brush to paint the house *with.* (It is not grammatically incorrect to end a sentence with a preposition, but this sentence is more effective if due emphasis is given the relatively important word *house:* He had no brush with which to paint the house.)
>
> Ineffective: *However,* he will die, the physician says.
>
> Better: The physician says, however, that he will die.

79b. Avoid frequent use of the passive voice.

The use of the passive voice often detracts from the emphasis of a sentence. Many sentences require a passive verb, but, as a general rule, the use of the active voice gives sentences greater force and strength.

> Unemphatic: The lecture *is scheduled to be given* by Professor Smith on Wednesday.
>
> Better: Professor Smith *will give* the lecture on Wednesday.

79c. Repeat important words to gain sentence emphasis.

Faulty repetition should be avoided (see Section 97), but the effectiveness of many sentences can be increased by repetition of "pivotal" words. Thus, the ideas are "driven home," clinched. Study the effect of repetition in the following: *"Give! Give* money when you see that women and children are hungry. *Give* sympathy when you can cheer a beaten man. *Give* time to study conditions in your own community. *Give* your whole self in an attempt to change and better the life of all humanity."

79d. Use periodic sentences to secure emphasis.

A periodic sentence is so constructed that its full meaning is not apparent until the end. Such a sentence creates suspense; something is held back, and the reader continues in a state of expectation. You should avoid a too frequent use of periodic sentences because an awkward and artificial style will inevitably result. But their occasional use is fully justified by the effectiveness of the suspense they achieve. Note the following:

> Tired, hungry, bewildered, and sick at heart, the derelict stumbled into the warm and brightly lit restaurant. At first hesitantly, then eagerly, then almost fiercely, he seized and drank a cupful of steaming coffee.

> On men reprieved by its disdainful mercy, the immortal sea confers in its justice the full privilege of desired unrest.

> When we are young and concerned with the overriding importance of the approaching football game, the class dance, the long summer vacation, with making an impression on

the new employer, passing the C.P.A. or the Bar examinations, getting married—the importance of knowing a great deal fails to disturb us.

—DEAN PAUL A. MCGHEE

As these three examples show, sentences introduced by phrases or by dependent clauses are periodic and may be effective.

In loose sentences—usually compound sentences or complex sentences with the dependent clause following the independent clause —complete meaning is possible before the end of the sentence. There is nothing wrong with loose sentences; they predominate in most writing. Because of this predominance, an occasional periodic sentence is especially effective.

79e. Arrange ideas in the order of their importance so as to secure climax.

Climax is attained when the ideas in a sentence are so arranged that each succeeding idea has greater force than its predecessor. You must avoid arranging the elements of a sentence so that it "sags," or loses force at the end. Consider the following:

Unemphatic: In this wreck, some died horrible deaths; some received serious injuries, and a few were barely scratched.

Better: A few were barely scratched in this wreck; but some received serious injuries; and some died horrible deaths.

Unemphatic: We were frightened by the noises: the crashing of the thunder, the pouring of the rain, and the steady blowing of the wind.

Better: We were frightened by the noises: the steady blowing of the wind, the pouring of the rain, and the crashing of the thunder.

CAUTION: The effectiveness of a sentence depends not entirely on the *position* of any single word or idea but on the arrangement of the whole sentence. The *sense* of the sentence must always be considered; the statement must be correct and clear. Effectiveness cannot be gained by a thoughtless or artificial attempt to employ the rules mentioned in this section. They will help to increase effectiveness only if their use does not destroy correctness, clearness, and naturalness.

EXERCISES

A. Increase the effectiveness of the following sentences:

1. This is not good soil to plant flowers in.
2. Accidentally, he was shot and seriously wounded by his friend.
3. In short, both platforms promised to help the farmer out.
4. He became better liked as more people came to know him and gradually his circle of acquaintances widened.
5. He started out to take a walk because he was desperate, unable to sleep, and tired of hearing the radio.
6. John's fender was bent when he did not have enough room to turn the automobile around in.
7. In order to accomplish this, you should be willing to give up honor, family, friends, and acquaintances, I think.
8. At first, she did not love him, but she came to like him as time went on.
9. You know that your bill will be paid by me as soon as I am able.
10. He came here to recuperate from a serious illness, play bridge, and have the sun brown him, I suppose.

B. Directions given in Exercise A.

1. I believe he said that he would go on his vacation August 1, as well as I remember.
2. Mr. Jackson was made treasurer of the company, although he has no executive ability, is in bad health, and his home is situated in another town.
3. This is not a bargain, if you ask my opinion.
4. There were summoned up in my recollection the exciting, gay, pleasant days spent by us in Ames, Iowa.
5. I saw the child run over and killed by a drunken driver who never even knew he had hit anything, perhaps.
6. I do not believe I wish to read this book if it is similar to all others written by the same author, in years gone by.
7. He quickly left the house, after putting on his hat and adjusting his collar.

8. According to many people, discretion is not possessed by many motion-picture directors, I read in a recent magazine article.

9. The barn was on fire, the horses were kicking and neighing, and confusion was apparent everywhere, it seemed.

10. He thought that everyone would have a good time on the picnic if there were ample food and a lake to swim in.

C. Make the following sentences more effective by changing them from loose to periodic:

1. I was awarded first prize after the judges had deliberated for a considerable time.

2. Bret Harte is still a favorite among short-story readers, since he portrayed the exciting life and conditions during the California gold rush.

3. Grandfather was known as a pioneer among pioneers, having crossed and recrossed the continent frequently during his lifetime.

4. We knew we had won the game when the kick sailed over the crossbar in the last three seconds of play.

5. Edward FitzGerald meant that the past can never be called back when he wrote, "The Moving Finger writes, and having writ moves on."

6. Decisive action is to be taken at the meeting, and everyone is urged to be present.

7. You have been admitted to the university, your high school principal having written you an excellent recommendation.

8. John knew that he had turned in the winning answer; so he wasn't surprised when the results were announced.

9. We braced ourselves for the shock as the car swerved and started to skid.

10. To be awakened from a sound sleep is startling, even though you realize immediately that what awakened you is the alarm clock ringing.

VARIETY

80. Sentences cannot be effective if they are monotonous in structure. The reader tires of a long succession of sentences which are identical, or nearly identical, in construction, just as he tires of sameness in anything. Variety is more than the "spice" of writing;

it is a quality which accurately reflects the mature or immature processes of the writer's mind.

Monotony may be caused by a series of short, simple sentences (see Section 78), by a series of "seesaw" sentences (see Section 76b), and by a series of sentences beginning with the same word (*this, these, it,* etc.).

The good writer will revise his sentences to make sure that they do have variety. He will vary their length, and, occasionally, their normal word order. He will avoid sentences which are similar in form; he will use periodic sentences as well as loose sentences (see Section 79d); above all else, he will properly subordinate ideas and thus construct complex sentences (see Section 77) to take the place of too many simple and compound sentences. Even a series of simple sentences can be given variety by using various kinds of phrases as beginnings or endings.

80a. Do not begin a number of successive sentences with the same word.

Avoid especially the outworn beginnings *there is, there are, it is, this, the, he,* and *we.*

> Awkward: It is just the trip he had planned. It is just the day for the trip. It is the consummation of all his hopes.
>
> Improved: It is just the trip he had planned and just the day for the trip, a consummation of all his hopes.

80b. Do not place the subject at the beginning of every sentence.

Occasionally change the word order of subject + verb + complement. A deviation from this order will avoid monotony and, if correctly done, will attract desired attention.

> Usual order: I saw that play when I was in Indianapolis.
> Position changed: That play I saw when I was in Indianapolis.
> Usual order: Those who can sleep through a dull lecture are fortunate.
> Position changed: Fortunate are those who can sleep . . .

80c. Vary the length and form of successive sentences.

Sentences which follow each other should not all be of the same approximate length. Likewise, they should not all be simple, or compound, or complex. Remember, sentences of the childish or immature person are likely to be predominantly simple or compound, whereas the work of the skilled writer will abound in subordination (complex sentences).

CAUTION: You should not consciously attempt to vary your sentences while you are composing the first draft of your composition. If you do so, you are likely to pay more attention to the structure of your sentences than to the ideas you are trying to express. After the first draft is completed, however, you should carefully revise sentences which are monotonously similar in beginning, length, and form.

The student who wrote this paragraph was quite properly concerned with developing the thread of the narrative, but he neglected revision:

We set out at dawn for the place where we were going to fish. We looked forward eagerly to a morning of real sport. The air was fresh and balmy. We reached the lake in about half an hour. First, we placed some moist earth in the cans in which we carried the bait. Then we set up our rods. Next we located a comfortable spot on the shore. At last we were ready to begin fishing.

EXERCISES

A. Rewrite the paragraph immediately above.

B. Rewrite the following to add variety to the structure:

1. The batter then tries to hit the ball the pitcher throws. He runs to base if he does hit it. He is out if he does not get to base before the ball is thrown there. He is safe if he does. He is out if he completely misses the ball three times.
2. I shall go if you will go with me. I shall stay if you refuse to go with me. I do not care to go unless I have company.
3. When the pan is warm, put the butter in. When the eggs are well beaten, pour them into the pan. Do not stir the eggs too vigorously while they are cooking. When they are cooked, serve them at once.
4. He was tired and so he left the office. He walked down the street

General Exercises

until he came to a park. He sat down on a bench and went to sleep. Later he awoke and went home for supper.

5. I tried to get the car started by rolling it down a hill. Then I looked at the carburetor, making sure it was in order. Then I cleaned the spark plugs, wiping them carefully. Then I telephoned for help, hoping it would come soon.

6. I lost my head. Why? I had been studying hard. My nerves were on edge. Besides, I dislike being scolded.

7. He went to the library. From there he returned to his room. Still later he took a walk. Then he ate supper.

8. The day was sunny. The coat was hot. The road was dusty. No wonder I needed a long rest in the shade.

9. My hat is five years old. It is spotted and worn. But I like it. I sometimes say it is a new hat. When I do, someone usually asks, "New what year?"

10. He can pass. He can punt. He can run in a broken field. He can block. He is, in short, quite a football player. But he just can't tackle.

GENERAL EXERCISES: THE SENTENCE

A. Correct all errors in structure in the following sentences. If necessary, refer frequently to Sections **61–80.**

1. There are three main types of essays. Reflective, informational, and personal.

2. He is a very good athlete, while I am not.

3. He says he only has three sentences to write before he will be through with the letter completely.

4. The writer who does not take account of this will result in monotony and dullness.

5. I really should not have gone to the play that night, as I had a lot of work to do.

6. Anyone who can master this theorem he should have no further difficulty with geometry.

7. He said he couldn't help but do what he did, disregardless of all our warnings.

8. He walked faster, he was already an hour late, he was afraid everyone would have left before he arrived.

9. This offer is absolutely free and will not cost anyone anything.

10. Some time ago I took a bus trip to Lansing. The bus was crowded.

399

The driver was not courteous. I did not enjoy the trip very much.

11. When he was in high school he was interested in dramatics, but athletics and dances occupied much of his time in college.

12. Glad to have your note. Sorry you have been ill. Hope you will soon be all right.

13. I wish to say that in the first place—and I am sure you will agree with me after you think it over—the suggestion is not worthy.

14. Engaging in daily exercise is done with several things in mind.

15. This automobile is prettier and will be able to be operated more economically.

B. Directions given in Exercise A.

1. Our hero slept far too long. And so he felt drugged and lethargic for the rest of the day.

2. Jack built a canoe like the one the Indian had described with the assistance of his father, it was a tedious job.

3. *Tom Jones* is an exciting book. He is such a "he-man" character is why.

4. Mother bid two hearts. I bid two spades. Dad decided to pass. Sis raised me to game.

5. When the bridge was washed away in the spring freshet is why the road inspector lost his job, probably.

6. Our cat only had three kittens in her litter this year, while last year she had six.

7. Any Bleaker College man is thoroughly trained and who is reliable.

8. Most savages are fond of hunting and to dance. Especially in the warm weather.

9. These "oriental" rugs aren't originals and the colors fast, they want to sell them for twice what they are worth, nevertheless.

10. She is the best dancer I know and lives with her widowed mother.

11. I did not like to pay more than a dollar; on the contrary, neither did Grace, who told the ticket scalper that (where she found the courage I can't imagine) he was a fraud.

12. After eating up lunch, the teacher made me sweep the whole classroom up.

13. Norm said that it was about opposite this house where he saw your dog.

14. Few sailors fail to somehow or other assume that they will be probably able to finally die on land.

400

General Exercises

15. It is the worst ice storm I have ever seen if we have a whole fruit tree left, we'll be lucky.

C. Directions given in Exercise A.

1. Jacques ate so much ice cream that he said he wished to never as long as he lived hear the word again.
2. With the more thoughtful and industrious farmer, he works at his job twelve months of the year.
3. It was this place in the experiment where I made a mistake.
4. While sitting in my room, four students came in with tickets for the basketball game.
5. I don't wish to unfairly give you the wrong impression, but she is one of those naïve persons.
6. As a young man he worked on farms, played professional baseball, and acted as a swimming instructor; this gave him a good physique.
7. The physician who treats his patients well deserves to be remunerated promptly.
8. Father did not wish us to go; on the contrary, neither did Mother, who said that (she is a cautious person) the roads were too icy.
9. They do not have the proper kind of equipment for us to work with.
10. He loved to play practical jokes and came from the city of Duluth.
11. There were at least a few of us who wondered what we were coming to.
12. The rooms are clean and the meal cooked, they won't arrive for another hour, however.
13. Della liked singing and to play the piano. For hours at a time.
14. The mechanic is a good workman and who is honest.
15. I have only bought two suits all year, while Peter has purchased four.

The Word

The word is the smallest grammatical element which can stand alone as an utterance. Problems with words involve spelling and diction; both are important and difficult.

Correct spelling is not yet old-fashioned, although comparatively little attention is currently paid to its teaching. Misspelling is not the most heinous sin which a writer can commit, and yet it is looked upon by readers, teachers, employers, and some friends as a serious fault.

Diction is the choice of words for the expression of ideas. Words are the only medium for the perception of ideas and are the most important medium for communicating thought from one person to another. Because there are many different ideas to express in many different shades of meaning and emphasis, because there are many words to choose from, and because there are many errors in word choice to be avoided, students frequently maintain that the most difficult part of composition to master is diction. But all good writing depends upon good diction; just as a good builder carefully selects the materials for the construction of a house, so must the writer make an earnest effort to choose painstakingly the basic materials which he puts into his theme.

Diction reveals the man even more clearly than dress or manners. A person's choice of words is not accidental but is an organic part of him. Listen to someone for a few minutes, or read something he has written, and you will learn much about the kind of person he is. Thus, we frequently say of someone, "He talks like a lawyer," or a physician, or a scientist, or a sailor. A novelist makes each of his characters use words that are suitable, "in character."

Since diction is basic in all writing, and since it is clearly indica-

The Word

tive of what we are and what we wish to express, all people, especially the student, must keep in mind the necessity for regular effort to improve in the choice and use of words. Improvement in diction is indeed a lifework, but you, as a college student, have an unusual opportunity to build a foundation.

Diction should be *correct, clear,* and *effective.* No standards of diction, however, can be absolute. Any rule or prescription concerning word usage must be modified by considerations of time, of place, and of situation. Our word choice is not inflexibly "good" or "standard." A word in "correct" use a generation or two ago may now be outmoded; a word appropriate in one section of the country or used before a particular group of hearers may not be correct, clear, or effective elsewhere. Diction, like women's hats, is influenced by many changes of taste; with diction as with hats, appropriateness is the only worth-while test.

Nor can the use of this or that word be justified by saying that it is seen frequently in print. Advertisements, newspapers, magazines, and even well-considered books may exhibit poor diction. You should aim to use words that are understandable in all sections of the country at the present time. The dictionary, therefore, must be constantly at your elbow (see Section **99**). Finally, you must be guided, even if the guidance seems to necessitate a blind and unsubstantial trust, by the practices of the standard authors of the past and those writers of today who command the respect of serious readers.

In short, correct English is that which is in present, national, and reputable use, and the use of such English is, in general, our safest guide. We should normally use words that are currently accepted and sanctioned, not archaic, obsolete, or newly coined words. We should use words which are generally understandable throughout the country, not provincialisms, technical terms, Anglicisms, or foreign words. And we should use only words which are established by good usage, that is, words accepted by that great body of accomplished speakers and writers who we have reason to believe know the language best and who set the standards for others to follow.

Correctness in the use of words is discussed in the following sections:

403

Spelling—Section 81
Archaic and obsolete words—Section 82
Provincialisms—Section 83
Colloquialisms—Section 84
Idiom—Section 85
Vulgarisms—Section 86
Improprieties—Section 87
Slang—Section 88

Clearness in word choice is treated in these sections:

Exact diction—Section 89
Jargon—Section 90
Mixed figures—Section 91

Effectiveness in word choice is developed in these:

Emphatic diction—Section 92
Appropriateness—Section 93
Triteness—Section 94
Fine writing—Section 95
Conciseness—Section 96
Faulty repetition—Section 97
Euphony—Section 98

Some of these sections simultaneously deal with correctness, clarity, and effectiveness. For example, incorrect idiomatic usage can be neither clear nor effective; mixed figures are incorrect, ineffective, and vague in meaning. But the outline above may be useful in keeping your attention focused on important principles.

Section 99 introduces you to, or reinforces your knowledge of, using the dictionary; Section 100, a "Glossary of Faulty Diction," contains a list, worth study, of common errors in the use of specific words.

SPELLING

81. Misspelling is not a problem in diction, but obviously it is an important initial phase of word study.

The spelling of English words is difficult. Some words, for example, are not spelled as they sound. Also, you cannot spell by analogy. It should, however, be comparatively easy to improve your spelling if you will habitually do these seven things:

1. Pronounce words correctly.
2. Mentally *see* words as well as hear them.
3. Use a dictionary to fix words in the memory.
4. Use memory devices to help remember troublesome words.
5. Learn a few simple rules for spelling.
6. Write words carefully in order to avoid errors due not to ignorance but to carelessness.
7. *List* the words most frequently misspelled.

81a. Pronounce words correctly.

Mispronunciation is responsible for a large number of misspelled words. Although pronunciation is not always a safe guide to spelling, it is difficult to spell correctly a mispronounced word.

1. Do not add vowels in pronouncing such words as *disastrous, similar, remembrance, hindrance,* and *athletics,* and you will not misspell them as disasterous, similiar, rememberance, hinderance, and athaletics (or atheletics).

2. Do not omit consonants in pronouncing such words as *eighth, library, government, environment.*

3. Do not omit syllables in pronouncing such words as *miniature, sophomore, laboratory, accidentally, criticism, convenience.*

4. Carefully examine words that contain silent letters: *psychology, pneumonia, ghost, aghast, condemn, exhaust, rhythm, column.*

5. Be suspicious of words containing lightly stressed syllables. The technical name, *schwa* (ə), is given to indicate the sound, a kind of "uh"; the vowel used may be any one of the six, *a, e, i, o, u, y: dollar, grammar, corner, model, nadir, peril, professor, sponsor, murmur, sulfur, martyr.* In such words, it may help to exaggerate the "trouble spots": *grammAr, sepArate, repEtition, mathEmatics, humOrous, existEnce, dEscribe.*

81b. Actually <u>see</u> words as well as hear them.

An important method of improving your spelling is to look at, or repeat, a word until you can really *see* it. Correct pronunciation will help an "ear-minded" person to spell correctly, but it is also important to visualize words. Frequently we say of a word we have written, "That doesn't look right." But many students constantly misspell words because they have never really learned to observe a printed page; their errors in spelling come from an unwillingness or apparent inability to observe, to *see*. Study words until you can *see* them anywhere: in the air, on the floor, or under the table.

The most frequent error in visualizing words is mistaking one for another. Observe carefully the pairs or triplets in the following list. Understand their meaning and do not use one when you mean the other.

accept, except	loose, lose
advice, advise	lose, loss
affect, effect	marital, martial
an, and	medal, metal
angel, angle	of, off
are, our	on, one
biding, bidding	passed, past
breath, breathe	personal, personnel
capital, capitol	precede, proceed
choose, chose	principal, principle
cite, sight, site	quiet, quite, quit
clothes, cloths	respectfully, respectively
coarse, course	shone, shown
conscience, conscious	shudder, shutter
counsel, council, consul	stationary, stationery
decent, descent	statue, stature, statute
desert, dessert	than, then
due, do	their, there, they're
ever, every	therefor, therefore
hear, here	thorough, through
hoping, hopping	to, too, two
human, humane	weak, week
its, it's (never *its'*)	weather, whether
know, no	were, where
later, latter	whose, who's
lead, led	woman, women
least, lest	wont, won't
lightening, lightning	your, you're

81c. Use the dictionary to help fix words in your memory.

A knowledge of the etymology (origin, derivation) of a word may help you to spell it correctly. For example, he who knows that *preparation* is derived from the prefix *prae* plus *parare* (to make ready) will not spell the word *preperation*. Similarly, a study of common prefixes and suffixes, such as *ante, per, fore,* and *cede,* will enable you to spell correctly by grouping similar forms in a way which will emphasize their resemblance.

Of course, a study of the dictionary will enable you to pronounce words properly and will give you an opportunity to *see* words (81a, 81b), and thus help you to spell correctly.

81d. Use memory devices to help remember troublesome words.

Some of these devices apply to groups of words, such as the common spelling rules (81e) and the rhyme for the *ei-ie* words (81e, 1).

Others that you may devise apply to specific words. For example: *PrepAration* is from the basic word, *prepAre; infinIte* and *definIte* are from *finIte.* (Four puzzlers to watch, however, are *explanation* from *explain, maintenance* from *maintain, procedure* from *proceed,* and *pronunciation* from *pronounce.*)

"Together" breaks into "to get her"; "piece" has "pie"; "tomatoes" and "potatoes" have "toes"; "pa" and "ma" appear in "se*pa*rate" and "gram*ma*r."

81e. Learn a few simple rules for spelling.

There are numerous rules for spelling certain words and classes of words, but it is doubtful that many of them are really helpful. Remember that the words came *first,* the rules *second,* and that the rules are generalized statements applicable to a fairly large number of words, but not all; consequently, there are exceptions to every rule.

For words ending in *-able* or *-ible, -ant* or *-ent, -ance* or *-ence, -ise, -ize,* or *-yze, -tion* or *-sion,* there is no safe guide except memory or constant reference to the dictionary. The seven rules which follow are simple and easily learned; mastering them will eliminate a larger number of recurring errors.

1. *Words in ei or ie.*

407

81e

> Write *i* before *e*
> Except after *c*,
> Or when sounded as *a*
> As in *neighbor* and *weigh*.

This rule applies when the pronunciation of *ei* or *ie* is a long *e* (as in *he*) or the *a* sound: *believe, chief, field, niece, piece, siege, yield, view, conceive, deceive, receive; eight, freight, reign, veil.*

A simple memory device for remembering whether the *e* or *i* comes after the *c* or *l* is the key word *Celia* (or *Alice*, or *police*, or *lice*).

NOTE: Exceptions often misspelled: *neither, leisure, seize.*

2. *Final y.*

Words ending in *-y* preceded by a consonant change *y* to *i* before any suffix except one beginning with *-i;* words ending in *-y* preceded by a vowel do not change *y* to *i.*

This, the most commonly illustrated of all spelling rules, is especially helpful in forming plurals of nouns ending in *-y* or in forming the third person singular present tense, the past tense, and the past participle of verbs ending in *-y.*

> *activity, activities; enemy, enemies; library, libraries; valley, valleys*
>
> *carry, carries; try, tried; modify, modifying; study, studied, studying; annoy, annoyed; stay, stayed, staying*
>
> *lucky, luckily; easy, easier; lovely, loveliest; empty, emptiness; lively, livelihood*

Important exceptions: *lay, laid; pay, paid; say, said.*

3. *Doubling final consonant.*

Monosyllables and words of more than one syllable accented on the last syllable, when ending in a single consonant (except *x*) preceded by a single vowel, double the consonant before adding an ending which begins with a vowel.

This rule is valuable in forming the past tense, past participle, and present participle of many regular verbs and in forming the comparative and superlative degrees of adjectives. Common endings beginning with a vowel are the following: *-ed, -ing, -er, -est, -able, -ible, -ance, -ence, -ish,* and *-y.*

408

*drop, dropped, dropping; plan, planned, planning; refer, re-
ferred, referring; admit, admitted, admitting, admittance; tax,
taxes, taxing; overlap, overlapped, overlapping; unforgettable;
red, redder, reddest; acquit (q equals kw), acquitted, acquitting*
Important exceptions: *transferable, transference, gaseous.*

NOTE 1: If the accent is shifted to an earlier syllable than it was
on in the basic word, the final consonant is not doubled:
refer, referred, referring—but *reference*
prefer, preferred, preferring—but *preference*
Exception: *excellence.*

NOTE 2: Derivatives from basic words that change pronunciation
from a long vowel sound to a short vowel sound follow the
doubling rule: *write, writing,* but *written; bite, biting,* but *bitten;
inflame, inflaming,* but *inflammable.*

NOTE 3: Observe also what the doubling-final-consonant rule does
not include:
Words ending in a final consonant preceded by *two* vowels do
not double the final consonant: *appear, appearing, appearance;
need, needing, needy; train, trained, training.*

Words which are not accented on the *final* syllable do not double
the final consonant: *happen, happened, happening; benefit, benefited, benefiting* (but *fit, fitted, fitting*).

A good key word for this rule is *combat.* It can be pronounced
with the accent on either syllable, but note the spelling:

combat'	combat'ted	combat'ting
com'bat	com'bated	com'bating

4. *The "one plus one" rule.*
When the prefix of a word ends in the same letter with which
the main part of the word begins, or when the main part of the
word ends in the same letter with which the suffix begins, be sure
that both letters are included.
dissatisfied, dissimilar, misspell, roommate, overrun (but *disappear, disapproval,* etc.)
*accidentally, cruelly, occasionally, brownness, meanness, sudden-
ness* (but *sadly, severely, greatness,* etc.)
5. *Silent e.*
Most words ending in silent *-e* drop the *e* before a suffix begin-

409

ning with a vowel but keep the *e* before a suffix beginning with a consonant.

> *believe, believing; live, livable; arrive, arrival; ice, icy*
> *sincere, sincerely; amuse, amusement; safe, safety*

NOTE: Two exceptions often misspelled: *argument, truly.*

Words which end in *-ce* or *-ge* retain the *e* when *-ous* and *-able* are added, in order to prevent giving a hard sound (*k* or *ga*) to the *c* or *g: notice, noticeable; service, serviceable; change, changeable; courage, courageous; outrage, outrageous,* etc.

6. *The inserted -k rule.*

In words ending in *-c* to which a suffix is added beginning with *e, i,* or *y,* insert *k* before the suffix in order to prevent mispronunciation: *picnic, picnicked, picnicking; panic, panicky; traffic, trafficked, trafficking.*

7. *The -eed, -ede rule.*

When words end in an *-eed* sound, remember that only three words are spelled with an *-eed* ending (*exceed, proceed, succeed*), only one word ends in *-sede* (*supersede*), and all other words in this group end in *-cede* (*accede, intercede, precede, recede, secede*).

81f. Do not carelessly misspell words.

Some spelling errors are caused by carelessness, not ignorance. Nearly everyone makes errors in writing, and the careful student, realizing this, will read and reread his written work to eliminate slips, sometimes rereading once or twice solely for the purpose of finding misspelled words.

Do not carelessly transpose letters of words or write two words as one when they should be written separately.

curl, *not* crul	Britain, *not* Britian
first, *not* frist	research, *not* reaserch
high school, *not* highschool	third, *not* thrid
in fact, *not* infact	thirty, *not* thrity
in spite, *not* inspite	wouldn't, *not* would'nt

81g. Keep a list of the words you most frequently misspell.

Learning to spell correctly seems a hopeless task because so many thousands of words must be mastered. But it is well to remember that no one is expected to be able to spell all words, on demand,

and that only a comparatively few words are the most persistent troublemakers. For, curiously enough, words like *Mississippi, Tennessee, literature, excommunicate,* and *Canaan* are not frequently misspelled, even when frequently used; rather, words like *too, all right, it's, its, there, their* most often are the offenders (see 81b).

Keep a list of words which you misspell and study them (perhaps according to 81a, 81b, 81c) until you thoroughly learn their spelling.

It has been estimated that a basic list of only 1,000 words appears in 90 percent of all writing, a basic list of only 2,000 words in 95 percent of all writing. Many of these words appear in the following group. Your own list will contain words not given here, but try to see that none of the following appears on your list. Master the spelling of these words but do not try to do so all at once; rather, try to master five words a day.

1. absence	21. advisable	41. antecedent
2. absolutely	22. afraid	42. anticipation
3. abundant	23. allotting	43. anxiety
4. accidentally	24. allowance	44. apology
5. accommodations	25. all right	45. apparatus
6. accompaniment	26. already	46. apparent
7. accomplishment	27. although	47. appearance
8. accumulation	28. altogether	48. appreciation
9. accuse	29. alumni	49. appropriate
10. achievement	30. always	50. approval
11. acknowledge	31. amateur	51. approximately
12. acquaintance	32. ambitious	52. argument
13. acquire	33. American	53. arise
14. acquisition	34. among	54. arithmetic
15. across	35. amusement	55. armistice
16. activities	36. analysis	56. around
17. actually	37. ancestry	57. aroused
18. adequate	38. announcement	58. arrangement
19. admiration	39. annual	59. association
20. advantages	40. answer	60. athlete

61. attempt
62. attendance
63. attitude
64. attractiveness
65. audience

66. autobiography
67. auxiliary
68. available
69. awkward
70. bachelor

71. barbarous
72. barely
73. bargain
74. basically
75. beautiful

76. becoming
77. beginning
78. believing
79. benefited
80. boundary

81. brilliant
82. business
83. calendar
84. campaign
85. candidate

86. career
87. carrying
88. celebrate
89. certain
90. challenge

91. changeable
92. characteristic
93. cheerfulness
94. chiefly
95. coincidence

96. college
97. column
98. comfortably
99. committee
100. community

101. comparatively
102. comparison
103. competence
104. competition
105. complexion

106. compliment
107. composition
108. comprehension
109. conceive
110. concentrated

111. concerned
112. condemn
113. conducive
114. confidence
115. congratulations

116. conscientious
117. consequently
118. considerable
119. consolation
120. contemporary

121. contemptuous
122. continually
123. continuous
124. contrary
125. contribution

126. controlled
127. correspondence
128. countries
129. courageous
130. courtesy

131. criticism
132. crowd
133. cruelly
134. curiosity
135. curtain

136. customer
137. dangerous
138. dealt
139. deceive
140. decision

141. defenseless
142. deficient
143. definitely
144. definition
145. delinquent

146. demonstrated
147. denied
148. depression
149. depth
150. descendant

151. descent
152. description
153. desperate
154. destruction
155. determination

156. difference
157. difficulty
158. diminish
159. dining room
160. director

161. disappear
162. disappoint
163. discoveries
164. disease
165. disguise

166. dissatisfied	201. everybody	236. gentleman
167. distinguished	202. evidently	237. gesture
168. divide	203. exaggerating	238. glorious
169. divine	204. excellent	239. government
170. dormitories	205. exceptionally	240. graduating
171. dropped	206. excitement	241. grammar
172. earlier	207. exercise	242. guarantee
173. easily	208. exhaust	243. handicapped
174. education	209. exhibit	244. happening
175. efficient	210. existence	245. happily
176. eighth	211. expectation	246. haughtiness
177. either	212. expenses	247. healthy
178. elementary	213. experience	248. heartily
179. eligible	214. experiment	249. heavier
180. eliminate	215. explanation	250. height
181. eloquently	216. extravagant	251. helpful
182. embarrass	217. faithfulness	252. heritage
183. emergency	218. familiar	253. heroes
184. emphasize	219. fascinating	254. hindrance
185. emptiness	220. February	255. history
186. encouragement	221. fiery	256. hopelessness
187. enemies	222. finally	257. hospitality
188. English	223. financially	258. hostile
189. enormous	224. finish	259. humiliate
190. enough	225. foreign	260. humorous
191. entertainment	226. forty	261. hungry
192. enthusiasm	227. fourth	262. hurriedly
193. entrance	228. fraternity	263. hypocrisy
194. environment	229. friendliness	264. ignorant
195. episode	230. frontier	265. imaginary
196. equipment	231. fundamental	266. immediately
197. equipped	232. further	267. important
198. especially	233. future	268. impossible
199. essential	234. gathering	269. inadequate
200. eventually	235. genius	270. incidentally

271. indefinitely
272. independent
273. individual
274. industrial
275. influenced

276. initiative
277. injured
278. innocence
279. inquiries
280. insistence

281. installation
282. instructor
283. instrument
284. intelligent
285. intensely

286. interesting
287. interfere
288. interpret
289. interruption
290. intolerance

291. introductory
292. invariable
293. invitation
294. justifies
295. knowledge

296. labeled
297. laboratory
298. language
299. lengthwise
300. liberal

301. libraries
302. license
303. lightning
304. listener
305. literature

306. livelihood
307. loneliness
308. lovable
309. loveliest
310. loyalty

311. luxuries
312. maintenance
313. majestic
314. managing
315. manufacturer

316. marriageable
317. mathematics
318. meanness
319. meant
320. medicine

321. mediocre
322. melancholy
323. mentality
324. merchandise
325. merely

326. metropolitan
327. millionaire
328. miniature
329. minutes
330. miracle

331. mischievous
332. misspelled
333. modifying
334. monotonous
335. month

336. multiplication
337. musician
338. mysterious
339. nationalities
340. naturally

341. necessary
342. negative
343. neighbor
344. neither
345. niece

346. nineteen
347. ninety
348. ninth
349. noisy
350. noticeable

351. notoriety
352. numerous
353. obsolete
354. obstacle
355. occasionally

356. occupying
357. occurred
358. occurrence
359. o'clock
360. offered

361. official
362. omission
363. omitted
364. operation
365. opinion

366. opponent
367. opportunities
368. optimistic
369. originate
370. overwhelming

371. pamphlet
372. parallel
373. paralyze
374. parental
375. parliamentary

376. participated
377. particularly
378. pastime
379. pattern
380. peaceable

381. peculiarities
382. penniless
383. performance
384. perhaps
385. permanent

386. permissible
387. perseverance
388. persistent
389. personalities
390. persuade

391. physician
392. picnicking
393. planned
394. pleasant
395. plotted

396. poignant
397. poisonous
398. politician
399. portrayed
400. possessions

401. possibility
402. poverty
403. practically
404. preceding
405. predominant

406. preferable
407. preference
408. preferred
409. prejudice
410. preparation

411. prevalence
412. previous
413. privilege
414. probably
415. procedure

416. proceed
417. professor
418. prominent
419. pronunciation
420. proved

421. provisions
422. publication
423. punctuation
424. pursue
425. qualities

426. quantity
427. quarter
428. questionnaire
429. quizzes
430. realize

431. really
432. rebellious
433. receipt
434. receive
435. recognize

436. recollection
437. recommend
438. reconciliation
439. reference
440. referred

441. refrigerator
442. register
443. regrettable
444. rehearsal
445. release

446. religious
447. remembrance
448. remodeled
449. rendezvous
450. renowned

451. repentance
452. repetition
453. replies
454. representative
455. requirements

456. research
457. reservoir
458. resources
459. respectfully
460. responsibility

461. restaurant
462. reverent
463. reviewing
464. ridiculous
465. righteous

466. rivalry
467. roommate
468. safety
469. sandwich
470. satirical

471. satisfaction
472. Saturday
473. scarcely
474. scenery
475. schedule

476. scholarship
477. scientific
478. secretary
479. selection
480. semester

81g

481. sensitive
482. sentences
483. separation
484. seriousness
485. severely

486. shining
487. shudder
488. siege
489. significance
490. similar

491. sincerely
492. situation
493. solution
494. somebody
495. sophomore

496. sorrowful
497. sovereignty
498. specialization
499. species
500. specifically

501. specimen
502. spectacle
503. speech
504. sponsor
505. statement

506. stopping
507. straighten
508. strength
509. strenuous
510. stretched

511. stubbornness
512. studied
513. studying
514. subscribe
515. substantiate

516. substitute
517. suburb
518. succeeding
519. successful
520. sufficient

521. summarize
522. superintendent
523. supersede
524. superstitious
525. surprised

526. surrounded
527. suspense
528. suspicious
529. swimming
530. system

531. tactfulness
532. technical
533. technique
534. temperament
535. temperate

536. temperature
537. temporarily
538. tendency
539. thankfulness
540. thieves

541. thirtieth
542. thirty
543. thoroughly
544. throughout
545. together

546. tomorrow
547. tradition
548. tragedy
549. training
550. transferred

551. transportation
552. treasurer
553. tremendously
554. tried
555. trifle

556. trivial
557. truly
558. Tuesday
559. twelfth
560. typical

561. unbelievable
562. uncivilized
563. unconscious
564. uncontrollable
565. undesirable

566. undoubtedly
567. undying
568. uneasiness
569. unforgettable
570. universities

571. unmanageable
572. unnecessary
573. until
574. unusual
575. usage

576. usually
577. varieties
578. vengeance
579. versatile
580. vertical

581. veteran
582. vicinity
583. victim
584. view
585. village

586. villainous	591. wealthiest	596. wonderful
587. virtuous	592. Wednesday	597. wondrous
588. visible	593. weird	598. writing
589. volume	594. wherever	599. written
590. warranted	595. witnessed	600. yield

EXERCISES

A. Pronunciation: Carefully pronounce the following words; then mark the division into syllables (see Syllabication, Section 22): *opportunity, conspicuous, February, accommodate, kindergarten, delicatessen, villain, maintenance, secretary, misspell, pronunciation, fourteen, sacrilegious, mischievous, laboratory, temperament, frantically, emperor, incidentally.*

B. Rules:

1. Insert *ie* or *ei* in the following:

bel___ve	n___ce	f___ry	f___rce
ch___f	s___ze	misch___f	f___nd
rec___ve	s___ge	l___sure	w___rd
gr___vance	th___r	th___f	w___ght

2. Form derivatives of the following words by adding *-ly, -ty,* or *-ment: commence, judge, argue, subtle, naïve, love, safe, extreme, acknowledge, like.*

3. Write the present participle of each of the following verbs: *hope, force, agree, argue, singe, die, dye, use.*

4. *Study—studies—studied.* Supply the same verb forms for the following: *hurry, stay, try, play, envy, tarry, enjoy.*

5. Add suffixes to the following words: *clan, gas, defer, bag, begin, hot, swim, split, transfer, cut.*

C. Dictionary study: See if a study of the derivations of the following words will aid you in spelling them correctly: *atonement, bilingual, assignee, nasturtium, precedence, nickname, saxophone, coexist, bungalow, senile, precancel, necrology.*

D. Some of the following words are misspelled; correct the misspellings: *exhilarate, tranquillity, batalion, parafin, ecstacy, excellant, liquify, retreive, supercede, irrelavant, stretched, transfered, enquiring, interrupted, unoticed, approximately, cleptomania, meddle-some, murmered, drunkeness, roommate, newstand.*

E. Some of the following proper names are misspelled. Correct the errors:

Amercian	Floridia	Phillippines
Britian	Hawaiian	Saterday
Britannica	Louisiana	Southren
Christain	McBeth	Tennessee
Cincinnati	Massachusetts	Teusday
Conneticut	Minnesota	Wendesday
Febuary	Pennsylvania	Wisconson

F. Some of the following names are misspelled; correct the errors:

T. S. Elliot	Guiseppe Garabaldi
Eleanor Wylie	Ernest Hemmingway
Walter Lippmann	Chiang Kaishek

G. Consult your dictionary to find the preferred spellings of *kidnaped, theater, centre, instalment;* the preferred plurals of *stratum, index, medium.*

ARCHAIC AND OBSOLETE WORDS

82. One of the requirements of good usage is that words must be intelligible to readers and hearers of the present time. Words are constantly going out of use because our language is constantly growing and changing. Except for somewhat doubtful purposes of humor, we should guard against using expressions which, though antiquated, persist in our vocabularies because of our reading of them in books written centuries ago.

82a. Avoid the use of archaic words.

An *archaic* word is old-fashioned; it may be retained in special contexts, such as legal and Biblical expressions, but has almost entirely passed from ordinary language. Examples: *enow* for *enough; eftsoon* (eftsoons) for *again;* to *glister* for to *glisten; gramercy* for *thank you; methinks* for *it seems to me;* to *jape* for

to *jest* (joke); *lief* for *willing; whilom* for *formerly; wight* for
person; wot for *know; y-clad* for *clothed; y-clept* for *named* or
called. Do not use archaic words except to achieve some particular
stylistic effect; even then, be certain this effect can be secured in
no other way. Words which are archaic are so marked in dictionaries.

82b. Do not use obsolete words.

An *obsolete* word is one which has completely passed out of use;
an *obsolescent* word is one which is becoming obsolete. Examples:
infortune for *misfortune; bene* for *prayer; dole* for *grief; permit*
for *commit; prevent* for *precede* or *anticipate*. Obsolete words and
obsolete meanings of words are so marked in dictionaries.

PROVINCIALISMS

83. Avoid the use of provincialisms.

A fundamental requirement of good usage is that words must be
in national, not merely sectional, use. A provincialism, or localism,
is a word or phrase used and understood in only a particular section or region of the country. Such words are difficult to detect
because a writer or speaker may have come to accept them as
reputable and to assume that they are nationally understood since
he himself has known them from childhood. The northeastern
(New England), southern, and western parts of the United States,
among others, are especially rich in colorful localisms which add
flavor to speech but which may not be immediately intelligible in
other areas. Such localisms are appropriate in informal writing
and conversation but should be avoided in formal writing. Examples: *chunk* and *chuck* for *to throw; tote* for *carry; tote* (noun)
for *a load; poke* for *a bag* or *sack; fatback* for *bacon; bunk into*
for *bump into; reckon* for *think* or *suppose; choose* for *wish;*
draw for *gully; chuck wagon* for a *supply wagon; selectman* for a
town official; to home for *at home; loco* for *crazy*. Linguists may
differ among themselves over which of such expressions are localisms and which are merely colloquial. In formal writing guard
against them, whatever their label.

A. Make a list of provincialisms heard in your neighborhood or vicinity.

B. Select some provincialisms from a dictionary. Can you recall any of them from your reading?

C. Discuss former President Coolidge's famous remark: "I do not *choose* to run."

COLLOQUIALISMS

A colloquialism is a conversational expression which is permissible in, and frequently indispensable to, an easy, informal style of writing and speaking. If it is used only in familiar talk and informal writing, there is no objection. Colloquialisms are necessarily used even in the formal writing of dialogue to aid in developing the characteristics of speakers.

Dictionaries mark words as colloquial (*Colloq.*) when in the judgment of the editors they are more common in speech than in writing or more appropriate in informal than formal discourse. Because editors differ in the interpretations of their findings and because formal English has a far wider range than formerly, this label may apply to many kinds of words. All contractions, for example, may be considered "respectable" colloquialisms, whereas some other kinds should be guarded against in even informal writing.

84. Avoid colloquialisms in formal writing.

The test for the use of colloquialisms is appropriateness. There is no objective test or exact rule to enable you to determine when colloquialisms may be used. Certainly it is better to employ them than to avoid them and make your writing seem artificial and awkward. But in formal, well-planned writing they should be avoided unless they are deliberately used to achieve some stylistic effect (see Section 93). Consult the dictionary to determine what words are considered colloquial.

Examples of colloquialisms: *don't, won't, phone, auto, ad, gumption, cute, Chink, in back of, show up, try and, brass tacks* (facts), *take a try at, alongside of, angel* (financial backer), *fizzle* (to fail), *goner* (a person lost or dead), *flabbergast.*

EXERCISES

A. Discuss the following expressions. On what levels of writing and for what purposes might they be used? *To put a bug in his ear, take it easy, every which way, laid off, get it across, grip (valise), fellows, holler, well-liked, bobby socks, jam session.*

B. Make a list of colloquial expressions which you have heard used by educated speakers. Add to the list colloquialisms you have read in books written by reputable authors. Bring in the list for class discussion.

IDIOM

Idiom means the forms or variety of expression of a language, the characteristic way in which it is put together. In speaking of French idiom, for example, we refer to such a distinct usage as putting the adjective after its noun or the fact that an adjective in French has forms for singular and plural and for masculine and feminine gender. An idiom, as distinct from idiom, is a structural form peculiar to a language. Normally, an idiom is an accepted word or phrase which violates grammar, or logic, or both.

Idiom is always familiar and deep-rooted. French and German or Spanish idioms are difficult for us to understand and master; likewise, English idiom is difficult not only for foreigners but for all who have not listened closely to the speech of acceptable speakers. For example, a foreigner has considerable trouble with *the,* using it where English-speaking people omit it and omitting it where we use it, as "When I came to the America, thing that impressed me most was vast distance between the New York and the San Francisco." Curious, too, is the use of *a* with a plural noun when a word like *few* intervenes: *a few apples.*

Many idioms defy grammatical analysis but, because they are sanctioned by current usage, are looked upon as correct. "How do you do?" is an accepted idiom, although an exact answer to the question would, of course, be ridiculous.

Despite the fact that idiom cannot be explained scientifically, you should make frequent use of idiomatic expressions. They are necessary short cuts in our language and make writing vigorous and picturesque. In fact, idioms are the essential material of which language is made: the widespread, everyday usage of people.

85. Use correct idiomatic words and expressions.

Although idioms cannot be justified grammatically, the careful writer will not therefore assume that he can use them as he pleases. His idiomatic usage should conform to the word links generally acceptable. A good dictionary will contain a statement of idiomatic usage following words which need such explanation. It should be noted, however, that dictionaries differ and that, for example, some of the expressions cited below are in controversial use. You should be especially careful to consult your dictionary when using certain word groups of *prepositions* with nouns, adjectives, or verbs. The following lists of idiomatic and unidiomatic expressions contain numerous examples of the use of troublesome prepositions:

Unidiomatic	*Idiomatic*
accord to	accord with
according with	according to
accuse with	accuse of
acquitted from	acquitted of
adverse against	adverse to
aim at proving	aim to prove
all the farther	as far as
among one another	among themselves
angry at (a person)	angry with
as regards to	as regards
authority about	authority on
blame it on me	blame me for it
cannot help but talk	cannot help talking
comply to	comply with
conform in	conform to, with
convince to	convince that
correspond with (a thing)	correspond to
desire of	desire to
desirous to	desirous of
die with (a disease)	die of
different than	different from
disdain of	disdain for

dissent with	dissent from
doubt if	doubt whether
enamored about	enamored of
feel of	feel
free of	free from
frightened of	frightened by, at
graduated (high school)	graduated from (high school)
have got to	must
identical to	identical with
in accordance to	in accordance with
in search for	in search of
jealous for	jealous of
kind of a	kind of
listen at	listen to
monopoly for, on	monopoly of
oblivious to	oblivious of
on line	in line
out loud	aloud
plan on going	plan to go
prefer (one) over (another)	prefer to
prior than	prior to
providing	provided
sensitive about (a stimulus)	sensitive to
superior than	superior to
tend to	attend to
to home	at home
treat on (a subject)	treat of
try and	try to
unequal for	unequal to
unmindful about	unmindful of
vie against	vie with

Certain words require different prepositions to express different meanings. Examples:

agree $\begin{cases} \textit{to} \text{ a proposal} \\ \textit{on} \text{ a plan} \\ \textit{with} \text{ a person} \end{cases}$

contend $\begin{cases} \textit{for} \text{ a principle} \\ \textit{with} \text{ a person} \\ \textit{against} \text{ an obstacle} \end{cases}$

$$
\text{differ} \begin{cases} \textit{with} \text{ a person} \\ \textit{from} \text{ something else} \\ \textit{about} \text{ or } \textit{over} \text{ a question} \end{cases}
$$

$$
\text{impatient} \begin{cases} \textit{for} \text{ something desired} \\ \textit{with} \text{ someone else} \\ \textit{of} \text{ restraint} \\ \textit{at} \text{ someone's conduct} \end{cases}
$$

$$
\text{rewarded} \begin{cases} \textit{for} \text{ something done} \\ \textit{with} \text{ a gift} \\ \textit{by} \text{ a person} \end{cases}
$$

EXERCISES

A. Correct the errors in idiom which occur in the following sentences:

1. Please listen at this music; it is superior than anything I've ever heard before.
2. He was initiated to our fraternity during his first year at college.
3. Oblivious to all sound, he concentrated on his studying.
4. She was enamored with the idea, but there was nothing she could do about it.
5. As I sat in the divan, I looked quietly about the room.
6. It must have slipped my mind for I don't remember of having said that.
7. If you will wait on me for only ten minutes, I'll be glad of an opportunity of going with you.
8. He was impatient at restraint and angry that the warden would not comply to his request for more freedom.
9. That is a trait which is peculiar with this race of people, but they seem to be unmindful to it.
10. If you don't plan on going with me, I shall be free of all future obligations to you.

B. Make the following sentences idiomatically correct by filling in the blanks with the proper prepositions.

1. This letter means that he will accede......your request.
2. Contrast this idea.......that one.
3. She does not adhere......that theory.
4. Mr. Bullock will compensate you......the work.
5. In this instance, the boys don't agree.......the girls.

6. Sarah was then admitted......the theater.
7. Are you really independent......your father?
8. Your mother is apprehensive......your safety.
9. Surely you can accommodate yourself......any plan.
10. What do you infer......that proposal?

C. Use correct prepositions with each of the following verbs: *acquiesce, center, collide, engage, initiate, sympathize, wait, part, concentrate, listen.*

D. Use correct prepositions with each of the following words: *peculiar, prodigal, independent, unmindful, glad, sympathy, angry, repugnant, vexed, hatred, ambitious, sick, careful, obedient, worthy.*

E. Collect examples of unidiomatic English from your reading of dialect stories or from the speech of others (children, foreigners).

VULGARISMS

86. Avoid the use of vulgarisms.

Vulgarisms (also called "barbarisms" and "illiteracies") are words and phrases not accepted in either colloquial or formal language. Characteristic of uneducated speech, they are always to be avoided in writing unless you put them into the mouths of people you are characterizing. Vulgarisms are not necessarily coarse and are frequently effective, but the careful writer does not use them.

Dictionary makers apply different restrictive labels to "vulgar English." What may be marked *illiterate* in one dictionary may be termed *colloquial* in another. And because most dictionaries primarily record "standard" usage, many vulgarisms are not listed at all. The following words and phrases should be guarded against: *hadn't ought, to burgle, boughten, borned, losted, drownded, mistakened, this here, disremember, irregardless, anywheres, nohow, couldn't of, hisself, being as, being as how, concertize, vacationize, still and all.*

EXERCISES

A. From what is the word *vulgarism* derived? What is the difference between a *vulgarism* and *vulgarity*?

B. Make a list of several vulgarisms heard in the conversation of others or reported in books.

IMPROPRIETIES

87. Improprieties are recognized English words which are misused in function or meaning. The word that constitutes an impropriety is acceptable; it is its misuse which causes an error in diction.

87a. Avoid improprieties in grammatical function.

A word may be transferred from one part of speech to another, but the careful writer will not employ such a word in its new function until it is sanctioned by good use. Examples of improprieties in function:

> Verbs used as nouns: *eats, an invite, a fix, a think, a combine* (combination).
> Nouns used as verbs: *to suspicion, to suicide.*
> Adjectives used as adverbs: *real* pretty, *sure, some* tall, etc. (See Section 13.)
> Other examples: *like* for *as* or *as if; don't* for *doesn't; except* for *unless.*

87b. Avoid improprieties in meaning.

Although some improprieties in meaning are the result of ignorance, most of them are caused by the misuse of words similar in form (see Section 81b), or even identical in pronunciation, such as homonyms (words pronounced alike but different in spelling and meaning). Examples:

accept, except	elude, allude
affect, effect	expect, suspect
all ready, already	farther, further
all together, altogether	formally, formerly
allusion, illusion	healthful, healthy
avenge, revenge	ingenious, ingenuous
complement, compliment	interest, intrigue (*v.*)
council, counsel	irritate, aggravate
disinterested, uninterested	later, latter

liable, likely
noted, notorious
principal, principle

respectfully, respectively
stationary, stationery
than, then

EXERCISES

A. Use correctly in sentences each of the pairs of words listed in Section 87b.

B. Use each of the following words correctly in a sentence: *continual, creditable, practicable, apt, continuous, vocation, consul, can, may, mad, conscious, conscience.*

SLANG

Slang is a particular kind of vulgarism (see Section 86). Formerly the term was applied to the cant of gypsies, beggars, and thieves, or to the jargon of any particular class of society. Now slang is defined as language which consists of widely current terms having a forced or fantastic meaning, or displaying eccentricity.

88. Avoid slang in formal writing.

Slang is very popular, but it has little place in formal writing. There are sound reasons for avoiding it. First, many slang words and expressions are ephemeral; they last for a brief period of time and then pass out of use, becoming unintelligible and violating the principle that words must be in current use (see Section 82). Who today uses such formerly popular expressions as "23 skidoo" and "Ishkabibble"? How many people would understand them if they were used? Numerous currently popular slang expressions will be outmoded in a very short time.

Second, the use of slang expressions may keep you from searching for the exact words you need to express your meaning. Many slang expressions are only rubber stamps; to refer to a person as a "peach" hardly expresses exactly or fully any critical judgment or intelligent description. To argue that such a word conveys precisely the intended meaning is to reveal a poverty of vocabulary, or careless thinking, or laziness. The most serious charge against slang is that it becomes a substitute for thinking.

Finally, slang is not appropriate in most formal writing because it is not in keeping with the context. Words should be appropriate to the audience, the occasion, and the subject matter (see Section 93).

Note these typical slang expressions: *grub, to get away (by) with it, bang-up, to get pinched, a bum hunch, to put it across, so what?, spuds, prexy, took the count, going some, a drugstore cowboy, put on the dog, have a heart, a lemon, attaboy, cut no ice, fall for it, hard-boiled, get the goods on him, talk through your hat, it's the berries, goofy, wacky, to crab, let it ride, stow the gab, jitterbug, what's cooking?, you said it, in the groove, a smooth number, to get hep, cooking with gas, to dig, sharp, a rat race, on the beam, sourpuss, cockeyed, good egg, mike, croak* (meaning *to die* or *to kill*).

There are good arguments in favor of slang and places where it should be used. Slang does express feeling, although explosively and sometimes grotesquely. It also makes effective short cuts in expression and often prevents artificiality in writing. Furthermore, it should be used in reporting dialogue to give the flavor of the speech actually used. But you should avoid an excessive or injudicious use of slang expressions, for the reasons already mentioned.

EXERCISES

A. Look up the meanings of *lingo, jargon* (cf. Section 90, as well as the dictionary), *argot, cant.*

B. Prove that slang expressions are short-lived by reading one of Dickens' novels, such as *Oliver Twist.* Can you interpret the thieves' talk?

C. Study the use of slang for purposes of characterization in a story by Ring Lardner.

D. A few words, formerly considered slang, have become legitimatized. Examples are *buncombe, hoax,* and *mob.* Try to find similar examples of words which have filled a real need and thus become acceptable. For example, how respectable have the words *graft, racketeer, bogus,* and *bootlegger* become?

EXACT DICTION

89. The primary purpose of writing is communication; therefore it is important for you to use words which will express *exactly* what you wish to convey. For each idea there is a word or phrase which expresses your meaning more exactly than all others. It is your task, your obligation, to find this word or phrase, and use it. Exactness in diction requires you to think clearly and carefully. Sometimes the first word which comes to mind is the most exact which can be used; more often it is not. The good writer always remembers that a word means to the reader what the reader thinks it means. Exact diction does not result when the writer knows precisely what he means, but only when the reader understands exactly what the writer intended to communicate. Mark Twain once wrote: "The difference between the right word and the almost-right word is the difference between lightning and the lightning bug."

89a. Avoid the use of vague, general words.

Try to be definite in your word choice. Use a specific word rather than one which only approximates the idea. Such vague, general words may be illustrated by these examples:

Fine—a fine day, a fine time.
Vital—a vital message, a vital game.
Thing—used for any idea or object.
Item, phase, nice, element, feature, interesting, factor, instance, nature, lot, job.

The best way to avoid the use of vague words is to think *carefully* what is meant. A study of the synonyms listed for an expression in a dictionary or thesaurus will enable you to choose a more exact term. For example, before allowing the word *jocular* to stand in one of your themes, find out if one of the following adjectives might not communicate your meaning more exactly: *blithe, joyful, joyous, jolly, jocose, jovial, jocund, gay, merry, sportive.*

89b. Avoid exaggeration.

Exaggeration, unless for deliberate effect, is misleading because

429

of its inexactness. An intelligent man once said that when his pastor started using the word *marvelous* over and over in a sermon, he knew that the preacher had run out of something to say. Do not inexactly use such words as *terrible, ghastly, horrible, thrilling, gorgeous, amazing, awful, splendid,* and *phenomenal.* Each of these words has legitimate uses but has been used inexactly so often that it is rarely effective.

EXERCISES

A. The following sentences have been selected from students' themes. Study the inexact diction in each and, with the aid of your dictionary, express the intended meanings more precisely.

1. He had lain ill for some time.
2. A period of despondency engulfed him.
3. Bill entered the house, wearing a sort of yellowish sweater.
4. He came on the field in a blind rage.
5. She looked at the species carefully.
6. Since it was a nice day for fishing, I bought a few items at the store and asked Henry if he was interested in accompanying me.
7. I thought it was a funny proposition and said so, in no uncertain terms.
8. One of his typical characteristics was that he was always pleasingly dressed.
9. It didn't take him long to fix the tire, I suppose, but it seemed ages to me.
10. Swimming was one of the things which helped him develop.
11. Her clothes were amazing creations, and she wore them regally, as if she were some kind of Greek goddess.
12. Since she had an utter horror of all insects, I bravely persecuted the spider until he expired.
13. Examinations are perhaps unavoidable elements of college life, but George swore that the anguish they caused him in bygone days was the deciding factor in his breakdown.
14. The dress looked fine, but I was horror-struck when I realized that all the girls might know that I had been cute enough to fix it out of a last year's number.
15. One thing in her favor was that she was as funny as a person can get to be.

B. Distinguish among the meanings of the words in each of these groups:

    argue, debate, discuss
    dislike, disgust, distaste
    feature, characteristic, peculiarity
    color, hue, tinge, shade

JARGON

Jargon may be defined as confused, unintelligible language. But the term has been amplified by Sir Arthur Quiller-Couch (in his *On the Art of Writing*) to include the use of long words, circumlocution, and other forms of clumsiness difficult to understand. The following discussion is based upon his comments.

90. Avoid the use of jargon.

1. The user of jargon dislikes to say things directly; he resorts to euphemisms and circumlocutions. Instead of saying "No," he says, "The answer is in the negative"; *worked hard* is *pursued his tasks with great diligence; bad weather* is *unfavorable climatic conditions; to get married* is *to enter a state of blessed matrimony.*

2. The jargoneer makes use of "vague, woolly, abstract nouns rather than concrete ones": *case, instance, character, nature, condition, persuasion, degree, quality, personality, asset, thing, state,* and *factor.* He employs such expressions as *along the line of, with regard to, in respect of, in connection with,* and *according as to whether.*

3. Another trick of jargon which Quiller-Couch discusses is "Elegant Variation," an unwillingness to repeat words already used. He cites Lord Byron as being called "that great but unequal poet," "the gloomy master of Newstead," "the meteoric darling of society," etc. Nearly all of you were at one time accustomed to reading of Joe Louis, the prize fighter, as "The Brown Bomber," "The Detroit Menace," "The Tan Terror," etc. Such variation looks affected; it should be avoided.

EXERCISES

A. Improve the wording of the following sentences:

1. The greatest factor in his success was that he had reached a man's estate in a healthy physical condition.
2. In the case of those not present, the nature of their offense will be judged as of a different character.
3. Ruth was one of baseball's greatest assets. The Sultan of Swat possessed ability to an unusual degree, and thousands of human beings in the environs of New York City thought that no one could ever rival the great Bambino. But by the very nature of things, the Bronx Behemoth entered a declining state over a long period of years. Later the fickle fans were of the persuasion that, with regard to baseball ability, Joe DiMaggio, the former San Francisco star, was of the same quality as the former home-run king.
4. With great diligence the student pursued his studies along the lines of medicine.
5. In this instance, his answer in the affirmative was a distinct asset to our business.
6. He was a serious type of student: he wished to major in the chemical field.
7. Illumination is required to be extinguished before this building is closed for the night.
8. In cashing checks, balance on deposit must cover checks to be cashed.

B. Read the section on jargon in H. W. Fowler's *A Dictionary of Modern English Usage,* pages 307–308.

C. Read the section on elegant variation in the same book, pages 130–133; and in *The King's English* (H. W. Fowler and F. G. Fowler), pages 184–189.

D. Distinguish the meanings of *jargon, argot, vernacular, cant, gibberish, lingo, parlance,* and *idiom.*

MIXED FIGURES

As is pointed out in Section **92b,** well-phrased similes and metaphors add clarity and effectiveness to writing. The chief value of such figures of speech is that, if successful, they suggest attractive associations in the reader's mind (see Section **92c**). But they should not be considered as mere ornaments of style; they should not be used too frequently; they should not be confused or inappropriate. To violate these principles is to be guilty of one kind of "fine" writing (see Section **95**).

91. Avoid the use of mixed and inappropriate figures of speech.

When using a metaphor or simile, you should sustain one figure of speech and not shift to another. Similarly, you should not shift too suddenly from figurative language back into literal speech. Finally, you should remember that direct, simple statement is preferable to a series of figures which are elaborate and artificial. Note these examples of inappropriate or mixed figures:

1. When his high hopes for the future were crushed to the ground, his friends forsook him like rats a sinking ship.
2. The road to dental school is straight, narrow, and strewn with rocks, but the diligent student must swim through it.
3. When she lost her job, she got into a rut and felt all at sea.
4. We stopped at the nearest garage, had the crankcase drained, and thus nipped our trouble in the bud.
5. Although I have no lamp to light my feet and feel as if I am up a tree, I shall fight desperately to the last ditch.
6. Directly behind her and pushing her along is the powerful magnet of modern advertising with its fangs of generalities and vague references.

EXERCISES

A. Improve the wording of the above six sentences.

B. Improve the wording of the following:

1. Although he put all his eggs in one basket, his business is built on a firm foundation.
2. She decided to put her shoulder to the wheel and refused to throw up the sponge.
3. The college's very lifeblood has been sapped because the trustees refused to turn over a new leaf.
4. Before the awful testing time of examinations he felt as if he were between two dilemmas: the Scylla of too little time for review and the Charybdis of other obligations. Nevertheless, he decided to put his hand to the plow, hope for the best, look for the silver lining, and try to lift high the lamp of learning.

92 a Emphatic Diction

5. The mainspring of his address hinged upon the fact that, like a
wolf in the fold, the administration had become firmly entrenched
in the hearts of the common people.
6. Like the faint whisper of spring, color began to flow back into her
cheeks.

C. Note that the sentences (above) contain numerous *trite
expressions* (see Section **94**). Try to rewrite some of the sentences,
substituting less worn phrases.

D. Make a list of *effective* figures of speech which you have
found in reading.

EMPHATIC DICTION

92. Words should be emphatic as well as clear. Certain words
are correct and clear but do not have strength or force; such expressions are abstract, or feeble, or worn out. Good writing is
positive and vigorous; it shuns tame, colorless diction.

92a. Prefer specific and concrete to general words.

A specific word names a narrow concept; a general word names
a broad concept. Thus *animal* and *land* are general words; *stallion*
and *pasture* are specific. Notice the greater effectiveness of the
second sentence following:

It was a noisy stream as it came running down the mountain.

Chestnut Creek felt its way down Mount Greybeard over
smooth, greenish-white stones.

The use of specific nouns and concrete phrases, and of specific
verbs which tell of action (motion) or relate to the senses (emotion) will help to make the whole theme more forceful. The diction of the following passage is so emphatic and exact that the
reader, with no further details supplied, can form a satisfactory
picture of Ichabod Crane:

The cognomen of Crane was not inapplicable to his person. He was
tall, but exceedingly lank, with narrow shoulders, long arms and legs,
hands that dangled a mile out of his sleeves, feet that might have
served for shovels, and his whole frame most loosely hung together.

434

His head was small, and flat at the top, with huge ears, large green glassy eyes, and a long snip nose, so that it looked like a weathercock perched upon his spindle neck to tell which way the wind blew. To see him striding along the profile of a hill on a windy day, with his clothes bagging and fluttering about him, one might have mistaken him for the genius of Famine descending upon the earth or some scarecrow eloped from a cornfield.

—WASHINGTON IRVING, *The Legend of Sleepy Hollow*

92b. Make occasional use of figurative language.

Effective writing frequently contains some figures of speech, usually metaphors or similes. A metaphor is a statement which implies a comparison between two ideas or objects; it is not literally true, but it has a genuine effectiveness in driving home an abstract idea. A simile is essentially the same as a metaphor, except that it expresses by means of such words as *like* and *as* a comparison which the metaphor only implies. The passage from Washington Irving quoted above suggests how apt and effective both metaphor and simile may be.

But you should not overload your work with figures of speech and, above all, you should not mix them (see Section **91**). Many of the most trite phrases are worn-out similes and, of course, should not be used (see Section **94**).

92c. Use words and phrases rich in suggestive values.

If your goal is utilitarian, you may use words which are as exact and specific as possible. But the conscientious writer should search for words which suggest more than they say, which stimulate the imagination. San Francisco is "a seaport city in California," but the name suggests such connotations as "Golden Gate," "The Gateway to the Orient," "Chinatown," and "earthquake of 1906." A dog is, according to denotative meaning, "a carnivorous, domesticated mammal," but the word suggests a wealth of associated meanings to anyone who has ever owned or loved a dog.

No rule can be laid down for the choice and use of words rich in connotative meanings. Skilled writers sense the suggestive powers of words, and a study of the language of such writers will aid more than any mere reading of the dictionary can.

435

92 d

Emphatic Diction

92d. Use direct and simple words.

The use of pretentious words is dealt with in Section **95,** but it should be noted here that simple, direct words add force to writing. Do not use *tonsorial parlor, purloiner, lubritorium, emporium, natatorium,* etc.; use the simpler words: *barber shop, thief, service station, store, swimming pool.*

Other means to attain emphasis in diction:

1. Prefer words that fit the context (see Section **93**).
2. Use fresh, unhackneyed words (see Section **94**).
3. Be economical in using words (see Section **96**).

EXERCISES

A. Make the diction of these sentences more emphatic:

1. He was a tall, thin person who looked as if he were tired.
2. As Dr. Jones rode about the country he saw many species of wild life.
3. As the train came closer, he became more and more frightened at the noise it made.
4. The sun was shining brightly, and the birds sang in the trees.
5. He was sorry he had to go—he knew the trip would be dangerous —but he bravely drove off as if nothing unusual had happened.
6. I liked to watch him as he went about the establishment checking up on the various items which were in stock.
7. She brought the fruit into the domicile, saying crossly as she did so that it had taken her a long time to gather it.
8. He asked the man for credit and said that if he didn't have some food to take home that night his wife would reprove him.
9. That book is just about the finest I have ever read, I daresay.
10. It was such a small room he was certain that it would not hold another thing.

B. With the aid of your dictionary, substitute more emphatic words for the following: *building, applause, task, utter* (verb), *sticky, flock* (noun), *loose* (adjective), *posterior, vicinity, run* (verb), *say, walk* (noun), *thing, hastily, instrument, comfortable, good, bite* (verb), *tired, careful.*

C. Substitute more emphatic verbs for those used in this paragraph:

436

In a few minutes, the sales manager came through the open door, hurriedly made his way through the cloud of cigarette smoke which had gathered, and sat down in the chair which had been left vacant for him. Immediately he began to give orders, asserting that the salesmen had not been working enough and that their efforts should be increased. He spoke on and on, becoming more insistent and more profane with each sentence. We were afraid lest he single out one of us for special attention. But he did not; he addressed the group as a whole.

D. Name several words which have the same general meaning as the word italicized but which are more exact and emphatic:

(1) A *tall* building; (2) a *vital* story; (3) your *nice* child; (4) a *talkative* man; (5) his *grave* condition; (6) a *brief* statement; (7) a *kind* person; (8) a *loud* noise; (9) he *worked* hard; (10) on the *boat;* (11) she *walked* in; (12) an angry *speech;* (13) a *leading* merchant; (14) I was *surprised;* (15) it's a *pleasant* room; (16) a *dislike* of war; (17) a good *pattern* to follow; (18) the bird *flew* away; (19) a *good* mind; (20) he *got* on the carousel; (21) he *ran* quickly; (22) a *small* animal; (23) a dilapidated *conveyance;* (24) the doorbell *sounded;* (25) a miserable *house;* (26) Dr. Jonas is a *specialist;* (27) a *warm* day; (28) a *delightful* book; (29) an interesting *trip;* (30) an *intelligent* student.

E. Make the diction of these sentences more exact and emphatic:

1. The best item among his amazing assets is his marvelous capacity for playing the piano.
2. "It's a fine day, of course, but I can't go swimming with you because someone has purloined my swimming attire."
3. Certainly I feel like playing tennis with you; the climate here is so enervating that I would like to play every day.
4. This is such a pretty red dress that I believe I adore it better than I do that one.
5. I did not pay much attention to that phase of his remarks, but I was later told that he adumbrated a most thrilling personality.
6. My heaviest task was to ascertain when this should be injected into the conversation.
7. I thought how thrilling it was for him to be preparing for a jaunt around the world while I had nothing to look forward to but a pilgrimage to the neighborhood drug store.
8. I felt certain that he was perturbed even before he offered to en-

gage in fisticuffs with my roommate, because his eyes were sparkling and his lips were moving with anger.

9. After every heat of the race (and each was vital) he would seat himself on the greensward, horribly tired.

10. It seemed ages before we could resume our hegira because I had a terrible lot of trouble fixing the tire.

F. Shakespeare's diction is especially noteworthy for emphasis and exactness. Point out the words in the following song from *Love's Labour's Lost* which seem especially vigorous and exact:

> When icicles hang by the wall,
>   And Dick the shepherd blows his nail,
> And Tom bears logs into the hall,
>   And milk comes frozen home in pail,
> When blood is nipped and ways be foul,
> Then nightly sings the staring owl,
> "Tu-whit, tu-who!" A merry note,
> While greasy Joan doth keel the pot.

> When all aloud the wind doth blow,
>   And coughing drowns the parson's saw,
> And birds sit brooding in the snow,
>   And Marian's nose looks red and raw,
> When roasted crabs hiss in the bowl,
> Then nightly sings the staring owl,
> "Tu-whit, tu-who!" A merry note,
> While greasy Joan doth keel the pot.

APPROPRIATENESS

93. Choose words which are appropriate.

The first essentials of diction are that it should be *clear* and *exact*. But as has been pointed out at various places in this book, diction can be clear and exact on one level of usage and yet be neither on other levels. Words should be appropriate to the audience, the occasion, and the theme. A word is wrongly chosen when it is out of harmony with either its context or the circumstances under which it is used.

You are not likely to use vulgarisms (Section 86) except, per-haps, in the most informal of informal conversations. But they do appear, and frequently with good reason, in reports of conversation given in narrative and also in certain comic strips and radio programs. If they aptly characterize or are used for other definite purpose, they are appropriate and hence may be said to "belong." Similarly, much slang and shoptalk appear in these media, in the conversation of fellow workers or close friends, and in informal letters.

Informal writing and speech are filled with provincialisms (Section 83), colloquialisms (Section 84), and slang (Section 88). Purposefully used, they aid communication of thought from speaker or writer to hearer or reader and are not to be condemned.

But remember that vulgar, colloquial, and slangy words and expressions seem as out of place in a formal theme as would learned and dignified words in an informal, humorous account of a dance. Such sets of words, however labeled, may express exactly what the writer means, but they should be in harmony with the subject, the occasion, and the context. A green bow tie does not belong with a full-dress suit, or a silk hat with slacks. Words, too, must be "in keeping."

EXERCISES

A. Discuss the appropriateness, and correctness, of:

nonsense, twaddle, buncombe, bunk
money, financial resources, legal tender, swag
talk, converse, chatter, gab
skin, complexion, pelt, hide
contemptible, shameful, unsatisfactory, lousy
combat, scuffle, tussle, scrap
osculation, caress, kiss, smack

B. Discuss the errors in the following sentences:

1. The milkman drove his courser through the streets.
2. The Waldorf dispenses excellent grub.
3. The cashier was personally responsible for all the jack in the bank.
4. The rivulet smashed the dam and flooded the town.
5. The conductor of the orchestra told the audience he was crazy about Beethoven's compositions.

C. Revise the wording of the following:

1. "Gosh," the barrister said, "I've never been to such a classy shindig."
2. It's a tasty, homey place but it scarcely seems suitable as the domicile of a bishop.
3. The girls all went for that punk in a great big way, but he was a pain in the neck to us boys.
4. The bookie suggested that I place a wager on the nose, but I scarcely thought the steed would even place.
5. At the meeting of the trustees, the prexy tergiversated following a dicker negotiated by two hombres from my natal village.

TRITENESS

Trite or hackneyed expressions, or clichés, are words which have lost their force. The origins of the words *triteness, hackneyed,* and *cliché* are illuminating: the first comes from the Latin word *tritus,* the past participle of *terere,* which means *to rub, to wear out; hackneyed* is derived from the idea of a horse, or carriage, let out for hire, devoted to common use, and thus worn out in service; *cliché* comes from the French word *clicher,* meaning to *stereotype.*

Thus trite words and phrases are similar to slang in that they are but rubber stamps, "stereotyped plates" of thought and expression. They may be tags from common speech, or overworked quotations, or outworn phrases from the newspapers. They save the writer the trouble of thinking exactly what he means, but their use results in writing which is stale and ineffective. Such words and phrases inevitably seem humorous; they are, indeed, regularly used for humor or irony by fiction-writers and columnists. Used seriously, they are signs that the speaker, or writer, is naïve.

94. Avoid hackneyed language.

Our familiarity with trite words and expressions is likely to cause them to occur to us more readily than others which are more effective. We should therefore look with suspicion upon each word or phrase which leaps to mind until we can assure ourselves that the expression is exact and unhackneyed. It is also well for us to remember that words and phrases which do not seem trite to us may be clichés to any reader more familiar than we with over-worked expressions.

Note this list of clichés:

a bolt from the blue
abreast of the times
aching void
acid test
after all is said and done
a long-felt want
all in all
along these lines
arms of Morpheus
artistic temperament
as luck would have it
at a loss for words
at one fell swoop
bathed in tears
beggars description
bitter end
blood is thicker than water
brave as a lion
brilliant performance
brown as a berry
budding genius
busy as a bee
by leaps and bounds
captain of industry
center of attraction
checkered career
clear as crystal
clinging vine
close to nature
cold as ice
conspicuous by its absence
Dame Fortune
deadly earnest
depend upon it
depths of despair
doomed to disappointment

drastic action
dull thud
each and every
epic struggle
equal to the occasion
eyes like stars
fair sex
familiar landmark
favor with a selection
few and far between
fiber of his (my) being
filthy lucre
flower of the Old South
fools rush in
footprints on the sands of time
force of circumstances
goes without saying
golden locks (tresses)
goodly number
green as grass
green with envy
gridiron heroes (warriors)
heartfelt thanks
heart's content
heated argument
he-man
holy bonds of wedlock
holy estate of matrimony
in great profusion
in the last analysis
In the spring a young man's
    fancy . . .
iron constitution
irony of fate
it stands to reason
last but not least

last straw
last white line
limped into port
looking for all the world like
mad as a wet hen
mantle of snow
meets the eye
method in his madness
monarch of all I survey
more in sorrow than in anger
Mother Nature
motley throng
myriad lights
needs no introduction
nipped in the bud
no thinking man
none the worse for wear
of the earth earthy
paramount issue
pending merger
picturesque scene
pleasing prospect
powers that be
promising future
proud possessor
psychological moment
red as a rose
reigns supreme
riot of color
ruling passion
sad to relate
sadder but wiser
sea of faces
(seething) mass of humanity
self-made man
shadow of the goal posts
sigh of relief

simple life
skeleton in the closet
sleep the sleep of the just
snow-capped mountains
soul of honor
strong as a lion
strong, silent man
struggle for existence
sturdy as an oak
take my word for it
taken into custody
tell it not in (Gath)
the happy pair
the plot thickens
the time of my life
the weaker sex
the worse for wear
thereby hangs a tale
thunderous applause
time marches on
tired but happy
too full for utterance
too funny for words
venture a suggestion
walk of life
wends his way
wheel of fortune
where angels fear to tread
where ignorance is bliss
with bated breath
words fail me
words fail to express
work like a Trojan
wrapped in mystery
wreathed in smiles
wrought havoc
wry countenance

EXERCISES

A. Consider the following piece of doggerel:

When will we cease to write in books
Of murmuring, gurgling, twisting brooks,
Of winds that sigh and moan and beat,
Of the beautiful maiden's dainty feet,
Of crowds that surge and wagons that clatter,
Of waters that swirl and birds that chatter,
Of his firm jaw and his modest ties,
Of her sunlit hair and her heavenly eyes,
Of fleeting clouds that fleck the sky,
Of loves that wait but never die,
Of lips that tremble and quiver and curl,
Of bosoms that heave, and teeth like pearl,
Of engines that puff and throb and groan,
Of the villain's hiss, and his low, tense tone,
Of the dying sun's last flickering beam,
Of the pale moon's mellow, tender gleam?
When, my friend? When the universe is dead,
When the brooks are dry, or gone instead,
When the sun doesn't shine, and the moon doesn't show.
There you have it, my friend—and now you know.

B. Rewrite the above doggerel, using other clichés. (Perhaps you can write a more hopeful, less truthful final four lines.)

C. Study O. Henry's ingenious short story, "Calloway's Code," from the volume entitled *Whirligigs*. (The entire story revolves about a reporter's use of newspaper clichés.)

D. Make lists of hackneyed expressions which you have used in recent themes or in conversations, or which you have overheard.

E. Read Gelett Burgess' little book, *Are You a Bromide?* (This is a very instructive and amusing discussion of triteness.)

FINE WRITING

"Fine writing" is writing which is thought to be free from all impurities because it has been brought to perfection; actually, it is writing which is affected or overcareful.

95. Avoid "fine writing."

The use of direct and simple words to gain effectiveness in writing is mentioned in Section 92d. You should avoid pretentiousness, artificiality, and affectation if you wish to be clear, exact, and emphatic.

1. *Polysyllabication*

The use of pompous and flowery words of several syllables is fine writing. To use the short word rather than the long, if it will serve as well, is sound practice. Short words are usually more understandable and less self-conscious than polysyllabic words. This does not mean that polysyllables should never be used; it means that they should not be used if they cause writing to sound high-flown, ostentatious, or pedantic. Note these examples: *auriferous teeth; savory repast* for *meal; retire* for *go to bed; prevaricate* for *lie; ratiocinate* for *think; pulchritude* for *beauty; inebriated, intoxicated* for *drunk; comestibles* for *food; devouring element* for *fire; obsequies* for *funeral.*

2. *The Use of Too Many Modifiers*

You should be careful to give your reader a clear, full understanding of your meaning, but avoid piling on descriptive words. Use adjectives and adverbs intelligently, not lavishly.

3. *The Use of Foreign Words and Anglicisms*

The inexperienced writer is likely to adopt a sententious style of writing because he is overwhelmed by the seriousness of his purpose. Frequently he will make the mistake of interlarding his work with foreign expressions or Anglicisms (English expressions rather than American) in a desire to convince the reader of his erudition and dignity. Examples: *chef d'œuvre, magnum opus, à bon marché, à propos de rien, dum vivimus vivamus, exempli gratia, garçon, morceau, robe-de-chambre, lift* for *elevator, petrol* for *gasoline.*

You should not hesitate to use the foreign word if it has been generally accepted or if there is no exact English equivalent. But you should not use such words too frequently or merely to show your erudition.

EXERCISES

A. The following sentences are taken from Newman's essay (lecture) printed in a volume called *The Idea of a University.*

Newman has been discussing the inseparability of thought and expression and is telling how in the Far East people engage professional letter writers.

The man of thought comes to the man of words; and the man of words, duly instructed in the thought, dips the pen of desire into the ink of devotedness, and proceeds to spread it over the page of desolation. Then the nightingale of affection is heard to warble to the rose of loveliness, while the breeze of anxiety plays around the brow of expectation. (This is what the Easterns are said to consider fine writing . . .)

Express these sentences in good English.

B. Improve the wording of the following sentences:

1. Your name's fair escutcheon has been tarnished beyond redemption.
2. His vitriolic discourse exacerbated the overweening students.
3. *Mirabile dictu,* he soon became convalescent and finally regained his strength, *peu à peu.*
4. He entered the sudatorium and, after leaving that, he plunged into the gelid natatorium.
5. He presaged the *Anschluss* because of an insidious *Weltschmerz* which had suffused his whole spirit.
6. He stretched his nether limbs on the downy couch just as Old Sol pierced the leafy fronds of the verdant foliage.

C. These three paragraphs are taken verbatim from a student theme. Rewrite them in clear, good English.

It was during my first year of high school that adolescent reason catapulted a mental conflict of doubtful victory—the attainment of a lifelong friend.

Succeeding years seemed quite remote from the momentum of the impending expectancy of a mutual comrade. Chums I had plenty, but the seemingly gripping void that only the reality of a lasting friendship could despatch, depressed me. I imagined myself forever walking companionless, alone.

In my persistent search I was rewarded with short-lived acquaintances with several of my classmates, but, slowly, the dream images I often found myself unconsciously forming, corporeally and facially resembling their likenesses, would crumble, become indistinct and nebulous, disintegrating into nothingness. Wraithfully vague, one face clung tena-

445

ciously, and it was from the pattern of its features that the process of creative reconstruction would begin all over again, fading and dimming, but bravely struggling for substantial visibility.

CONCISENESS

Diction, to be effective, must be as economical as possible. This does not mean that writing should be sketchy or that necessary words may be omitted (see Sections **66, 61**). But avoid wordiness because it lessens the force of expression.

In forceful writing, the ratio of ideas to words is high. In poetry, which consists of "words in their best possible use," "each word must carry twenty other words upon its back." Conciseness alone does not achieve effective writing, but it is extremely difficult for you to write forcefully if you use two or three words to convey the idea which one word would express.

Two types of wordiness which apply particularly to sentence structure are mentioned in Section **73**. But redundancy, the use of more words than are needed to express your meaning, applies to diction.

96. Avoid wordiness.

1. Do not use words which are superfluous. Note these examples:

Christmas Eve evening	absolutely parallel
endorse on the back	first beginnings
someone I met up with	free gratis
more paramount	recur again
unusually (most) unique	resume again
perfect circle	from whence
repeat it again	fellow classmates
return back	connect up with
the sunset in the west	join together
many in number	complete monopoly
round in form	each and everyone
coöperate together	this afternoon at three P.M.

You will find him *in back of* the house.
The coach *he* has a difficult job.

There *were* three books lying open on the table. (Three books lay open on the table.)

2. Do not use two or three words where one will serve.

Give your directions very definitely and precisely. (Give definite directions.)

John is going to plan to write you tomorrow. (John will write you tomorrow.)

3. The use of jargon (Section **90**) also frequently results in wordiness. Example:

He pursued his course of studies along the lines of mechanical engineering. (He studied mechanical engineering.)

4. The use of too many modifiers (especially adjectives and adverbs) results in wordiness (see Section **95**, part 2). Example:

It was a cold, bleak, gray day. John walked home nimbly and briskly. He felt full of life, keenly alert, and far from sluggish, despite the gloominess and cloudiness of his immediate surroundings.

EXERCISE

Improve the following sentences:

1. Although we were many in number, there were a few of us who felt close; and so we decided to correspond with each other in future years to come.

2. I do not wish one which is square in shape; I want one oval in form.

3. In the case of those culprits, there are not many people who would judge them solely and completely responsible for their cruel, thoughtless, and heinous misdeeds.

4. It is undeniably true that once you start to study in earnest that your troubles will be lessened and mitigated.

5. When he combined together the events of the autobiography of his life, he saw that the important essentials would have to be repeated again.

6. The end of the corridor terminates at a small green door.

7. His desire to express himself is a universal craving which is common to all people.

8. After his death he received the award posthumously.
9. The company had a complete monopoly in that territory, but there were unfavorable climatic conditions which prevented the factory from resuming production again.
10. In this day and age any girl with the necessary financial resources can keep her hair neat and attractive in appearance.

FAULTY REPETITION

Some repetition is effective, particularly in sentence structure (see Sections **66, 74**). But faulty repetition of words, phrases, or sentence structure is always objectionable. (See Sections **78, 80** for comment on monotonous sentence structure.) Careless repetition of words or phrases is caused by an unwillingness to search for a substitute, or by a limited vocabulary.

97. Avoid objectionable repetition of words and phrases.

Repetition is faulty unless a word or phrase is repeated for effectiveness or for clarity. Faulty repetition may be corrected by using pronouns more liberally, by substituting equivalent expressions (synonyms), or by recasting the sentence. Note the following examples of objectionable repetition:

1. *Since* several weeks have elapsed *since* you wrote, I have decided not to repeat the offer.
2. He *thought* everyone would *think* his act to be generous.
3. Each of you must *study* hard in order to finish your *studies* by noon.
4. He *said that* you *said that* we should apply promptly.
5. She *placed* the box in another *place*.

NOTE: Repetition, even if faulty, is preferable to artificial and awkward avoidance of it.

Jargon and "fine writing" (Sections **90, 95**) make use of elaborate and strained variation.

> Awkward: It was my privilege to deliver the lecture; it was his prerogative to listen to the oration.
> Some newspapers publish news; other organs

issue material which frequently has only an approximate degree of timeliness.

EXERCISES

A. Correct the faulty repetition in the following sentences:

1. The book is covered with a green cover.
2. This is the toy that Bill said that he had bought in France the last time that he was there (see Section **77c**).
3. You will soon find it will be difficult to find ways to avoid repetition.
4. He had but ten cents, but he was determined to go, anyway.
5. The writer of this story has a good sense of drama, but he has not sensed the real conflict so well as the other writer.
6. For days I was unable to pay for it, for my allowance was a few days late.
7. This statement states that the country that has plentiful resources should not seek new territory.
8. The height of the desk is about three feet high.
9. When he kicks the ball, he kicks it with all his force, but his kicks are not high enough to allow the ends to make forcing tackles.
10. This room does not have as much room as my former room had.

B. Correct the objectionable repetition in the five illustrative sentences in Section **97.**

C. Remove the strained variation from the last two sentences in Section **97.**

EUPHONY

Euphony means "pleasing sound." Diction should be euphonious; good prose is pleasant to the ear. Writing consists of wriggly black figures spread across pages and can hardly be called a beautiful image. Writing which is beautiful, therefore, symbolizes sounds which please the ear, not the eye. Beautiful prose contains words which have pleasing sounds that are harmonious with the sense. Good writing excludes disagreeable combinations of sounds (cacophony) because they are likely to distract the reader's attention. Of course, the *sense* of words is more important than their *sound,* but really good prose contains words whose sound and sense are harmonious. Reading aloud is a good method of detecting uneuphonious sounds.

98. Avoid awkward and harsh combinations of sounds.

Good prose rarely contains *rhyme* or *alliteration;* it also shuns the frequent repetition of *unpleasant sounds.* Note the following examples:

1. The balmy winds blew warmly over the bay.
2. The statistics of this strange situation certainly seem correct.
3. He could not pay the bill until he opened the till.
4. These apples the boys packed into boxes for the railroads to carry away.
5. Analytics is the science of analysis.

EXERCISES

A. Make the sentences above more euphonious.

B. Improve the following sentences:

1. John does not care if you cut your hair.
2. Sixty sons of Central College sang songs on the library steps.
3. Song-singing, hip-swinging dancing, and walking and talking are special delights of our sophisticated seniors.
4. In a blind fury he flew into the fray.
5. Scenes such as these are best seen at sunset from some lofty parapet.

C. Which of these words are pleasing to your ear? Which are harsh-sounding? *Spinach, cacophony, pavement, vermilion, melody, parsnips, jazz, nevermore, diaphanous, luxury, lyrical, haughty, democracy, cabbage, cranberry, moon, shrimp, sap, cuspidor.*

USING THE DICTIONARY

99. Knowledge of a foreign language, listening to good speakers, and carefully reading the works of good writers are effective aids in improving and enlarging your vocabulary. Building an adequate vocabulary is not the work of a month or a year, but your intelligent use of a good dictionary will accomplish much for you in a comparatively short time.

You should heed one caution: do not try to "swallow the dictionary." To do so will result in an artificial "bookishness" (see Section 95). It is good fun to browse in a dictionary and discover its amazing resources, but to memorize words merely for the sake of impressing others will act as a boomerang.

99a. Choose a good dictionary.

A pocket dictionary is well-nigh worthless, except as a guide to spelling and pronunciation. Many very small dictionaries are actually false guides. Equip yourself with a sufficiently large dictionary (approximately 100,000 entries) published by a reliable firm. Examples of such dictionaries are the following:

> *The American College Dictionary* (Text Edition).
> *Webster's New Collegiate Dictionary.*
> *The Winston Dictionary* (College Edition).
> *The Concise Oxford Dictionary.*

Excellent larger dictionaries, preferable to those mentioned above except that they are more expensive and are difficult to carry, are *Webster's New International, The Shorter Oxford Dictionary* (2 vols.), Funk and Wagnalls' *New Standard Dictionary,* and the monumental *New English* (Oxford) *Dictionary.*

99b. Learn how to use a dictionary.

Many students use a dictionary merely to learn the spelling, pronunciation, or one definition of certain words. The careful writer will *study* each word he looks up; that is, he will read carefully the entire entry under the word and thus make it a real part of his vocabulary. Time spent in studying words thoroughly will save time and errors later. This applies to English words fully as well as to foreign words. Who has not had to look up the same French, or German, or Latin, or Spanish word many times when translating, simply because he did not master the word at first?

99 b

Here is the entry under the word **rival** in *The American College Dictionary* (Text Edition).[1]

> **ri·val** (rī/vəl), *n., adj., v.,* **-valed, -valing** or (*esp. Brit.*) **valled, -valling.** —*n.* **1.** one who is in pursuit of the same object as another, or strives to equal or outdo another; a competitor. **2.** one who or that which is in a position to dispute preëminence or superiority with another: *a stadium without a rival.* **3.** *Obs.* a companion in duty. —*adj.* **4.** being a rival; competing or standing in rivalry: *rival suitors, rival business houses.* —*v.t.* **5.** to compete with in rivalry; strive to equal or outdo. **6.** to prove to be a worthy rival of: *he soon rivaled the others in skill.* **7.** to equal (something) as if in rivalry. —*v.i.* **8.** *Archaic.* to engage in rivalry; compete (*with*) [t. L: s. *rīvālis,* orig., one living by or using the same stream as another] —**Syn. 1.** competitor, contestant, emulator, antagonist. See **opponent.** —**Ant. 1.** partner.

From such an entry may be learned:

1. Spelling.
2. Syllabication.
3. Pronunciation.
4. Part(s) of speech.
5. Meanings.
6. Level(s) of usage.
7. Derivation.
8. List of synonyms and, frequently, definition of synonyms.
9. Antonyms.

1. *Spelling*

Ordinarily the basic word is given in black type. Also, in an attention-attracting type (blackface or capitals), the spelling of the word with its various endings may be given. Note especially:

a. The plurals of nouns are given, if the noun forms its plural other than by adding *-s.*

b. The comparative and superlative degrees of adjectives and adverbs are given, if there is a spelling change in adding *-er, -est.*

c. The past tense, past participle, and present participle of verbs are given if these forms differ from the present tense form or if there is a spelling change in adding the ending.

When a word has two or more spellings, the preferred spelling form is given first.

. The spelling of proper names (people, places, etc.) is given either in the regular place in the alphabetical listing or in a special section or sections at the back of the dictionary, depending upon the dictionary that you own.

[1] *The American College Dictionary,* Copyright, 1947, 1948, 1949, 1950, 1951, by Random House, Inc.

2. *Syllabication*

Learn to distinguish between the light mark (·) used to separate syllables (e·jac′u·late—written solid) and the hyphen (-) used to show that the word is a compound *(well-known)*. (Different dictionaries use different methods of marking syllabication; find out what system your dictionary uses.)

3. *Pronunciation*

Learn to distinguish the accent marks: primary stress is indicated by a heavy mark (′) and secondary stress by a light (′) or double (″) mark: search′light′, search′light″.

Pronunciation is usually given in parentheses. Study the key to pronunciation and learn to interpret diacritical marks.

When two or more pronunciations are given, the preferred pronunciation is given first.

4. *Part(s) of speech*

The part of speech of an entry is usually given. If the word can be properly used as more than one part of speech, such information is always provided. But check the meaning under each such listing. Also indicated is the correct use of verbs as transitive or intransitive, or both. Learn the more common abbreviations used by your dictionary: *n.* for noun, *v.* for verb, *v.t.* for transitive verb, etc.

5. *Meanings*

Note the different meanings given for a word, both the usual and the specialized meanings. Observe carefully all homonyms and words that have a superficial resemblance; although they may be spelled nearly alike, or pronounced alike, their meanings are quite different.

Abbreviations and foreign words or phrases are explained either in the regular alphabetical listing or in special sections in the back of the dictionary.

6. *Level(s) of usage*

Remember that mere entry in a dictionary does not guarantee that a word is in good use or that special meanings of the word are proper in current English. Your dictionary enables you to distinguish between the usage levels of words. Any word not supplied with a restrictive label may be regarded as appropriate to formal English. But watch for warnings (restrictive labels) before certain words or certain definitions of words: *Colloq., Slang, Dial., Brit., Scot., Archaic, Obs., Poetic,* etc.

Correct idiomatic usage, especially combinations of verbs and prepositions, is indicated in your dictionary. For example, look up the illustrations of *agree to* and *agree with.*

7. *Derivation*

Study the derivation (usually in brackets) of a word; the derivation may help to fix the meaning and spelling of the word in your mind (see Section **81c**). Learn the more common abbreviations used by your dictionary: L. (Latin); G. (German); Gk. (Greek), etc. Every dictionary contains a table of abbreviations.

8. *Synonyms and antonyms*

Study synonyms; frequently these "approximate equivalents" have significant differences in meaning which will enable you to choose more exact and emphatic words (see Sections **89, 92**). Antonyms can be used effectively to express contrast.

For example, study this treatment of synonyms of the word *plastic:*

> **Syn. Plastic,** pliable, pliant, ductile, malleable, adaptable mean susceptible of being modified in form or nature. Plastic suggests qualities, such as those of wax or clay, soft enough to be molded yet capable of hardening into desired form; pliable and pliant, the quality of willow twigs, supple enough to be easily manipulated and, therefore, yielding and compliant; ductile, the quality of that which can be drawn out at will and therefore responding to influences upon it; malleable, the quality of some metals after being heated, of being readily beaten or hammered into shape or form; adaptable, that of being easily modified to suit other conditions, needs, or uses.

99c. Make frequent use of your dictionary.

It is not enough to own a dictionary and know how to use it. Do not study the dictionary in an attempt to master every word it contains, but use it *intelligently.* Perhaps these two suggestions will help:

454

1. Either read with a dictionary at hand, examining words about which you need information, or, if that is not possible, make lists of unfamiliar words and look them up later.

2. List words which you hear in lectures or conversations, study them in a dictionary, and thus add them to your active vocabulary by using them in your conversation and in your writing.

An effective step toward building an active vocabulary is checking your list of words periodically (perhaps once a week) for words which appear twice or oftener. These are likely to be met over and over; they should become part of your speaking and writing vocabulary.

Following are seventy-five not uncommon words which any student, adopting this plan, can add to his vocabulary:

1. altruistic	26. gregarious	51. nocturnal
2. antithesis	27. hallucination	52. obsequious
3. apotheosis	28. immolation	53. omniscient
4. ascetic	29. impeccably	54. pedantic
5. atavistic	30. imperturbable	55. peremptory
6. autocratic	31. impotent	56. perfunctory
7. capricious	32. innocuous	57. petrified
8. circumambient	33. insatiable	58. precocious
9. conflagration	34. insidious	59. procrastinate
10. contamination	35. iridescent	60. propitiate
11. cynical	36. irrelevant	61. recantation
12. desiccate	37. lachrymose	62. resplendent
13. dogmatic	38. lassitude	63. restive
14. eccentric	39. loquacious	64. reticent
15. edification	40. lucrative	65. saturnine
16. efficacious	41. lugubrious	66. scintillating
17. enigmatic	42. malevolent	67. sententious
18. ephemeral	43. mellifluous	68. sinister
19. eradicate	44. mendacious	69. stertorous
20. eulogy	45. meretricious	70. superannuated
21. exotic	46. meticulous	71. surreptitious
22. extraneous	47. misanthropic	72. taciturn
23. facetious	48. mitigation	73. tenacious
24. futility	49. mollifying	74. vacillation
25. garrulous	50. monotonous	75. vindictive

455

EXERCISES

A. Find out the pronunciation of the following words: *adult, amateur, egotist, data, imperturbable, maraschino, subtle, often, superfluous, literature, valet, advertisement, italics, suite, coupon.*

B. What is the pronunciation of each of the following proper names? *Tschaikovsky, Robespierre, Wagner* (Richard), *Molière, Nietzsche, Socrates, Blasco Ibáñez, Lafayette.*

C. How should these words be written: as one word, with a hyphen, or as two words? *twenty one, hand ball, cater cornered, horse laugh, castor oil, runner up, court martial, hand made, well nigh, ante chamber, boll weevil, out of date.*

D. Of the twenty words on this "demon list," which are misspelled? *liquify, battallion, ecstasy, villian, diptheria, supersede, rarify, mosquitos, wierd, questionnaire, sacriligious, sieve, merangue, perseverance, morgage, seige, naptha, exhilerate, temperament, sargeant.*

E. Give the derivation of the following words: *buncombe (bunkum), lynch, boycott, tantalize, matinee, jovial, watt, quixotic, stirrup, guerrilla, subterfuge, English, ballot, gerrymander, pandemonium, bourgeois, tragedy, herpetology.*

F. Give the meaning of each of the following: *spurious, obstreperous, voracious, succinct, dolorous, querulous, elysium, urbanity, flippant, redolent, turbid, lurid, nomenclature, legerdemain, refractory.*

G. To what levels of usage (bearing what restrictive labels) does each of the following belong? *prithee, lam, elevated, osier, eftsoon, pica, evolute, osmosis, lumberjack, smog.*

H. What is the English equivalent of the following foreign phrases? *répondez s'il vous plait, a priori, auf Wiedersehen, banzai, haut monde, con amore, je ne sais quoi, per diem, quid pro quo, multum in parvo.*

I. Give synonyms and near-synonyms for the following words, explaining different shades of meaning: *defeat* (v), *perseverance, laugh* (v), *dismay* (v), *agree, simple, redress* (n), *empty* (adj.), *apology, noise, eminent, person.*

J. Prepare a vocabulary exercise or test, for class use, containing twenty-five items similar to the "General Exercise in Vocabulary" given below.

GENERAL EXERCISE: VOCABULARY[2]

Select in each series the word or word group which is closest in meaning to the word italicized in the phrase.

[2] Used with the permission of the compiler, Dr. Hans J. Gottlieb, New York University.

General Exercise

1. He *abetted* the conspirators.   summoned/foiled/aided/imprisoned/beheaded
2. The clerk *absconded*.   disagreed/forgot/disappeared/swore/resigned
3. A sharp *acclivity*.   slope/practice/criticism/pain/response
4. Spoken with *acerbity*.   authority/bitterness/ease/hesitancy/pride
5. An old *adage*.   house/utensil/saying/chamber/dance
6. *Adroitly* argued.   calmly/awkwardly/cleverly/hotly/frequently
7. The *altercation* was settled.   transaction/problem/territory/dispute/bill
8. An *antipathy* for war.   preparation/demand/aversion/cause/enthusiasm
9. A *babel* of languages.   similarity/decay/study/confusion/ignorance
10. His *baleful* influence.   inspiring/helpful/constant/evil/welcome
11. With *benign* thoughts.   sly/lofty/hypocritical/kindly/bitter
12. The teacher *berated* them.   graded/tested/scolded/dismissed/lauded
13. His *blatant* stupidity.   loud-mouthed/childish/obvious/inherent/pathetic
14. A *bucolic* scene.   touching/lively/warlike/rustic/deplorable
15. They *cached* their supplies.   consumed/stored/purchased/lost/discarded
16. He was a *charlatan*.   actor/impostor/spy/half-breed/officer
17. With great *chagrin*.   vexation/fuss/amusement/courage/ignorance
18. A *circuitous* route.   forbidden/hazardous/short/roundabout/unused
19. They use *coercion*.   hypnotism/coöperation/care/force/discretion
20. *Commiserate* with me!   dine/sympathize/share/celebrate/compete
21. He *conciliated* his rival.   congratulated/feared/rebuked/pacified/met
22. She *condoned* the offense.   resented/endured/denounced/punished/forgave
23. It ended in a *debacle*.   fight/debate/panic/temple/celebration
24. His *debonair* manner.   distracted/genial/brusque/serious/efficient
25. They *desecrated* the temple.   destroyed/cleaned/dedicated/profaned/built
26. His *diatribe* offended them.   race/abusive-speech/morals/views/behavior
27. He writes *drivel*.   satire/light-verse/fiction/nonsense/drama
28. They thanked the *donor*.   priest/Spanish-lady/lord/giver/owner
29. The *dowager's* claim.   queen's/orphan's/lawyer's/prospector's/widow's
30. Her *ebullient* spirit.   wrathful/enthusiastic/kindly/calm/charming
31. An *egregious* fool.   extraordinary/joking/blind/ignorant/old
32. It *engenders* hatred.   lessens/breeds/resembles/ends/presupposes
33. A curious *enigma*.   disease/species/riddle/name/medicine
34. The *excerpt* is typical.   excuse/slogan/extract/symptom/condition
35. He *expiated* his sins.   confessed/boasted-of/regretted/atoned-for/saw
36. A *factious* person.   practical/materialistic/quarrelsome/shy/vital
37. The *fecund* earth.   barren/damp/rotting/fertile/chilly
38. In a *fitful* fashion.   appropriate/noisy/irregular/hasty/novel
39. He has a *flair* for art.   passion/contempt/market/taste/respect
40. He acted with *fortitude*.   courage/foresight/haste/imagination/greed
41. Her desire was *frustrated*.   fulfilled/disregarded/thwarted/known/shared
42. Known for his *garrulity*.   stinginess/severity/charm/talkativeness/taste
43. A different *genus*.   spirit/life/species/deity/ability
44. A *graphic* description.   vivid/rapid/involved/technical/vague

457

45. *Gratuitous* advice.   sane/uncalled-for/moral/wished-for/helpful
46. A *grisly* spectacle.   ridiculous/immoral/sad/hideous/boring
47. He visited the *grotto*.   palace/singer/slum/art-gallery/cave
48. The *halcyon* days.   peaceful/turbulent/foggy/ancient/festive
49. Stored in a *hamper*.   closet/bin/attic/warehouse/basket
50. Its body is *hirsute*.   compact/tough/slender/hairy/bearlike
51. His *hoary* head.   tousled/noble/gray/broad/shaven
52. A *homogeneous* group.   dissimilar/biological/small/uniform/select
53. An *iconoclast* in politics.   veteran/mixer/beginner/radical/leader
54. *Immutable* destiny.   cruel/unknown/fickle/unchangeable/blind
55. His *impeccable* attire.   informal/shoddy/faultless/somber/careless
56. The valley was *inundated*.   inhabited/isolated/bombarded/flooded/surveyed
57. An *irascible* parent.   unreasonable/proud/strict/irritable/indulgent
58. Found himself in *jeopardy*.   difficulty/prison/danger/love/need
59. A *judicious* selection.   prejudiced/sensible/unique/surprising/random
60. A *laconic* response.   drawling/evasive/hesitant/sarcastic/concise
61. An amusing *lampoon*.   comedian/dialect/satire/game/puzzle
62. His *latent* abilities.   remarkable/potential/creative/many/obvious
63. The *limpid* pool.   murky/deep/chilly/secluded/clear
64. His *lithe* physique.   muscular/healthy/flexible/thin/youthful
65. The work is *lucrative*.   heavy/dishonest/enjoyable/profitable/easy
66. The *lush* foliage.   green/juicy/strange/tropical/poisonous
67. A *magnanimous* victor.   famous/proud/exhausted/generous/modest
68. Her *malevolent* attitude.   spiteful/gracious/spoiled/indifferent/placid
69. The story is *maudlin*.   exciting/funny/sentimental/plotless/coarse
70. A *mendacious* witness.   belligerent/silent/unwilling/shy/untruthful
71. His motive is *mercenary*.   humane/selfish/idealistic/clear/secret
72. *Meticulous* conduct.   irregular/overcareful/lax/moral/bashful
73. His *mimicry* is remarkable.   vocabulary/memory/insight/imitation/taste
74. He is a *misanthrope*.   misfit/soothsayer/miser/man-hater/cannibal
75. She *mitigated* his suffering.   lessened/pitied/regretted/rejoiced-in/shared
76. A *moribund* institution.   stable/ancient/dying/necessary/respected
77. They believe in *necromancy*.   monarchy/fables/anarchism/magic/luck
78. A *neurotic* disposition.   egotistical/balanced/nervous/amiable/giddy
79. A *nomadic* people.   pagan/romantic/peace-loving/primitive/roving
80. The effect is *nullified*.   destroyed/magnified/designed/retained/altered
81. An unfortunate *obsession*.   occurrence/loss/delusion/mistake/choice
82. An *officious* relative.   close/legal/important/meddlesome/considerate
83. This *onerous* routine.   necessary/thankless/daily/wearisome/endless
84. His *overt* confession.   detailed/public/forced/shocking/belated
85. A *palsied* old woman.   shriveled/sickly/bent/shaky/quarrelsome
86. Her *petulant* answer.   tactful/embarrassed/prompt/shrewd/peevish
87. A *predatory* tribe.   uncivilized/wandering/plundering/lost/ancient
88. His *recondite* knowledge.   superficial/exact/limited/profound/pretended

89. A *rigorous* climate.	bracing/harsh/torrid/temperate/wholesome
90. He found *sanctuary*.	happiness/fame/refuge/health/assistance
91. They *stipulate* cash.	squander/invest/borrow/specify/promise
92. She *surmised* the ending.	changed/feared/omitted/knew/guessed
93. The *tenets* of his faith.	brethren/churches/critics/sources/doctrines
94. A *travesty* of justice.	miscarriage/burlesque/triumph/court/symbol
95. Viewed with *trepidation*.	sorrow/interest/amazement/alarm/caution
96. His writing is *turgid*.	simple/interesting/pompous/dramatic/clear
97. With *unalloyed* pleasure.	complete/forbidden/sudden/apparent/renewed
98. Their *uncouth* neighbors.	hostile/boorish/inquisitive/foreign/snobbish
99. *Unequivocal* proof.	uncertain/false/definite/insufficient/necessary
100. His *vaunted* superiority.	recognized/boasted/decided/disputed/deserved

GLOSSARY OF FAULTY DICTION

100. The following glossary contains words and expressions often misused. The list is not comprehensive, but it does contain some of the most common violations of good usage.

A few of these expressions are always to be avoided, but many are incorrect only on the level of formal English. You should be careful to apply the dictates of Section **93,** page 438, as you interpret the comments provided for these words and expressions. Especially remember that no stigma attaches to the label "colloquial"; it merely indicates that a given expression is more appropriate in conversation and in informal discourse generally than in formal writing. In your formal theme work, however, you should think carefully before using a word or expression on the following list which bears a restrictive label.

Usage is so constantly changing that expressions which are now restricted in some way may later be considered standard. Furthermore, because no dictionary or grammar is a final authority, some usages are disputed. Probably no two linguists would agree on all the comments which follow. But this illustrative list of 100 items should be serviceable as a starter; to it you may add from time to time other words and expressions.

> **1. A, an.** *An* should be used before an initial vowel sound, *a* before a word beginning with a consonant sound: *an* adult, *a* problem. See page 43.

2. **Accept, except.** *Accept* means "to receive"; *except* means "to exclude."

> He *accepted* the nomination.
>
> I agree to the conditions if I may *except* the fourth in the list.

3. **Accidently.** A vulgarism (see Section 86). Use *accidentally*.

4. **Ad.** Colloquial abbreviation for *advertisement*. In formal writing avoid such colloquialisms as *ad, exam, phone,* and *prof*.

5. **Advise.** Use sparingly for "inform," "tell." Questionable:

> *I beg to advise* you that your letter has been received.

6. **Affect, effect.** *Affect* means "to influence" or "assume"; *effect* means "to cause" and, as a noun, means "result."

> This essay has *affected* student thinking.
>
> His speeches *effected* a political scandal.
>
> What *effect* has low temperature on iron?

7. **Aggravate.** Used colloquially for "irritate," "provoke," or "annoy." Specifically, *aggravate* means "to make more severe or intense."

> His disease was *aggravated* by this recent accident.

8. **Alibi.** Used colloquially to mean an excuse or any kind of defense. Properly, "a plea or fact of having been elsewhere when an offense was committed."

9. **All right, alright.** *All right* is overworked to mean "very well." *Alright* is not an acceptable word.

10. **All together, altogether.** The former means "everybody (or everything) in one place"; *altogether* means "wholly."

11. **Already, all ready.** *Already* means "previously"; *all ready* (two words) means "everything (or everyone) is ready."

12. **Among, between.** The former shows the relation of more than two objects; *between* refers to only two.

> He distributed the prizes *among* the five winners.
>
> He divided the prize *between* Jack and Joe.
>
> That is the road *between* Fort Worth and Dallas.

13. **And etc.** Redundant. *Etc.* is the abbreviation for *et cetera,* meaning "and so forth."

14. **Apt, liable, likely.** *Apt* suggests "fitness" or "tendency"; *liable* implies "openness or exposure to something burdensome or disadvantageous"; *likely* means "expected," "probable." *Apt* and *likely* are often interchangeable.

She is *apt* in mathematics.

You are *liable* for damages.

It is *likely* to rain.

15. As. (1) Overworked as a conjunction for *since, because, when,* etc.:

As it was raining, we decided . . . (See Section **72b.**)

(2) Misused as a substitute for *that* or *whether:*

I doubt *as* I can.

(3) In strictly formal English, prefer *not so . . . as* in negative comparisons:

He is *not so* wealthy *as* she.

16. Awful, awfully, abominable, abominably, terribly, etc. Loose, overworked intensives for *very,* etc. (See Section **89b.**)

17. Beside, besides. *Beside* is a preposition meaning "by the side of"; *besides* is both a preposition and an adverb meaning "moreover," "except."

18. Bursted, bust, busted. Vulgarisms for *burst.* The principal parts of *burst* are *burst—burst—burst.*

19. Can, may, might. *Can* suggests "ability," physical and mental:

He *can* make good grades if he tries hard enough.

May implies permission or sanction:

The teacher says that you *may* leave.

The distinction between *can* and *may* ("ability" vs. "permission") is illustrated in this sentence:

I doubt that you *can,* but you *may* try if you wish.

May also expresses "possibility" and "wish" (desire):

It *may* rain today. (Possibility.)

May you have a pleasant trip! (Wish, desire.)

Might is used after a governing verb in the past tense, *may* after a governing verb in the present tense:

He *says* that you *may* go.

He *said* that you *might* go.

20. Cannot help but. A double negative (*cannot help* + *can but*). See Section **71c.**

21. Can't hardly. A double negative. Preferable:

> *I can hardly* hear you. (See Section **71c.**)

22. Complected. Vulgarism. Correct:

> He was *dark-complexioned,* or (better) . . . a man of *dark complexion.*

23. Contact, contacted. Overworked business terms. Use such phrases as "get in touch with," etc.

24. Continual, continuous. The former implies a "close recurrence in time"; *continuous* means "without interruption."

> The ticking of the clock was *continuous.*
> They refused her *continual* requests.

25. Cute. An overworked colloquialism for *attractive, pleasing,* etc.

26. Don't, done. *Don't* is used incorrectly as a contraction in the third person singular, present tense. The correct form is *doesn't.* *Done* is incorrectly used as the past tense of *do.* Principal parts: *do, did, done.*

> It *doesn't* make any difference.
> He *doesn't* know any better.
> We *did* our work yesterday.

27. Due to. An adjective phrase; should not be used adverbially in formal English. The same principle applies to *owing to, caused by.* Adverbial phrases begin with *because of, on account of,* etc.

> His hoarseness was *due to* a cold.
> He was hoarse *on account of* (because of) a cold.

28. Either . . . or, neither . . . nor. *Either* and *neither* are singular; the former means "one of two"; *neither* means "not one of two." *Or* is used with *either, nor* with *neither.*

29. Enthuse. A colloquial substitute for "to be enthusiastic."

30. Farther, further. *Farther* is preferably used to indicate "space," "a commensurable distance"; *further* indicates "greater in degree, quantity, or time" and also means "moreover," "in addition to," etc.

> He walked one mile *farther.*
> Let us speak *further* on this topic.

31. Fellow. Colloquial for "individual," "person," "one," "man," etc.

32. Female. Always stresses the idea of sex and applies to animals, plants, and human beings. Its use as a synonym for *woman* is generally tabooed.

33. Fine. A colloquial term of approval. It specifically means "delicate," "refined," "sensitive," "subtle."

34. Fix. Colloquial as a verb for "to arrange matters"; colloquial as a noun for "predicament."

35. Folks. Colloquial for "relatives," "people."

36. Formally, formerly. *Formally* means "in a formal manner"; *formerly* means "in the past."

37. Funny. Colloquial for "strange," "queer," "odd," "remarkable," etc.

38. Good, well. *Good* is an adjective: "to have a *good* time," "to give a *good* performance." *Well* functions as either adverb or adjective:

I feel *well* (adjective).
He plays the violin *well* (adverb).

39. Got, gotten. *Got* is colloquial in the sense of "must" or "ought," as:

He *has got* to go.

Gotten is less used than formerly as the past participle of *get—got —got*.

40. Guess. *Guess* means "to conjecture" and is colloquial when used to mean "believe," "think," "suspect," etc.

41. Healthful, healthy. Often used interchangeably. *Healthful* means "conducive to health"; *healthy* means "possessing health."

He is a *healthy* person.
She lives in a *healthful* section.

42. Home, homey. Do not loosely use *home* for *house*. Do not omit the preposition in such an expression as, He was *at home. Homey* is a provincial substitute for *homelike.*

43. Human(s). Properly used in a collective sense, *humans* is sometimes vaguely substituted for *persons, people,* etc.

44. If, whether. Prefer *if* for conditional ideas, *whether* for alternatives.

If he is in, I mean to call on him.
I don't know *whether* he is in, but I mean to find out.

45. Imply, infer. To *infer* is to draw a conclusion from statements, circumstances, or evidence. To *imply* is to suggest a meaning not explicitly stated.

> The detective *inferred* from the position of the fingerprints that the man who fired the shot was left-handed.
> What you say *implies* that you think me a liar.

46. In, into. Verbs indicating a motion to a place are generally followed by *into:*

> When he walked *into* the room, he found us ready.

In is used to indicate motion within relatively narrow limits:

> She paced up and down *in* the classroom for the whole period.

In is used when the place is not mentioned:

> He came *in* after we finished the dishes.
> The train came *in.*

47. Ingenious, ingenuous. The former means "talented," "resourceful"; *ingenuous* means "frank" or "naïve."

48. Irregardless, disregardless. The prefixes *ir-* and *dis-* are superfluous. See Section **71b.**

49. Its, it's. *Its* is the possessive form of "it"; *it's* means "it is."

50. Job. Frequently and inexactly used in the sense of achievement. Questionable:

> The coach has done a good *job.*
> Hemingway does a splendid *job* in his novels.

51. Kind of, sort of. Colloquial when used in such expressions as "I am *kind of* weary tonight"; "he is *sort of* glad you spoke." Correct:

> He is a queer *sort of* person.

52. Kind of a, sort of a. Colloquialisms; the *a's* are superfluous.

53. Liable, likely. See Apt.

54. Lie, lay. The former, meaning "to recline," is intransitive, the latter, meaning "to place," transitive.

> I shall *lie* down.
> Please *lay* the book on the desk.

55. Like. Should not be used as a conjunction. Substitute *as* or *as if.* See Section **14d.**

56. **Loan.** As a verb, *loan* is a synonym for *lend*. Either may be used, but *lend* is preferred in most formal writing.
57. **Locate.** A provincialism when used to mean "remember" or "settle." Use the exact word.
58. **Lots of, a lot of, whole lot.** Colloquial for "many" or "much."
59. **Mad.** *Mad* means "insane," is colloquial when used to mean "angry."
60. **May, might.** See **Can.**
61. **Most, almost.** *Most* is an adjective, or an adverb modifying an adjective or adverb to form the superlative; *almost* is an adverb. In the meaning of *nearly*, use *almost*.

> *Most* games are entertaining.
> Mary is the *most* beautiful girl here.
> You have acted *most* wisely.
> He has *almost* finished his work.

62. **Muchly.** A vulgarism. Substitute *very, greatly.*
63. **Nice.** Colloquial for "agreeable," "pleasant," etc. *Nice* actually means "precise," "fastidious."
64. **Notorious, noteworthy, notable.** *Notorious* means "infamous"; *noteworthy* and *notable* mean "remarkable," "worthy of note."
65. **Nowheres, anywheres, somewheres.** Vulgarisms. Omit the *s's.*
66. **O, oh.** The former is usually a vocative, always capitalized, and is rarely followed by a mark of punctuation:

> O Richard! Come here, please.

Oh is an interjection, may be followed by punctuation, and follows the usual rules for capitalization.

> But, oh, what trust we placed in him!

67. **Oral, verbal.** *Oral* means "by mouth"; *verbal,* coming from *verbum,* meaning "word," means "by words."
68. **Party, person, individual.** *Party* implies a group and, except in legal and telephonic language, should not be used to refer to one person. *Individual* refers to a particular or single person.
69. **Pass out.** Slang in the sense of "faint."
70. **Pep, peppy.** Slang. Use *zest, energy, vivacity, animation,* etc., and corresponding adjectives.
71. **Plenty.** A noun. As an adverb or adjective, *plenty* is colloquial.

Colloquial: He was *plenty* angry.
Correct: The dairy has *plenty* of milk.

72. **Practicable, practical.** *Practicable* means "capable of being put into practice"; *practical* means "concerned with practice rather than theory."

The housewife should be *practical*.
The proposal is not *practicable*.

73. **Pretty.** Provincial or colloquial for "rather," "moderately," "somewhat." Questionable:

That is a *pretty* large order.

74. **Principal, principle.** *Principal* is a noun ("sum of money" or "teacher") and an adjective meaning "chief" or "main." *Principle* is always a noun meaning "a governing rule or truth."

75. **Proposition.** Business cant for "proposal" (offer, affair, etc.).

76. **Quite a.** Colloquial in phrases such as *quite a few, quite a bit, quite a lot.*

77. **Raise, rear, bring up.** *Raise* in the sense of "rear" or "bring up" is frequently used, but it is still considered provincial by some of the best writers. Preferable:

The mother *reared* (*brought up*) the children.

78. **Raise, rise.** The former requires an object, the latter never takes one:

As I *rise* from the chair, I shall *raise* my hat.

79. **Refer back.** *Refer* means to direct attention or to make reference; *back* is therefore superfluous. (The same kind of faulty diction is evident in *repeat again*.)

80. **Relation, relative.** *Relation* used to refer to a member of one's family is colloquial. Use *relative* in this sense.

81. **Respectfully, respectively.** *Respectfully* means "in a respectful manner"; *respectively* means "severally," "each in the order given."

82. **Right along, right away, right then,** etc. Colloquialisms. Substitute *directly, immediately,* etc.

83. **Said, same, such.** Do not use as pronouns. Objectionable:

Although the *said* plan was feasible, I decided not to adopt *same*.

Use *it, that, this,* etc.

84. Seen, saw. The principal parts of *see* are *see, saw, seen. Saw* is improperly used as a past participle; *seen* is improperly used as the past tense.

> I *saw* him yesterday.
> We have *seen* the exhibit.

85. Shall, will. The distinctions in the use of *shall* and *will* have broken down somewhat, but a few careful speakers and writers still observe them. (1) Use *shall* in the first person and *will* in the second and third persons to express *simple futurity.* "I *shall* go"; "you (he) *will* go." (2) For *emphasis* to express *determination, command, intention, promise,* etc., use *will* in the first person and *shall* in the second and third persons. "I *will* speak, no matter what the result may be." "You *shall* speak" (meaning "you must speak"). (See p. 80.)

86. Should, would. In general, use *should* and *would* according to the rules for *shall* and *will.* (See p. 80.)

87. Sign up with, sign up. Colloquial for *join, enroll, hire, engage.*

> Faulty: He has not *signed up with* any club.
> The coach *signed up* two assistants.

88. Sit, set. The former is predominantly an intransitive verb, the latter transitive.

> I shall *sit* down.
> Please *set* the vase on the table.

89. So. Avoid overuse of *so* as a conjunction; excessive use of *so* is a mark of immaturity, of childishness. Use more exact connectives. If a clause shows purpose, use *so that:*

> Martha went with Fred *so that* she could be sure to catch the bus.

Do not use *so* as a general substitute for *extremely, indeed,* or *very.* Correct:

> He is very kind. (See **Very,** below.)

90. Sure. Colloquial for "certainly," "surely," "indeed."

91. Suspicion. Used as a verb colloquially or in dialect for *suspect.* Better:

> I *suspected* that he was lying.

92. **Taste of.** Frequently misused for *taste*, which means "to experience the flavor of"; *taste of* means to eat or drink a little only.

93. **Transpire.** In the sense of "to happen" considered a colloquialism or vulgarism by some grammarians. *Transpire* strictly means "to become known." Questionable:

    An exciting baseball game *transpired* yesterday.

94. **Unique.** *Unique* means "having no like or equal" and logically should not be accompanied by *more, most, very,* etc.

95. **Very.** *Very* has been so overused that it has lost much of its value as an intensive. Use sparingly and thoughtfully.

96. **Wait on.** *Wait on* means "to attend," "to serve"; it is provincial when used to mean "wait for." Incorrect:

    I *waited on* him an hour before he came.

97. **Where at.** Colloquial (and redundant) for *where.* Avoid such a statement as "He did not know *where* he was *at.*"

98. **Worst kind, worst sort, worst way.** Misused for "very much."

99. **Would of, could of, might of,** etc. Vulgarisms for "would have," "could have," etc. *Would had, could had, might had,* etc., are also vulgarisms.

100. **You all.** In the sense of "all of you," this phrase has a recognized plural meaning. When used to refer to one person it may be considered either provincial or vulgar.

GENERAL EXERCISES: THE WORD

A. In the following sentences correct the errors in diction.

1. I don't understand your illusion to that poem, but I guess it must be some clever.
2. I disremember what grub we had, but I can't ever forget the dame that fixed it.
3. I couldn't of figured out what funny doings were going on in Columbia if you hadn't fetched me this paper.
4. The player, hight Red Smith, was the screwiest guy I ever saw.
5. The farmer was plumb tuckered out after his day's work, but he managed to enthuse a little over the chow his old lady had fixed for supper.
6. As soon as you give me your ascent, I'll pop the question to her.
7. I think you'll find the fellows concertizing in back of the house.

General Exercises

8. He doesn't cut a bit of ice in this burg, but on the campus of the state univ. I reckon he must be pretty hot stuff.
9. The prof's council was good, but Henry was a stubborn egg except you treated him easy and confidential-like.
10. I never was much good at telling antidotes, but I'll take a try at this one anyway.
11. Melton had all ready left for the barn, where the vet was trying to doctor a sick calf.
12. Divers people have suspicioned him, but he ain't let on that he knows a thing about it.
13. I know you are intrigued with the car, but it's too expensive for you, and I don't calculate on loaning you the money for it.
14. I don't care if he is a good fellow; he's a sucker to let himself be taken in that away.
15. He remained perfectly stationery while I toted in the whole load of packages.

B. In the following sentences correct the errors in diction.

1. In spite of the favorable factors in your case, I shall have to answer in the negative.
2. In the sea of ruthless competition one can climb to success only by seizing the golden flower of opportunity.
3. In connection with the degree of his guilt, I am of the persuasion that we are not certain as to whether we are fully conversant and acquainted with all the facts of the case.
4. The president's attention was arrested by Mr. Blaine's ability to cope with any situation that might arise.
5. Before giving the glass of milk to the little lass I placed a box of crackers before her.
6. My fellow classmates average in height a height of sixty-eight inches.
7. In these respects, laboratory sciences are of a notoriously trying nature.
8. With bated breath we watched that miserable specimen of humanity go to his doom.
9. The comestibles served in this refectory possess a high degree of noisomeness.
10. Concentrate on the coverage and do not concern yourself with minor, petty details.
11. As soon as I saw that sleek roadster in the showroom, I felt a weak moment coming on.

12. Those who take rooms in this house will have more than enough room in which to house their appurtenances.
13. The sheer force of his personality beggars description.
14. In connection with her other traits I should mention her pulchritude, which is of a very high order.
15. With regard to gardening facilities, there is an empty, vacant piece of unused land in back of the house.

C. The following sentences contain examples of archaic and obsolete words, provincialisms, improprieties, colloquialisms, vulgarisms, and slang. Identify the expressions in each sentence which would be incorrect in formal English; make appropriate substitutions.

1. He was whilom a brilliant lawyer.
2. Will you be in the dorm then?
3. The poor student always gets it in the neck.
4. He never let on he knew about it.
5. She was an earthly angle, but one without wings.
6. That is an expensive pair of pants.
7. They walked up to the alter and got married.
8. What do you reckon he meant by that?
9. Dick had a bad case of the jitters.
10. Please proceed me into the room.
11. She took on when I told her of the accident.
12. I never would have suspicioned it.
13. He had to accompany a dumb bunny to the dance.
14. The latch is broken off the gait.
15. George should never have tooken her skating.
16. Leave go of me at once.
17. He was goodnatured ordinarily, but sometimes his choler rose.
18. The ship was sunk in the Straight of Magellan.
19. Why did you fall for that?
20. Now you will have to work extra hard.

D. The following sentences contain examples of triteness, "fine writing," jargon, mixed figures, wordiness, faulty repetition, lack of euphony. Rewrite each sentence, keeping as close as possible to the intended meaning.

General Exercises

1. Rod decided to seize the bit in his teeth and come down like a wolf on the fold.
2. At the institution of higher learning which he favored with his presence, he was justly proud of his rugged individualism.
3. After spending much time preparing to leave, and after many fond goodbye's, we decided to proceed on our journey.
4. Although he ordinarily liked the succulent bivalve, he picked up one of the delectable morsels in a gingerly fashion and devoured it with a wry smile.
5. Not all widow women regard their lot with apprehension, but those who are left with small children are prone to view their status with alarm.
6. Sitting in his room alone by himself, he repeated her name over again and again.
7. A raging conflagration all too soon destroyed the edifice which with loving hands we had erected that sunny afternoon.
8. Sweetly scented school sashes worn by the fair sex added to the riot of color on the crowded dance floor.
9. Full steam ahead! In this storm of controversy, you must not let your hand falter on the plow.
10. After serious financial reverses, he attempted to misappropriate funds from the bank.
11. We followed the speaker's line of reasoning to a very great extent.
12. Our gridiron warriors were tendered a banquet at the conclusion of their victorious season, and after the sumptuous repast each gladiator spoke a few well-chosen words.
13. The nature of the outside reading in English Composition is something of an added attraction.
14. When asked if he wished to be the recipient of our offer of a position, he replied in the affirmative.
15. We beg to state that your valued order will receive prompt attention along the lines which you suggested.

Appendices

Appendix A

WRITING LETTERS

The letter is the most widely used of all forms of written communication. Each of you, during your college years, probably will write several times as many letters as formal themes. And after graduation you will perhaps find it necessary to write even more letters than you did in college. Surely so widely used a form of writing deserves attention; from the standpoint of utility only, training in no other form is so important. For the ability to write a good letter indicates much more than we are likely to realize. You will find that important businessmen and firms waste little time, for example, on applications written in slipshod style; friends frequently drift away from us when we persist in writing them hurried notes instead of sincere, attractive, detailed letters; only too often our social contacts are affected by our ignorance of proper forms and conventions.

It must be remembered that the letters we write are an unfailing reflection and representation of ourselves. What we say and how we say it, the paper and ink we use, even the way in which we address the envelope and affix the stamp reflect our personalities just as do our diction, our smiles, our gestures.

This universally used, important, and highly personal form of communication which we call the letter is, in a sense, a theme which is governed by the same rules and principles as other kinds of composition. A letter should be *correct, clear,* and *effective.* Good letters are rarely "dashed off"; usually they are the result of careful planning, writing, and rewriting.

There are two main kinds of letters: business letters and informal, friendly letters. A third kind is formal invitations and replies, but the conventional patterns of formal correspondence may be

475

Appendix A

found in any standard book of etiquette. Business letters and informal letters, however, are more variable; each deserves attention. And each illustrates admirably the process of communication: you, *the writer,* send some specific question or information, *the subject,* to some specifically named person or company, *the reader.*

BUSINESS LETTERS

The business letter is largely utilitarian: its object is to convey information by precise exposition. In writing business letters one is primarily concerned with *presentation* (the way in which what one has to say is arranged and expressed) and *content* (the subject matter that is to be included).

1. Presentation

A good business letter creates a pleasing impression the moment it is taken from its envelope. Physical appearance—quality of paper, neatness of typing or writing, arrangement of letter parts—is almost as important as content to the total effect. Correctness and attractiveness in form reflect a courteous attitude toward the reader.

STATIONERY

Business letters should be written on good-quality white unruled paper, preferably of the standard $8\frac{1}{2}$ x 11-inch size, although the half-size sheet ($8\frac{1}{2}$ x $5\frac{1}{2}$) is acceptable, using either the longer or the shorter measurement for the horizontal lines. Colored and unusual-sized sheets are in doubtful taste for business correspondence, as is fraternity, club, and hotel stationery.

TYPING

Letters should be typewritten if possible, but neat longhand, in black or blue-black ink, is permissible. For typing, a black ribbon fresh enough to insure legibility should be used. The letter must be neat in every detail; never strike over or leave a visible erasure.

FORM

Good business letters are arranged in a form which has now become so standardized that it is easy to follow. It consists of six parts:

476

Writing Letters

1. The Heading
2. The Inside Address
3. The Greeting, or Salutation

4. The Body
5. The Complimentary Close
6. The Signature

Each part has certain set forms which must not be ignored or altered if your letter is to be attractive and easy to read. Study the letters on pages 482–485, not only for observing the position of the parts but also as an illustration of the correct use and balanced arrangement of these conventionalized forms.

The Heading. The heading contains the sender's full address—street, city, postal zone, state—and the date of writing. It is usually placed in the upper right-hand part of the sheet (but see p. 482), several spaces below the top edge, and flush with the right margin of the letter. It is single spaced. Abbreviations should be avoided, and *st, nd, rd,* or *d* should not follow the day of the month. On stationery with a letterhead, the writer need add only the date, which he places flush with the right-hand margin of the letter or centers directly beneath the letterhead. For position of lines and punctuation, see "Indented and Block Systems" and "Open and Closed Systems," page 482, and the letters on pages 482–485.

The Inside Address. The address of the person or company that the letter is written to should appear at least four spaces below the heading and flush with the left-hand margin of the letter. It is usually single spaced and harmonizes with the heading in that it conforms to it in having either block or indented form and in being punctuated according to the open or closed system.

Some title should always precede the name of the person addressed: *Mr., Mrs., Miss, Messrs.,* etc. A business title should never precede the name, but a person of professional standing may be addressed as *Dr., The Reverend, President* (of a college), *Dean, Professor, General,* etc. The title *Honorable* is widely used for a person holding an important government position.

If you know only the last name of the person to whom you are writing, direct your letter to the firm, adding *Attention: Mr. —* or *Attention of Mr. —.* The attention line usually appears directly above the greeting or flush with the right-hand margin; it has no bearing on the greeting itself, which is always determined from the first line of the inside address.

477

Appendix A

The following list indicates proper forms for addressing various persons:

	INSIDE ADDRESS	GREETING
One man:	Mr. James T. Wilcox 49 Nottingham Road Silver Spring, Utah	Dear Mr. Wilcox:
One woman:	Mrs. Robert Fitch Two Park Place Troy 65, Ohio	Dear Mrs. Fitch:
Partnership:	Messrs. Herd and Tims 1350 Sumter Boulevard Tallahassee, Florida	Gentlemen:
Firm of women:	The Dora Dress Shop 14 Wilton Boulevard Portland, Maine	Ladies:
One man in a firm:	Mr. Victor C. Woll Art Printing Company 332 Aiken Building Nashville 10, Florida	Dear Mr. Woll:
An officer in a firm:	Mr. Lee Fox, Treasurer The Mayo Corporation West Falls, Montana or Mr. Walter Stephens Treasurer, Lea & Sons, Inc. 1659 Glenham Street Oak Park 4, Illinois	Dear Mr. Fox: Dear Mr. Stephens:
A college official (with professional standing):	President Roy G. Wild Charlotte College Jackson, Arizona	Dear President Wild:
An officer in an organization, when individual name is unknown:	The Registrar Polk University Brighton, New York	Dear Sir:
PUBLIC OFFICIALS:		
The President	The President The White House Washington, D.C.	Mr. President: or My dear Mr. President:

478

Writing Letters

	INSIDE ADDRESS	GREETING
Cabinet member	The Secretary of — Washington, D.C. or The Honorable John Foy Secretary of — Washington, D.C.	Dear Sir: or My dear Mr. Secretary:
Senator	The Honorable John Rae The United States Senate Washington, D.C.	Dear Sir: or Dear Senator: or Dear Senator Rae:
Representative	The Honorable R. B. Burns The House of Representatives Washington, D.C.	Dear Sir: or Dear Mr. Burns:
Governor	The Honorable Paul Key Governor of Colorado Denver, Colorado	Dear Sir: or Dear Governor Key:
Mayor	His Honor, the Mayor City Hall	My dear Mr. Mayor: or Dear Mayor Woods:

The Greeting, or Salutation. The greeting, or salutation, should be placed two spaces below the inside address and flush with the left-hand margin. It is punctuated by a colon only, never a comma, semicolon, dash, or colon and dash. The following forms of salutation, arranged in decreasing formality, are correct. Select the one which corresponds to the first line of the inside address and to the general tone of your letter. However, for most business correspondence, the last form listed in each group is preferable (see also greetings shown above with the list of inside addresses). Notice that "dear" is capitalized only when it is the first word.

TO A MAN:
    My dear Sir:
    Dear Sir:
    My dear Mr. Pollock:
    Dear Dr. Bard:

TO A WOMAN:
    Dear Madam:
    My dear Mrs. Lord:
    Dear Mrs. Lord:

TO A FIRM OF MEN:
    Dear Sirs:
    Gentlemen:

TO A GROUP OR FIRM OF WOMEN:
    Mesdames:
    Ladies:

Appendix A

NOTE: The more personal form using the name of the person addressed is now preferred to the older, more formal *My dear Sir, Dear Sir(s)*, or *Dear Madam*. Use the person's name if it is known to you, except in letters to public officials or church dignitaries. However, *Dear Sir* and *Dear Madam* are commonly used for addressing officials. A minister may be addressed *Dear Sir, Dear Mr. —*, or *Dear Doctor* — (if he is a Doctor of Divinity); a priest is *Dear Father* — or *Reverend and dear Sir;* a nun or a sister is *Dear Sister* or *Dear Sister* —; a rabbi is *Dear Sir* or *Dear Rabbi* —.

The Body. The body of the letter contains the message and begins two spaces below the greeting. Most business letters are single spaced, although an extremely short message may be double spaced for attractive arrangement on a large page. Single-spaced letters require two spaces between each paragraph. Paragraphs may be in block form (if the heading and inside address correspond in form) or indented. They *should be* indented when the indented system is used. They *may be* indented, for clearness and effectiveness, even when the block system is used in the other parts. If double spacing is used in the body of the letter, paragraphs are more clearly separated by double spacing and indentation. On the typewriter, indentation may be five or ten spaces, or one space beyond the length of the greeting line.

Messages which are too long for one page should be continued on a second page (never write on the back of a sheet). However, the second page must contain at least two lines, preferably more, in addition to the complimentary close and signature. A paragraph may be continued from one page to another, but at least two lines of the paragraph should appear on the page on which it begins. Each additional page should carry a top line containing some sort of identification, such as the addressee's initials or name, the page number, and the date.

The Complimentary Close. The close is placed slightly to the right of the middle of the page, two or three spaces below the last line of the body of the letter. Only the first word is capitalized. The punctuation mark is a comma, even though open punctuation is used in the heading and inside address. Correct forms, arranged

480

Writing Letters

in decreasing formality and used to harmonize with the formality or semi-informality of the greeting, are as follows:

Respectfully yours,	Yours very truly,
Yours truly,	Yours very sincerely,
Very truly yours,	Sincerely yours,
	Cordially yours,

The close should be independent of the last paragraph of the letter. Do not link the last paragraph and the close by a participial phrase such as *Thanking you in advance, I remain,* or *Hoping for an early reply, I am.* Avoid "clever" or "original" forms such as *Enthusiastically yours, Apologetically yours, Yours for lower taxes, Yours for a cheery Homecoming.*

The Signature. The signature is placed directly below the complimentary close. If the signature (name) is typewritten, leave four spaces for the insertion of the handwritten signature. Unless a letter is mimeographed or is plainly a circular letter, it should always have, in ink, a legible, handwritten signature.

A married woman should sign her own full name, followed by her married name:

Anne Marie Shelton

(Mrs. Paul R. Shelton)

An unmarried woman places the title *Miss* in parentheses before her name:

(Miss) Elizabeth West

Academic degrees and courtesy or professional titles—*Mr., Dr., Rev., Litt.D.,* etc.—should not be used with a signature.

MARGINS

Balanced layout of the letter on the page is determined by the length of the message. The entire letter (including heading, inside address, complimentary close, and signature) should have the appearance of a rectangle, with top and bottom margins slightly wider than those at the side. Side margins should be at least an inch wide, and particular care must be taken to maintain as even a right margin as possible. If necessary, long words should be divided, always according to their proper syllables. Short letters should be approximately centered, with wide margins.

INDENTED AND BLOCK SYSTEMS

Arrangement of the lines of the heading, as well as those of the inside address and the outside address on the envelope (see below), may follow the *indented* or the *block* system. In the first of these methods, each line is indented a few spaces to the right of the preceding line. In the block form, which is now more widely used, the lines begin at the same margin. The block form may be one of two kinds: In the "modified block" form, the lines of each part are blocked, and the various parts of the letter are placed in the positions indicated above. In the "full block" form, all the parts of the letter, including the heading, the complimentary close, and the signature, begin at the left-hand margin. For an example, see below.

OPEN AND CLOSED SYSTEMS

Punctuation of the heading and inside and outside addresses may follow the *open* or the *closed* system. In the open system, no commas or final periods (except after abbreviations) are used after the separate lines. In the closed system, commas are used after each line except the last; a period is used after the last line. Both methods are acceptable, although the open system is now more widely used.

```
1934 Travis Street
Louisville 8, Kentucky
February 3, 19--

Miss Lucy Irwin
Secretary, Society of Commerce
375 East Boone Street
Arlington, Kentucky

My dear Miss Irwin:

This letter is an illustration of the "full
block" or the "modified military" form, since
all the parts of the letter, including the
```
482

Writing Letters

heading, complimentary close, and signature, begin flush with the left-hand margin. Where there are two or more lines in a part, each line begins directly under the line just above. Note also the space between the various parts of the letter.

The paragraphs illustrate block form; that is, each paragraph begins flush with the left-hand margin. Division between paragraphs is indicated by double spaces. Within the paragraphs and within each part of the letter, single spacing is used.

No punctuation marks are used after the lines in the heading, inside address, and signature. This system, called open punctuation, does not apply, however, to the greeting and the complimentary close, which are followed by a colon and a comma, respectively.

This letter form--full block and open punctuation--is becoming increasingly popular among business men, secretaries, and stenographers, for it saves considerable time and trouble by its elimination of indentions and some of the end-punctuation marks.

Yours very truly,

Wilson F. Johnson

Wilson F. Johnson
Correspondence Consultant
Louisville Mercantile Corporation

"FULL BLOCK" FORM

Appendix A

516 Tudor Place,
Detroit 22, Michigan,
November 2, 19--.

Rinebeck & Company,
1224 East Denver Avenue,
Chicago 12, Illinois.

Gentlemen:

This letter is an example of "modified block" or "semi-block" form; that is, the heading, complimentary close, and signature are on the right side of the letter, the other parts on the left. But within the parts the block form is used.

The paragraphs are indented here, but they could be block form. In fact, blocked paragraphs are optional: indented paragraphs can be used, if the writer so desires, with any type of letter, including even the full-block form.

Closed punctuation is used here: commas at the end of each line in the heading and the inside address except the last, which has a period. Such punctuation, too, is optional, for open punctuation could be used.

These three letters--this one, the one preceding, and the one following--also illustrate variety in the use of the greeting and the complimentary close. The tone of the complimentary close likewise is in harmony with the tone of the greeting, in each of the letters.

Very truly yours,

Rodney R. Rhodes

Rodney R. Rhodes

"MODIFIED BLOCK" FORM

Writing Letters

Mr. Harrison McWilliams,
   Supervisor of Correspondence,
      Washington High School,
         Clearwater, Indiana.

Dear Mr. McWilliams:

    This letter illustrates "indented" form,
both in the various parts and in the paragraph
beginning. Such indentation is somewhat
troublesome, although preferred by some letter-
writers. Closed punctuation is used in the
heading and inside address, but open punctuation could be used. Since this is a one-paragraph letter, notice that it has larger margins
at left and right, and more white space at top
and bottom.

             Sincerely yours,

Jane Ferguson

           (Miss) Jane Ferguson

       "INDENTED" FORM

THE ENVELOPE

The envelope carries the sender's return address in the upper left-hand corner and the addressee's name slightly below center and to the right. The full address should be used in harmony with the inside address on the letter, although double spacing of a three-line address on the envelope is helpful to the Post Office Department, as are indented lines regardless of the system used in the inside address.

Folding of the letter depends upon the size of the envelope. When the large No. 10 ($9\frac{1}{2}$ x $4\frac{1}{8}$) envelope is used, the lower third of the sheet should be folded over the message, the upper part folded down to within a half inch, and the upper folded edge should be put in the envelope first.

Appendix A

For a No. 6¾ (6½ x 3⅝) envelope, fold the lower part of the letter page over the message to within approximately one-half inch of the top of the page. Next, fold from the right slightly more than one third, then from the left, leaving the left flap edge slightly short of the right folded edge. Insert the left folded edge in the envelope first.

The reason for these folds is obvious—courtesy to the reader. If he opens your letter in the conventional way, the letter comes out of the envelope literally half-unfolding itself, top edge and written face up, ready to be read.

2. Content

In addition to adhering to general principles of effective writing, business letters should always be clear, concise, complete, and courteous. As has been noted, the object of a business letter is to convey information by precise exposition. Since the writer hopes to secure the reader's careful attention, every letter should be carefully planned and phrased with its reader in mind.

OPENING SENTENCE

Open the letter with a statement of its subject or its purpose, a courteous request, a direct question, a simple direct important statement, or several of these in combination. Avoid such opening abbreviations, terms of jargon, and rubber-stamp expressions as *enclosed please find, your recent favor to hand and in reply would state, I beg to advise, yours of the 8th inst. recd.* Include briefly in the opening sentences or paragraph any pertinent "background" information which will clarify your message. Make the purpose of your letter evident and arrange your thoughts in logical, easy-to-follow units. Separate ideas require separate paragraphs and should be developed according to the principles discussed on pages 308–310.

PARAGRAPHING

Business-letter paragraphs are shorter than paragraphs in most other kinds of prose. They usually vary in length from two to six lines. Longer paragraphs are rare; not infrequently one-line paragraphs are used. The reason for such paragraphing is to enable

Writing Letters

the reader to get the message of each paragraph, and of the letter, easily, quickly, clearly, and effectively.

CLOSING SENTENCE

Your letter should close strongly and effectively. As indicated above under "The Complimentary Close," avoid weak participial or prepositional phrases. Make your last group of words a complete sentence: an invitation, a direct question, a courteous request, a restatement of the subject of the letter, or a significant and important statement.

LANGUAGE

Remember your reader: avoid using too formal English, but at the other extreme avoid using trite, outworn, "business" expressions, such as *recent date, contents noted, as per, past favors, wish to advise, in receipt of, valued wishes, according to my records, attached hereto, enclosed herewith, under separate cover, beg to acknowledge, your kind indulgence, we trust, permit us, at your earliest convenience, as soon as possible, thank you in advance.*

Use instead an informal and soundly idiomatic style. Colloquialisms are permissible, but avoid using a telegraphic style. Someone has said that effective business letters use the same courteous and friendly language that is used in a business conversation over the telephone.

TYPES OF BUSINESS LETTERS

There are numerous kinds of business letters, classified according to their content, or message. The most common of these are

1. Order letters and acknowledgments of orders.
2. Inquiries and replies.
3. Sales letters.
4. Credit letters (designed to encourage buying now and paying later).
5. Collection letters (designed to encourage paying *now*).
6. Claims and adjustments.
7. Letters of application.
8. Letters of introduction or recommendation.

Appendix A

The four types you are most likely to use, now and later, are represented below. (For more detailed discussion of all the various types of letters used in the transaction of business, the student is referred to *Business Letters,* by W. K. Smart and L. W. McKelvey.)

ORDER LETTERS

Make your order letter (if you do not have a printed order blank available) brief, clear, and exact. Give a full description of the goods which you wish to buy, including quantity, size, color, price, and any other available identifying data such as catalogue number and trade name. Two or more items ordered in the same letter should be listed separately to facilitate reading. Always specify methods of shipment and payment and remember to mention any special wish (delivery of the order by a certain date, etc.).

In the lower left-hand corner, several spaces under the last line of the body, write "Encl." (i.e., enclosure) if something is to be sent with the letter (check, sample, etc.). Whenever this is done, it serves to remind you, or whoever folds the letter, to be sure that the enclosure mentioned in the body of the letter is made; it is also a further indication, to the reader, of the enclosure.

ORDER LETTER

240 King Street,
Maryville, Delaware,
June 9, 19—.

White Garment Company,
8639 West Street,
New York 17, New York.

Gentlemen:

Please send me, by parcel post, six pairs of ladies' nylon hose, 15 Denier, size 9, medium length, suntan color. In payment I enclose a money order for nine dollars ($9.00).

Yours very truly,
(Miss) Jane Smith

Encl.

Writing Letters

INQUIRIES

Most inquiry letters are written to obtain information about the products or services of a business firm. Some may be written to an individual for information concerning a subject on which he is an authority. Always make your request understandable; avoid vague and general questions. Supply any information the reader may need in order to answer your questions definitely.

Routine requests for catalogues, price lists, or other prepared data may be limited to a one-sentence letter clearly identifying the desired material. If your letter is phrased as a question (*Will you please send me* . . .), it should close with a period instead of a question mark.

Nonroutine inquiries require more detailed letters. For example, a letter asking about an organization's policies must explain the use to which the information will be put. A request stemming from a personal problem must give a clear explanation of the problem and an indication of the type of help needed.

The general plan for the inquiry letter (usually from two to four paragraphs) is as follows: (1) reason for the inquiry, (2) the inquiry, (3) expression of appreciation (*never* a "thank you in advance"). Sometimes material may be included to show the reader how he will benefit by replying. If the inquiry includes several questions, these are more effective when numbered and paragraphed separately.

If the person or firm addressed will eventually profit, no postage should be enclosed. Otherwise, apply this principle: When you ask for that which is of benefit only or primarily to you, enclose a self-addressed stamped envelope.

Study the example on page 490.

Appendix A

919 Fowler Avenue
Athens 12, Indiana
September 25, 19--

Secretary-Treasurer
American Institute of Electrical Engineers
33 West 38th Street
New York 18, New York

Dear Sir:

As a student in the College of Electrical Engineering at Athens University, I am interested in eventually obtaining full membership in the American Institute of Electrical Engineers.

Will you please answer the following questions:

(1) Is it possible for an undergraduate student of electrical engineering to obtain a junior membership in the A. I. E. E.?
(2) What is the cost of such membership?
(3) Is such junior membership transferable to full membership upon the student's graduation from college?
(4) Does the junior membership fee include a year's subscription to the official magazine, Electrical Engineering?

Your sending me this information will be greatly appreciated.

Very truly yours,

Wilson Hargrove

Wilson Hargrove

CLAIMS AND ADJUSTMENTS

The claims, or complaint, letter is written not to accuse, blame, or threaten but to point out an error, such as shipment of wrong

490

Writing Letters

goods, damaged goods, failure to ship goods, an overcharge in a bill, and the like. Clarity is essential, brevity is desirable, and courtesy is diplomatic. Present the necessary facts fairly; identify the unsatisfactory article or service, explain how it is unsatisfactory, and suggest or give the reader an opportunity to suggest adjustment. (The letter he writes to you is the adjustment letter.)

If you have to write an angry letter, by all means write it, but lay it aside for a day; then destroy it and write the kind of letter you would like to receive if your position were that of the reader.

Usually your claims letter will consist of two to four paragraphs containing (1) a specific explanation of what is wrong, (2) the course of action you desire the reader to take, (3) sometimes, the inconvenience resulting to the writer, and (4) sometimes, the gains to be won by the reader's making prompt adjustment. Circumstances will determine the order in which these paragraphs come.

CLAIMS LETTERS (1)

```
                         R.F.D. 6,
                           Lansom, Pennsylvania,
                           November 15, 19--.

The Tryco Department Store,
    49 East Tenth Street,
      New York 10, New York.

Gentlemen:

          On November 9 I purchased in your
radio department a Vinson radio, table model
R-350, with brown plastic case. The radio
arrived promptly, but I am disappointed to find
that it does not operate on DC current. It was
my understanding that the Model R-350 is de-
signed to operate on either AC or DC, but I
find that the accompanying instructions indi-
cate only AC. I am returning the radio at once
in the hope that it can be exchanged for a set
suitable for DC wiring.
          If there has been a misunderstanding
and the R-350 does not operate on DC current, I
```

491

Appendix A

shall have to choose another model. If that is
the case I hope that I may have a refund, since
I shall not be in New York again for several
months. I hope, however, that you will be able
to supply an R-350 model which will fill my
needs.

Very truly yours,

Edward J. Ryan, Jr.

Edward J. Ryan, Jr.

(2)

240 King Street,
Maryville, Delaware,
June 23, 19--.

White Garment Company,
8639 West Street,
New York 17, New York.

Gentlemen:

On June 9 I ordered from you six pairs of
ladies' nylon hose, 15 Denier, size 9, medium
length, suntan color, total price $9.00. I de-
sired to give these hose to a friend who was
leaving on June 20 for a trip abroad.

The hose arrived on June 18, and I was
greatly disappointed to find several mistakes
in the order: they were size 10, short length,
gunmetal in color.

As it is too late to have the error corrected, I am returning the hose to you parcel-
post insured and am asking that you return to
me the purchase money of $9.00.

Yours very truly,

(Miss) Jane Smith

(Miss) Jane Smith

Writing Letters

LETTERS OF APPLICATION

An effective letter of application stresses, throughout, the applicant's desire and ability to be of benefit to the prospective employer. Always emphasize what you, the applicant with your qualifications, can do for the employer, not what the latter can do for you. The letter must be courteous, straightforward, and sincere in tone, offering services without pleading or demanding.

Open your letter by applying for a specific position and indicating how you learned of the opening (from a friend, an agency, a classified advertisement, etc.) or your special reason for applying (if the application is unsolicited). Present qualifications (education, interest, aptitude) and experience honestly, emphasizing those which will be particularly useful to the employer's firm. Devote a brief paragraph to personal information: age, health, and any other pertinent details. Include two or three references, listing them separately, either in the body of the letter or immediately after the close, with full names, titles, and addresses. Close your letter by requesting an interview at the employer's convenience. If you are in the same city, indicate where you may be reached by telephone. (See an example of a letter of application below.)

NOTE: Always secure permission from the persons whom you wish to suggest as references and remember that it is courteous to write letters thanking them for their help.

Letters Accompanying Data Sheets. Many applicants prepare a separate data sheet (which should be labeled "Information Record Concerning . . ."), listing education, experience, personal information, and references. Such a record can be a full page (or even more) of information pertinent to the position desired; it will also have room, preferably in the upper right-hand corner, for the pasting of a good photograph. Subheadings should be used for ready reading. The letter accompanying such a sheet should not repeat information. It is usually in three paragraphs. The first applies for the position; the second points out the information on the data sheet which especially qualifies the applicant for the position; the third requests an interview.

Letters Replying to Newspaper or Magazine Advertisements. In responding to "Help Wanted" advertisements in newspapers or in

493

certain professional magazines, the applicant must first analyze the information given to determine the required qualifications. *Blind advertisements* give neither name nor address of the advertiser and often provide scant information about the opening. The applicant must judge as best he can the qualifications needed and offer in his letter whatever details seem pertinent.

Here is an example of a blind advertisement:

Stenographer: Good beginner considered. 5 day week. Opp. for advancement. M4089 Tribune.

The applicant has no way of knowing the name of the firm, the kind of business, or exactly what "advancement" is suggested. It is likely that the work does not require knowledge of technical terminology since a beginner will be considered. In replying, the applicant can only express interest in a position which offers further opportunity and give details about her stenographic skill. She should of course include past experience in stenography, usually without referring to employers by name.

Classified advertisements ordinarily include the name of the firm and more detailed information about the position. The following advertisement clearly outlines the employer's needs:

Wanted: Young man to check reports of public accountants, prove figures, check references, etc. Prefer accounting education and background, ability to assist in preparing reports. Excellent opportunity young man studying for CPA. Reply in detail. Brown, Merrill and Scott, CPA, 35 National Bank Building.

The applicant analyzes the advertisement by listing in detail the qualifications desired; his letter, if he expects it to gain him an interview, must show precisely how he meets these qualifications. For the position just quoted, an applicant must indicate (1) strong interest in an accounting career; (2) experience, if any, in checking reports, etc.; (3) education; (4) ability to compile data and write reports.

Unusual Letters of Application. The usual purpose of the letter of application is to gain for its writer an interview. Therefore, make your letters of application effective by making them unusual.

Writing Letters

Do not be vain, assertive, overconfident, but try to convey routine information in an unusual way. For example, you can use subheads: centered, or in the left margin, or on the left third of the page with the material developing the subheads filling the right two-thirds. One attention-getting letter of application had the applicant's picture centered at the top, with position desired at the left and date available at the right; a three-paragraph letter occupied the center of the page, enclosed by ruled lines; surrounding the letter were statements of the applicant's attainments and qualifications: educational background, campus activities, business experience, personal data, and references. Your own ingenuity may suggest other unusual letters of application.

LETTER OF APPLICATION

```
                              961 Boulder Drive
                              Atlanta 21, Georgia
                              October 21, 19--


Mr. David Carr, Office Manager
Textile Products, Inc.
16 Whicher Street
Nashville 8, Tennessee

Dear Mr. Carr:

          Through the courtesy of Professor
A. D. Dwyer, I have learned that you are con-
sidering employing an office assistant. I
should like to apply for this position.

          Under Professor Dwyer, I took
several courses in office management at Black
University. In addition to the usual classroom
work, I had an opportunity to analyze various
problems of office management as a part of my
senior research work. This study was carried
on in the model business office conducted by
the University's College of Commerce and also
```

in the offices of the Alliance Chemical Corporation.

As background for my major studies, I have taken courses in business law, accounting, stenography, and typing. I can take dictation rapidly and am an accurate, though not rapid, typist.

For the past four summers I have been employed as a "relief" secretary at the Dow Smelting Company of this city, substituting for other girls while they were on vacation. At present, I am working as a typist with this same company, but I believe that my college training and practical background of experience have fitted me for duties of greater responsibility.

My age is twenty-two; I am in excellent health. My parents are native-born Americans. You can depend upon my working intelligently and diligently.

I shall arrange to come to Nashville for an interview at any time agreeable to you. When would be most convenient?

Very truly yours,

(Miss) Frances Whirter

(Miss) Frances Whirter

References:

Professor A. D. Dwyer, Black University, Columbus, Georgia.

Mr. James Ragsland, Personnel Manager, The Alliance Chemical Corporation, Columbus, Georgia.

Dr. Rufus J. Smythe, Plant Director, Dow Smelting Company, Atlanta, Georgia.

496

Writing Letters

There is an old saying: "The best way to have a friend is to be one." This adage applies particularly to the writing and receiving of friendly letters. All of us are prone to say, "I love to get letters but, oh, how I hate to write them!" It is unfortunately true that good informal letters require careful planning and writing; they can no more be "dashed off" than can effective business letters. Writing letters is not exactly an art, but many of us can approximate artistry in our personal correspondence *provided* we take the time and pains to plan and write our letters thoughtfully. They should, however, never seem or sound labored, strained, or artificial.

Conversation is no more a "lost art" than is friendly letter writing. We tend to live so hurriedly these days that we feel we have actually written a letter when all that we have done is to dash off a few hastily scrawled notes on a half-dozen random subjects. We can somewhat restore the "lost art" of friendly letter writing by practicing the following suggestions:

1. *Give details.* The full, clear description of one person or one place is likely to prove far more interesting than a series of choppy notes on numerous people or places. The detailed account of one interesting conversation which you have had will be far more revealing and entertaining than a kaleidoscopic series of random comments quoted from a dozen people whom you have met. The vivid narration of a single experience which you have had will prove more readable than scrappy accounts of several incidents. Try to write letters made up of unified details, not random notes which really are only topic sentences needing expansion. Think of each letter as a *theme* with a central purpose. Keep your central purpose in mind, reject all irrelevant details, and focus attention upon one primary incident or one piece of conversation, upon description of one person or place or exposition of one idea. Of course, a letter may discuss more than one topic, but the topics should be clearly related and each should be fully developed. In writing informal letters follow the principles of paragraph development mentioned on pages 308–310.

2. *Vary your letters.* Our friends differ somewhat in their tastes and interests. An incident Sue would enjoy reading about might

497

Appendix A

not be particularly interesting to George. Jack is a music lover: he will enjoy full details of that concert which you attended; Henry is not especially interested in music, but he will read avidly an account of the last fraternity dance that you went to. Friendship implies many obligations, one of which is to detect and respect individual differences. Rarely is it possible to give all our friends the same Christmas present. It should be equally obvious that the recipients of our letters have a right to expect individual treatment. In other words, adapt each letter and its content to your specific reader.

3. *Take time.* No one can write a long, interesting letter in five or ten minutes. The best friendly letters are usually written by people who plan their letters before attempting to write them. They don't sit down to write a letter, saying, "Well, I owe Bill a letter and I can't put it off any longer. What can I tell him?" They sit down to write Bill about people, places, and events in which they know he will be interested and about which they have made mental notes for the very purpose of using in a letter to him. Nor do good letter writers try to write six or eight letters at a sitting. They write only one or two, and thus give each letter all the freshness, spontaneity, and chattiness which they can. Few of us can write good letters when we consider the task tiresome and laborious. Each of us can write letters with charm if we don't stint the care which we expend upon them. Friendships, often kept alive necessarily through the medium of correspondence, are too precious for us to throw away for the lack of a little time. Each of us is occasionally irritated at receiving a long-expected letter which begins "I am sorry that this letter will be brief for I am in a great rush" or ends with a "Hastily yours." We may expect that those who receive from us letters beginning or ending in the same manner will be similarly nettled.

4. *Don't write illegibly or sloppily.* The friendly letter is different in form and purpose from business and formal correspondence. It is more intimate, much more informal. But hastily scrawled notes on odd pieces of paper do not show much interest in or respect for the persons to whom we are writing. Informality is not only permissible but desirable in friendly letters, but liberty must not become

498

Writing Letters

license. The illegibility and general carelessness which fairly scream "I haven't time to write you a good letter—take this or leave it" are not permissible.

Use letter paper of good quality and in good taste. White or cream or pale gray paper is preferable to that of other colors. Avoid the use of heavily perfumed paper. Don't use violet or red or green ink. Your letters, even in their paper, ink, and handwriting, reflect your possession or lack of good taste and refinement.

Types of Friendly Letters

Each of us is called upon to write various kinds of friendly letters. There is the "thank you" letter in which we express our appreciation for a favor or a gift. There is the informal invitation to attend, let us say, a house party, and the informal reply to that invitation. Letters of congratulation, of sympathy, letters to the family, "travel" letters, "bread and butter" letters are other types.

These types are so varied that no single rule or suggestion can be offered to cover them all. But for each of them, follow the directions given above; for each, make mental or written notes of the details you plan to include and the order in which you will treat them.

Remember also that the *form* of friendly letters is not nearly so important as their *content*. It should be noted, however, that a comma, not a colon, usually follows the greeting. It is suggested, too, that the writer's address and the actual date (not just the day of the week) be given in the usual place for the heading or in the lower left-hand corner of the last page of the letter. No inside address is necessary, but the outside address on the envelope of the friendly letter must be as accurate and full as that on a business letter.

The letters that follow may be helpful to you in suggesting solutions to some letter-writing problems, but do not follow any models slavishly.

A "Thank You" Note

Dear Uncle Jim,

I know that I wasn't the prettiest girl at the dance (although Jack, who took me, said I was); and I didn't get the biggest rush either, but

499

Appendix A

then again I wasn't exactly a wallflower. And yet I'm positive about one thing—I was the happiest girl there. No one else was wearing such beautiful costume jewelry, and I could just see the looks of envy on the other girls' faces. I have always known that you knew the way to a girl's heart, but what I didn't know was that you thought enough of me to take the time and trouble to select and send me such an exquisite gift. I'm very grateful and the next time that I see you I'll tell you in person just how happy you have made me.

> Your devoted niece,
> Louise

923 Athens St.
New Orleans 6, La.
January 20, 19—

A Note of Congratulation

> McWhorter Apartments,
> Des Moines 14, Iowa,
> May 10, 19—.

Dear Fred,

I was delighted to learn that you had been elected the president of your class. Because I have known you for a long time as a sincere, hard-working, and completely honest person, I am certain that you richly deserve the honor and that you will prove worthy of the position which is yours. If I had been fortunate enough to be a classmate of yours at — College, I should have voted for you, too. I congratulate you sincerely and I congratulate your class.

> Your old friend,
> Joe

A Note of Sympathy

Dear Barbara,

As I sat in the church today, a whole host of memories came crowding about me. I remember so well when I met your mother; she received me, as your friend, with her arms literally open. And for all the months that I have been privileged to know her, she has always been graciously hospitable to me. I recall dozens of good times which she made possible for us; I remember especially how she helped me with that fancy dress costume when I was almost in tears because I couldn't get it to hang just exactly right.

Nothing which I can say will lessen either the shock of her passing

500

Writing Letters

or your grief. But I want you to know that as I paid her my last respects this afternoon, my own heart was heavy with a sense of personal loss. Her kindliness, thoughtfulness, and complete integrity will serve as a constant challenge to you and to me.

With sincere sympathy,
Alice

Hamilton Hall
Lake College
October 9, 19—

An Informal Invitation

Blake University
130 Haven Hall
April 2, 19—

Dear Jane,

I haven't forgotten your interest in our annual Campus Carnival, and now that the big day is rolling around, I want very much to have you come for a visit. Then you can see for yourself how much fun the Carnival is.

The date is to be April 23, a Saturday, and I hope that you can spend the entire week end as my guest in the dormitory (special privileges for Carnival week end!). Please do plan to come on Friday afternoon or early Friday evening so that we can go to the informal Paddy dance. There's a handsome law student who's heard about you and thinks that's a wonderful idea.

If you'll just let me know which bus or train you'll arrive on, I'll be waiting for you at the station. And I'll be looking forward eagerly to seeing you again. It's been much too long now.

Sincerely,
Sarah

A "Bread and Butter" Letter

26 Burton Place
Chicago, Ill.
July 21, 19—

Dear Helen,

I want to tell you again how very much I enjoyed spending these past four days with you. The train arrived in the city about ten minutes late, but Dad was waiting for me and brought me home in the car.

Mother was glad to see me, for my sister, Marion, is giving a party

Appendix A

for the neighborhood "gang" this afternoon; you can imagine that Mother is doing most of the work!

Tell your brother that I'm going to plan on three or four tennis matches this week, so that next time I play him I may be able to win *two* games!

Thank you for such a good time, Helen. Let me know when you come to town on your next buying spree; perhaps we can arrange to get together for lunch and our usual window-shopping afternoon.

Sincerely,
Martha

EXERCISES

1. Collect and bring to class at least ten examples of business letters. (Perhaps you can supply these from your own correspondence; or a relative or business acquaintance may lend you some letters from his files.) Study the letterheads used; note especially both the usual and unusual features about the six parts of the letters (heading, inside address, greeting, body, complimentary close, signature). Notice the stock of paper used, the spacing and length of the paragraphs, the tone of the letters.

2. Classify the letters in your collection (Exercise 1) according to the types of business letters listed on page 487. For one example of each type that you find, make a paragraph outline of the content. Compare this outline with the plan of organization given for the order letter, inquiry letter, claims letter, and application letter (see pp. 488–496).

3. Write a letter answering an advertisement in a magazine, in which you request a catalogue.

4. From a magazine advertisement, write a letter ordering the item or items advertised.

5. You notice the announcement of an essay contest for college students being sponsored by a national publisher. Write a letter asking for details.

6. Assume that you are preparing a paper or a speech on the history of your home town. Write a letter to the state historical society asking for information on the early shops and industries in the town.

7. Write a letter asking an entertainer or a guest speaker to appear on a program sponsored by your class or some organization of

which you are a member. Then assume that the entertainment has been given; write the speaker a "thank you" letter.

8. Write a formal letter to the editor of your local newspaper, calling attention to some matter which you believe will interest your fellow-townsmen or fellow-students.

9. Write a letter to a railroad or bus company asking for a refund on an unused ticket.

10. Assume that some of your luggage has been lost on your way to or from college. Write a claims letter to the railroad or the express company.

11. Write a letter applying for a summer job on a cruise boat or at a summer camp (or some other kind of summer employment).

12. Write a letter of application in answer to an advertisement in the "Help Wanted" section of a newspaper or magazine. Choose an advertisement giving a reasonable amount of information.

13. With a specific position in mind, prepare a record sheet giving pertinent information about yourself. Write a letter of application to accompany the record.

14. Write a completely self-contained letter of application (i.e., without use of a record sheet). Use one or two unique or unusual devices to make your letter distinctive.

15. Write a letter to a high school teacher or former college instructor, asking permission to use his name as reference in your application for a position.

16. Write an informal invitation to a friend, asking him to join you and your family on a week's automobile tour.

17. Write a "bread and butter" letter to a friend who has entertained you for a week end in his (her) home. Write a letter also to your friend's mother.

18. Write a letter to a friend who is in the hospital for a long stay following a serious operation.

19. Assume that you are spending some time in a foreign country or in a section of the country considerably removed from your home. Write a "travel" letter to a friend at home.

20. Write a "thank you" note to a friend's parents who have given you a "going-away-to-college" present.

21. Write a letter of advice to a friend who is a high school senior and who plans coming in the fall to the college which you are attending.

Appendix A

22. Write a letter to a friend attending another college, inviting him (or her) to one of the important social functions of your college.

23. Write a letter to a relative, asking him (her) to be your guest at some college activity in which you know that he (she) is greatly interested.

24. Send a letter of information to your high school principal, or your favorite high school teacher, giving your impressions of some phase of college life.

25. Write a letter to a former high school friend reminding him of, or suggesting, a reunion of your class or some other organization during the next vacation period.

Appendix B

SENTENCE ANALYSIS AND DIAGRAMING

Theoretically, one who knows grammar should be able to analyze a sentence both by words and by groups of words (phrases and clauses).

Consider the following sentence:

The little old lady across the street is carefully knitting a sweater for her grandson, who is a freshman.

A grammatical analysis of this sentence is as follows:

The is a definite article modifying the noun *lady.*

little and *old* are adjectives modifying the noun *lady.*

lady is a noun used as *subject of the sentence.*

across is a preposition introducing the prepositional phrase; *the,* a definite article modifying the noun *street; street,* a noun used as object of the preposition *across.* The entire prepositional phrase, *across the street,* is used as an adjective modifying *lady.*

is is an auxiliary verb which with the present participle *knitting* forms the present progressive tense, active voice, and is the *predicate of the sentence.*

carefully is an adverb modifying the verb phrase *is knitting.*

a is an indefinite article modifying *sweater,* which is a noun used as direct object of the verb phrase *is knitting.*

for is a preposition; *her,* the possessive pronoun, third person singular feminine, referring to *lady* and modifying *grandson; grandson,* a noun, the object of the preposition *for.* The entire prepositional phrase, *for her grandson,* is used as an adverb, modifying *is knitting,* if we think of the phrase as being closely associated with and tied to the verb phrase *is knitting;* if, however, we think of *for her grandson* as closely associated with *sweater,* then both by logic and common sense we can call it a prepositional phrase used as an adjective, modifying *sweater.*

505

Appendix B

who is a relative pronoun, nominative case, referring to *grandson* and used as the subject of *is; is* is a linking verb; *a* is an indefinite article modifying *freshman;* and *freshman* is a predicate noun after a linking verb. The group of words, *who is a freshman,* is an adjective clause modifying *grandson.*

Lacking the skill (or knowledge) needed to analyze sentences as indicated above, many students find diagraming of value. This is a mechanical device by which you are aided in identifying words as parts of speech, in identifying phrases and clauses, and in indicating the uses or functions in a sentence of these words, phrases, or clauses. These purposes of diagraming are accomplished through the use of lines: horizontal lines, perpendicular lines, slanting lines, curved lines, and dotted lines.

But remember that diagraming, although it seems like a game, is only a *means* to an end, not an *end* in itself; it is simply a device to help you identify and see the relationships between various parts of a sentence.

The important parts of the sentence are put on lines in the positions indicated in the following skeleton diagram.

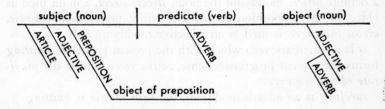

Filled in, such a diagramed sentence might read:

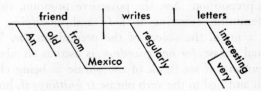

The simple subject, the simple predicate, the direct object, the object complement, the predicate noun (or pronoun), and the

506

Sentence Analysis and Diagraming

predicate adjective are written on the main long horizontal line. Subject and predicate are separated by a perpendicular line intersecting the horizontal line. The direct object is separated from the verb by a short perpendicular line extending up from the horizontal line. The object complement, the predicate noun or pronoun, or the predicate adjective is separated by a short slanting line extending leftward from the horizontal line.

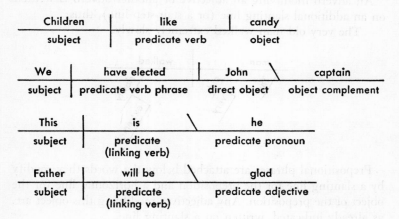

Dashes or dotted lines (usually perpendicular) are used to join, and the conjunction is written along or across such a line. In the following sentence, notice the compound subject, the compound predicate, and the compound object.

Freshmen and sophomores read or write stories and essays.

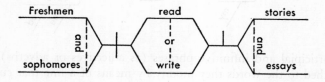

Slanting lines below the horizontal line are used for adjective and adverbial modifiers. Each adjective or adverb is on a separate slanting line.

507

The old man slowly but carefully signed his name.

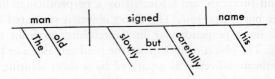

An adverb modifying an adjective or another adverb is written on an additional slanting line (or a stair-step line), thus:

The very old man walked extremely slowly.

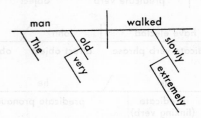

Prepositional phrases are attached below the words they modify by a slanting line for the preposition and a horizontal line for the object of the preposition. Any adjectives modifying this object are, as already indicated, written on a slanting line.

A friend of my father gave me the book with the red cover. (Note how *me*—the indirect object—is diagrammed.)

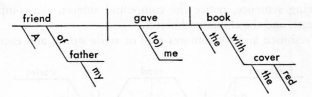

Participial and infinitive phrases (as adjectives or adverbs) are attached to the words they modify by means of a line that curves into a horizontal line. Any objects, adjectives, or adverbs in these phrases are placed as indicated above.

The man wearing the brown hat is the man to be nominated for president.

508

Sentence Analysis and Diagraming

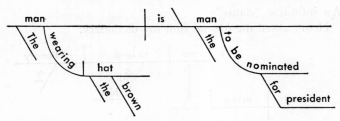

A gerund phrase or an infinitive phrase used as a noun is put on a horizontal line supported by a vertical line placed to indicate whether such phrase is the subject, object, predicate noun, etc. A noun clause or an infinitive "clause" is similarly supported. Within these phrases or clauses, objects, adjectives, adverbs, and the like, are placed as indicated above.

Gerund phrase as subject of a verb:

Occasionally reading a good book is a worthy achievement.

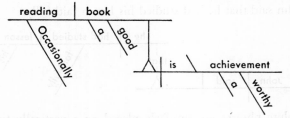

Infinitive phrase as predicate noun:

A precept worthy to be followed by everyone is freely to forgive your enemies.

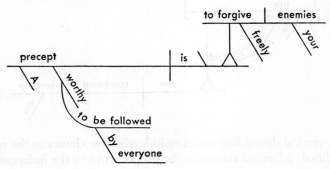

An infinitive "clause":
Henry asked me to lend him my dictionary.

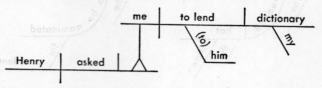

Noun clause as subject:
What you say has convinced me.

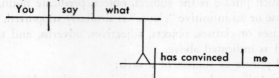

Noun clause as object:
John said that he had studied his lesson faithfully.

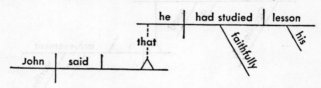

Absolute phrases are similarly placed on a vertically supported line but are enclosed in brackets:
The tire being repaired, we continued our journey.

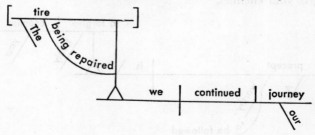

A vertical dotted line serves to link adjective clauses to the noun modified; adverbial clauses to the proper word in the independent

Sentence Analysis and Diagraming

clause; and one independent clause to another. Any conjunction expressed is written across the dotted line.

Adjective clauses:

Men who work diligently usually succeed.

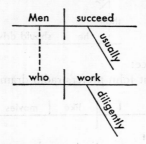

I met a friend whom I like.

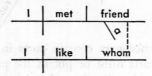

Adverbial clauses:

We won the game because we had the better team.

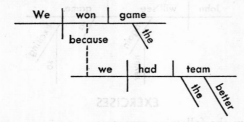

Mary is taller than her mother is.

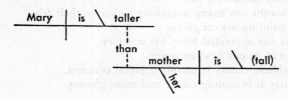

511

Appendix B

John drives faster than he should drive.

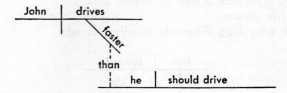

Compound sentence:
I like movies, but John prefers radio dramas.

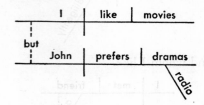

Sometimes a sentence may contain parts in inverted or trans-posed order; these parts must be put in the proper places in the diagram according to the directions already given.

Never again will John see so exciting a game.

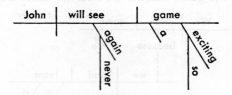

EXERCISES

A. Diagram the following sentences:
1. You may borrow my pen.
2. The Smiths saw many interesting sights on their trip.
3. I am painting my car green.
4. Father has appointed Mary his secretary.
5. You will be our next treasurer.
6. An athletic victory is usually a joyful occasion.
7. The day is becoming colder and more gloomy.

Sentence Analysis and Diagraming

8. Edison has been famous for a long time.
9. Books, magazines, and newspapers are available in the library.
10. Busy people receive and send many letters.

B. Diagram the following sentences:

1. Henry has worked faithfully to achieve his ambition.
2. Your winning the election so easily surprised everyone.
3. Tomorrow I shall begin taking regular exercise.
4. To recognize one's errors is to take the first step toward improvement.
5. The host invited us to come early and to stay late.
6. That I might have the pleasure of your company is my desire.
7. Father wrote that he would arrive on Friday.
8. We returned to college yesterday, our vacation having ended.
9. The college which I am attending is a small one.
10. To thoughts of love, in the springtime, often turns the fancy of a young man—and that of some old ones, too.

Index

515

Index

516

Index

517

Index

Index

519

Index

Index

521

Index

Index

523

Index

Non sequitur error, 14–15

Notorious, noteworthy, notable, 465

Note-taking, 284–287; lectures, 286–287; reading, 284–286

Noun clause, 49–50, 125; phrase, 47; subject or complement, 356

Nouns, abstract, 34; capitalization, 185–187; collective, 34–35; common, 34; concrete, 34; defined, 34–35, 125; number of, 35; plurals of, 35–36, 65; possessive case formation, 36, 171–172; predicate, 129; proper, 34

Nowheres, 465

Number, 125–126; shift in, 384

Numbers, commas, 193; dates, streets, telephone, highway, book chapters, 192; fractions, 192–193; italics, 182; parentheses, 175; plurals, 172; punctuation, 146–147; words or figures, 192

O, oh, 465

Object, 126; compound, 126; indirect, 123

Object complement, 60, 126

Objective case, 60–62, 126–127

Obsolete words, 419

Of, used for *have,* 78, 468

O'Mahoney, Joseph C., quoted, 234

Omissions, asterisks, 177; caret, 176; ellipsis periods, 176; use of dash for, 166; wrong, 360–361

Only, position of, 364

Op. cit., 293

Open punctuation, 482

Opinion, 13, 14

Oral, verbal, 465

Order, exposition, 259; paragraph, 330–333; themes, 223–224

Order letter, *see* Business letters

Ought as auxiliary verb, 81

Oursler, Fulton, quoted, 234

Outlines, 223–229; aid to proportion, 230–231; form, 224–228; logic, 227–228; mechanics, 224–227; paragraph, 224–227; research paper, 289–290; sentence, 224–225; subheads, 224–228; theme, 223–229; topic, 224–225

Overstreet, H. A., quoted, 320

Paper, 204

Paragraph, 307–347; appropriateness, 340–343; business letters, 486–487; characteristics, 309–310; defined, 308–309; development, 316–326; effectiveness, 332–333; faulty, 23; importance, 307–308; indentation, 205, 310; isolated statements, 343; length, 335–337; mechanics, 310–311; order, 330–333; outline, 224–227; proportion, 334–335; quotation marks, 178; substance, 315–326; topic sentences, 311–315; transition, 338–340; unity, 327–329

Paragraph outline, *see* Paragraph

Parallelism, 127; correlative conjunctions, 381; outlines, 227–228; sentences, 380–382; structure, 249; verb use, 105

Paraphrase, 269–272; example, 271–272; suggestions, 270–271

Parentheses, 139, 174–175; misuse, 175, 205

Parenthetical material, 127, 174; punctuation, 149–150, 166, 174

Participial phrase, 48, 127

524

Index

525

Index

Profile, 257

Progressive verb form, 87–89, 92, 97, 129

Pronouns, 129; agreement with antecedent, 69–72; agreement with predicate, 65–66; correct case forms, 27; defined, 36–37; demonstrative, 38–39; indefinite, 39, 71–72; intensive, 39, 72; interrogative, 39; kinds of, 37–40; objects of verbs or prepositions, 27, 60–61; personal, 37; possessive case, 173; reciprocal, 40; reference of, 71–72, 369–370; reflexive, 39, 72; relative, 38; shift, 384

Pronunciation, 453

Proof, paragraph development by, 320–322

Proofreading, 207, 251–252

Proper nouns, 34, 130; capitalization, 185–187

Proportion, paragraph, 334–335; theme, 229–231

Proposition, 466

Provincialisms, 419

Punctuation, 134–181, 197–202; business letters, 482; defined, 134–135; glossary of applied punctuation, 197–202; marks, 135; purposes, 135–136; to enclose, 136; to end or terminate, 135; to introduce, 135; to separate, 135–136
See also individual marks of punctuation

Pure conjunction, *see* Conjunctions

Purpose, central, 216–217, 239–240

Putnam, Nina Wilcox, quoted, 234

Question, direct, 53; indirect, 123; punctuation, 138–139

Question mark, 138–139, 180

Quiller-Couch, Sir Arthur, quoted, 431

Quite a, 466

Quotation marks, 177–181; chapter headings and titles, 179; dialogue, 178; direct quotation, 177–178; misuse, 180–181; paragraphing, 178; position with other marks, 180–181; quotation within quotation, 179–180; single, 179; titles, 179; technical terms, 178

Quotations, 130; capitalization, 184; colon, 141, 161; comma, 141; direct, 177–178; indirect, 180–181; within quotations, 179–180

Radio listening, 9–10

Raise, rear, bring up, 466

Raise, rise, 41, 466

Rambling sentences, *see* Sentence

Readers, consideration and study of, 206, 208–209, 216

Reader's Digest, 266

Reading, as communication, 6–8; suggestions for, 6–8

Rear, 466

Reciprocal pronouns, 40, 130

Recommendations, paragraphing for, 342

Refer back, 466

Reference books, 277–280

Reference of pronouns, 130, 369–370

References, parentheses and, 174–175

Reflexive pronouns, 39, 72, 130

Refutation, paragraph development by, 322

Relation, relative, 466

Index

Index

Index

Index

Index

170; effectiveness, 404; emphatic diction, 434–436; euphony, 449–450; exact diction, 429–430; faulty repetition, 448–449; fine writing, 443–444; foreign words, 444; glossary of faulty diction, 459–468; idiom, 421–424; improprieties, 426–427; italics, 182; jargon, 431; joining, 45–47; misplaced, 364; mixed figures, 432–433; modifying, 43–45; naming, 34–40; order, 363–365; parts of speech, 33–47; plurals of, 172; provincialisms, 419; slang, 427–428; spelling, *see* Spelling; triteness, 440–442; vocabulary exercise, 456–459; vulgarisms, 425; wordiness, 446–447

See also Grammar

Worst kind, worst sort, worst way, 468

Would, 467; as auxiliary verb, 80–81

Would of, could of, might of, 468

Writing, autobiographical, 256; as communication, 4–5; fine, 443–444; purpose, 216–219; readers, study of, 206, 208–209, 216; traditional forms, *see* Argument; Description; Exposition; Narration

See also Paraphrase; Précis-writing; Research paper

You, indefinite use, 71, 72, 370

You all, 468

531